Michael Glover

111 Hidden Art Treasures in London That You Shouldn't Miss

Photographs by Benedict Flett

111

emons:

For Tudor Wallis Fox Glover
newly leaped into
this dangerous world

Bibliographical information of the Deutsche Nationalbibliothek
The Deutsche Nationalbibliothek lists this publication in the Deutsche Nationalbibliografie; detailed bibliographical data are available on the internet at http://dnb.d-nb.de.

MIX
Paper from responsible sources
FSC® C043106

Layout: Eva Kraskes, based on a design
by Lübbeke | Naumann | Thoben
Maps: altancicek.design, www.altancicek.de
Basic cartographical information from Openstreetmap,

Edited by: Ros Horton
Printing and binding: Grafisches Centrum Cuno, Calbe
Printed in Germany 2024
ISBN 978-3-7408-1576-9
First edition

Foreword

London is a mega-city, more than 2,000 years in the making. Londinium, the Roman city, and now the financial district, is still defined by its original boundaries, proudly guarded by dragons. It is also a city made up of many distinct differences. Why? Because it is an accumulation of distinctive villages and settlements which, over time, became knitted together as the fields and the marshlands between those population centres disappeared.

Its hidden art treasures are scattered too. This is not a book about London's great museums, of which there are so many, but about the art to be found beyond their doors – though some of them do sneak in when there is something hidden in plain view that you may never have spotted. Did you know, for example, that you are likely to have walked over Virginia Woolf on one or other of the many occasions when you have visited the National Gallery, in spite of the fact that no image of her exists on its walls?

Yes, this is a book that will find you serendipitously wandering the streets and the parks, looking as much at the outdoors as the indoors, looking up at the face or the top of a building. It is an exercise in art-sleuthing and close-looking. It is a way of training the eye to seek out the unusual, to visit an alley here or a forgotten church there, a statue, or a grand ceramic mural beside an unglamorous road that harbours so much history. It is an exercise in finding things in unexpected places. Would you have expected to discover a chapel designed by Picasso's friend Jean Cocteau just off Leicester Square, that hub of entertainment?

The hidden art of London is everywhere once you begin to look closely, in small parks, down cul-de-sacs, in a little-known triangle of park beside the River Thames at Vauxhall. This book will help you to discover a multiplicity of stories of which you have been barely aware.

111 Hidden Art Treasures

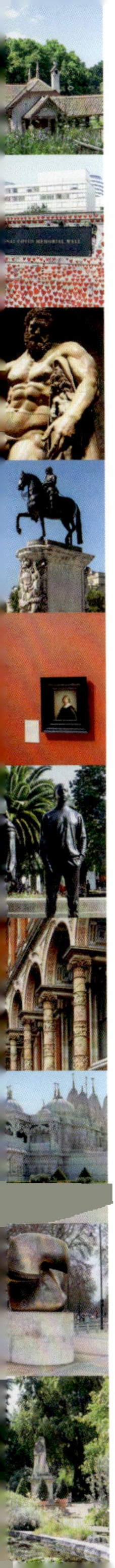

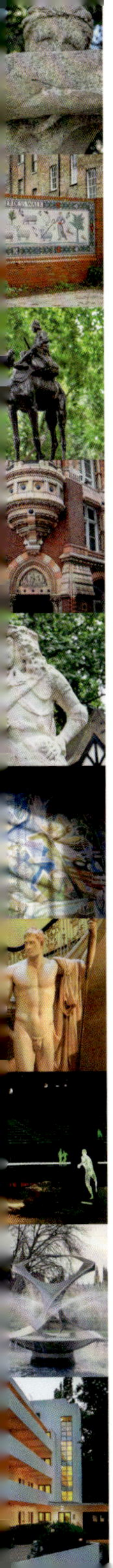

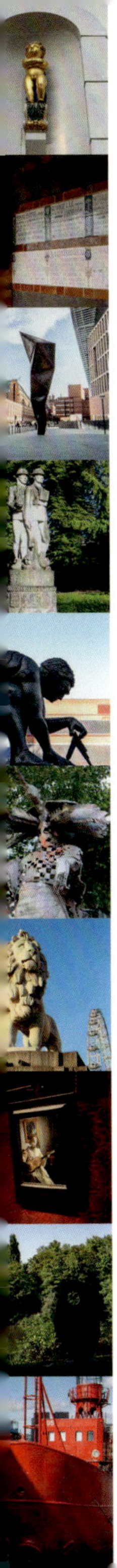

1 45 St Martin's Lane

Hotel lobby as art installation

What kind of strange apparition is this? we ask ourselves as we begin to walk up St Martin's Lane from Trafalgar Square. The building we are staring at is unlike any other in these Victorian streets. It resembles a stacking of giant cubes of colourless perspex, one balanced upon another. Is it finished? Or is it perhaps still in the making?

We are in the heart of Theatreland – the Duke of York's Theatre is almost directly opposite – so could these perhaps be props or crates to do with some forthcoming theatrical performance? It looks that makeshift.

On either side of the double-height revolving entrance doors (their colour is a softly dreamy combination of greens and oranges), there are two plant pots, far too big for their own good. Each one of them is taller than a human being. Quite ridiculous. All that colourless, boxy plainness falls away as soon as we enter the lobby of the hotel itself.

The place is as bizarre as anything that Philippe Starck, the hotel's French designer, has ever made. Starck is known for his outlandishness, and this lobby is one of the best examples you could ever see of his surreal work. It is not so much a hotel lobby as a giant art installation, and every visitor is free to wander through it, admiring its strange runway lighting at floor level (which makes the corridors look as if they might be receding as far as infinity), its giant gilded mirrors leaning nonchalantly against the walls, or the malign-looking, claw-footed chair that was surely never designed to be sat on. Or this gilded chair, whose legs end in high-heeled shoes. It combines the brashness of Versailles with *Alice in Wonderland*. If you peer into the restaurant, you will notice that all the paintings are on the tilt, as if they are being tossed about in a cabin out at sea. And why, when you reach for a door handle, do you find yourself clasping a golden hand?

Address 45 St Martin's Lane, London WC2N 4HK, +44 (0)207 300 5500, www.stmartinslane.com | **Getting there** Underground to Leicester Square (Northern and Piccadilly Lines), then a five-minute walk | **Hours** Hotel opening hours | **Tip** Walk down towards Trafalgar Square for the National Portrait Gallery and the National Gallery.

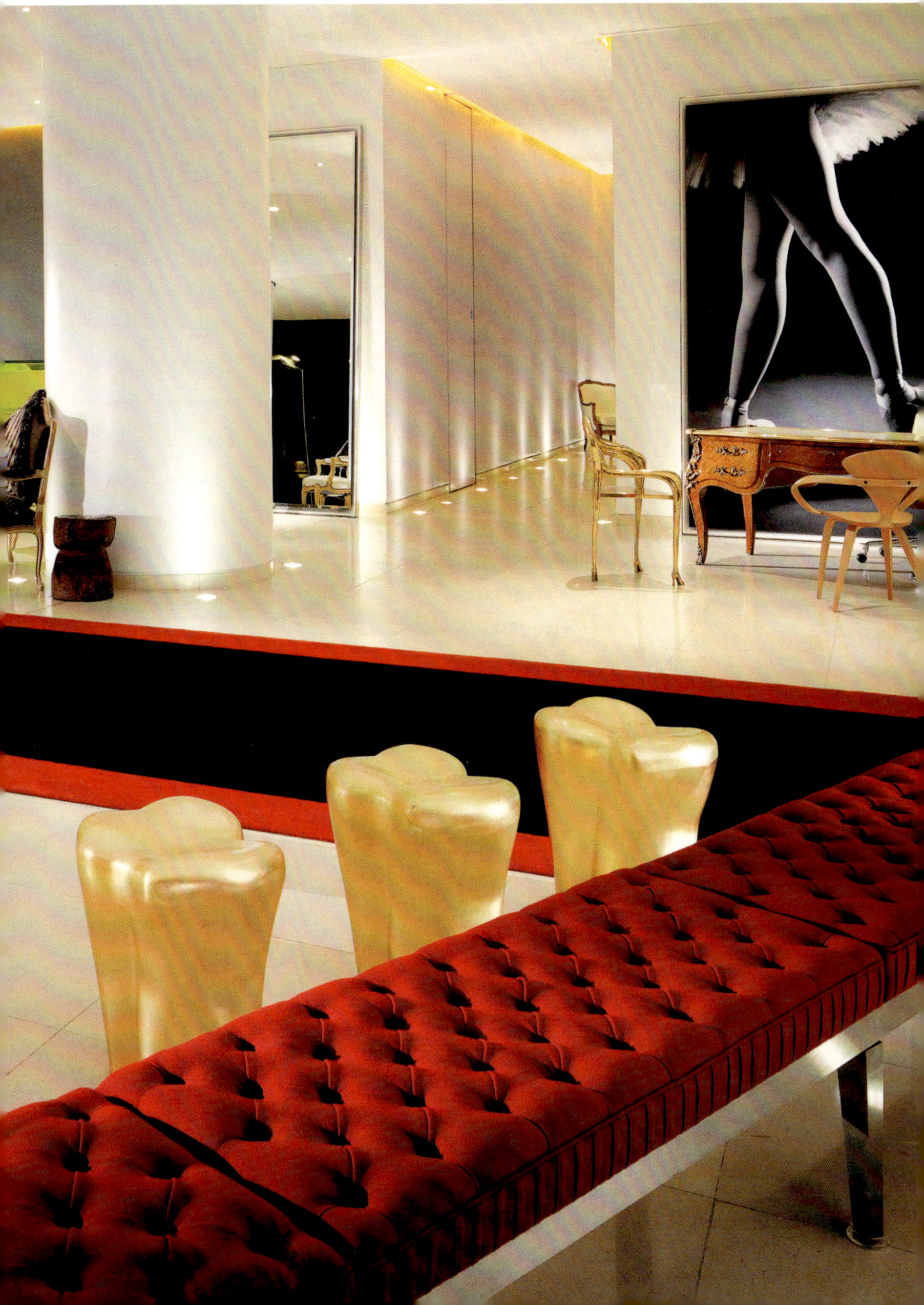

2 575 Wandsworth Road

The transforming power of fretsaw work

Anonymity. That is the message given off by this modest, well-proportioned, 18th-century house that sits a small front garden's width back from the noise of the Wandsworth Road in south London, where red London double-decker buses roar through in the general direction of Clapham Junction and beyond. Glance across the road in the general direction of the new, upscale glitz and glamour of the freshly renovated Battersea Power Station, and you will see two famous tower blocks, once painted by an artist called David Hepher.

Our house has no number. In order to determine that number, you have to look at the number on the door of the house next door, and add two – this is the uneven side of the street. If that is 573, this must be it. A flight of five fairly steep stone steps leads up to a beige door with a silver letter box, but no knocker. This little front garden was once a very dark and sequestered spot, nearly overwhelmed by trees. Now they have been pruned back so that the house is in full view and lets in much light. The façade of the house is stuccoed on the ground floor, and exposed London brick on the first floor.

There is no signage to alert you to the fact that something rather remarkable happened here. Well, looking a little more closely at the exterior of the house, there is in fact *something*: a display of even geometrical patterning that seems to rise up from the bottom of the handsome Georgian window upstairs, and then creeps up the left-hand side, somewhat thinly. Is it Islamic in inspiration?

The interior reveals all, and almost at a glance. The house is indeed modest in size, but the marquetry, delicate wooden fretsaw work, seems to engulf every climbing surface in almost every room. What an obsessive labour of love! This was all the work of a young Kenyan-born civil servant and poet called Khadambi Asalache. It took him two decades.

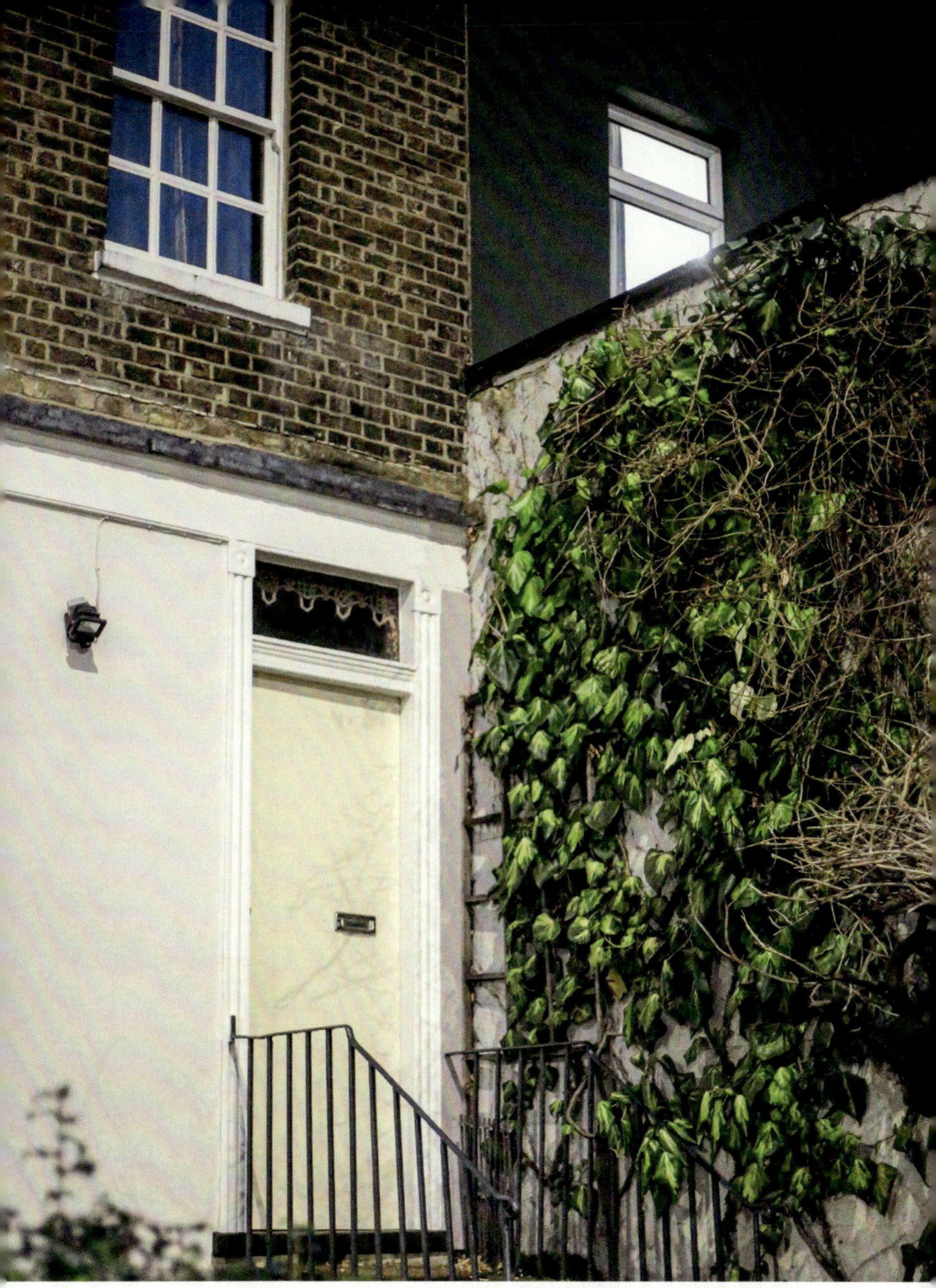

Address 575 Wandsworth Road, Lambeth, London SW8 3JD, +44 (0)207 720 9459, www.nationaltrust.org.uk/visit/london/575-wandsworth-road | Getting there Train to Wandsworth Road (London Overground) | Hours Thu & Fri 11am–4pm | Tip Turn left out of the house and walk up to Matrimony Place (next to St Paul's Church) and the Eden Nature Garden, a delightful miniature wildlife reserve.

3 Anthony Caro Centre

The sculptor who bent steel to perfection

Anthony Caro, who died in 2013, was one of the great post-war sculptors, and one of the defining figures of post-war abstraction. Where to go to find out about him? His former studio is in Camden, tucked away in a yard with an arched entrance (high enough to admit horse-drawn carriages), off a very characteristic 19th-century London terrace. This yard has been full of makers of this and that for at least 150 years. Once upon a time, Camden was famous for its piano makers – one of them had its factory in this yard. Now it is more likely to accommodate architects, designers and sculptors. The Anthony Caro Centre is at the far end of the yard, and you will recognise that you have almost reached it by the presence of a huge red, abstract sculpture fabricated from steel, Caro's material of first choice.

The centre, which comprises offices (look out for his handsome wooden workdesk with the steel spiral at one corner to accommodate his stick), and his archives in grey filing cabinets (open one up and find out about one or another of his many exhibitions, for example). In this room, along shelves ranged around the walls, you can also see dozens of small-scale models of his sculptures, which, rather surprisingly, he always made *after* the work was finished.

And then there are also, here and just across the yard, several galleries that display changing exhibitions of his works, from the 1960s and on, which give you a sweeping overview of his entire, long career – it went on for more than half a century – as a fabricator. Look out too for the many browsable catalogues of his exhibitions, and posters on the walls that show you when he had a show in New York, London or Tokyo.

Caro's former studio is on the left as you leave the yard, and it is still in use to this day by a sculptor of international importance. Her name is Rachel Whiteread.

Address Barford Sculptures Ltd, 38a Georgiana Street, London NW1 0EB, +44 (0)207 482 2871, www.anthonycaro.org | **Getting there** Underground to Camden Town (Northern Line), then a five-minute walk | **Hours** Mon–Fri 10am–4pm (by appointment only) | **Tip** Great street food and much else at Camden Market, 10 minutes from here.

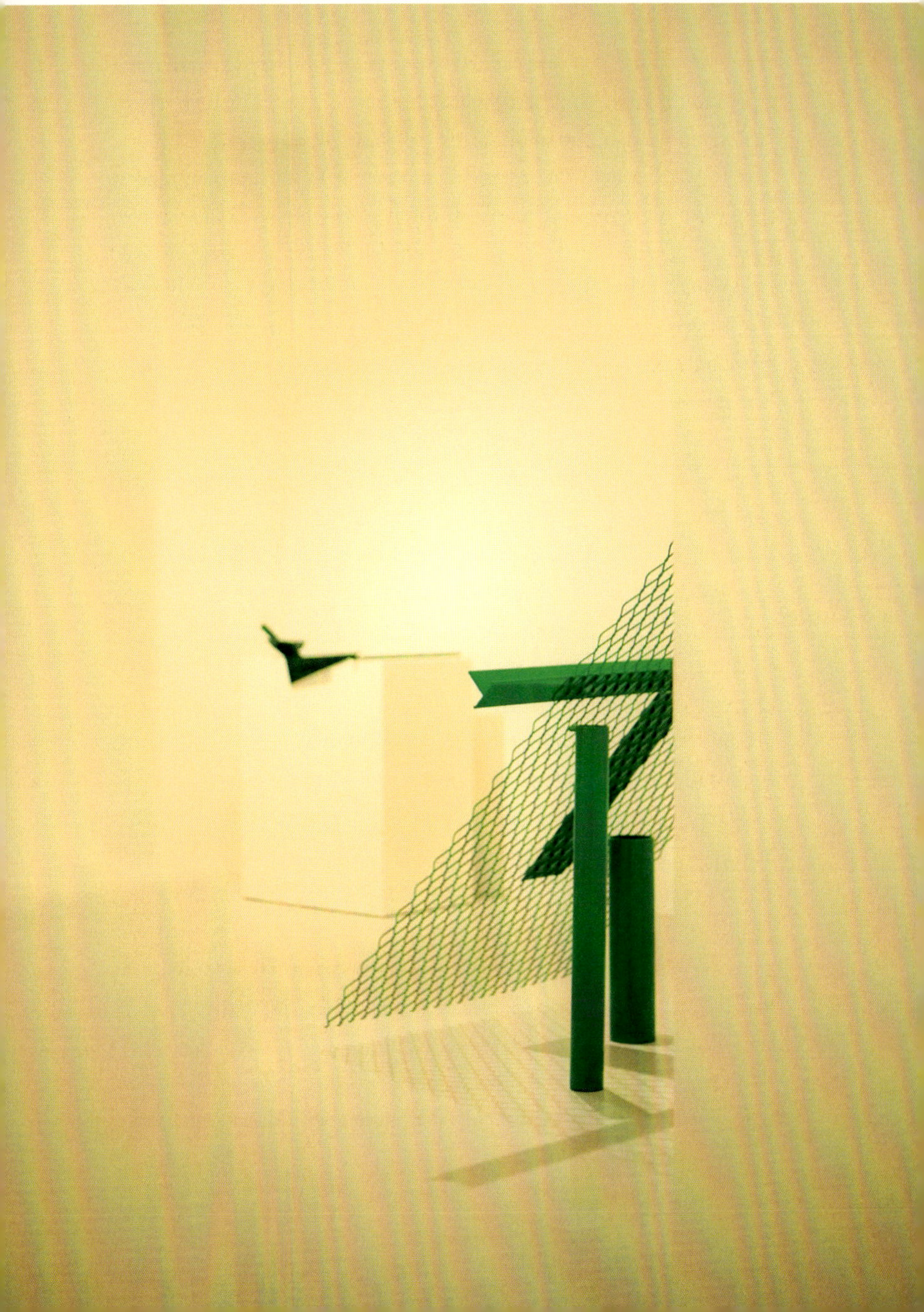

4 Apsley House

Napoleon, nude and vanquished

Apsley House, the home of the Dukes of Wellington that now presides over a tumult of traffic at Hyde Park Corner, is full of artistic treasures, many of them gifts from the grateful monarchs of Europe. The Iron Duke had vanquished Napoleon at Waterloo (with a little help from his Prussian friends) in 1815, putting an end to the Napoleonic Wars, which had dragged on for more years than the combined durations of World Wars I and II.

But perhaps the most extraordinary fact about these collections is quite how much memorabilia about Napoleon himself they contain. The fact is that although Wellington purported to despise the short (five-foot-five inch) Corsican upstart, he was also obsessed with his greatest and most dangerous enemy. Napoleon stuff is everywhere, from the Empress Josephine's great dinner service (gifted to Wellington by Louis XVIII), to a rather teary-eyed genre painting by Edward Matthew Ward of the young Napoleon being held prisoner in Nice in 1794.

But quite the most extraordinary item of Napoleon memorabilia does not live in the great picture gallery upstairs amongst masterpieces by Goya and Velasquez at all. It is downstairs, at the foot of the stairwell, and it can be seen very soon after you enter the house. To call this nude, neo-classical sculpture in marble by Canova extraordinary is a bit of an understatement. It stands almost 12 feet high. The emperor flourishes a golden figure of Victory. Is there not a hint of homo-eroticism about it? A brick column was built beneath the staircase hall to support the sculpture's great weight. Commissioned in 1806, at a point when Napoleon seemed to be the master of all he surveyed, he never put it on public display. Did he hate it? Probably. In public, he called it too athletic. Did the Iron Duke smirk or roar with laughter every time he passed it? Even if he didn't, his friends probably did.

Address 149 Piccadilly, Hyde Park Corner, London W1J 7NT, +44 (0)207 499 5676, www.wellingtoncollection.co.uk | Getting there Underground to Hyde Park Corner (Piccadilly Line) | Hours Wed–Sun 11am–5pm | Tip The Hyde Park Screen (to the left of the house), designed in 1828 by Decimus Burton, is well worth a look.

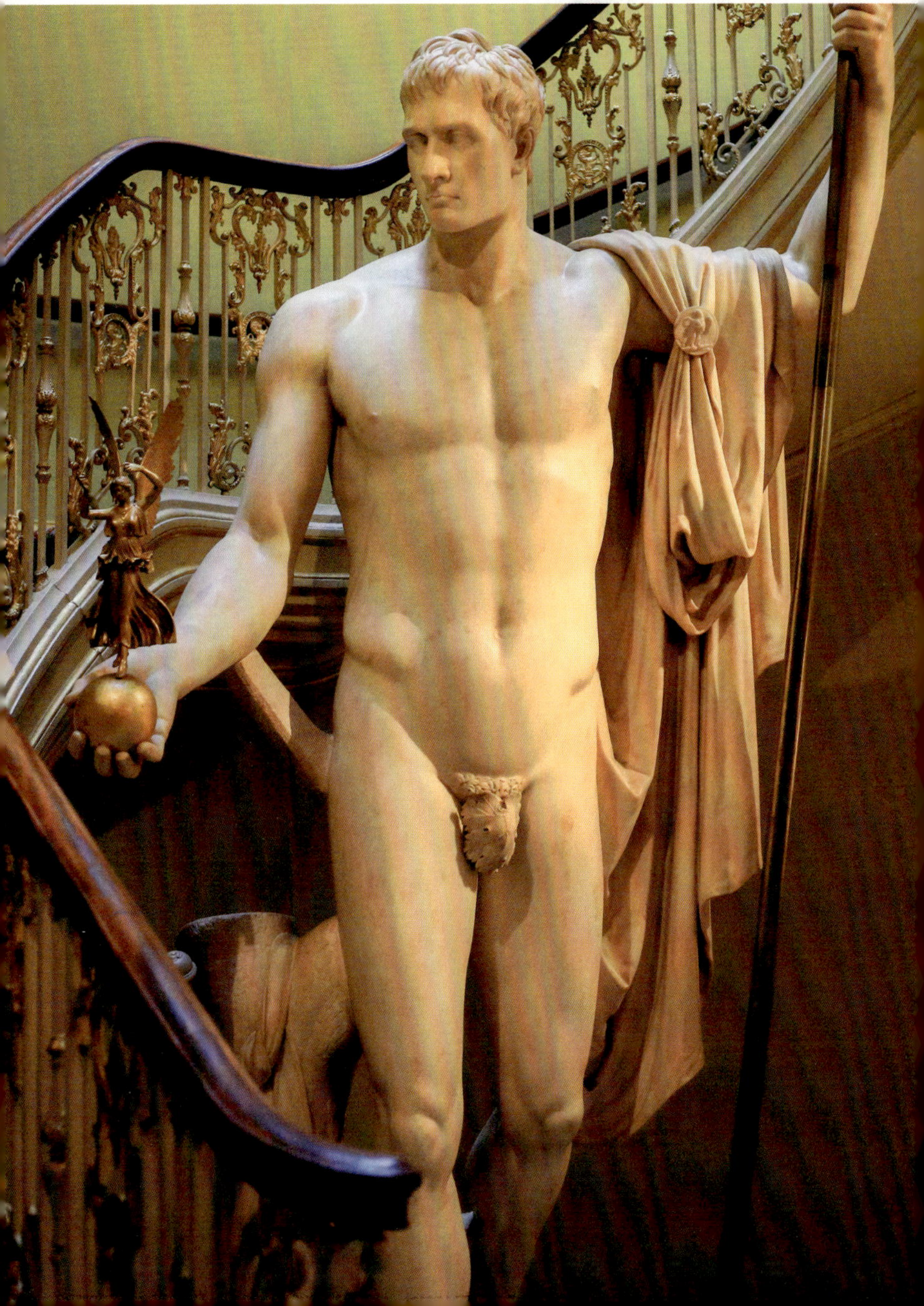

5 The Art of Bellenden Road

Peckham's magical street art

Sometimes, almost as if by magic, art accumulates along a suburban street little by little, at street level, on gaping gable end walls, and even high in the air above where the cars nose past…

This is the case with a stretch of Bellenden Road in Peckham, between the junctions with Choumert Road and Maxted Road. This is a people-busy location packed with delis, restaurants, coffee shops, a general store where vegetables spill out onto the pavement, pubs – and much surprising art too. Not necessarily art of a predictable kind either. There is, granted, some good and fairly predictable-looking street art here, a fine mural on a side wall, for example, but there is also street furniture and restaurant signage, all made by artists too. Why? Because this is also a street where artists have – or have had – their studios, and to leave art here represents a legacy, and perhaps even a thank you, to the neighbourhood.

Look carefully, for example, at the junction where Choumert meets Bellenden. What do we make of these smooth and unusually shapely bronze bollards outside the Victoria pub, and on other nearby corners too? They are not the usual, forgettable kinds of bollards at all. These are basic sculptural forms, sculptural building blocks if you like, showing off spheres balanced one upon another or double cones or a lovely gherkin shape. The one outside the general store is phallic. This is Brancusi country, we think, at first glance. In fact, they were all made by a celebrated sculptor called Antony Gormley – he of *The Angel of the North* – during the time that he had a studio in the neighbourhood. Tom Phillips, a multi-media artist of some renown, made his mark here too. The lights that curve over the street were designed by him, along with the mosaic sign on the curved wall above a restaurant called The Begging Bowl, where the lettering is sheer playfulness.

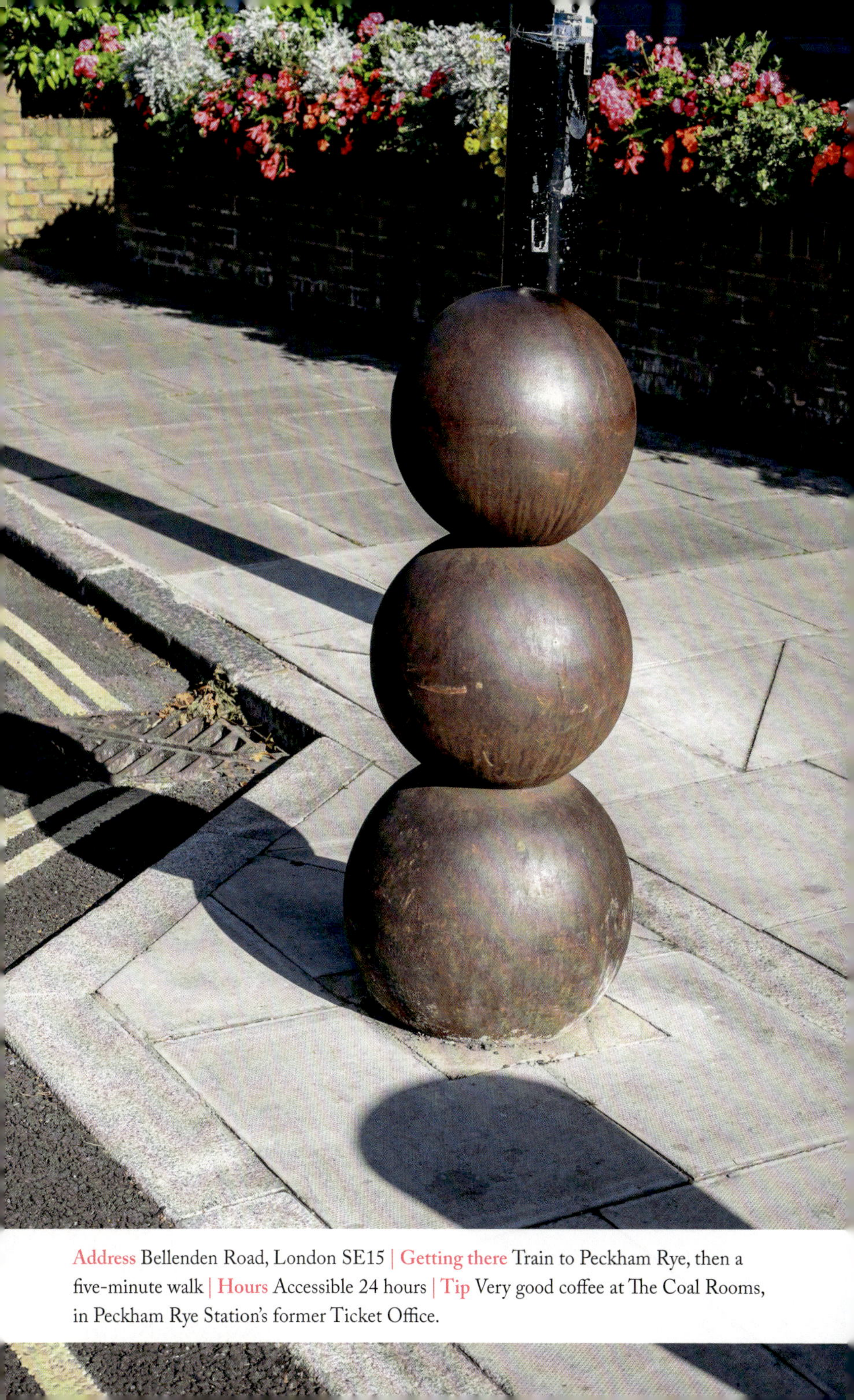

Address Bellenden Road, London SE15 | Getting there Train to Peckham Rye, then a five-minute walk | Hours Accessible 24 hours | Tip Very good coffee at The Coal Rooms, in Peckham Rye Station's former Ticket Office.

6 The Artist's Garden

A trace of psychedelia underfoot

Where might a garden in the centre of a city grow? The Artist's Garden, which prospers on the long roof above Temple Underground station, is reached up a steep flight of stone steps from pavement level. Having reached it, you stare across at a long rectangle of level ground bounded by stone balustrades. The view from the southern side shows you the Thames in full spate, with the Hayward Gallery off to the right, and a little further along the South Bank, the London Eye.

Vents from the Underground erupt from time to time, enclosed by railings. We hear hissing and the squeal of brakes as the trains draw in and out. This is not quite a garden as we usually know it though. It is, being artist-made, a painted rather than a planted garden, more a slightly hallucinogenic use of space than a natural one – it is painted in bold stripes, cubes and ziggurats, all rendered in extraordinarily bright and eye-beguiling primary colours. The colours remind you of Lego bricks. It feels slightly soft. Everything looks heightened and intensified. Almost psychedelic in fact. A hut some way along is also painted in the same bright stripes. A few ceramic sculptures, raised up on brick plinths, also punctuate the space.

There is some grass towards the far end, you do notice (and some greenhouses too), but it is not really grass at all because its colour is not quite nature's. It is astro turf. And at your feet, for the most part, almost everywhere you walk, there is underfoot this extended exercise in Op Art painting, bold works of abstraction that put you in mind of the works of Bridget Riley (although actually by Lakwena Maciver). One of the four greenhouses at the far end contains a display of micro-organisms as we have never before seen them with the human eye. They look like psychedelic landscapes. Blown up to giant size, they are brilliantly decorated with sequins.

Address Temple Underground Station Roof Terrace, London WC2R 2PH, www.thecolab.art | Getting there Underground to Temple (Circle and District Lines) | Hours Daily 8am–dusk | Tip A short walk along the Embankment will bring you to Cleopatra's Needle in Victoria Embankment Gardens. A gift from the Sultan of Egypt, it was transported from Alexandria in 1877.

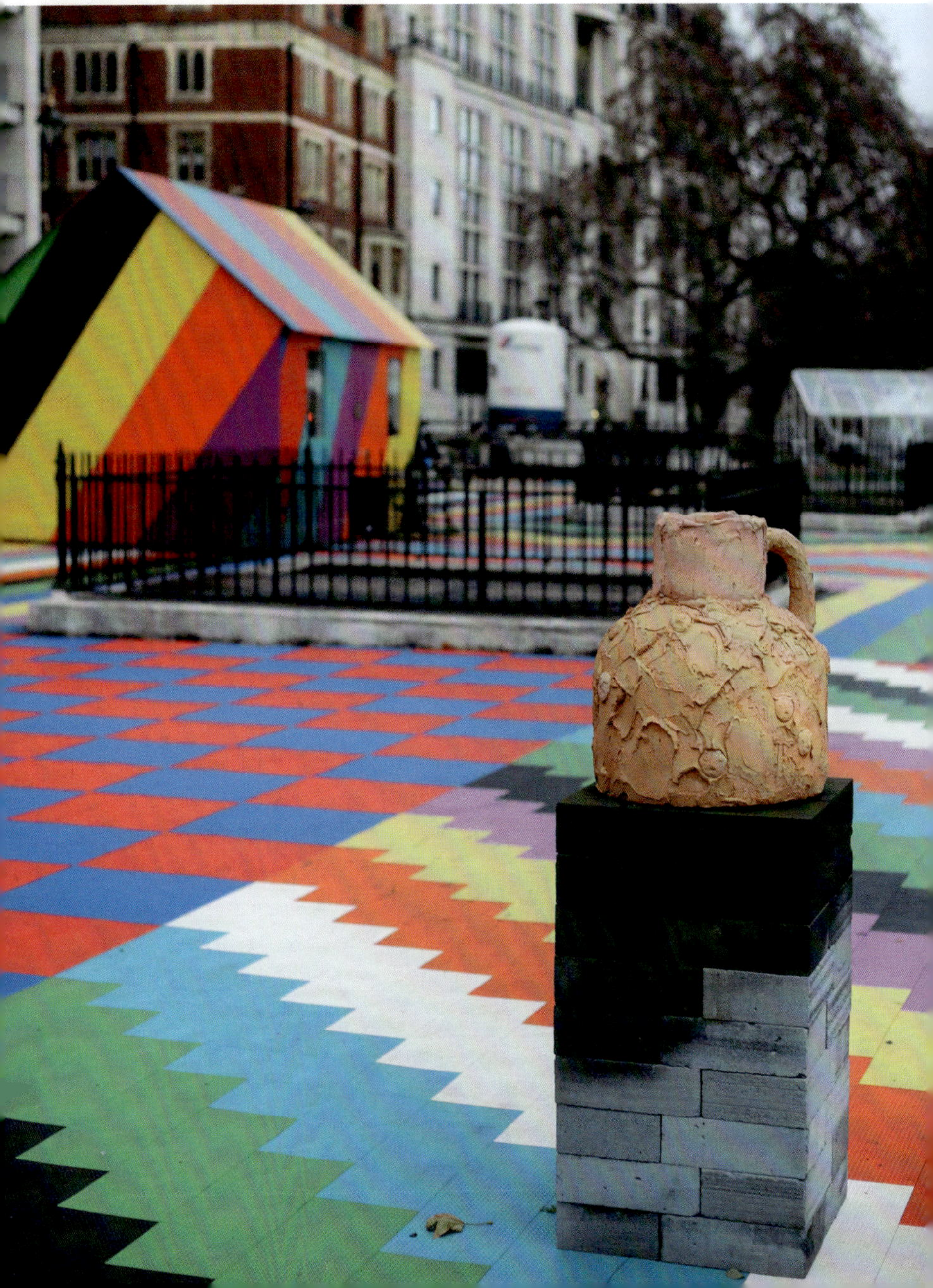

7 Banksy meets Basquiat

Street art at the Barbican

The street art of Banksy, that famously anonymous prankster, usually turns up unexpectedly, and often in response to quite particular situations. He does like to have his say. His is an art of often quite subtle protest, political without being stridently so. Sometimes he seems to be in humorous conversation with other artists. In 2018, for example, the Barbican Centre in the City of London staged a huge retrospective by the New York artist Jean-Michel Basquiat, who began life as a graffiti artist and later took the gallery world by storm. The Barbican development itself is a sleek concrete jungle of a place, and Banksy dived into the midst of it just a few days before the Basquiat show was due to open in order to make a point about the relationship between art and politics.

The work itself is in the most relentlessly urban of settings, at the point where two streets meet, at the junction with an underpass that forever roars with the relentless and unforgiving noise of passing traffic. The work itself, having arrived as if by magic (no one ever seems to spot Banksy doing his stuff), was quickly covered by bolted-on sheets of Perspex so that it would not suffer damage – or get stolen. Was it really genuine though? There are many fake Banksys in the world. Banksy's Instagram account quickly confirmed it to be an original.

The work looks like something of a collaboration between Banksy and Basquiat, but this was impossible because Basquiat was long dead. It shows two cops frisking a black man with wild dreadlocks. Hang on a minute though. This is not really a man. It is a copy of an image by Basquiat that two numbskull cops have mistaken for a dangerous prowler. The sobering joke is at the expense of the cops for being such fools, far too quick to frisk a man of colour. The cops have such subtlety of line and tone. The Basquiat looks wild, and even skeletal.

Address At the junction of Beech Street and Golden Lane, London EC2Y 8HD | **Getting there** Underground to Barbican (Circle, Hammersmith and City and Metropolitan Lines) | **Hours** Accessible 24 hours | **Tip** The Barbican Centre is great for coffee, art and music.

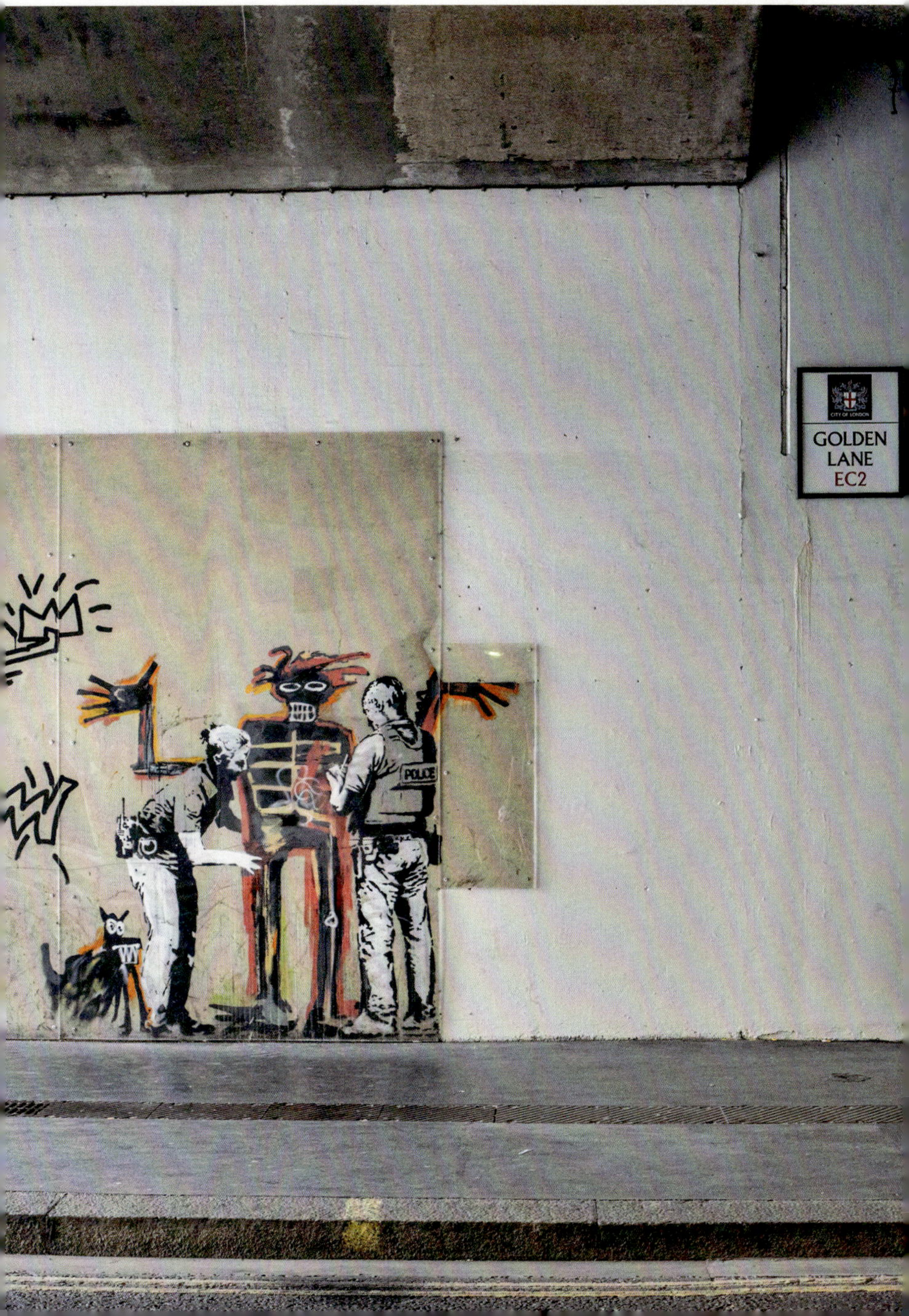

8 Banner Repeater Gallery

Radical art at a train station

You don't normally take a mainline train directly to an art gallery. But then Hackney Repeater, insofar as it lives in a couple of rooms on Platform One at Hackney Downs Station on the outskirts of London, is no normal gallery by any stretch of the imagination. It's also quite easy to miss: the sign on the white door is not difficult to walk past, though an opened billboard just outside the door may help – if it's not raining.

Once inside, things clarify somewhat. There may be a librarian-cum-archivist called Carl with a ring in their ear and a very friendly manner sitting across from you, tapping away at a keyboard, when you visit.

You are now standing in the first of the gallery's two long and narrow rooms. Behind you there's a long grey sofa, a little desk on wheels, and some book-shelving straight across from you full of books made by artists. There's a small library in here, and some cutting-edge art magazines on a spinner with a queer/radical and/or feminist slant. There's also a digital archive of artists' publishing you can access if you wish. No pressure. Everything is very relaxed and unhurried. No one tries to get you outdoors again any time soon. Every now and again a train squeals by, and the room judders, gently.

The second room – it's an extension of the first really – is an exhibition space, and an animated film is running on a big screen. The text accompanying the images is vaguely philosophical. Banner Repeater project space, with its programme of alternative art, queer studies and radical feminism has been out here on Platform One since 2010, quietly getting on with its mission. A young woman walks in wearing a cycle helmet, and pushing a bike. Can she bring it in while she looks? Sure, says Carl, giving her a kindly smile before resuming tap-tap-tapping on the keyboard. They are a librarian and an artist when they're not working here.

Address Platform One, Hackney Downs Network Rail, Dalston Lane, London E8 1LA, www.bannerrepeater.org | Getting there Network rail from Liverpool Street to Hackney Downs | Hours Sat noon–6pm, closed Aug | Tip A 12-minute walk away, on Reading Lane, is the Hackney Museum, which focuses on the rich and diverse history of the area.

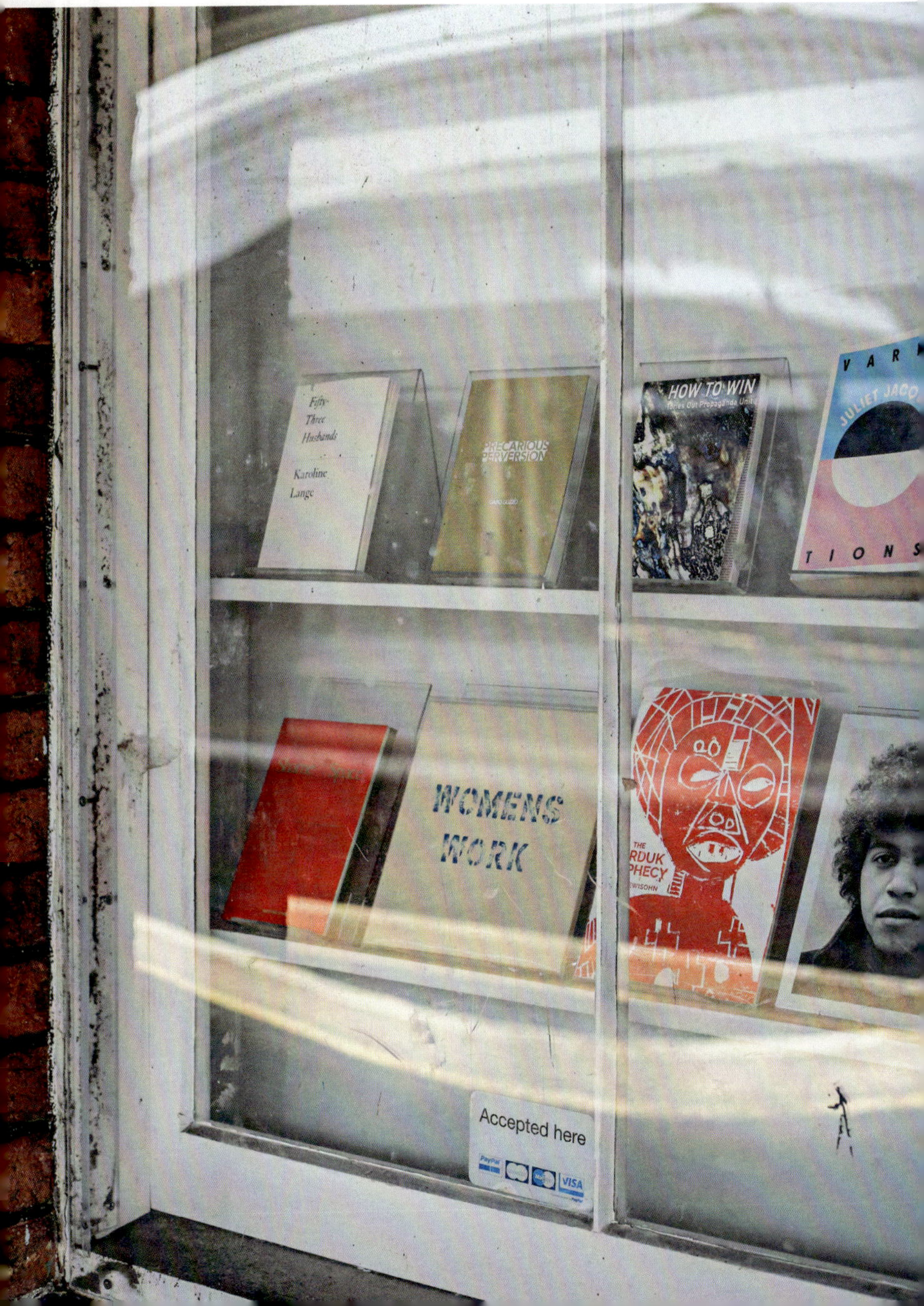

9 The Blasted Crosses

A ghosting of the wreckage

The dramatic, central siting of these two artworks by the Jewish sculptor Gerry Judah adds to the drama of their presence here in St Paul's Cathedral, perhaps London's most magnificent Christian basilica. White and more than a little fragile looking, one of them descends at medium height from a great left-hand pier just before the nave reaches the church's crossing point, where the transepts feed in from left and right. In their form they resemble a roughly made cross with some odd, additional out-juttings, the whole structure leaning out towards us, rather in the way that a body might lean out in supplication.

And yet, on closer inspection, there is nothing of the human body about them at all – apart from this cruciform shape, which appears almost ready to accommodate the presence of a body. Except that it does not, not really, because attached to this surface are what look like blasted remnants of buildings, ruined or part-ruined remnants. In fact, what we see here, in this rather sacralised form, is what Judah has often shown us in the past – terrible fragments of pulverised and perhaps war-charred architectural landscapes. We look down on crushed and tumbling tower blocks, bent aerials, shattered windows – and the fact that they are all accommodated within this symbolically potent shape, and indeed even seem to grow out of it, adds a tremendous touch of poignancy to what we are seeing.

It is as if the ghostly presence of the crucifixion at its back is adding its support, offering it all up for our contemplation, giving relief, before bearing all this tragedy away, and perhaps asking us to regard it all as only superficial damage. The sculptures are here to help us remember the dead of World War I. Their presence is a reminder that across the cemeteries of Europe, the fact of the un-numbered dead is marked by seas of white crosses stretching away as far as the eye can see.

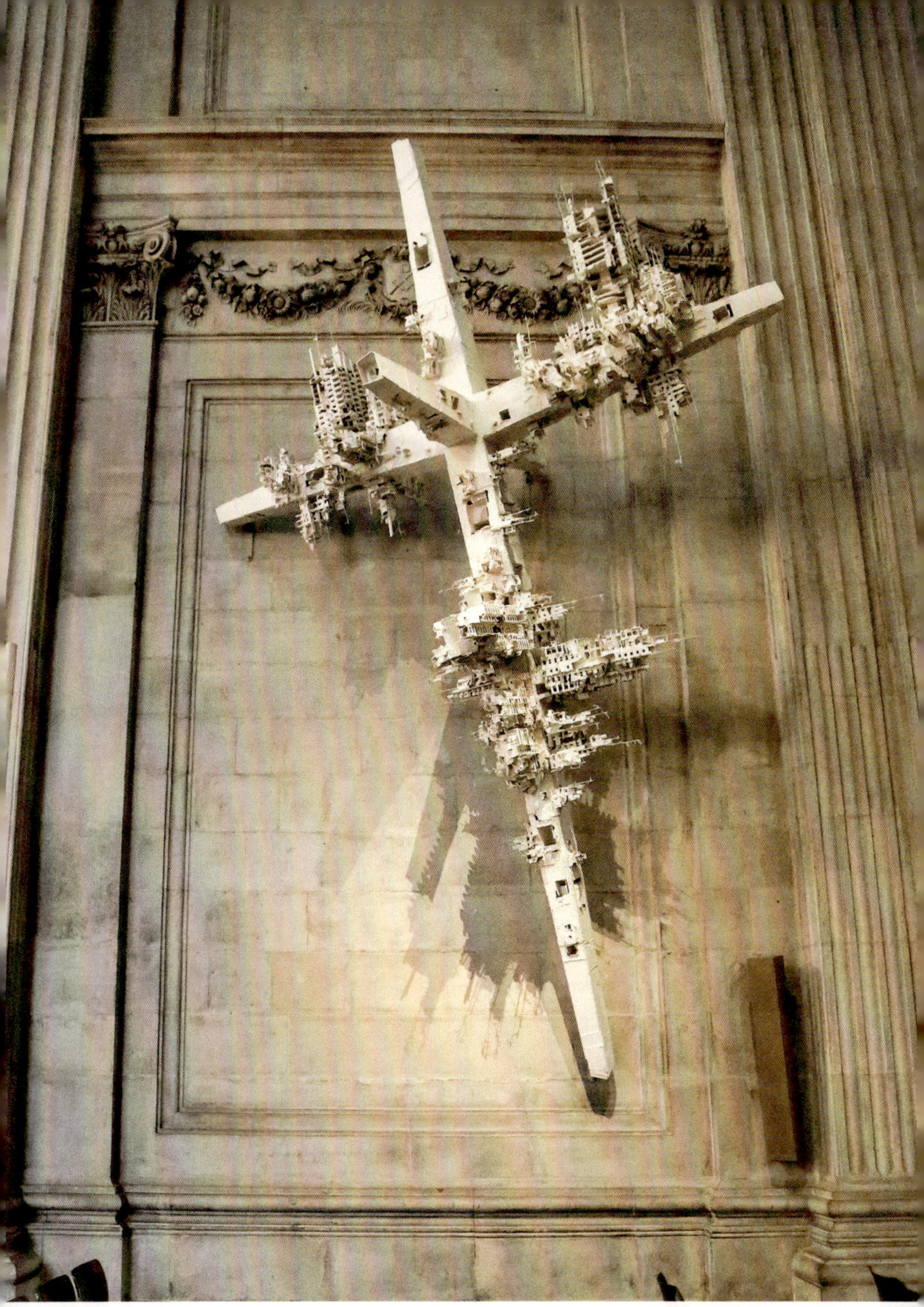

Address St Paul's Cathedral, St Paul's Churchyard, London EC4M 8AD, +44 (0)207 246 8350, www.stpauls.co.uk | Getting there Underground to St Paul's (Central Line) | Hours Mon, Tue, Fri & Sat 8.30am–4.30pm, Wed 10am–4.30pm; open Sun for worship only | Tip Good street food is generally available in Paternoster Square just across the churchyard.

10 Blue Sky Players

How to beautify the plainest of façades

The French artist Yves Klein was a stunt man – as so many artists often tend to be. The best-known image of the man shows him seeming to fly horizontally, arms spread, with all the confidence of a bird, out of a first-floor building in Paris. He came to no harm. It was all a carefully staged shot.

Yves Klein comes to mind for two reasons when we stand opposite an otherwise unremarkable building at the lower end of Borough High Street in Southwark, where Shakespeare once had his company of players. It is not the exciting end of this street by any means. We have to walk a little way north towards the river, and the promise of the beauty of Southwark Cathedral (you can see its tower), the marvellous hubbub of Borough Market, and the allure of the City with all its high-rise glister – on the northern bank of London Bridge, to find that. Here, instead, we have the oddly misnamed Maya Building, a rather faceless structure, with routine beige concrete panelling. And yet, if you look up, you will see that it has been transformed by the unexpected presence here of three blue figures, all naked and slender, and all painted, quite distinctively, in that blue we have come to know as Yves Klein Blue, which means that, in its richness and its intensity, it seems to possess an almost other-worldly lift.

These three figures seem to be climbing the building's façade with apparent ease, stepping up towards the roof so lightly, and they are all carrying instruments. One of them, the man closest to the top, has a large golden drum strapped to his back as if it were a knapsack; another flourishes a trumpet in his right hand, almost flinging it away as his left leg kicks back from the wall. They look like fantastical versions of steeplejacks, steeplejacks wholly unsupported by pulleys or planks or ropes. And when they reach the flat roof, they will presumably play for us.

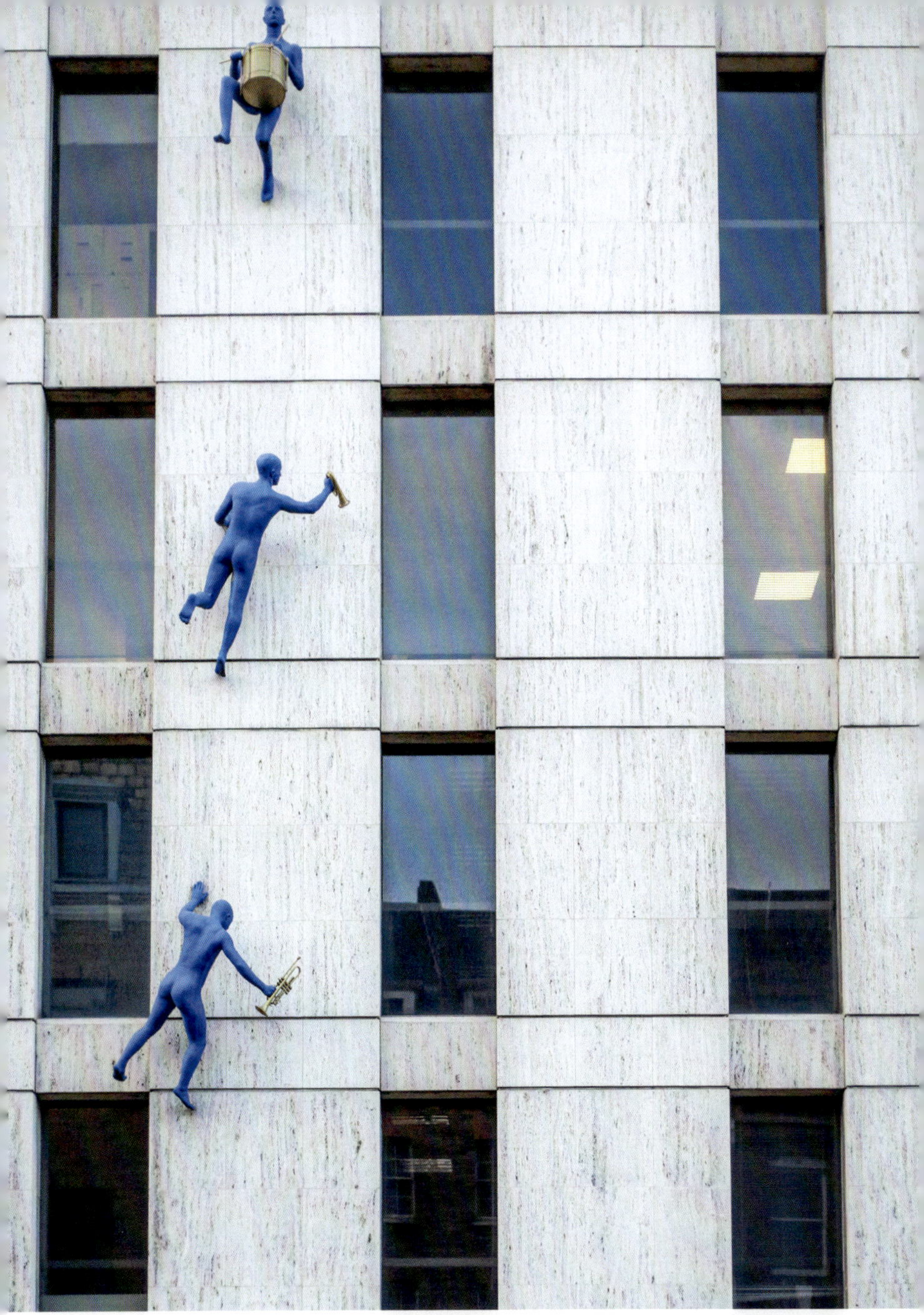

Address Maya House, 134–138 Borough High Street, London SE1 1LB | Getting there Underground to Borough (Northern Line), then a five-minute walk | Hours Accessible 24 hours | Tip Enjoy an excellent lunch of haddock and chips at award-winning restaurant Fish! on Cathedral Street in Borough Market, five minutes' walk away.

11 The Bridge of Aspiration

In flight as any ballet dancer

Bridges, often objects of utility, seldom position themselves as if to welcome admiration and slow appraisal as works of art in their own right.

One exception is a short and dramatic intervention, which can be seen high in the air above Covent Garden, so far above the street in fact that it could almost be cloud-borne. It connects two built structures: Covent Garden's Royal Opera House, and the school where ballerinas learn to leap and pirouette and curtsey to each other. The bridge is at the eastern end of a little cobbled side street just off the main piazza called Floral Street, that name reminding us of the fact that this is where the market sellers would once have dragged great barrow loads of fruits, vegetables – and, of course, flowers – to Covent Garden Market, a labour that went on from the time of Charles II in the 1670s to the 1960s.

The bridge is a creation by the WilkinsonEyre partnership, one of London's most excitingly innovative of architectural practices, whose built structures can be seen across the world: they are currently involved with a major development at Sydney Harbour.

This tiny jewel of a bridge seems to embody the spirits of dance and music which, given where it is, is exactly what should be happening, we feel. As it arcs over the space, flinging itself in a single mighty leap through the air, it seems to be giving a bit of a quarter twist, as if it is the bellows of a concertina opening out to let in air before it blows out its long rasping chords. So, the bridge somewhat resembles an instrument. But it also suggests the movement of a dancer too, as she takes flight. You can see into and even through the bridge, to a degree. If you are lucky, you might even spot a ballerina crossing from side to side. So, you can also call the bridge wonderfully fanciful, an acknowledgement of the perpetual restlessness of dance.

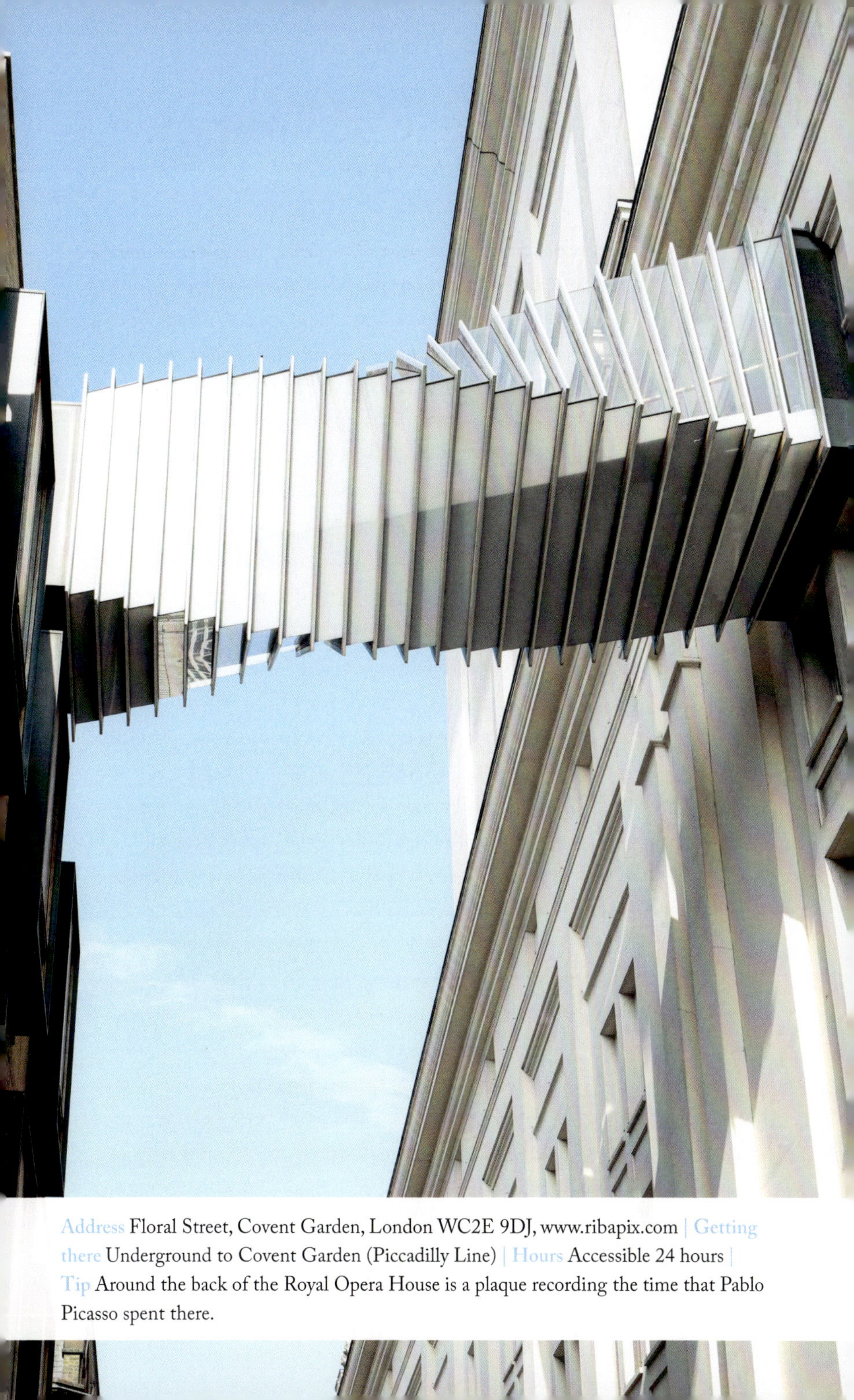

Address Floral Street, Covent Garden, London WC2E 9DJ, www.ribapix.com | Getting there Underground to Covent Garden (Piccadilly Line) | Hours Accessible 24 hours | Tip Around the back of the Royal Opera House is a plaque recording the time that Pablo Picasso spent there.

12 The Broody Pelican

An 18th-century masterwork

Some ancient churches look so squeezed in beside other buildings that they barely seem able to breathe. Such is St Michael's, Cornhill, in the City of London, which was made by a pupil of Wren's, and whose magnificent tower, the work of Sir Nicholas Hawksmoor, closely resembles the one at Magdalen College, Oxford. This church is famed for its long history of choral music, which continues to this day – some of the organ pipes would have been in place when Henry Purcell played it in the late 17th century.

The church was much remodelled in the 19th century, but its finest art is to be found at the west end, hidden away in semi-darkness, beneath a scene of Christ's crucifixion. And it is directly beneath this scene of Christ's agony on the cross that we spot a magnificent wooden Pelican in her Piety, raised up on a high shelf, fabricated late in the 18th century by an artist called Joseph Glazeley. The pelican seems to be feeding her young brood. Five of them surround her feet, beaks raised.

In fact, the pelican is an ancient symbol of Christ the Saviour, denoting his own sacrifice for mankind – he has chosen to pierce his own breast with his beak, thus shedding his blood. The young brood is feeding off this blood.

Though not well lit, we take in the drama of the scene – the pelican's wings are wide spread, as if protecting her young. She is rearing up and back, dramatically, as if almost mindful of the symbolic importance of her act. The pelican's beak is slightly agape – we see the long lash of her tongue. Her layered feathers are individually carved and highly stylised, as if they were elements of an armorial shield – it looks almost as if she is armoured against adversity. She stands on a woven bed of dark osier, which is the nest in which she protects her young from harm. The work is badly in need of cleaning and restoration.

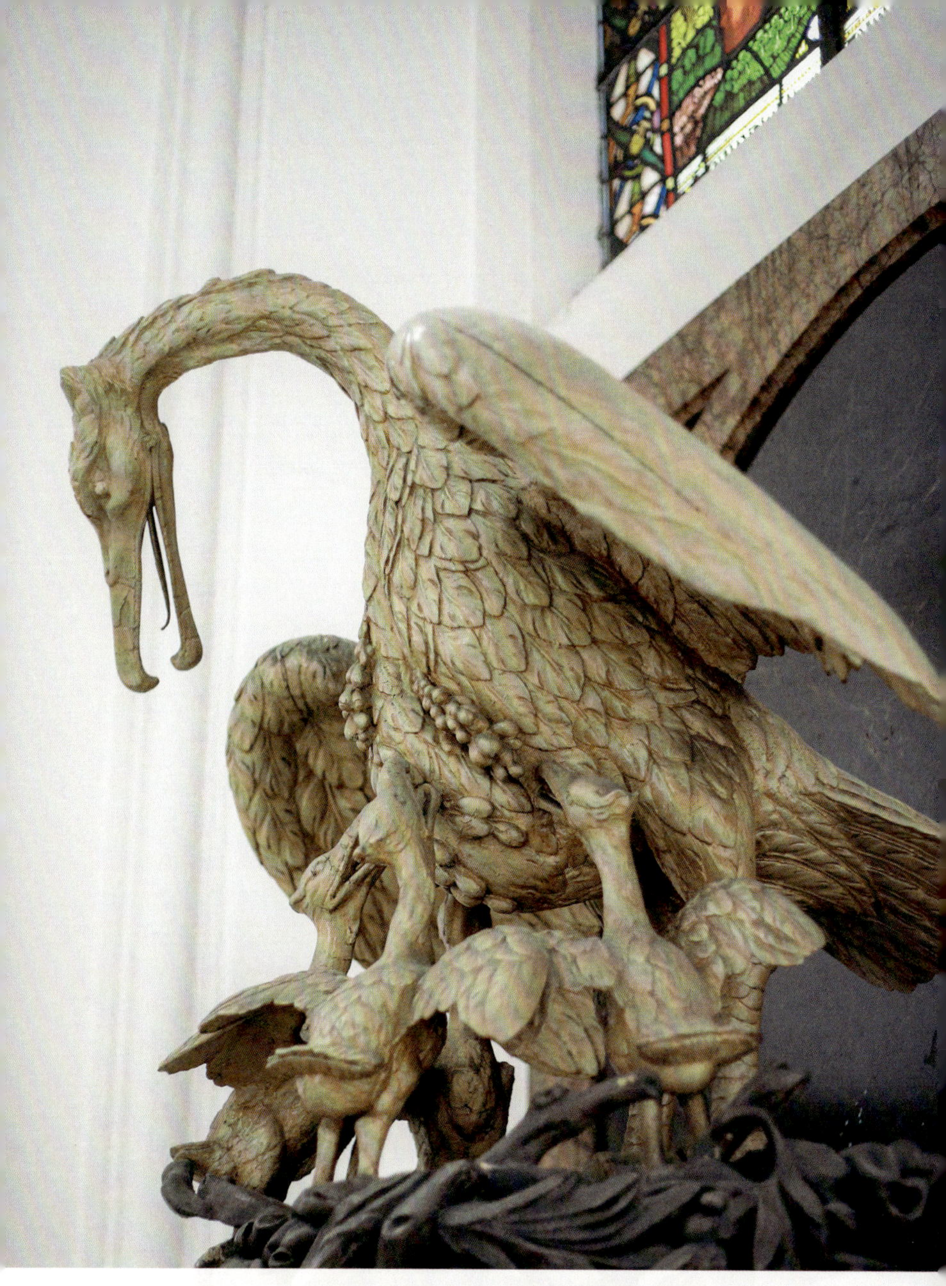

Address St Michael's Alley, London EC3V 9DS, +44 (0)207 283 3121, www.st-michaels.org.uk | Getting there Underground to Bank (Central, Northern, Waterloo and City Lines and DLR), then a five-minute walk | Hours Mon 10am–7pm, Tue–Fri 10am–4.30pm | Tip Visit the magnificent covered Leadenhall Market in Gracechurch Street, which sells mainly fresh food and flowers. It was used in *Harry Potter and the Philosopher's Stone* to represent Diagon Alley and the Leaky Cauldron.

13 The Burghers of Calais

Sacrificial victims on display

London is lucky to have so many sculptures by Auguste Rodin. Luck? The tragedy of war helped a little too. In 1914, 18 works by him were put on display at the Grosvenor Gallery in London as part of an exhibition of French sculpture. A little later, war broke out. The sculptures found themselves stranded. They were loaned to the Victoria and Albert Museum for six months. Then Rodin, in a gesture of Anglo-French amity, donated them to the museum as a way of commemorating the fact that French and British soldiers were dying side by side on the battlefields of France. In 1915, he made a further gift of a bronze cast of a figure group created for Calais. *The Burghers of Calais* was set on a low plinth in Victoria Embankment Gardens, a long, tapering park bordered by avenues of London planes, beside Parliament's Victoria Tower.

When Rodin first displayed the group at his studio in Meudon, it was raised up on a high wooden plinth, so that onlookers could stare up into the anguished faces. The sculpture group is a sustained piece of story-telling. The date is 1346–47. The port of Calais was under sustained siege by the forces of Edward III of England. In order to avoid the wholesale butchery of the citizenry of the town, he invited six prominent citizens to volunteer for death. These six men are the ones, all preparing for the afterlife. In the end, they were spared.

Rodin's work is so often about bodily contortion, the writhing of limbs. He liked nothing better than to put together body parts at striking angles. And so it is here. There is some exaggeration in the anguish – the bare, damaged feet are over-large, for example. The bodies are almost on the shrivel. The faces contort horribly. At every angle from which we view it – and it is very important to circle it and circle it – we seem to happen upon a slightly different take on the tragedy.

Address Victoria Tower Gardens, London SW1P 3JU | **Getting there** Underground to Westminster (District, Circle and Jubilee Lines), then a seven-minute walk | **Hours** Daily 7am–8.30pm | **Tip** As well as Rodin's sculpture, you will find a statue to the suffragette leader Emmeline Pankhurst, and a fountain commemorating the emancipation of slaves in 1834.

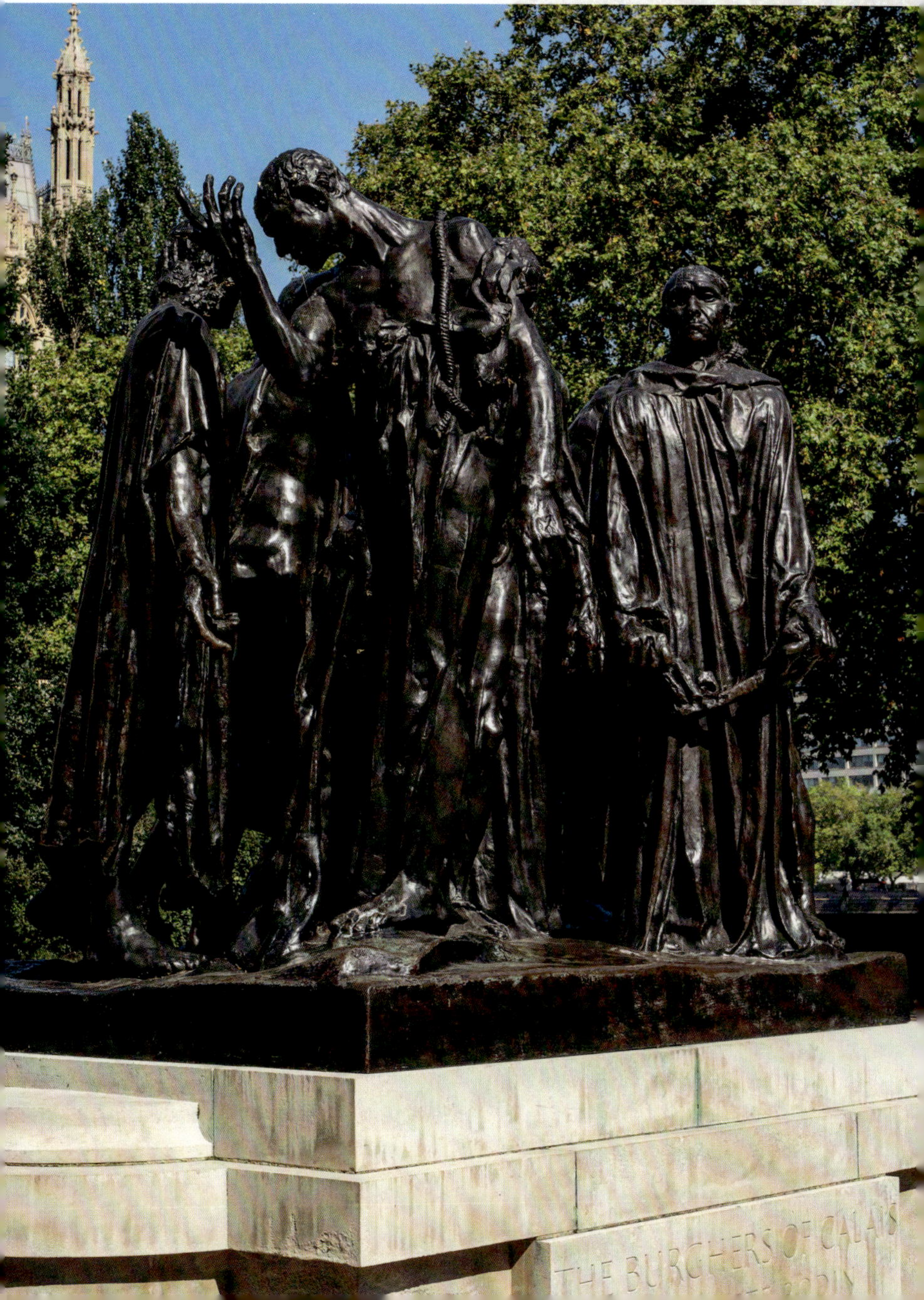

14 Canterbury Tales Retold

Canteen walls turned stage set

You can often find some very good art in a student canteen. Take Morley College in south London, for example, which was founded to give educational opportunities to working people at the end of the 19th century. It has had some famous teachers in its time – Bertrand Russell, Virginia Woolf and the composer Holst are amongst them – and there have been fine artists at work on the walls of the refectory on the third floor.

In fact, its cycle of murals was painted not once, but twice. The first ones – created by Eric Ravilious and others during the 1930s – were obliterated during the Blitz, when the building took a direct hit. After the war, the college was rebuilt, and by 1962, plans were hatched to prettify the walls of the refectory once again. This time four huge murals were created by the artist Edward Bawden and his student son Justin Todd. They were painted on wooden panels in a converted piggery in Essex, and then transported to London, to this delightful, light-flooded, L-shaped room.

There are fine views from the windows onto the gardens of a very characteristic, 19th-century London terrace. Bawden's wish was to create a cycle of story-telling paintings that would induce a mood of good cheer, and he chose scenes from Chaucer's *Canterbury Tales*, often slotting several tales into a single wide narrative scene. To see the best of them, you need to carry your tray of coffee and sandwiches down to the end of the room and turn left. Two murals face each other on the walls, and the more delightful and more vigorously painted of the two is on the left. It shows scenes from the Reeve's Tale and the Miller's Tale, the second of which is a highly coloured, raunchy romp. And all is enclosed within a castle courtyard that is pure stage set. Food is being scoffed at the table, buttocks are exposed, knights descend steep stairs, swords at the ready. What a romp!

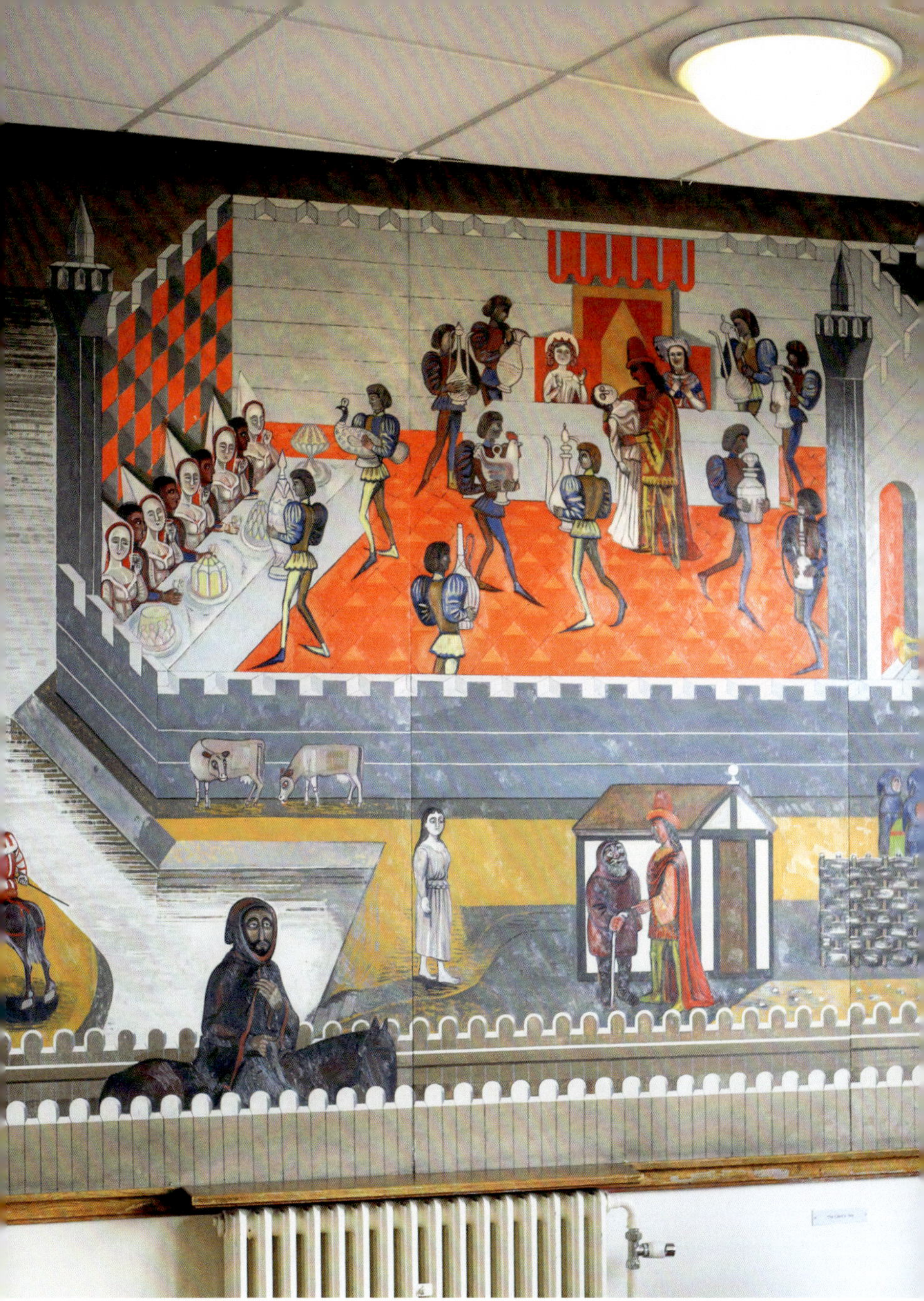

Address Morley College, 61 Westminster Bridge Road, London SE1 7HT, +44 (0)207 450 1889, www.morleycollege.ac.uk | Getting there Underground to Lambeth North (Bakerloo Line), then a five-minute walk | Hours Mon–Fri 9am–8pm, Sat 9am–4pm | Tip Look out for changing exhibitions at the Morley Gallery (www.morleygallery.com).

15 Captain Coram

Saviour of London's orphans

The Foundling Hospital in Bloomsbury was created in the 18th century by a philanthropical sea captain and shipwright called Captain Coram. It existed to save the unwanted babies of the poor from near certain death – they could be handed over to the hospital by their mothers for nurture and safe-keeping. Not all, alas, could be accepted.

The Foundling Museum was built on part of the site of the hospital (the rest of it is a public park called Coram's Fields to which adults can only by admitted if accompanied by children), and its picture gallery on the first floor (a replica of the original) displays the collection of paintings that were donated to that first institution, which include a painting of the original building by a youthful Thomas Gainsborough, and a bust of Handel (another benefactor).

We approach the gallery up the sweep of a grand staircase. The portrait of Captain Coram himself, which was the first painting to enter the hospital's collection, is a near perfect embodiment of his swashbuckling character – and it is also, incidentally, the only full-length portrait ever made by William Hogarth. The picture is still on display in its original frame. The seated captain, gripping his gloves, is brought so vividly alive – admire the glitter of his buckled shoes, the huge globe, the various scrolled maps to remind us of his exploits at sea, and the sheer display of his magnificently epauletted frock coat. His grey hair puff-billows out, as if tempestuously tousled, and his legs are spread as if he is ready to take on all comers.

On display we also see the Royal Charter that was granted to enable the founding of the hospital. There is even a view of the sea. A classical column adds a touch of gravity to the occasion, as does the fact that the scene is raised up on a dais – another indication that this is a man of some clout and status.

Address 40 Brunswick Square, London WC1N 1AZ, +44 (0)207 841 3600, www.foundling museum.org.uk | Getting there Underground to Russell Square (Piccadilly Line), then a five-minute walk | Hours Tue–Sat 10am–5pm, Sun 11am–5pm | Tip Skoob Books, London's finest second-hand bookshop, is five minutes' walk from here.

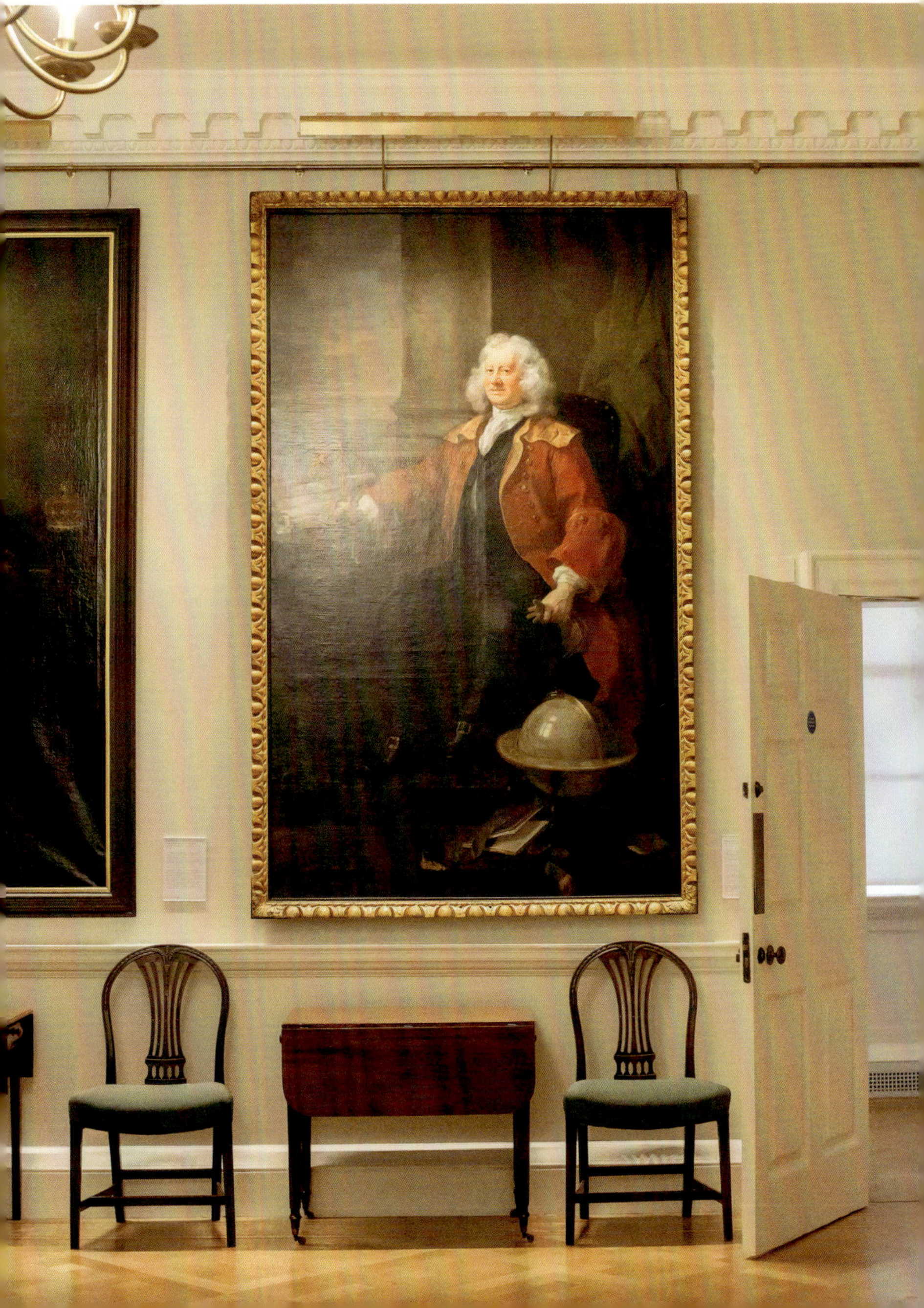

16 Caulfield's Last Laugh

A gravestone unlike any other

There are many distinguished permanent residents who sleep in peace at Highgate Cemetery East. Those buried there include Colnaghi the art dealer, Alan Sillitoe the novelist, Edward Elgar the composer, and that international rabble-rouser Karl Marx, who has not one memorial there but two: a modest grave and a triumphally immodest memorial in marble topped by a bust of his tremendous bearded head, around which cluster, as if in homage, such stalwart men of the left as Michael Foot, former leader of the Labour Party, and the great historian Eric Hobsbawm.

But there is one grave here that is so unlike any other, it makes you almost blink in disbelief when you spot it. It's almost directly opposite the grave of the actor Ralph Richardson, two-thirds of the way along the avenue that leads to the Chester Road Gate, and on the right-hand side.

It is not sited in plain view, and it is not beside the avenue, so you could say that it is not seeking to draw attention to itself. Patrick Caulfield is described in the key to the cemetery's inhabitants as a pop artist, but that is to do him something of a disservice, because his paintings were more formally subtle and richer in their use of colour than anything that the pop artists ever managed.

The gravestone, which is set side on to the avenue, is a single upreared stone slab out of which four letters have been cut. Those letters simply read: DEAD. The letters seem to be stepping down, letter by letter, as if stepping into the grave itself. The visual impact is that of a concrete poem – a kind of writing that was very popular in the 1960s, when Caulfield was making some of his best work. It enacts its meaning with dignity. It is a little lugubrious. It is also very funny. We almost laugh out loud when we spot it playing its marvellous visual joke. It reminds us of Spike Milligan, another great man who took death lightly.

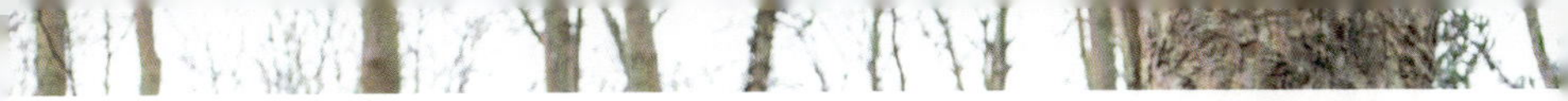

Address Highgate Cemetery East, Swain's Lane, London N6 6PJ, +44 (0)208 340 1834, www.highgatecemetery.org | **Getting there** Underground to Archway Station (Northern Line), then a 15-minute walk uphill – or you could take the 143 or 271 bus up the hill to Waterlow Park | **Hours** Daily Mar–Oct 10am–5pm, Nov–Feb 10am–4pm; guided tours are offered daily | **Tip** Lauderdale House, in Waterlow Park, is an elegant house dating from 1582. Now run as an arts centre, it has a theatre and holds exhibitions, concerts and family fun days. There is also a good café.

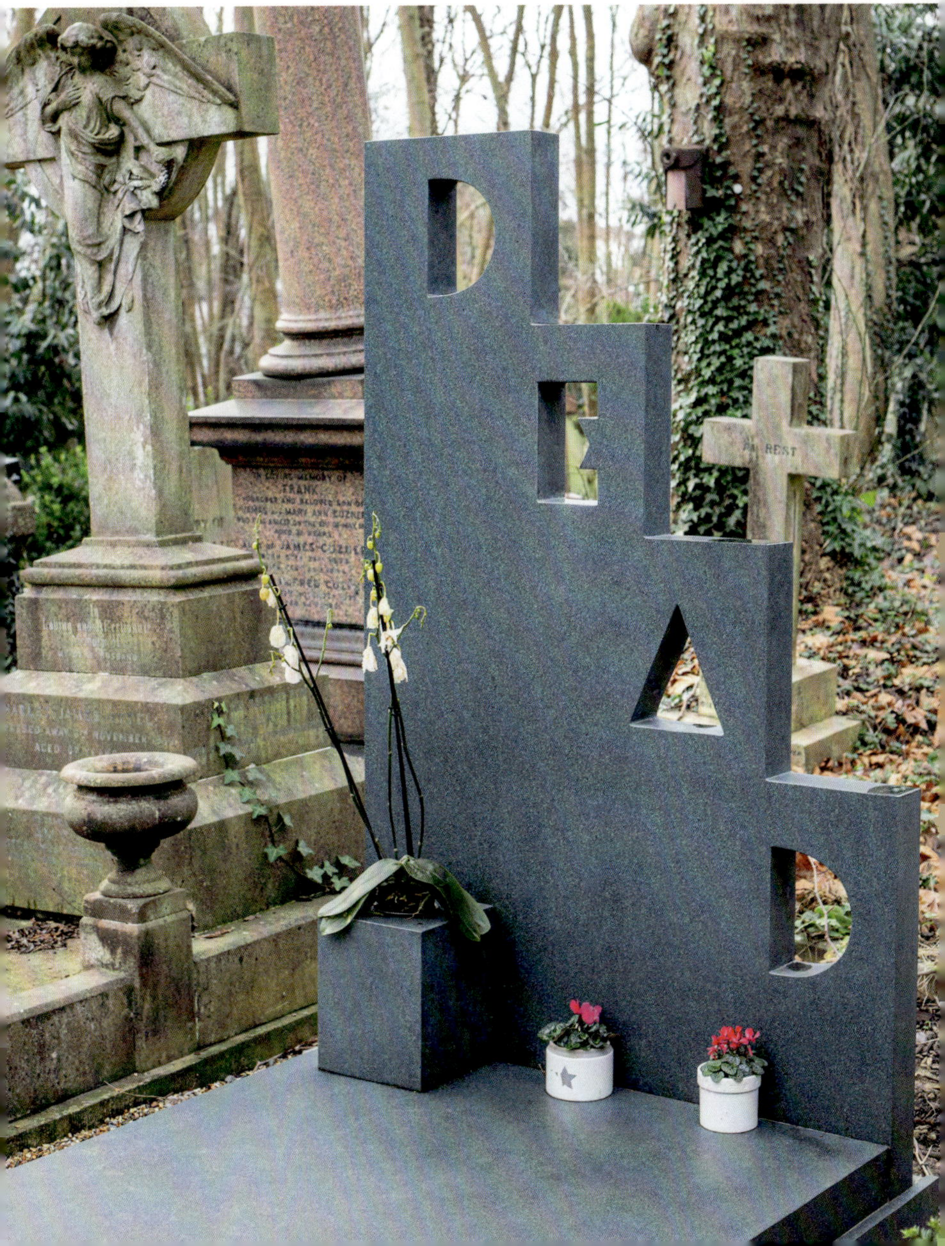

17 Charles I on Horseback

A masterpiece saved from destruction

There are far too many mediocre equestrian statues in central London. This one, by contrast, deserves our attention. It is just beyond the southernmost tip of Trafalgar Square, sitting on its own circular island these days, facing downhill towards Whitehall. Unlike all the other public monuments near this square, this statue has no name, no date of fabrication, and no acknowledged maker. How perplexingly sad.

Its identity, and its positioning here, give it especial poignancy. This is Charles I, that autocratic, Parliament-defying Stuart king (and great art collector) who was beheaded a few hundred yards away from here outside Inigo Jones' Banqueting Hall in 1649. He stares down towards the place of his own beheading. The statue itself, by a Frenchman called Hubert Le Sueur, is a remarkable survival, from the fourth decade of the 17th century. Many images of the Stuart kings were destroyed by the regicides. This one was hidden away, and eventually found its way back here…

In Daniel Mytens' portrait of the king of 1631 at the National Portrait Gallery, Charles stands on his own two feet. We admire his magnificent, trowel-shaped beard, extended moustaches and shoulder-length hair. Physically, he is undeniably a weakling whose body was always likely to profit by the puffing out of a suit of armour. In Trafalgar Square he's in armour too, but less of an attempt has been made to suggest that he is a powerful physical presence. Luckily, he is raised up high, far beyond the reach of mere mortals, which always helps to dignify. We recognise that same beard. The ends of his moustache prick the blue sky. He is carrying what to the ignorant may look like a long police baton – in fact, it is his commander's baton. The sculptor has not troubled to flatter him or make him seem an unusually commanding presence. This is a small man, raised up on a large, frisky horse.

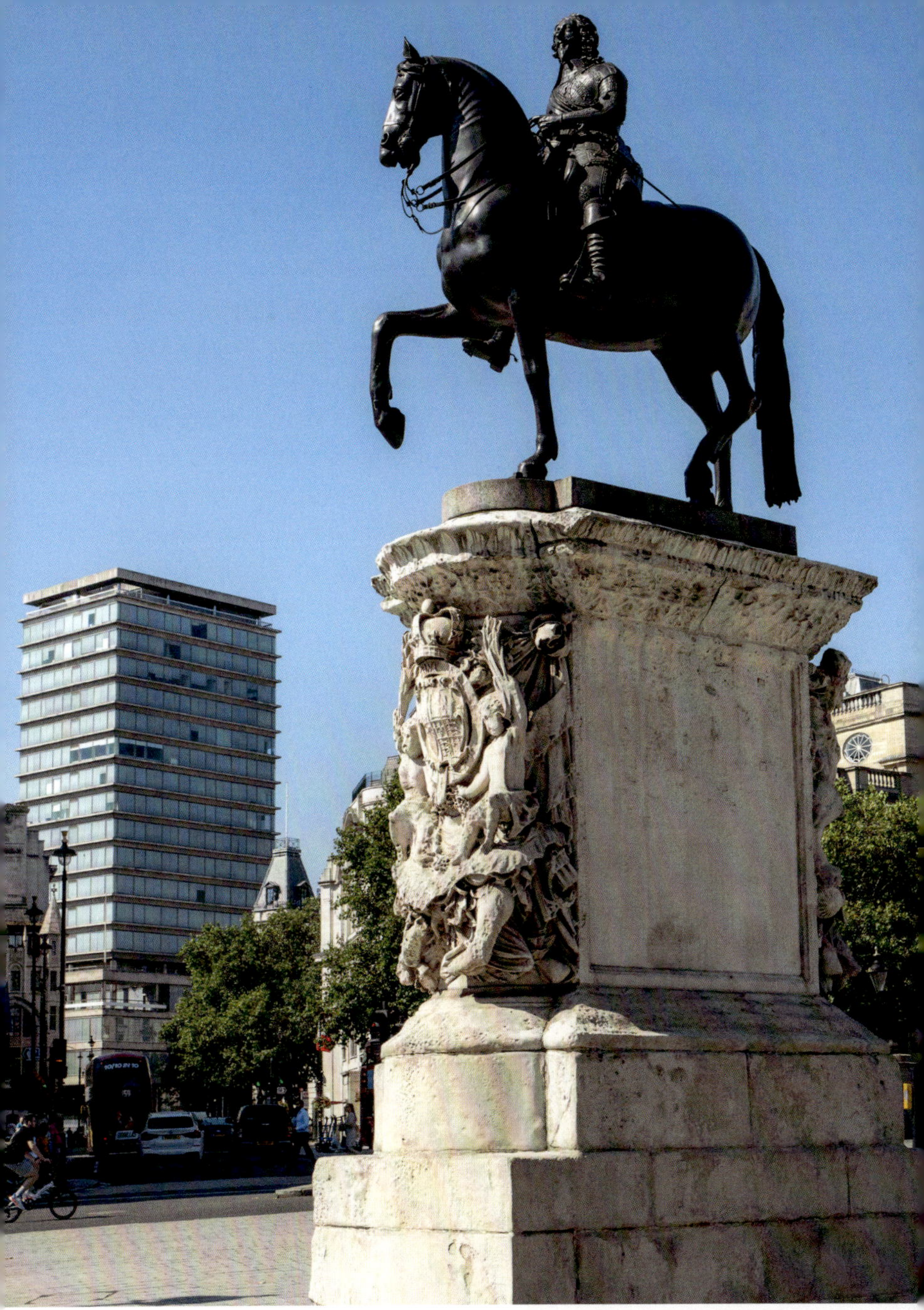

Address Top of Whitehall, London SW1A 2DX | Getting there Underground to Embankment (District, Circle, Bakerloo and Northern Lines) | Hours Accessible 24 hours | Tip Spot the plaque to Ho Chi Minh, founder of modern Vietnam, on New Zealand House, just off Pall Mall.

18 Charles II Steps Out

The monarch of Soho night life

Even raffish Soho has its quiet quarter-acres of green set-apartness. Such is Soho Square, at the northern end of Frith Street, just a short walk up from the famous Ronnie Scott's Jazz Club, where horn players have been blowing their lungs out for decades.

The square itself, unlike so many, is a public park where people lounge around on the grass munching sandwiches, or sit on one of the many stout wooden benches, and wonder which building on this square is home to Paul McCartney's recording studio. There are two delightful curiosities at the square's centre. One looks like a tiny half-timbered market hall of the kind that might have been built in Tudor times. It appears weathered, and slightly on the tilt as you might well expect of an old wooden structure. Pure fakery. It was built in 1926 to disguise essential council maintenance work.

The other curiosity is original to the square, and has done some travelling over its long life. This is the statue of the Stuart monarch Charles II, which was fabricated by a jobbing Danish sculptor called Caius Gabriel Cibber, and placed here in 1681, soon after the square itself was created – and not long after the monarchy was restored, and the monarch himself returned from exile in France. The statue spent much of its life languishing on a country estate, and was restored to its rightful place here in 1938, thanks to the generosity and determination of a Lady Gilbert. In spite of the fact that it has suffered damage over the years – Charles' face looks as if it might have been knocked about in the boxing ring – the figure is imposing.

The fact that the figure stands, unhorsed, on a relatively low plinth means that we can get a very good view of it. The sculptor does not seek to flatter. The legs are armoured and well modelled. The posture – left leg thrust forward – is relatively casual. A sandwich perhaps, sire?

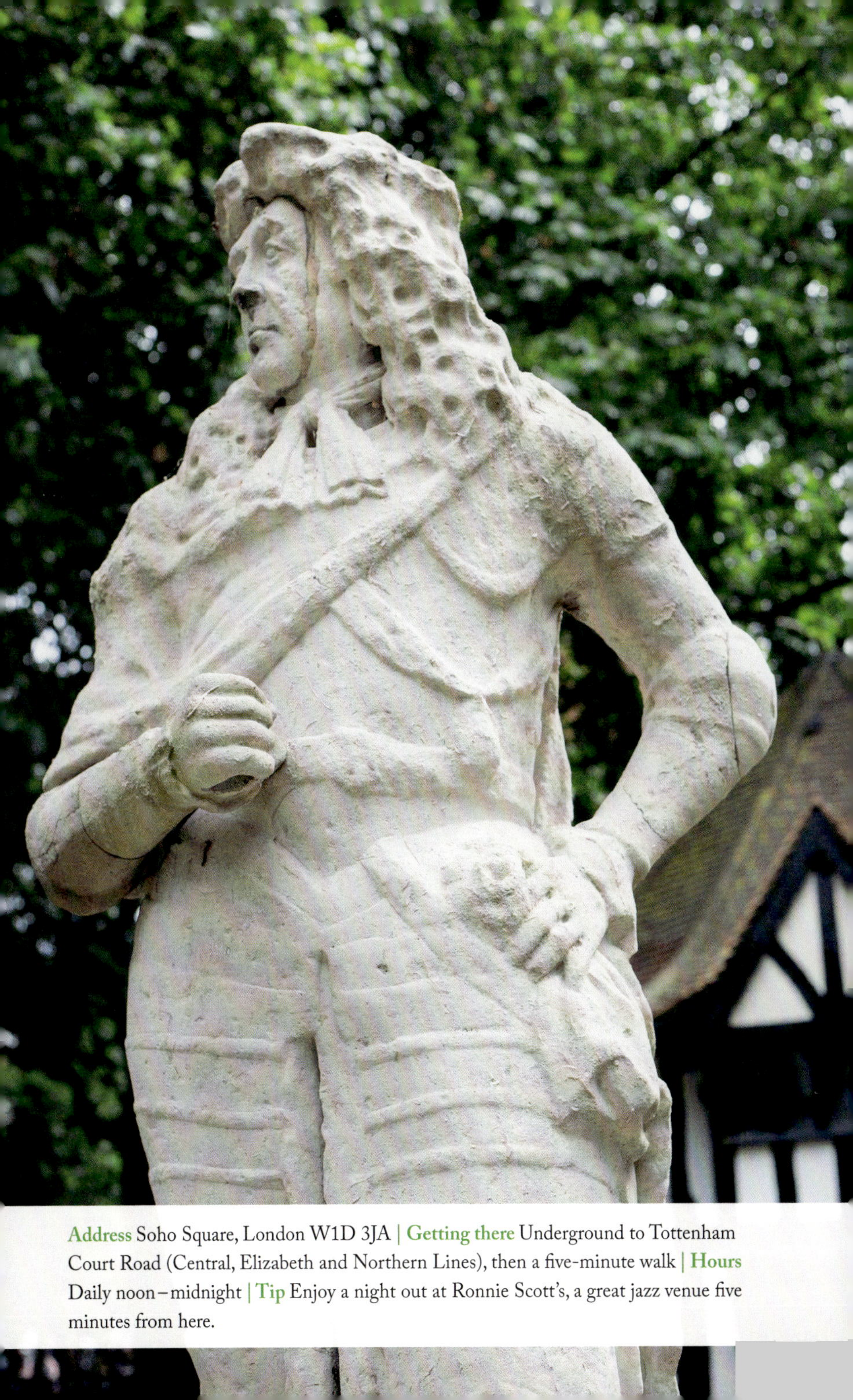

Address Soho Square, London W1D 3JA | **Getting there** Underground to Tottenham Court Road (Central, Elizabeth and Northern Lines), then a five-minute walk | **Hours** Daily noon–midnight | **Tip** Enjoy a night out at Ronnie Scott's, a great jazz venue five minutes from here.

19 Christ the Healer

The young Hogarth paints history

To find the art we are looking for, you will first need to pass through the Henry VIII Gate – admire the statue of that Tudor monarch displayed above you, in a niche, as you go. The oldest surviving part of St Bart's Hospital is the North Wing, which was created in the 18th century, and its finest room the picture-bedecked Great Hall, where the names of all those who paid to create this great institution are listed, one by one, together with the sums that they contributed.

But the art that deserves most attention in this building overlooks the great staircase you would have ascended to reach this grand reception room on the first floor. Two large-scale narrative paintings can be seen on the walls as you climb the stairs, and they were both made by a man called William Hogarth, who had been born in a street nearby (his mother and his sister were living within the precincts of the hospital in 1720), who was to become in time one of the greatest painters of that century. The larger of the two paintings, which engulfs the entire end wall of the building, is on a biblical theme, but its story also relates directly to the fact that the painting is being displayed in a hospital.

It shows Christ healing the sick at the Pool of Bethesda in Jerusalem, a scene described in the Gospel According to St John. Christ stands at the centre of the painting, hand extended in welcome, bathed in a pool of light, overlooking the sick, who are collapsed, and near naked, beside the pool. Other needy people – a woman, a babe in arms – are approaching; an angel watches over the scene from on high. It is all very busy and rather crowded. Hogarth was a young man when he did this work in the 1730s, with little experience of painting at such a scale. It seems likely that he used patients from the hospital's wards as models for the sick and the injured. He took no payment for his work.

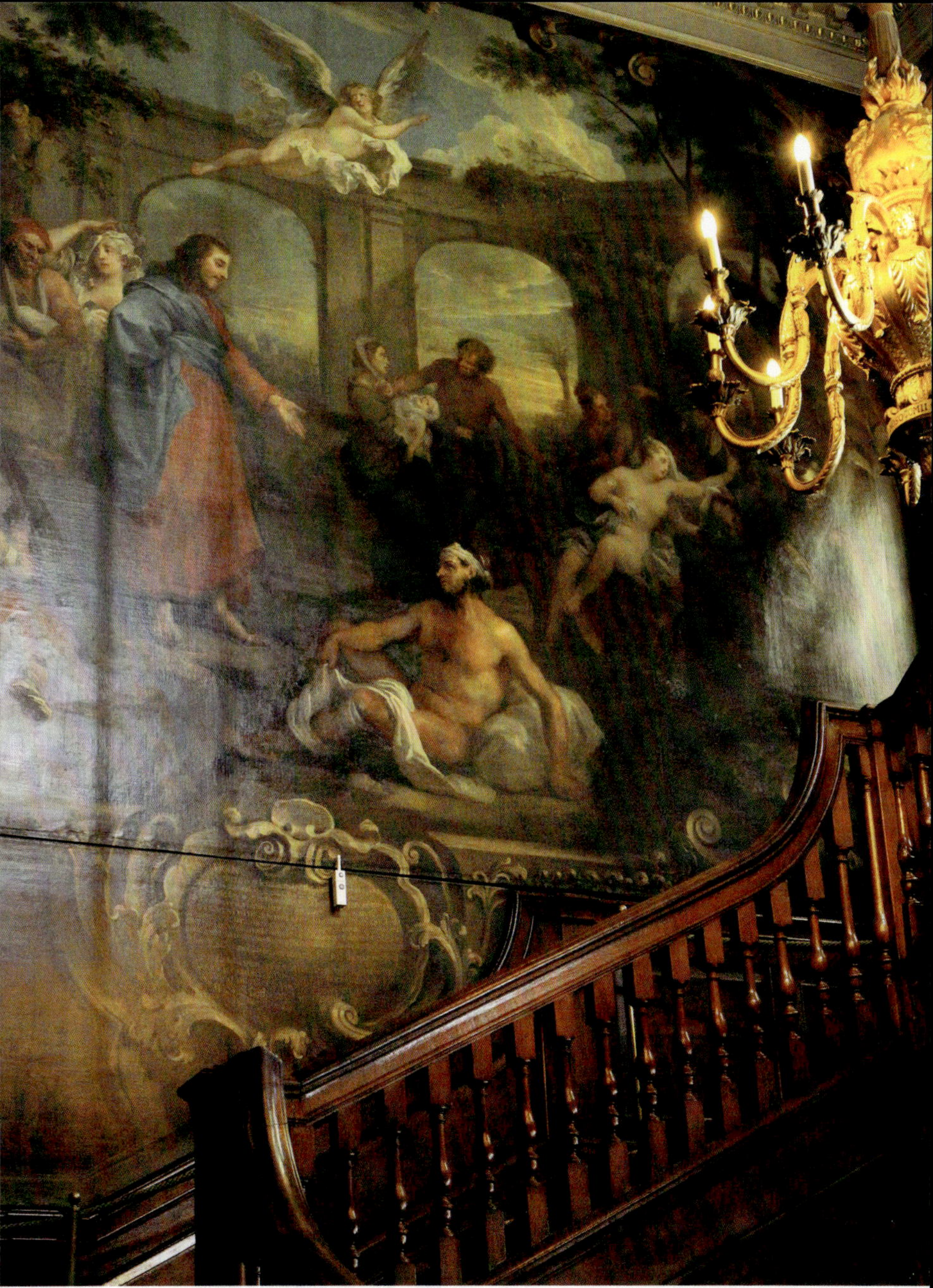

Address West Smithfield, London EC1 7BE, +44 (0)203 465 7608 (for St Bartholomews Hospital Museum), www.medicalmuseums.org | Getting there Underground to Barbican (Circle, Hammersmith and City and Metropolitan Lines), then a five-minute walk | Hours Hospital Museum Tue–Fri 10am–4pm (check visiting hours of staircase with museum) | Tip Visit historic Smithfield Market facing you as you leave the hospital.

20 The Coade Stone Lion

The regal upgrading of a pub mascot

When the English Lion roars, the world looks on in trepidation. Or perhaps not? The delightful, outsized lion that sits high on its magnificent stone plinth on the south side of Westminster Bridge has more than a touch of the comic about it. Its ringleted mane is positively baroque. Its downturned mouth reminds you of a disgruntled judge in his chambers. Its huge legs – almost elephantine in their girth – are massively rooted. It looks as much pantomimic as regal. It is well positioned to be impressive, nudging up as it does against County Hall (now a Marriott Hotel), which was the seat of London's government until Margaret Thatcher did away with such a pesky thing. And it's within full view of Big Ben on the north side of a bridge, which is now, thanks to its processional of stout bollards, a wonderfully safe and broad pedestrian walkway.

Many great public monuments are tailor-made for the plinths on which they come to rest. Not so this chunky, muscly lion, which has done a bit of roaming in its time. It is also not quite what it seems. It is, for a start, not made from quarried stone at all. Modelled by W. F. Woodington, it is fabricated from an artificial material called Coade stone. From 1837 onwards, it stood on a parapet above the river entrance to the Lion Brewery, which was in Lambeth. It had the luck and the fortitude to survive World War II. And after the preparations were made to build the Royal Festival Hall and the South Bank Centre, it was preserved at the express wish of King George VI. So, though a pub lion, you could argue that it is also, by favour, a regal beast.

Its name – you can read it, picked out in gold, on the side of the plinth that faces towards St Thomas' Hospital – is The South Bank Lion. It therefore gives its blessing to all the theatre and the music that goes on…at its back. Why is it turned away quite so disdainfully?

Address Westminster Bridge (south-east side) | **Getting there** Underground to Westminster (Jubilee, District and Circle Lines), then a five-minute walk over the bridge | **Hours** Accessible 24 hours | **Tip** Next to Lambeth Palace is the Garden Museum, Britain's only museum that celebrates the history, art and design of gardens.

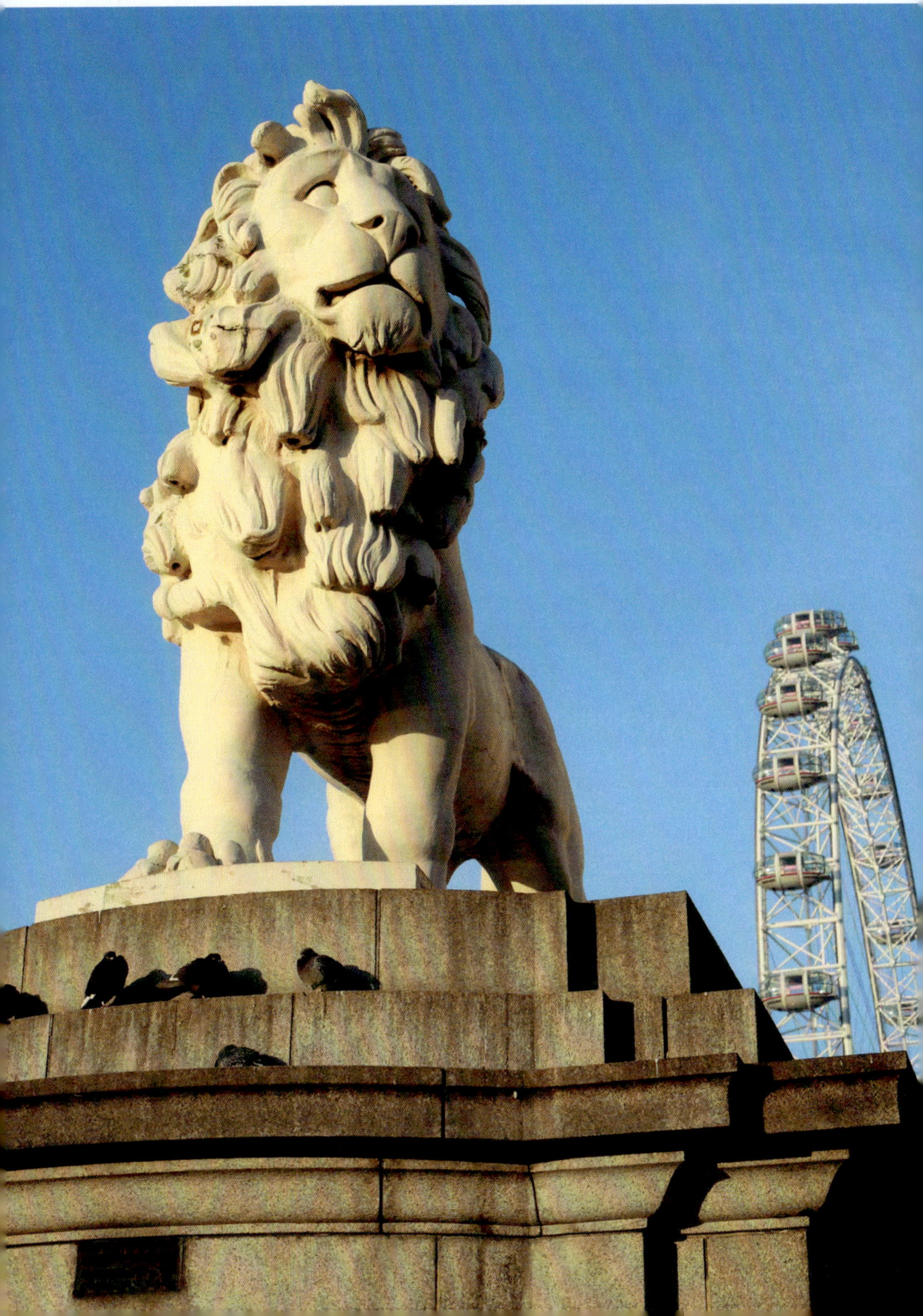

21 The Cocteau Chapel

The gadfly's bold, quick strike

A statue of Shakespeare dominates the little garden at the centre of Leicester Square, the fizzy epicentre of light entertainment in London's West End. Nonchalantly leaning on his elbow, he looks north in the direction of restaurants, cinemas and umpteen casinos – at the roof level of the grandest, the Hippodrome, sculptures of wild horses, desperate gamblers all, launch themselves into the air.

What he appears not to see is the modest, pedestrianised street which, were he to raise his eyes, would be almost facing him. Its presence amidst all this raucousness would surprise him too because it is here that one of London's hidden artistic jewels is to be discovered, in a small, red-brick Catholic basilica called Notre Dame de France. You will recognise it by the many flags that it flies: six flagpoles, two apiece! A few yards north of the church, the fragile red lanterns of London's Chinatown pitch and swing in the wind. In a lovely statue above the main door, the Virgin fans out her skirts to accommodate the apostles, who stare up at her worshipfully.

Inside this elegant and becalming circular church there is a chapel decorated by one of the 20th-century's most energetic gadflies, Jean Cocteau, a man who managed to be so many people in one: *cinéaste*, playwright, novelist, poet, painter and irrepressible Parisian socialite. It was Cocteau who persuaded his friend Pablo Picasso to design the costumes for a revolutionary theatre production called *Parade* in 1917, sending his friend thundering off in yet another creative direction.

By comparison with *Parade*, the chapel feels calm and sequestered. Why here though? You might well ask. Cocteau was in London in 1959 on film business. The drawings of the crucifixion and the assumption are characteristic of Cocteau's style: bold, spare and linear. The work was done with speed and assurance. One week sufficed.

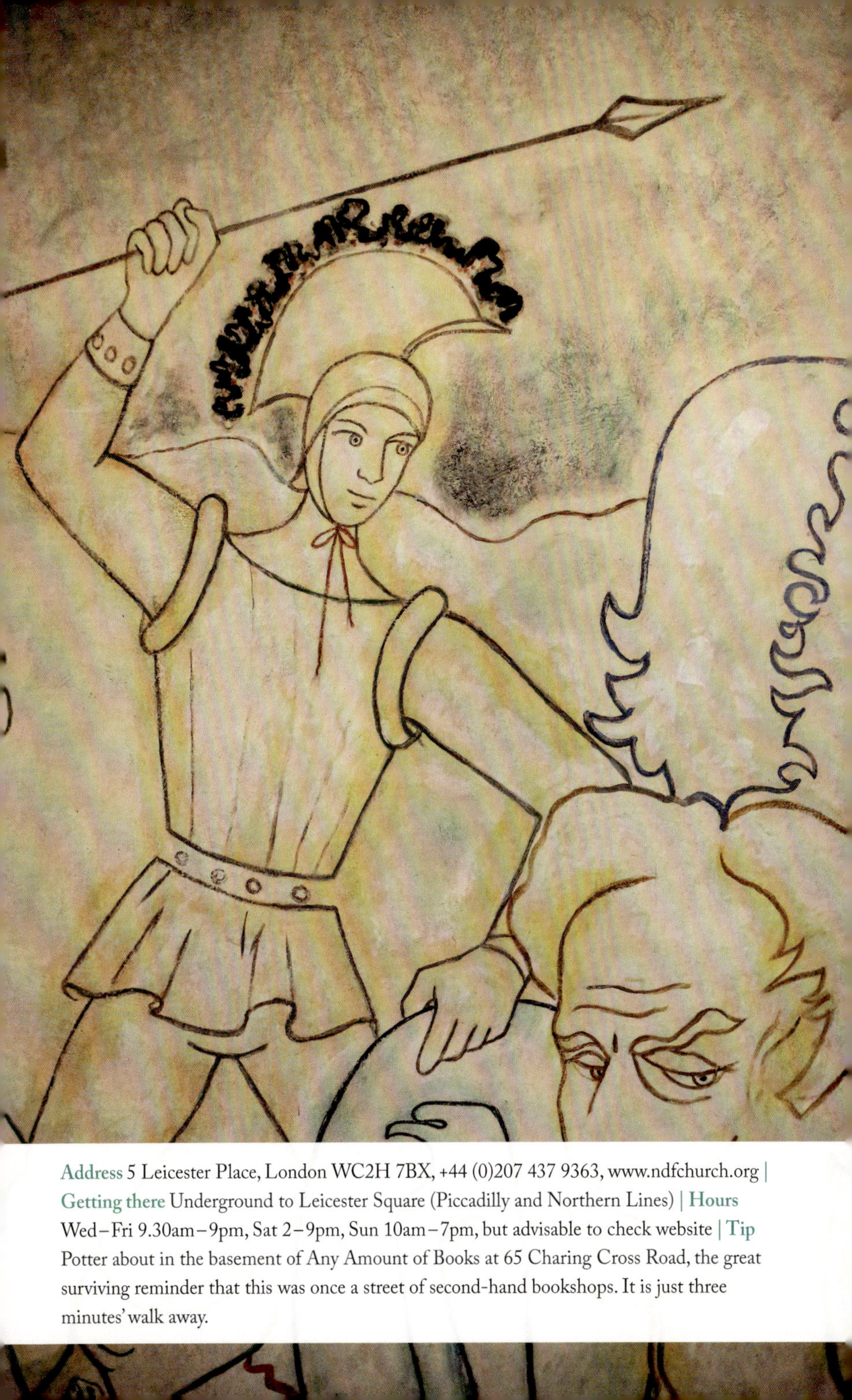

Address 5 Leicester Place, London WC2H 7BX, +44 (0)207 437 9363, www.ndfchurch.org | Getting there Underground to Leicester Square (Piccadilly and Northern Lines) | Hours Wed–Fri 9.30am–9pm, Sat 2–9pm, Sun 10am–7pm, but advisable to check website | Tip Potter about in the basement of Any Amount of Books at 65 Charing Cross Road, the great surviving reminder that this was once a street of second-hand bookshops. It is just three minutes' walk away.

22 Communing With Angels

The visionary fervour of William Blake

William Blake (1757–1827), visionary painter and poet, lived in London for all but three years of his relatively long life, principally in the boroughs of Lambeth and Westminster. Born near Golden Square in what is now the heart of Soho, his father was a hosier by trade. Blake was sent to Henry Par's Drawing School in the Strand at the age of ten, and then went on to become an apprentice engraver to the celebrated James Basire in Great Queen Street, east of Covent Garden. Blake worked as a jobbing engraver and printmaker all his life, earning the most meagre of livings.

But it is for his extraordinary visions, the fantastical works of art, and the enigmatic and paradoxical poems that flowed from his pen, that he is known, and now widely regarded as England's greatest painter-poet. According to the man himself, he regularly communed with angels and such figures of great renown as Aristotle, Jesus and Newton. Many thought him insane. A small coterie of faithful collectors regarded him as a genius, and bought his paintings and prints.

He had just one exhibition of his works during his lifetime, in a room above his brother's hosiery shop in Golden Square. The few critics who bothered to visit condemned it with a mixture of scorn and mockery. Blake, wounded by the ferocity of the condemnation, withdrew from public life for almost a decade.

Blake lived at many different addresses in London – Marshall and Poland Streets in Soho, and South Molton Street in Mayfair, for example – but it is beneath some railway arches close to Archbishop's Park in Lambeth, south London, within a short walk of Hercules Road where he had his studio for upwards of 20 years, that his presence currently sings out most fully.

An entire series of murals, some by professional artists, others by local enthusiasts, have recreated some of his best known and most cherished images.

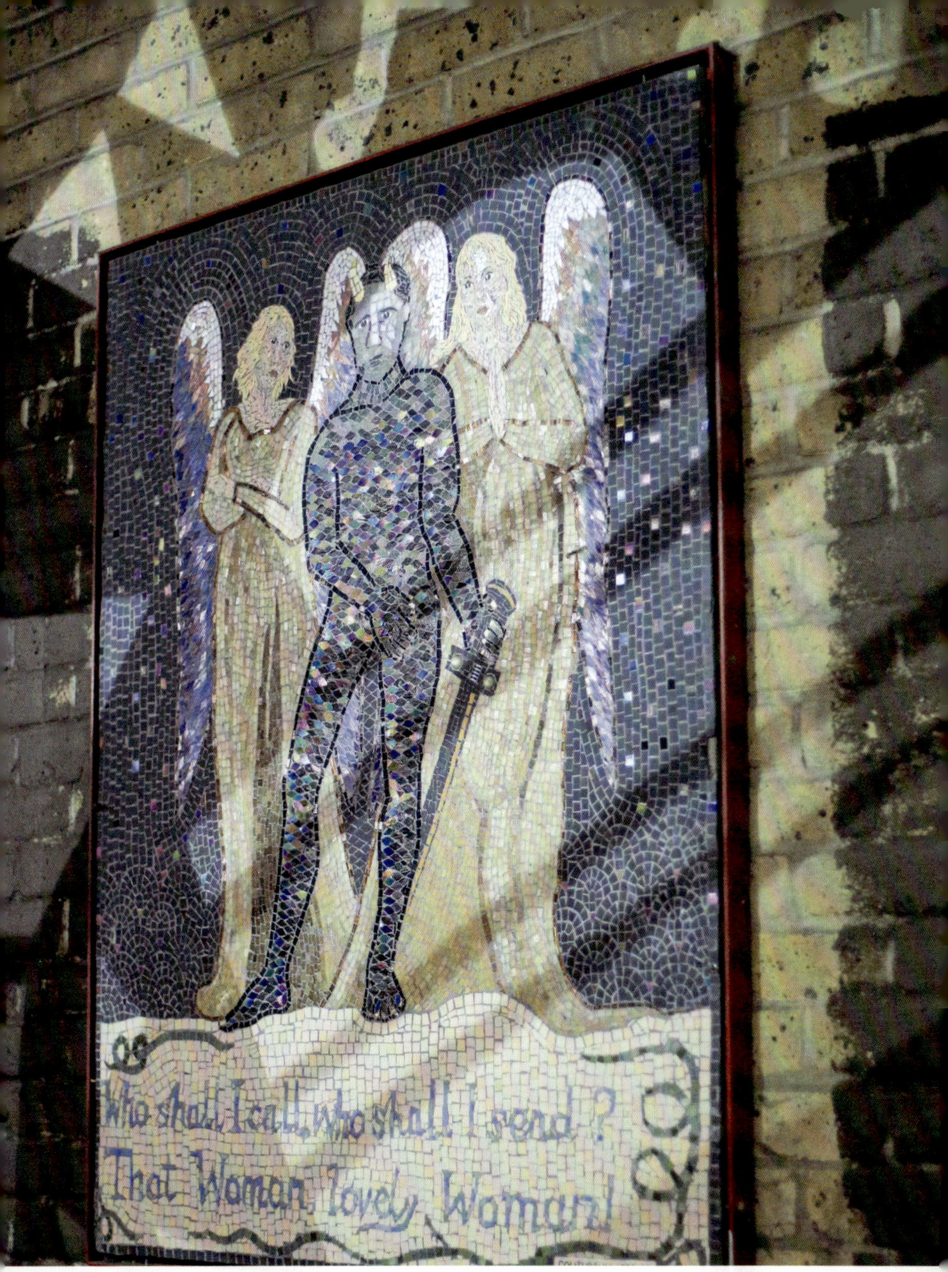

Address The arches, in Carlisle Lane, Virgil Street and Centaur Street, are adjacent to Archbishop's Park (40 Carlisle Lane, London SE1 7LE) | Getting there Underground to Westminster (Circle, District and Jubilee Lines), then a 10-minute walk | Hours Accessible 24 hours | Tip Liberated from the confines of Lambeth Palace, and now sited in the Palace gardens, the new Archbishop's Library is open to all. It describes itself as 'the largest religious collection outside of the Vatican' and includes books dating back to the 12th century.

23 The Crossbones Graveyard

Where the unloved of London are remembered

The name is ominous, almost piratical: the Crossbones Graveyard. It is a graveyard unlike any other in London, overlooked by the Shard, London's tallest and swankiest building. Modest and humble by comparison with such evidence of wealth, it recognises tragedy and injustice by its very presence here, but it is also a kind of joyous, defiant, colourful and loudly demonstrative tribute to thousands of lives that went unremarked and unloved for so long.

You first recognise its presence (almost directly across from a fine vintner called the Boot & Flogger) through the power of art to bring joy along an unlovely stretch of street. A riotous, rag-tag-and-bobtail display of streamers, knotted silks, ribbons, toys, ties, scarves, crushed cans, garish plastic flowers, photographs, paper hearts, hand-written messages on paper saggy with rainwater, and even a single battered boot, hang and swing and blow in the wind across the long length of a tall and forbidding metal fence on Redcross Street in the borough of Southwark.

Sited at the junction of Union Street and Redcross Street, it occupies one small corner of what is currently a great development site, screened off from the world by hoardings. Part the streamers with your fingers and peer through the fence, and you will see a small garden of remembrance, somewhat haphazardly laid out and impromptu in feel. There are stackings of bricks beside bits of cheap religious iconography.

It opens its doors to the public intermittently, currently up to three times a week – everything depends upon the goodwill and the availability of volunteers. This garden covers the site of an ancient burial ground where prostitutes and other unloved and long-neglected social outcasts were once laid in the ground without ceremony, or even a name to be remembered by. It was not officially recognised as a Garden of Remembrance until 2004. Crossbones Graveyard is cared for and managed by many local volunteers and Bankside Open Spaces Trust.

Address Crossbones Graveyard, Redcross Way, London SE1 1TA, www.bost.org.uk | Getting there Underground to London Bridge (Northern and Jubilee Lines), then a five-minute walk | Hours Wed–Fri noon–2pm, but check info@bost.org.uk first | Tip Have a drink at the Boot & Flogger wine bar opposite. Opened in 1965 as Davy's Wine Bar, it became the model for all later wine bars in the capital.

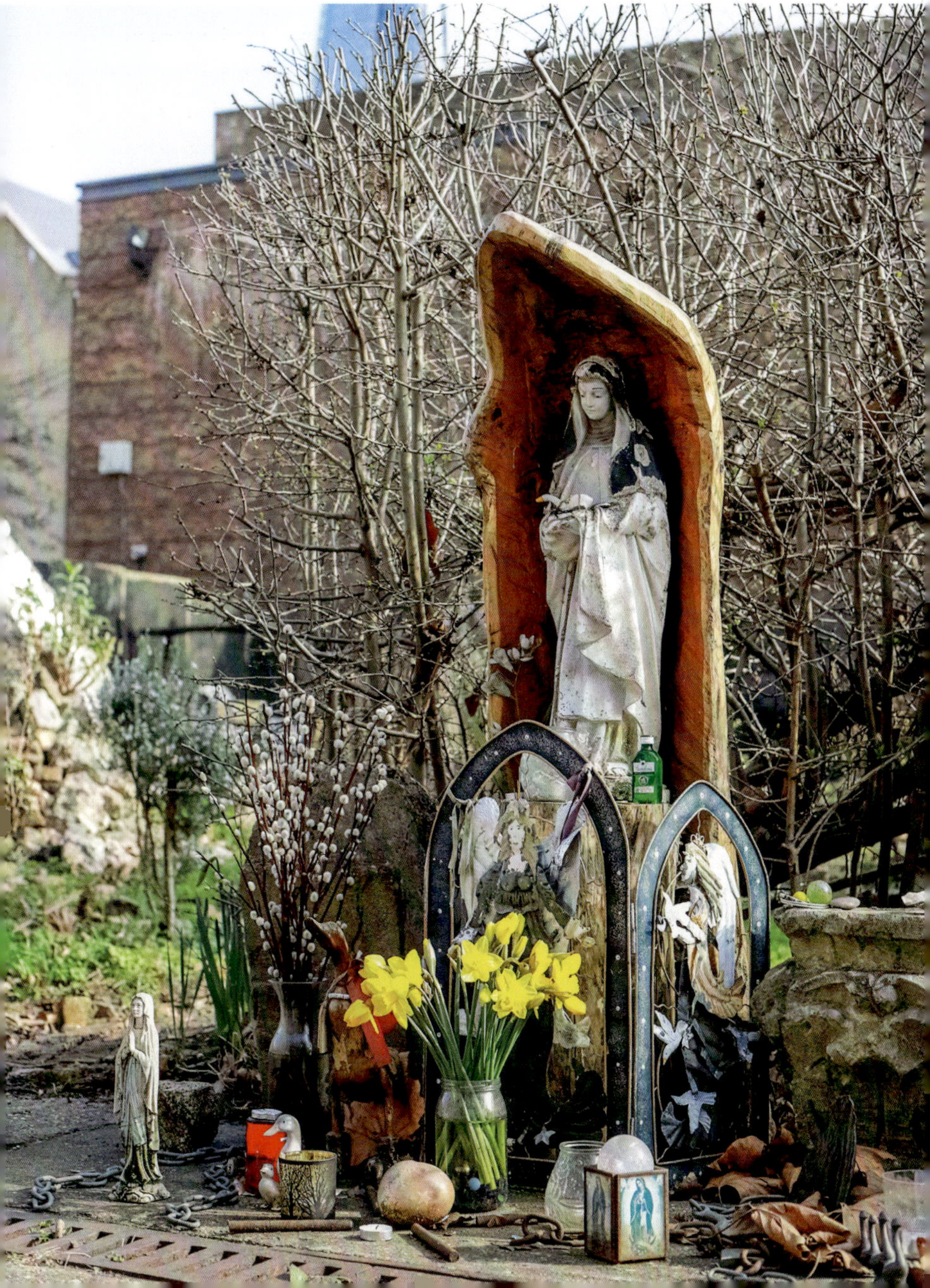

24 Deacon's Cornice

A hangover to savour

We spend too little time looking at the surprises to be found at the tops of buildings. Yes, you often need to look *up* to catch some of the best hidden art in the streets of central London.

Take Piccadilly, for example, as you are approaching Piccadilly Circus from the general direction of Hyde Park Corner. Glance to the right. You are now close to the corner of a recent development called St James's Gateway. At street level this building's windows show off all the restrained sartorial swank that Barbour International can muster.

Now raise your eyes and admire its façade. The architect Eric Parry has embellished it with smooth faience tiles, grey at the start. When you reach the upper range, the colour changes to a rather startling red, and the entire façade also seems to be dusted with snow as if every passing day might just be an excitable child's idea of Christmas.

Then look up further still, to the startling jazzy overhanging cornice. (Above this there is an open arcade.) The cornice is by an internationally celebrated British sculptor called Richard Deacon, but it is much more colourful and flamboyant than his most characteristic work. He often bends wood into mesmerisingly complicated and elegant loopings, as if he is in the throes of proposing some geometric puzzle that no one will ever answer, not even Euclid. These loopings of wood are never painted. Unlike this long cornice, which looks as if it has been tamped in colours we might more readily associate with the snappy rhythms of the Notting Hill Carnival – yellow, red and green. It looks like fabric onto which these colours have been sponged. And then there is the falling movement of its blockish facetings. It is segmented in such a way that it seems to be perpetually rolling or cascading forward – like the movement of a fruit machine in a fairground when you slip in a coin and yank on the arm.

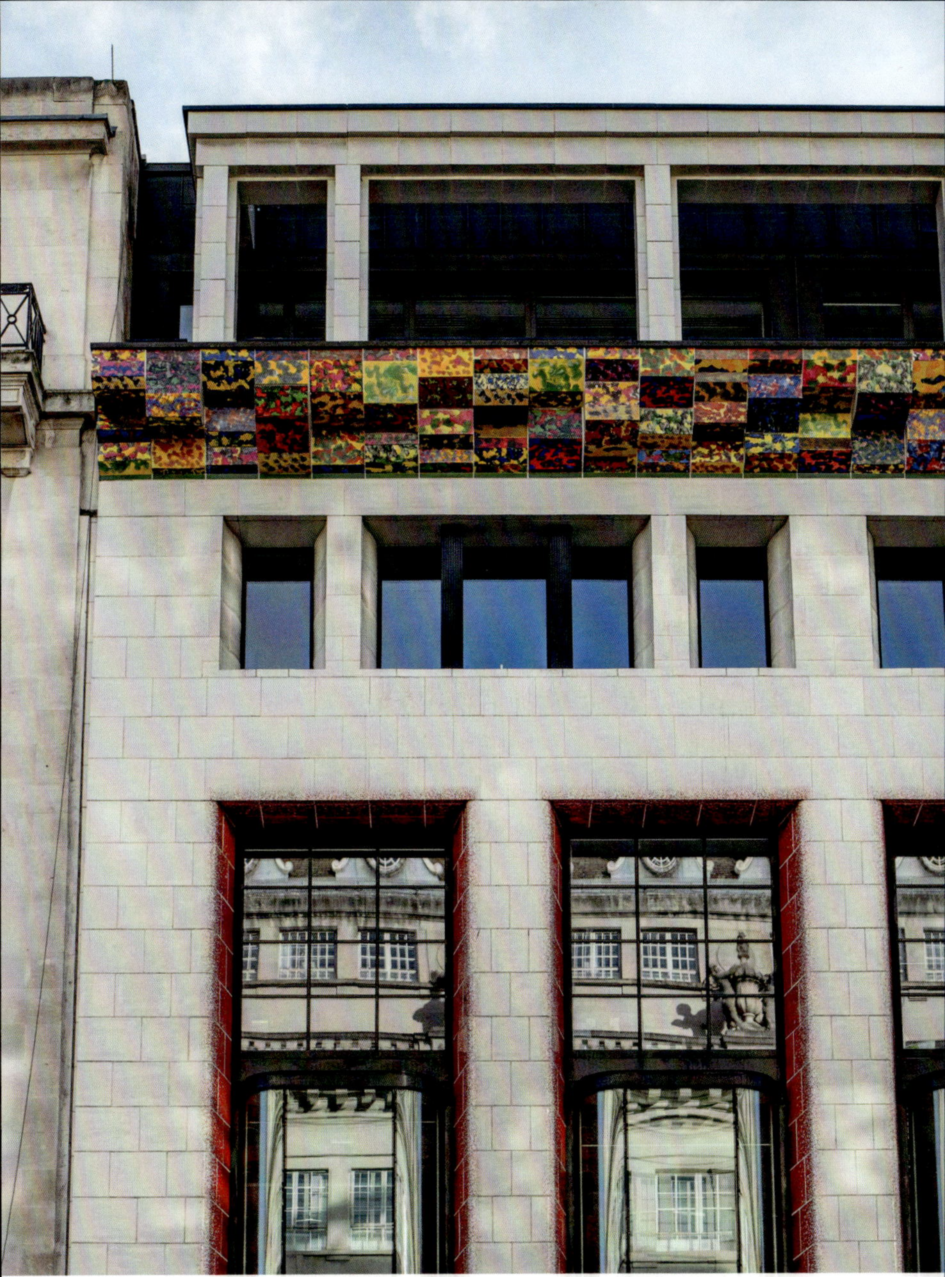

Address 214 Piccadilly, St James', London W1J 9HL | Getting there Underground to Piccadilly Circus (Piccadilly and Bakerloo Lines) | Hours Accessible 24 hours, though best seen when illuminated at night | Tip The churchyard of nearby St James', Piccadilly, is a delightful place to relax away from all the hubbub. Most days you can find either a food market or a craft market there.

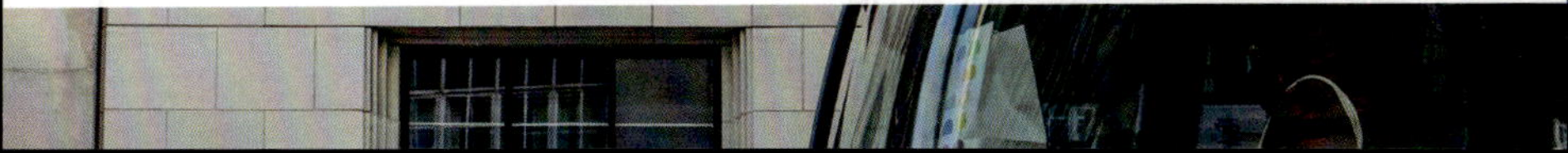

25 Decorating the World

'A living advertisement'

The Royal Doulton Pottery, which bordered the Thames close to Lambeth Bridge, was one of the great industrial enterprises of Victorian England. It did not finally close its doors until 1956. Its offices, created in a style of architecture that we would now describe as High Victorian Gothic, still survive at the river's end of Black Prince Road.

This is an astonishingly ornate building, and a major piece of public art into the bargain. It is also one that shows off on the outside what is being manufactured indoors, on the factory's floors. The window ledges seem to push outwards at an exaggerated angle in order to allow us to see samples of the range of styles of decorative embellishment that the factory could offer any potential customer. Samples of wonderful individual tiles are embedded into the walls – it is a little like looking into a kaleidoscope. Best of all is to position yourself at the main entrance, exactly where Lambeth High Street meets Black Prince Road, and look up.

Every inch of the building has been attended to – the sides of the windows are decorated with ceramic sheaves of gleaming corn. Gargoyles project from close to the roof. You will see a lovely scene above the old main entrance, a ceramic panel – it is a little like a biblical scene carved into the pediment above the principal doorway of a church – which shows Mr Doulton cradling and examining one of his own urns in a crowded work room. He is surrounded by dutiful overseers and some workers. To his left, a young woman is seated on a stool, hand-decorating an urn. He himself is standing beside her, with others looking on. Other Doultonware is ranged along a shelf at his back. Above this pediment the architecture takes flight once again – into lovely semi-circular offices that project over the street. Mr Doulton used to watch his barges leaving from one of these upper windows.

Address 26 Black Prince Road, London SE11 6NF, www.victorianweb.org | **Getting there** Underground to Vauxhall (Victoria Line), then a 10-minute walk | **Hours** Accessible 24 hours | **Tip** Look at the ceramic mosaic portraits in the nearby railway tunnel that show the life of Edward, the Black Prince, and a range of typical Doulton designs.

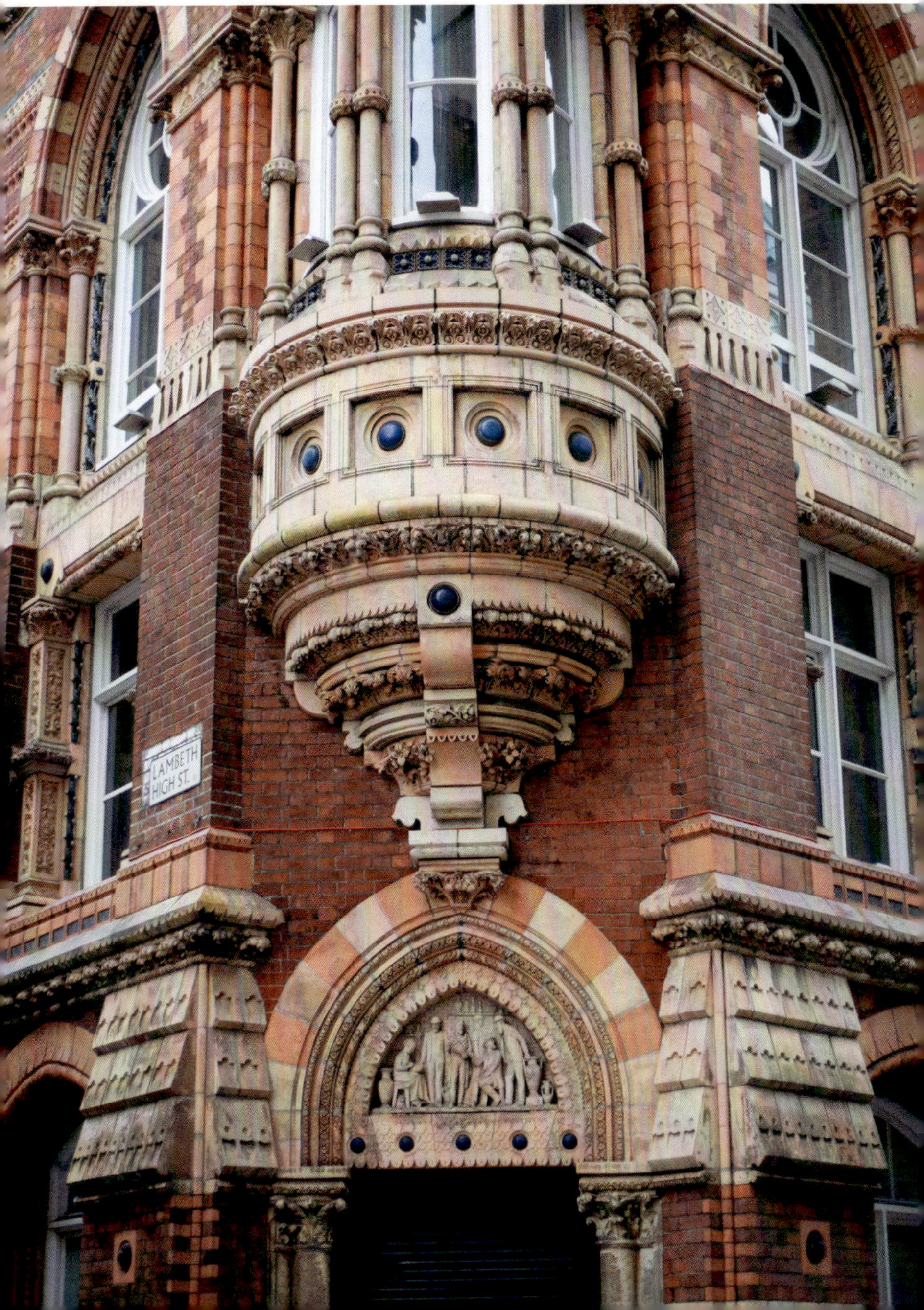

26 Diana, Queen of Hearts

With jaunty umbrella fit for a princess

Covent Garden and the environs of its great fruit and vegetable market were once all about hard human labour and making ends meet – coster-mongers, in their filthy aprons, heaving giant wooden carts behind them, overladen with turnips, spuds and carrots, for sale as quickly as maybe.

These days it's a frenziedly buzzy, chi chi place for tourists, all tarted up to appeal to passing prosperity. The veg has been swapped, in the beautifully colourful environs of Neal's Yard, for example, where all the walls have been painted in bright, summer-sippy colours, for deep massage, giant pizza slices, herbal remedies by the sackful, and the choicest of fresh ground coffees, whose aroma lingers in the air. Flowers now hang in baskets from the walls of the old warehouses.

Just as you leave Neal's Yard through the arch that takes you into Monmouth Street, just to the right of you, opposite a sign that reads 'Neal's Yard, formerly King's Head Court', you will spot a lovely mural that shows us a very familiar face. The slender young female, dressed in her bonnet, holding up a black umbrella against the rain that doesn't seem to be about to fall any time soon, has an air of Mary Poppins or the Von Trapp family about her – that promise of carefree, skippy fun, enjoyed to the accompaniment of a tune we all must surely know... Yes, it's her again, Princess Diana, that sometime media-savvy, pretty queen of all our hearts. The heels of her out-turned black boots – a dancer's pose – are painfully pointy. She's carrying a Harrods bag as she gazes down at her two adoring wee' uns, who stare back up at her. Is she hovering in the air, as if she is more magical than real? There's a caption just to the right of her, which is something that the real Diana once said to one of her children: 'You can be as naughty as you want just don't get caught'. What a fun/sinister thing to say! Who made her? Bambi.

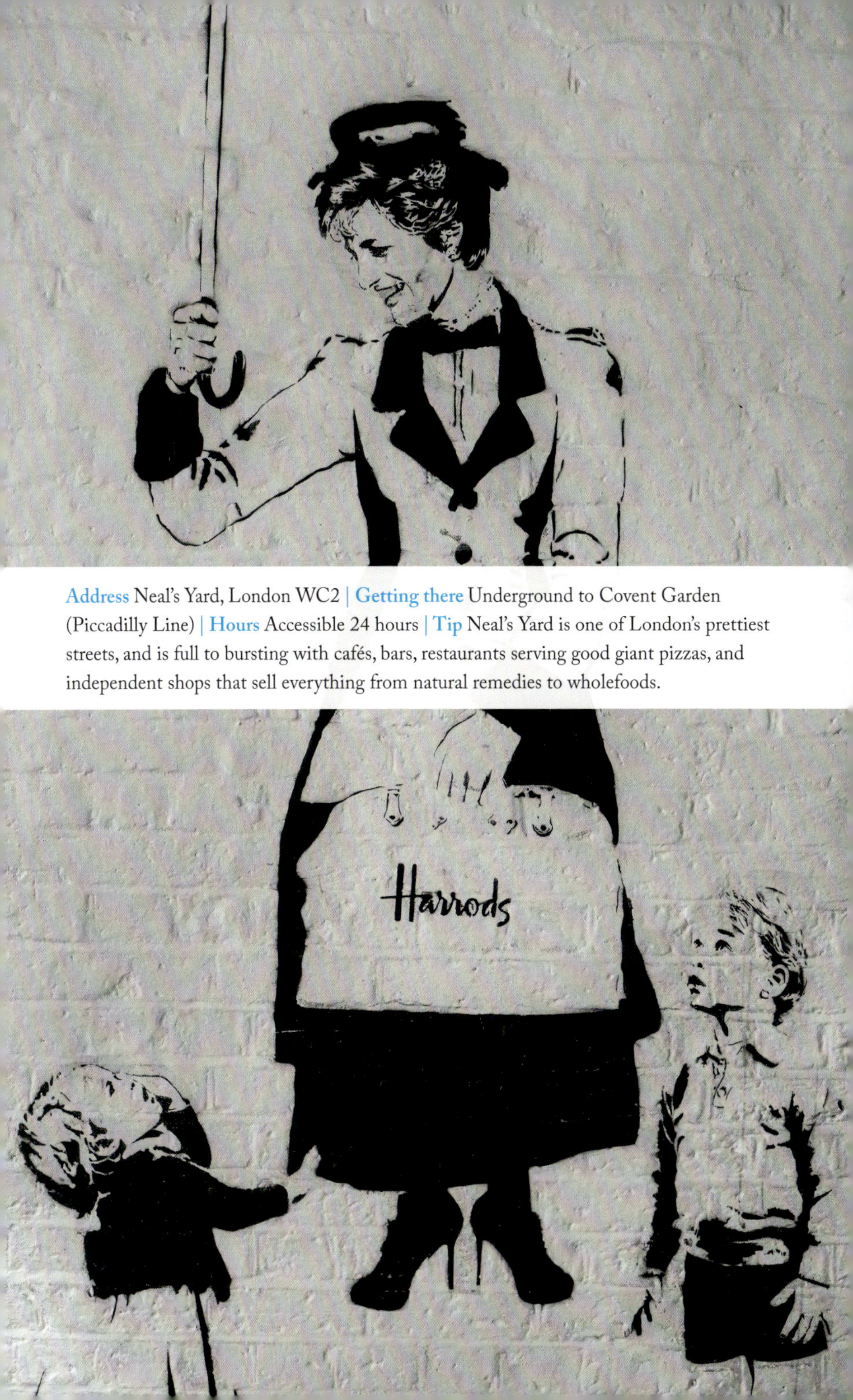

Address Neal's Yard, London WC2 | Getting there Underground to Covent Garden (Piccadilly Line) | Hours Accessible 24 hours | Tip Neal's Yard is one of London's prettiest streets, and is full to bursting with cafés, bars, restaurants serving good giant pizzas, and independent shops that sell everything from natural remedies to wholefoods.

27 Duck Cottage

In the playpark of monarchs and their proxies

It is to the beautifully manufactured landscape of St James' Park, one of the most charming royal parks of the capital, that you must go to enjoy some of the best performance art London has to offer. And it is entirely free of charge. Start at the east end of the park, at an unpretentious place called Duck Cottage (which is overlooked by the Treasury). The name has a whiff of the Marx Brothers about it, which feels entirely appropriate. This is a modest and charming Victorian cottage made for the use of the park's gardeners; in fact, it contains a cultivated garden within its boundaries. Stride along the path and up to the building itself, and then onto the balcony that overlooks a little man-made island that sits in the lake.

This is where the park's pelicans most often gather. These huge, gorgeous, ungainly birds, flushed almost pink in colour in the summer (their colour changes with the season), favour this island and the nearby cottage as places in which to stand around and be admired in all their wonderful and exaggeratedly comical finery. This park has been the plaything of monarchs and their toadies for centuries.

Before it was made more beautiful in the early 19th century by the architect John Nash – he turned the canal that once ran through it into a looping and sinuous lake – it was more French in style. The canal bisected it like a ruler, bordered by rigid avenues of trees. Charles II swam in that canal, having first carefully removed his wig. Monarchs filled the parks with the species of exotic birds that inhabit it to this day, delighting us all with their idling, carefree monarchical behaviour.

A heron, for example, stands on a single leg for hours on end, showing it off, as gracefully thin as the leg of Charles I that you can see on horseback in the National Gallery. He was the man who lost his head by overreaching himself.

Address 69 Horse Guards Road, London SW1A 2BJ, www.royalparks.org | **Getting there** Underground to St James' Park (Piccadilly Line), then a seven-minute walk | **Hours** Not open to the public, but viewable from the outside when the park is open, 5am–midnight | **Tip** A short walk down Horse Guards Road, to King Charles Street, will take you to the Churchill War Rooms at the north-east corner of the park.

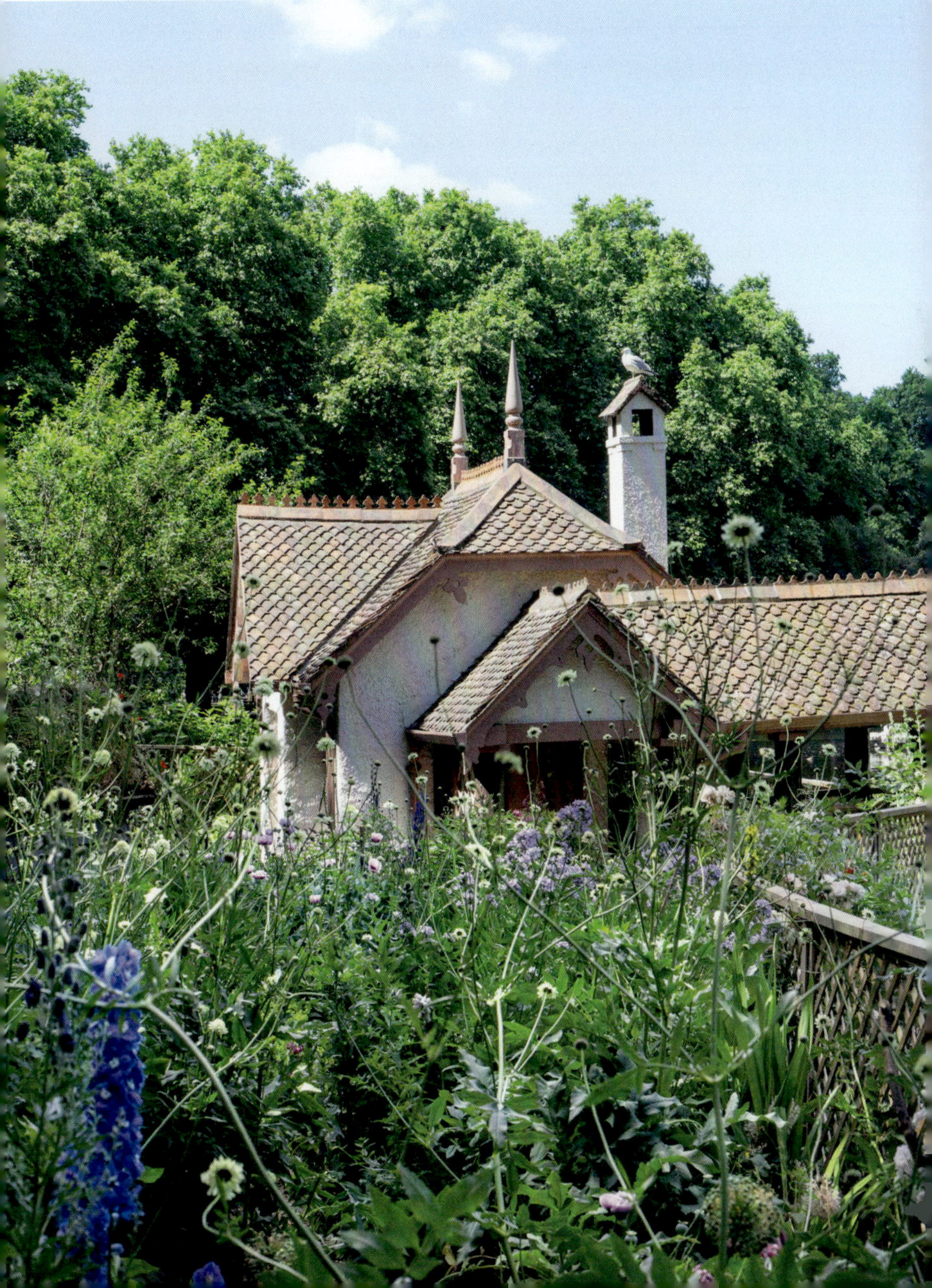

28 The Elegance of a Camel

The Camel Corps remembered

Eager sculpture-watchers will spot many fine examples of horses, dragons and lions in central London, from the great quartet of hugely over-sized lions by Edwin Landseer that protects Nelson's Column (and gives umpteen free rides to children, though its back is rather slippery) in Trafalgar Square, to the great, uprearing silver dragons that guard the entrance to the City of London at the top of Fleet Street. (Most of the horses are human weight-bearing, of course.) But what of camels?

Of sculptural camels of any significance, there is only one in the capital, and it lives at the western end of Victoria Embankment Gardens, almost overlooked by the trains that slide smoothly into Charing Cross Station.

It is not immediately within our line of sight when we enter those gardens from Villiers Street because it is hidden from view by a great, gnarled London plane tree. Once found, it surprises and delights on several counts at once. For a start, it is something of an exquisitely modelled miniature of a camel, so much smaller than we might have expected, and made to look even smaller by the fact that a huge statue of a seated Robert Burns lives so close by, eyes heavy lidded in poetic rapture.

Our camel, who faces away from Burns, carries a member of the Camel Corps on its back, who seems to sit casually, if not wearily, atop his mount. He is in no hurry, it seems. He is wearing a hat against the sun, and he is carrying a rifle and a great deal of other clobber. The camel, whose fine head twists to show off the ripple of its neck muscles, is part turned towards Cleopatra's Needle, which is entirely appropriate, of course, because others of his kind would have seen much service in Africa. The camel's legs are long, slender, bowed a little, and exquisitely modelled. In fact, the camel's legs are so long that the man he is carrying almost looks like a miniature.

Address Victoria Embankment Gardens, Villiers Street, London WC2N 6NS, +44 (0)207 641 6000, www.londonremembers.com/memorials/imperial-camel-corps | Getting there Underground to Embankment (District, Circle, Bakerloo and Northern Lines) | Hours Daily 7am–9pm | Tip Established in 1890, Gordon's Wine Bar in Villiers Street is London's oldest and is an experience not to be missed.

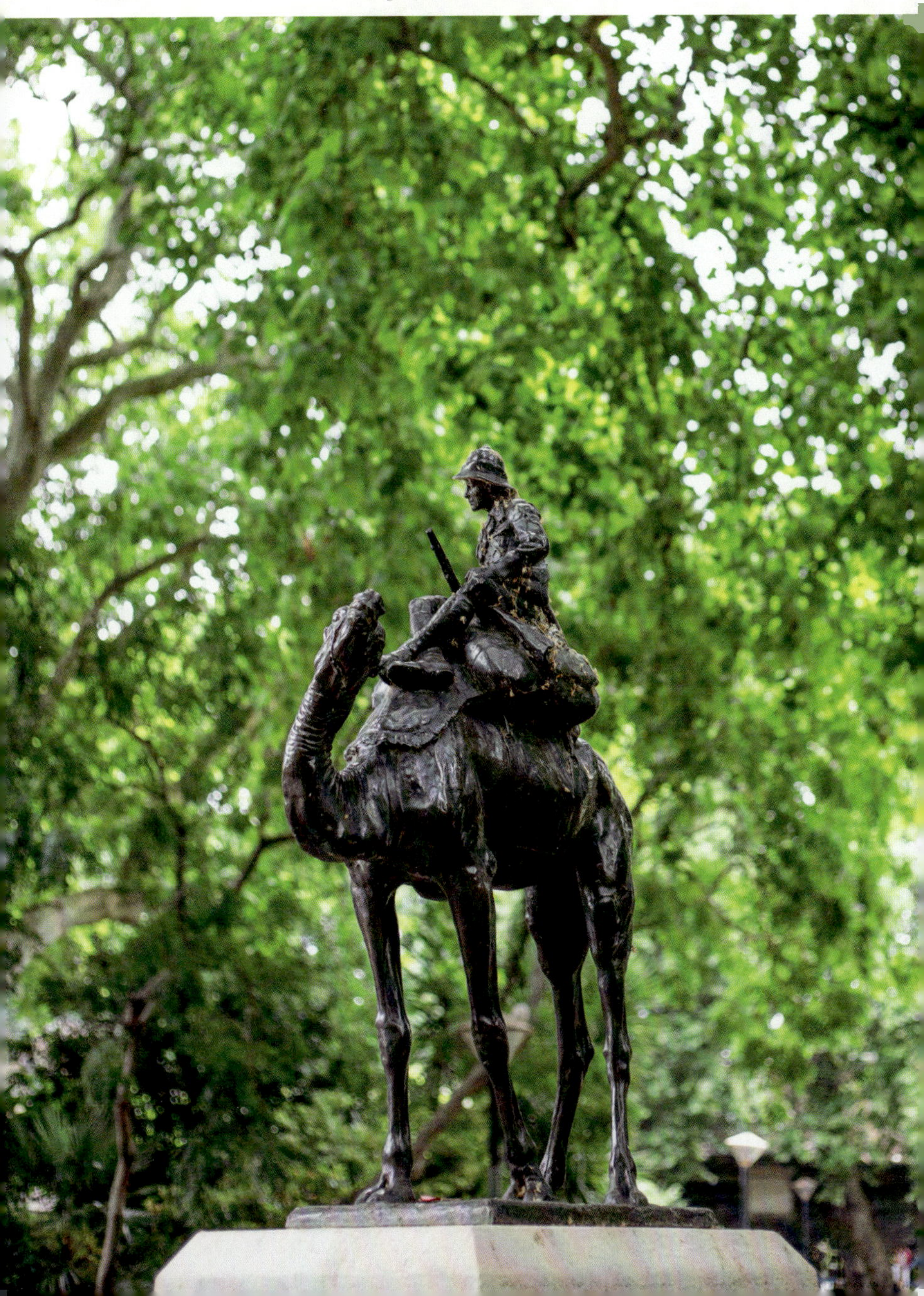

29 The Estorick Collection

The roar of Italian Futurism and more

The Estorick Collection of modern Italian art is tucked away in a fine, early 19th-century Georgian town house on one corner of an elegant north London square. It is the only museum in the country devoted solely to Italian art of the recent past; the paintings, prints and sculptures that it contains, about 120 pieces in all, were once the private collection of its founder Eric Estorick, an American sociologist who came to live in England after World War II, and made many trips to Italy during the later 1940s and 1950s with his wife, the textile designer Salome Dessau. He befriended many of the artists whose works he later acquired, which explains why the works feel like such excellent, hand-picked examples of their kind.

The permanent collection is on two floors of the house. It ranges from such masterpieces of the Futurist movement as Giacomo Balla's *The Hand of the Violinist* (1912), in which the player's frantic bowing is suggested by a fracturing of the image of the hand in motion. What was it about the Futurists that appealed to him so? Their evocation of the speed and the frantic pace of modernity put him in mind of his early years in New York. 'Boyhood life in the metropolitan oasis of New York was Futurism in action,' he once remarked.

On the topmost floor, more contemplative works by Giorgio Morandi are usually on display (though things do move around), including a celebrated still life with bottles, a subject to which he returned throughout his life. Eric Estorick made repeated visits to Morandi's studio in Bologna during the late 1950s, and the collection includes landscape etchings and drawings from all periods of the artist's career. In addition to key Futurist works by Giacomo Balla, Gino Severini, Umberto Boccioni and Carlo Carrà, the collection includes figurative works from the 1890s and on, including a remarkable sculpture by Medardo Rosso.

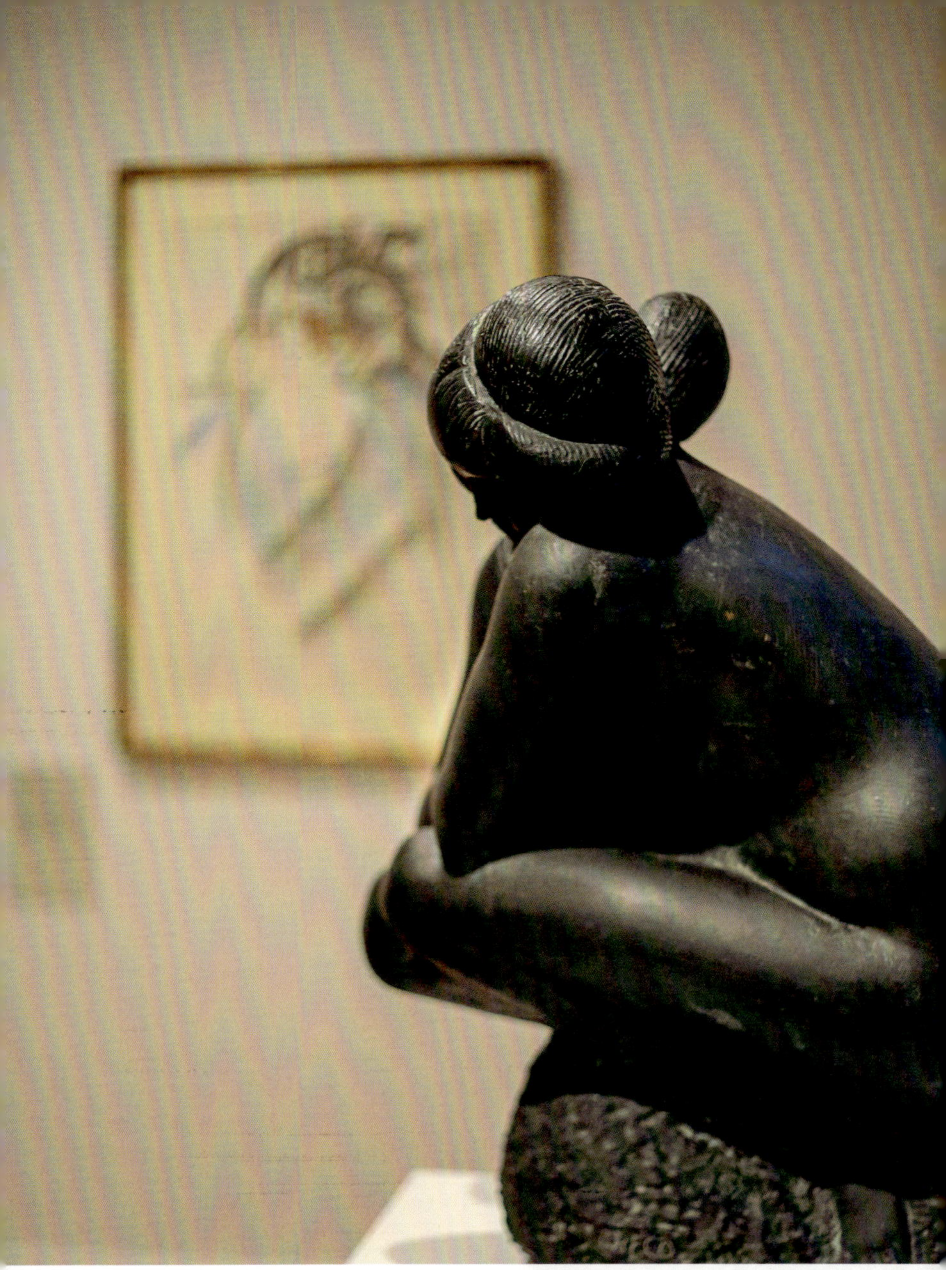

Address 39A Canonbury Square, N1 2AN, +44 (0)207 704 9522, www.estorickcollection.com | Getting there Underground to Highbury and Islington (Victoria Line), then a seven-minute walk | Hours Wed, Fri & Sat 11am–6pm, Sun noon–5pm | Tip Take a picnic to lovely Highbury Fields, five minutes' walk from the gallery. Admire the elegant Georgian and Victorian town houses nearby, once home to the artist Walter Sickert and the cleric John Wesley.

30 Flat Time House

Where books burst through windows

Books are not necessarily docile things. Some of them even explode through windows. Take the front window of Flat Time House in Peckham, for example. It is like no other window you are ever likely to see. Two interleaved books – they are facing towards each other – seem to be hovering horizontally, half in and half out of the house. Are they yearning to take flight? This modest, two-storey building was occupied by the conceptual artist John Latham for the last 20 years of his life, and it has been preserved in his memory as a gallery and a research centre. Latham was a wild and unconventional thinker and maker, much consumed by abstruse musing about physics, cosmology and the nature of time – one of his many correspondents was Stephen Hawking.

He regarded the house itself as a body in which various rooms represented the mind, the soul, etc. The studio at the back of the house contains his library of books. To Latham, books themselves fell into two categories: books to be read and books to be burnt. Many of Latham's works of art – one such example is in the house – include charred remnants of books with blackened and singed pages. Why burn books? Because knowledge was an ever-changing thing. No answer to the problems of the universe could ever be complete or unchallengeable – so Latham burnt books, not in order to destroy dangerous or heretical knowledge (as Savonarola once did), but to remind us that all book learning is open-ended and soon to be superseded.

Latham was an unruly creature to encounter, a smelly jabberer of a man whose words were always on the edge of incomprehensibility. This house, now that he is dead, is a much-tamed version of himself. We pass from room to room – all the rooms have clinically white walls – staring at books, stackings of plastic boxes containing his voluminous correspondence. These books contain combustible thinking.

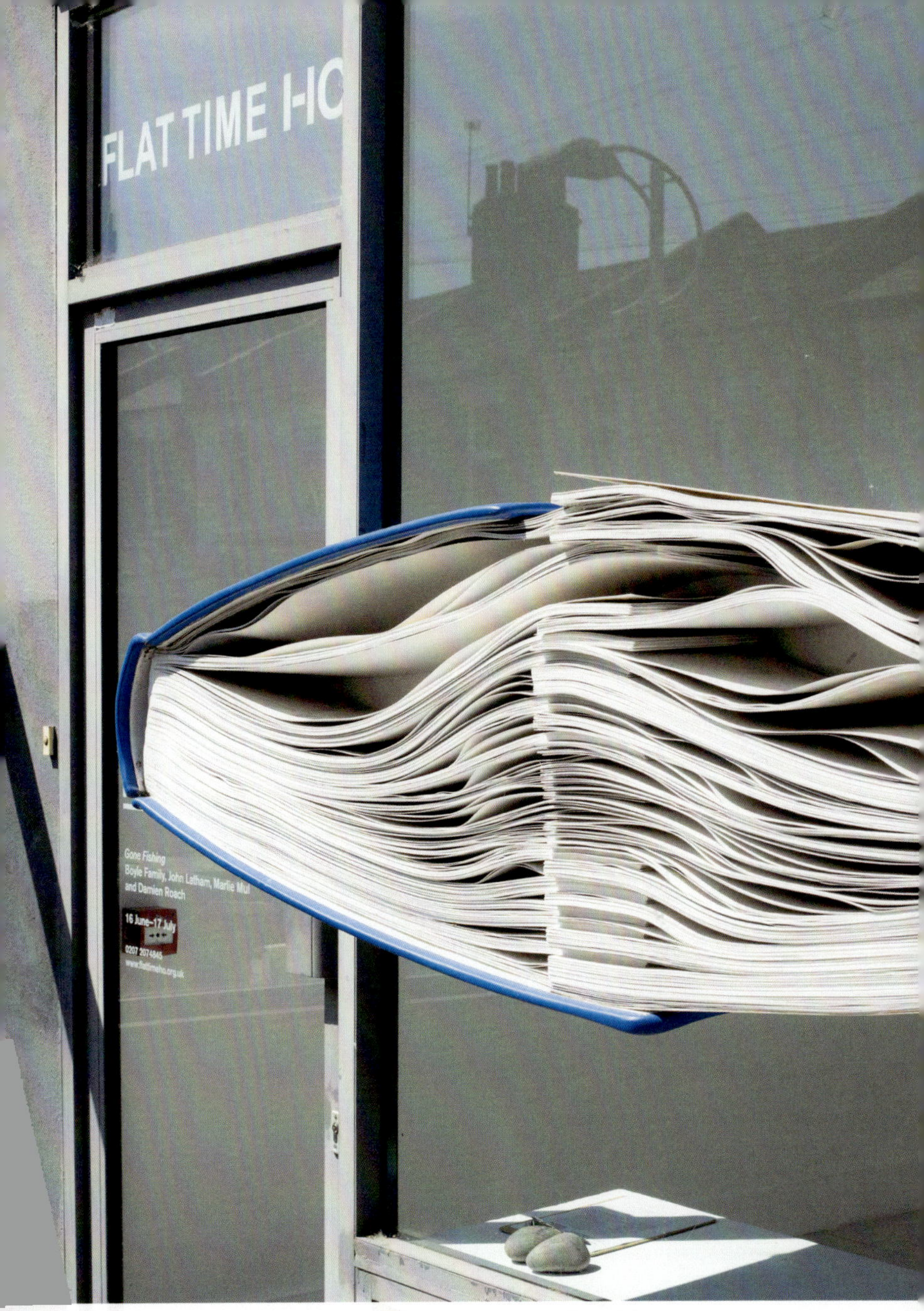

Address 210 Bellenden Road, London SE15 4BW, +44 (0)207 207 4845, www.flattimehouse.org.uk | Getting there Overground to Peckham Rye, then an eight-minute walk | Hours Thu–Sun noon–6pm, and at other times by appointment | Tip Visit the Hannah Barry Gallery, 4 Holly Grove, London SE15 5DF.

31 The Flayed Saint

Damien Hirst's dramatic exposure

St Bartholomew the Great is the oldest church in the City of London, and its surrounding streets have seen much bloodletting in their time. Wat Tyler's Peasants' Revolt was enacted outside its walls in 1381; William Wallace, Scottish patriot, was put to death here in 1305; and several martyrs were burned at the stake – a plaque giving all their names is set into the wall of St Bartholomew's Hospital, which is adjacent – in the 16th century.

Inside the church itself, very close to the font, there is yet more dramatic evidence of human suffering, this time created by Damien Hirst, *enfant terrible* and general provocateur of British art. The work is called *Exquisite Pain*, and it is a slender, full-length human figure of St Bartholomew, the apostle of Christ who went to Armenia to spread the gospel there, and was flayed alive for his pains.

Flaying is a terrible business. It means meticulously removing the skin with a knife – in Titian's great painting *The Flaying of Marsyas*, we see how the victim hangs upside down while several work on the task simultaneously – to expose everything that lies beneath.

The figure is gilded, and we see through to the anatomical details of the flayed saint. His skin hangs loosely down from his right arm like a Macintosh. The way its feet seem to step down from the gilded table on which the saint is posed makes the skin look like a simulacrum of the figure. He holds up the flayer's knife to show us to what torture he has been subjected. But this knife is in fact a scalpel of the kind used in a hospital – which makes for a neat nod in the direction of the hospital already mentioned. Hirst has always been fascinated by religion, science and medicine, and in this dramatic work – for all that it is a demonstration of suffering – St Bartholomew seems to rise up and pose like a hero. All these preoccupations seem to coalesce.

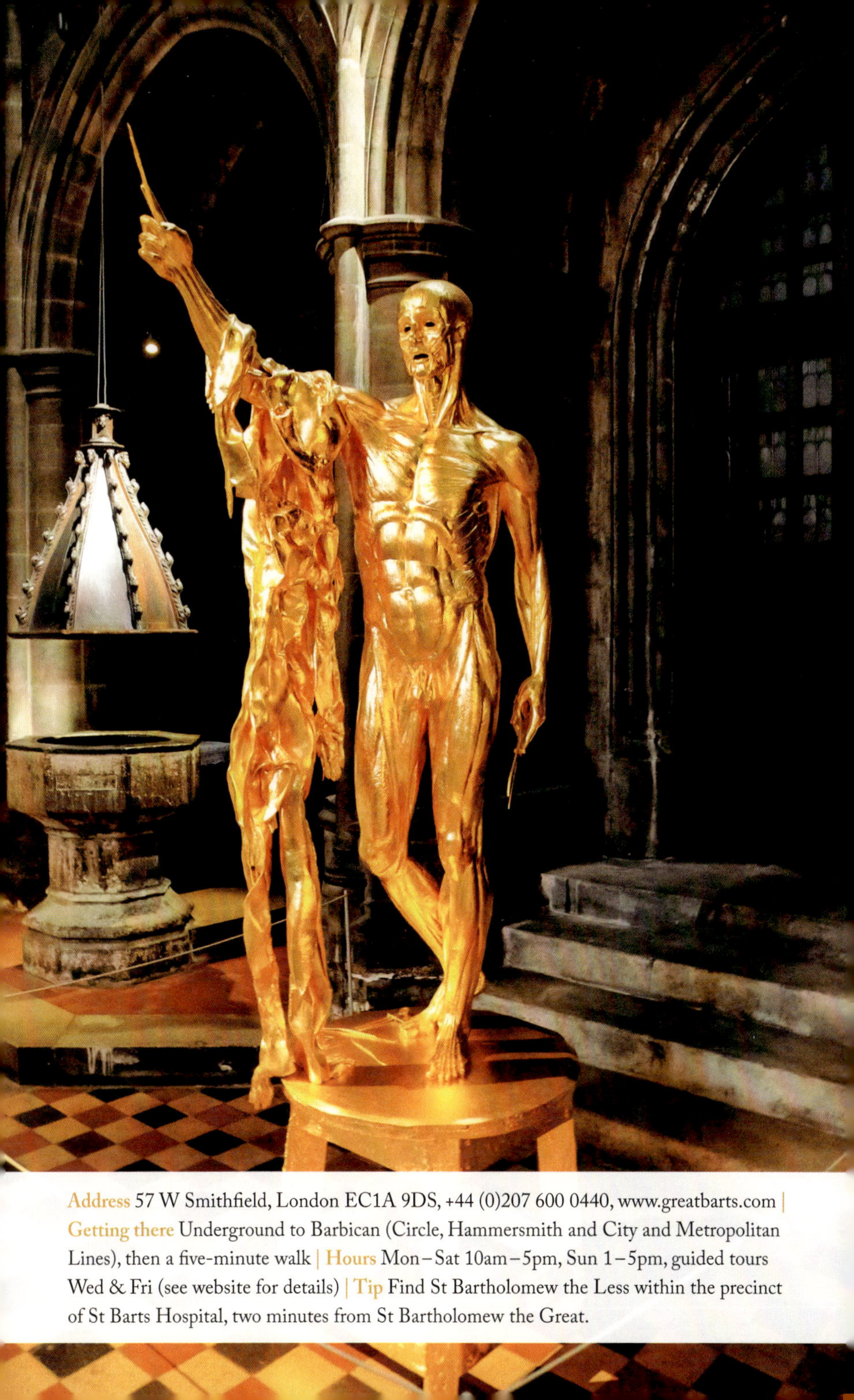

Address 57 W Smithfield, London EC1A 9DS, +44 (0)207 600 0440, www.greatbarts.com | Getting there Underground to Barbican (Circle, Hammersmith and City and Metropolitan Lines), then a five-minute walk | Hours Mon–Sat 10am–5pm, Sun 1–5pm, guided tours Wed & Fri (see website for details) | Tip Find St Bartholomew the Less within the precinct of St Barts Hospital, two minutes from St Bartholomew the Great.

32 Fortnum's Monarchs

Piccadilly's hourly spectacle

One of London's most delightful spectacles can be enjoyed hourly, out on the pavement in Piccadilly, not far from Eros at Piccadilly Circus, that small figure so full of flourish and confidence. For the best viewing point, stand outside the Royal Academy and look across the road in the general direction of Fortnum and Mason, one of London's best-loved luxury stores, where a gentleman in a frock coat will be more than delighted to guide you towards the finest quality chocolate you might ever wish to eat.

What you will see as you stare across at the rather elaborate canopy above the entrance to the shop is a game of sorts that is played between an immobile sculptural group of two seated figures and the two standing, mobile figures (mobile in so far as they move in and out of their hiding places) of a magnificent cuckoo clock, from which two figures slide out and then withdraw again when the clock strikes and chimes.

The sculptural group that sits on the canopy against the red-brick façade consists of a king and queen, in bronze, by the celebrated artist Lyn Chadwick. His head is rectangular, hers triangular, and their bodies consist of flat, faceted triangles – a little like a formal cape worn against a London downpour. They look very severe, imperious and watchful, as if they might be the sombre guardians of some sacred shrine. And why shouldn't a luxury goods store be a sacred shrine? The clock and its two magnificent painted boxes from which the figures emerge stand a good yard above the king and queen, as if having a bit of a tease at their expense – or perhaps looking down on them, rather sneeringly, as recent interlopers, which of course they are. This figure group is on long-term loan from a collector called Frank Cohen, who has in the past populated the front windows of Fortnum and Mason too with a selection of the paintings that he owns.

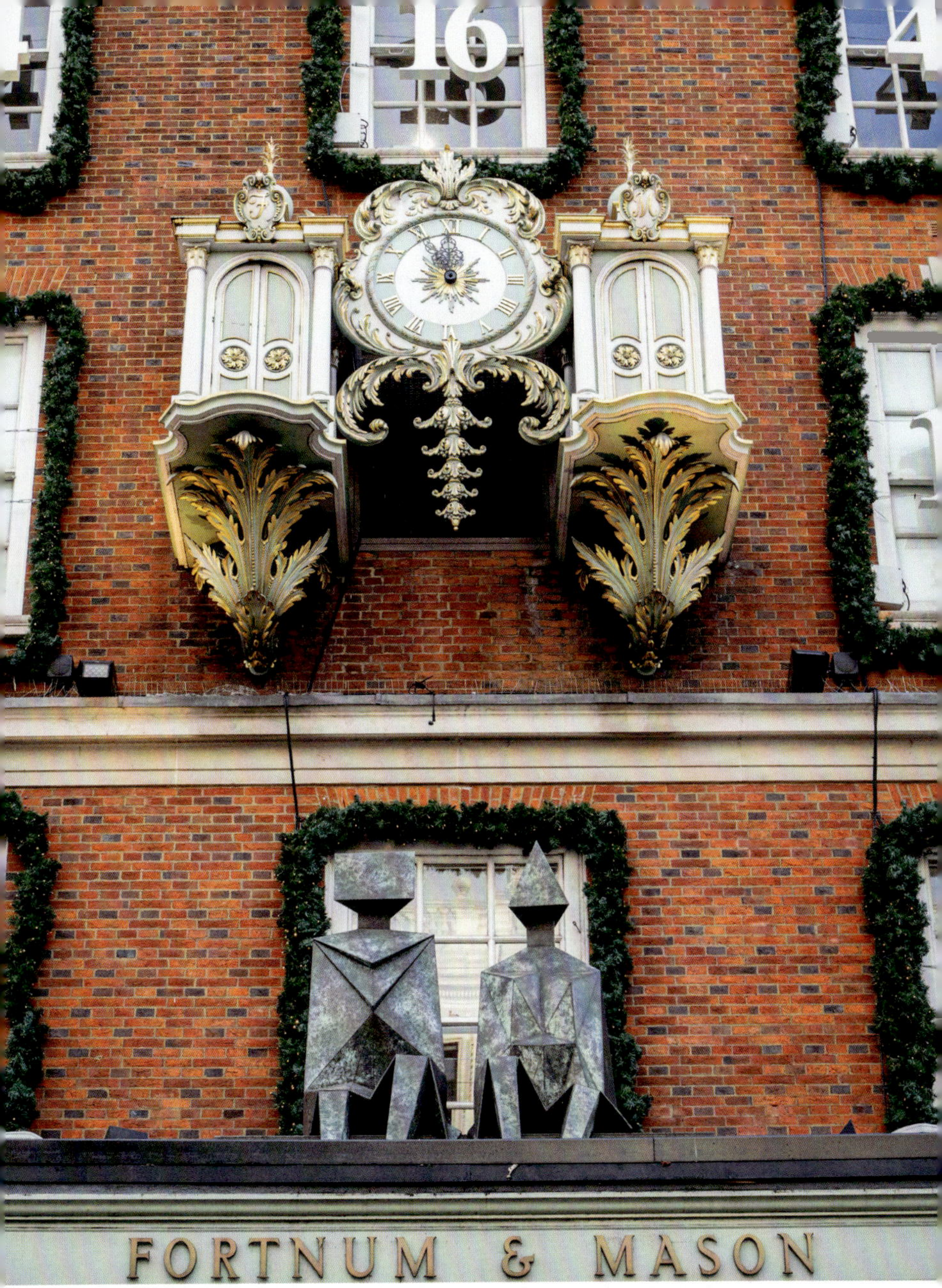

Address 181 Piccadilly, St James, London W1A 1ER, +44 (0)207 734 8040, www.fortnumandmason.com | Getting there Underground to Piccadilly Circus (Piccadilly and Bakerloo Lines) | Hours Visible from the street 24 hours | Tip Jermyn Street, the original home of gentlemen's clothing, is also the place to find some fine (albeit not cheap) galleries, bars, restaurants and cafés.

33 Fountain Play

The graceful promise of lift-off

A sculpture is best seen in the round. An aerial view can help. Begin at the northern end of Westminster Bridge – Big Ben is over your right shoulder. This is the bridge that was celebrated by William Wordsworth, in a famous sonnet. All the out-flung beauty of London is still visible from it. As you walk towards the southern end, look to your right and down.

You will see the modern buildings of an ancient foundation called St Thomas' Hospital. Its two wings part to enclose a square garden named after Florence Nightingale. In the centre of that garden, you will notice a circular pond. A fountain unlike any other you may have seen, with a silvery sheen, set on a circular base – it is made from overlayerings of polished steel – spews out thin, regularly spaced jets of water. It looks almost weightless. It has none of the ponderousness and weight that we so often associate with the idea of a monumental public fountain.

Standing as it is amidst water, it looks as if it ought to be a kinetic sculpture, which means a sculpture that is in perpetual motion. The fact is that it once was, and that the mechanism is now broken. Money should be raised to repair it as quickly as possible because this fountain is an important piece of public sculpture by a famous Russian-born artist called Naum Gabo (1890–1977). His work is in the Tate Gallery. Gabo was a Constructivist – and an idealist into the bargain – who believed that the purpose of art was to do us some good, raise us up. He often worked with transparent materials such as Perspex, in combination with string, creating tensions between the two, linking them somewhat in the way that a harp is tensioned by its stringing.

The play of these water jets reminds us of regularly spaced lengths of string arcing through the air. The whole thing has a promise of gracious lift-off. Its name is *Revolving Torsion* (1971–72).

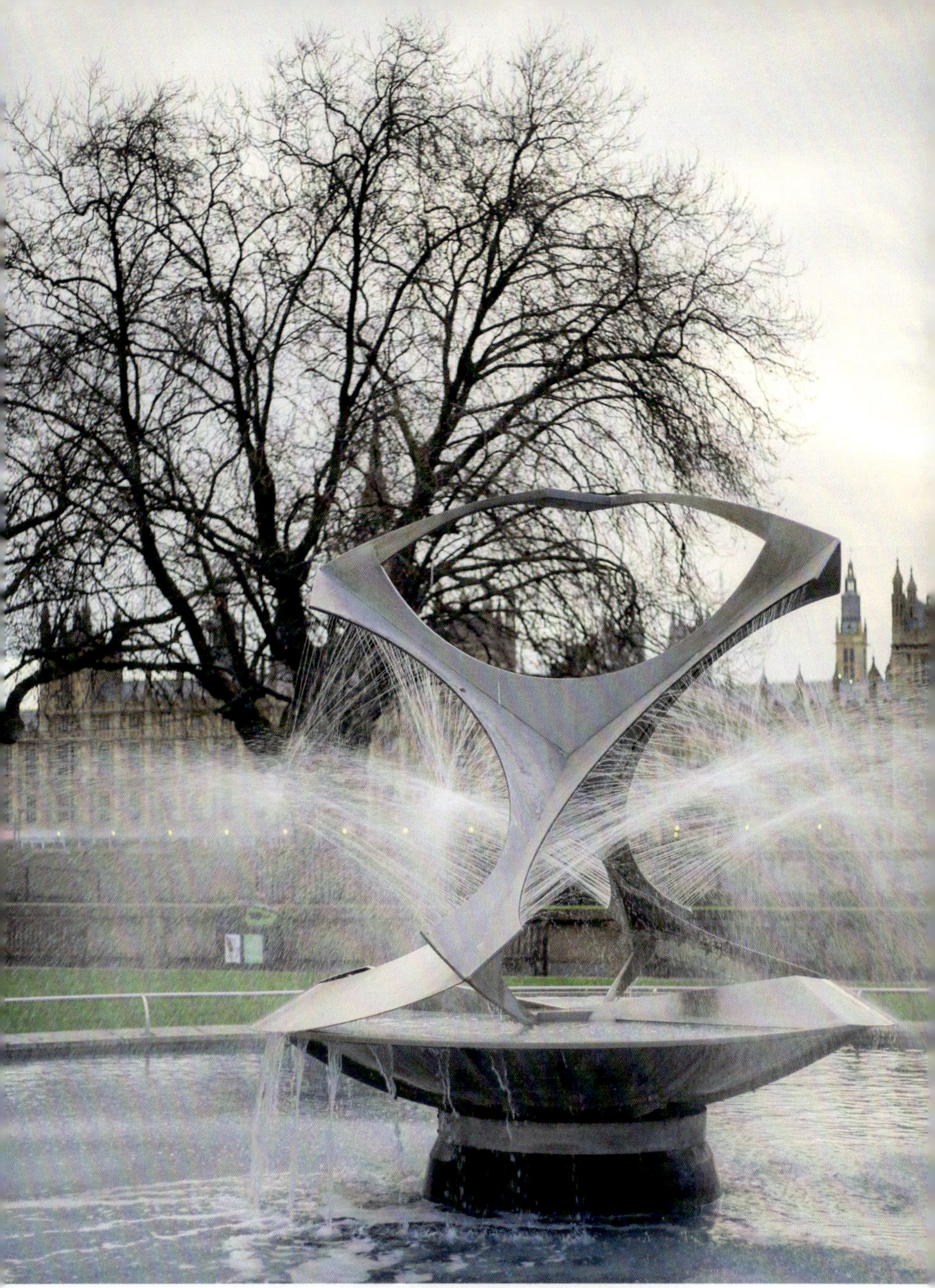

Address St Thomas' Hospital, Westminster Bridge Road, London SE1 7EH, +44 (0)7188 7188, www.guysandstthomas.nhs.uk | Getting there Underground to Westminster (Circle, District and Jubilee Lines), then a five-minute walk | Hours Accessible 24 hours | Tip The Thames walkway is on the northern side of the garden wall. Try beachcombing at low tide…

34 Freedom from Fear

Children dancing up a brick wall

For two centuries, from the middle of the 17th century on, Vauxhall Pleasure Gardens was one of the greatest entertainment meccas of London, with a range of extravagant architectural pavilions to match. Samuel Pepys couldn't get enough of it. Now it is a small park, bounded by a railway viaduct that carries trains into Waterloo station, with a city farm at its outer southern edge. The flame throwers, the jugglers and the dancing girls have been replaced by the relative sobriety of llamas, an avenue of flowering cherry trees, and a special variety of elm that resists the blight of Dutch elm disease.

There is some lovely public art here too, but it has its back to the gardens. In order to see it – it is on the side of a building called Darley House, which forms part of a post-war housing development called the Vauxhall Gardens Estate – you have to walk around the building until you reach a car park that overlooks a few allotments and an ambitious children's play park. Now look up at the back of this block of apartments, and especially at what embellishes the wall of the blockish square brick tower enclosing the staircase. On its flank, more than half way up, you will see a teem of climbing, dancing humans (a mother, with her children), all linking hands. It is called *Following the Leader*, a memorial to children who died in the Blitz. It seems to celebrate the old freedoms of everyday life – including the right to play out in the street again without the fear of being obliterated by a bomb. The mother has gained a bit of a lift-off from a brick ledge that runs just above the name of the block.

This work, in coloured concrete, was made by a Hungarian refugee called Peter László Péri. The oldest son of a Jewish family, he was raised in relative poverty. The children leap. Their legs are out-flung. What a joy to be alive!

Address Darley House, Laud Street, London SE11 5HW | **Getting there** Underground to Vauxhall (Victoria Line), then a five-minute walk | **Hours** Accessible 24 hours | **Tip** The Teahouse Theatre, where you can enjoy a meal and a play, is just 55 yards away.

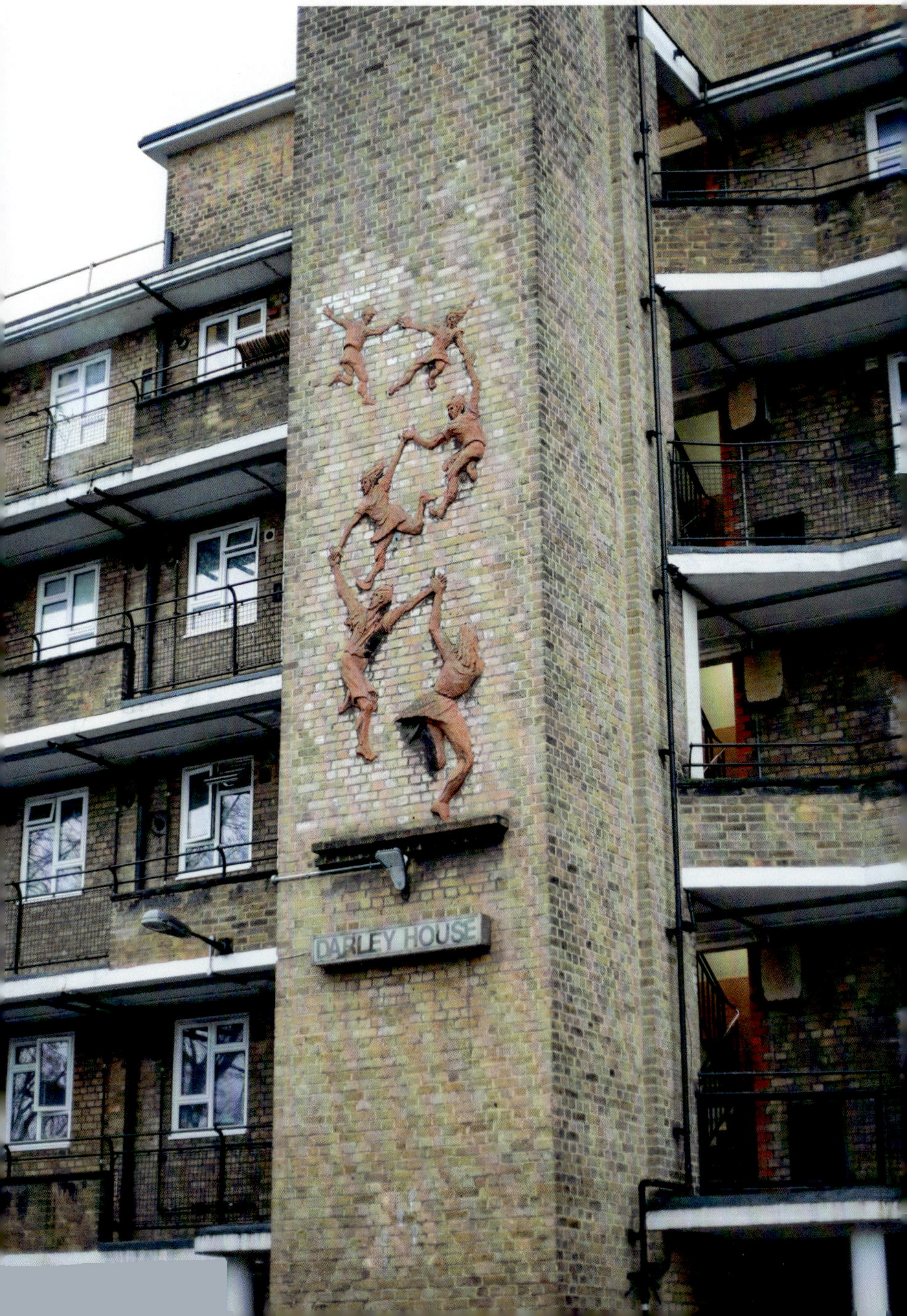

35 The Fulcrum

The massive poise of metal on metal

Richard Serra's magnificently bullish sculptural forms in weathered steel – this is the only example of its kind on public display in the United Kingdom – alarm and challenge and unnerve almost as much as they enthral and invigorate.

This one at Broadgate Circle is sited a very short walk from the roar and the life and the bustle of the concourse of Liverpool Street Station, at the end of a clean-lined, high-end shopping mall, solidly settled within a circle of space that has been carved out for it – there is a flight of steps leading down to it from street level. The fact that it sits at the centre of this tiny circus of space makes it feel slightly gladiatorial.

At first glance, and from the way that its massive leaning plates of gently oxidising metal seem to almost taper to a point at its apex, it could be a giant weathering teepee of sorts. It also looks simple; as if we could encompass its shape at a glance. This is not true, of course. It is never quite true of this man's sculptures. They always slightly wrong-foot us.

They are never quite what they seem. No matter from what angle we look at it as we circle its exterior, it always looks slightly different from how we imagined it was going to look – oddly unanticipated juttings and comings together. We can enter it, by a kind of slit in its side. Entering feels like a slightly illicit game. The metal walls loom over us as they soar and soar upwards. The fact that there is no evident welding of plate-to-plate troubles. All seems to depend on each thinnish flank of metal leaning against its neighbour, in a kind of mutually sustaining act of precarious balance. Precarious? It rather feels that way. One of Serra's sculptures did once fall on a man, killing him. When we look up, we can see out, to thin slivers of the sky beyond. Beyond its walls, we can hear the sound of skateboarders flashing by.

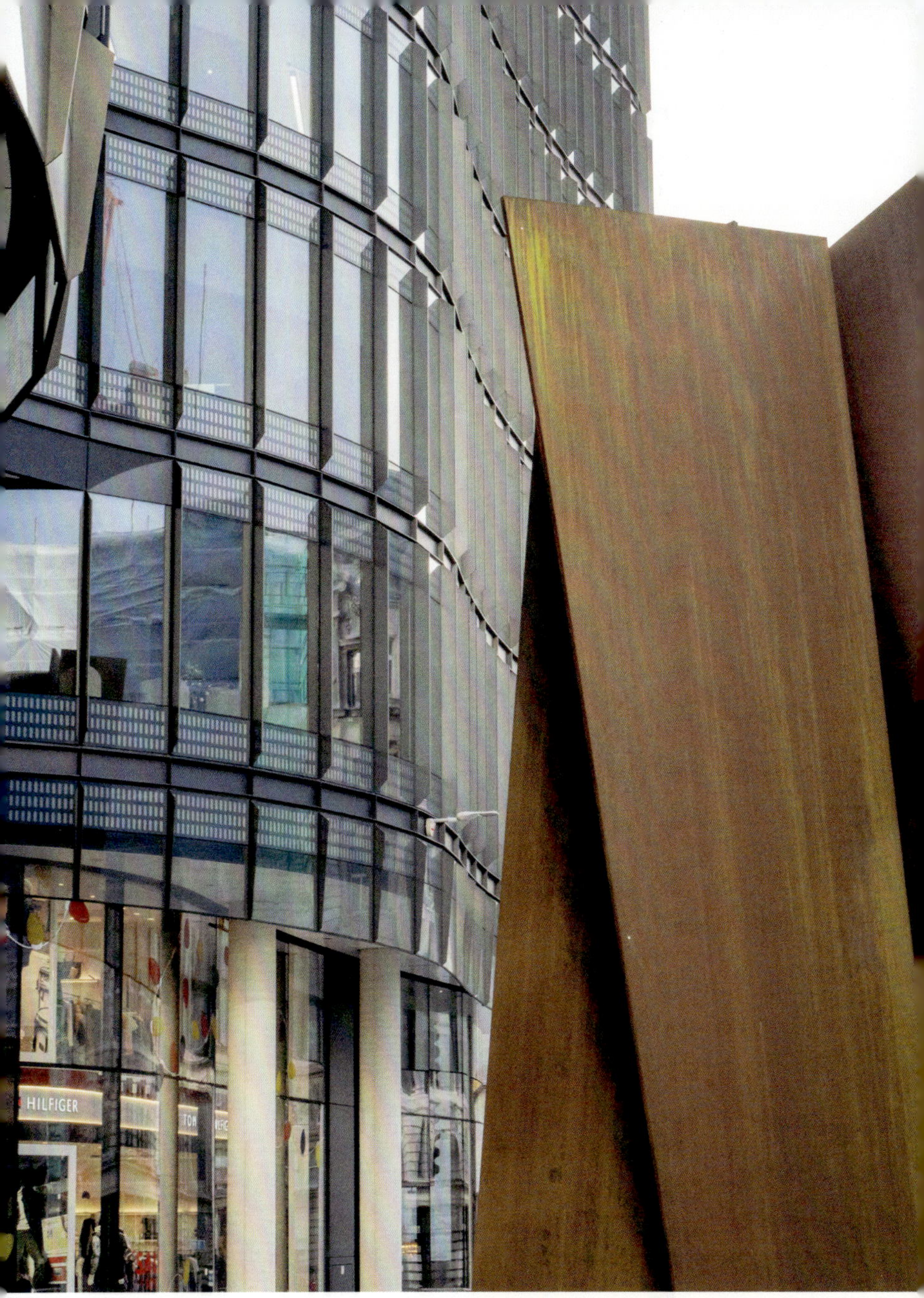

Address Broadgate Circle, 22 Eldon Street, London EC2M 7LA (adjacent to Liverpool Street Station), www.broadgate.co.uk | Getting there Underground to Liverpool Street (Circle, Central, Hammersmith and City and Metropolitan Lines) | Hours Accessible 24 hours | Tip For more contemporary art, a 15-minute walk away is the Whitechapel Art Gallery.

36 The Gallery of Everything

Encountering the outsiders indoors

What would Sherlock Holmes (whose fictional presence hovers close by, in Baker Street) have made of this oddly compelling little gallery with the strangest of names? It looks, with its brilliant red blind, like a street-fronting shop, but above that blind we are told that it is (or perhaps once was) a BARBER SHOP. And inside, it feels a bit like a house – there are remnants of fading wallpaper on the walls and, downstairs, after you have braved the horribly steep and twisty old wooden staircase that takes you down to the basement level, there is a fireplace and a coal hole, and, at the back, a very old-fashioned, pull-chain WC… And what would a Gallery of Everything contain anyway? Everything? Impossible, surely.

In fact, it is an adjunct to, or a spirited little growth off, something bemusingly called The Museum of Everything. That museum has in the past shown off parts of its collection in galleries and museums around the world, but it does not do so any more. Now, for the moment at least, it is this small gallery. And its collections are stored goodness knows where.

What does it show? The word EVERYTHING offers – does it not, Watson – a compelling clue? The works it puts on show are all examples of what has variously been called raw art, Outsider Art or even Art Brut, which means that the artists are not formally tutored, nor graduates of any academy except perhaps the Academy of Life, to which we all belong.

Many of these artists feel like solitary visionaries. Today, on these walls, I am staring at dozens of photographs, by an American from the late 19th century, who first had the wit and the wisdom and the visionary fervour to photograph snowflakes. And what dazzlingly symmetrical marvels snowflakes are! Someone else, on the opposite wall, is into rackety, free-floating angels. Exhibitions change frequently, at the whim of the world…

Address 4 Chiltern Street, London W1U 7PS, +44 (0)207 486 8908, www.gallevery.com | **Getting there** Underground to Baker Street (Bakerloo Line), then a five-minute walk | **Hours** Tue–Sat 11am–6.30pm, Sun 2–6pm | **Tip** Il Blandfords just up the street is a lovely, traditional Italian eatery.

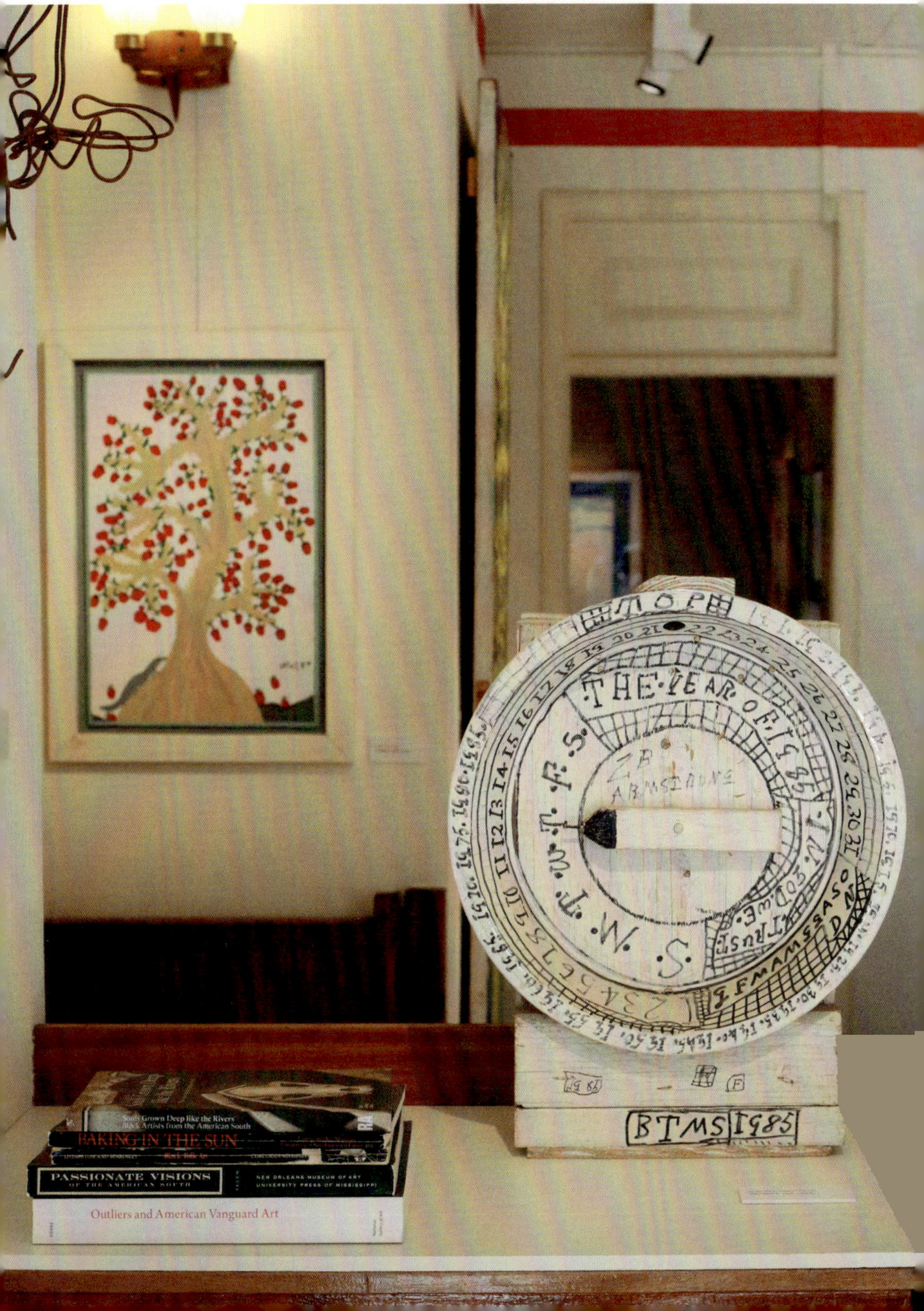

37 The Golden Boy of Pye Corner

Displaying the dangers of over-indulgence

He is popularly known as the Golden Boy of Pye Corner, and he lives in a niche close to Smithfield Market, at the point where two streets intersect, Giltspur Street and Cock Lane. Both these streets are within the boundaries of the old Roman City of London, which is of course both the capital's historic heart – everything grew out, to north, south, east and west, from here – and its financial quarter.

You could call the boy's positioning at this corner site, raised up high in the air as he is (you have to look up to see him), a cheeky, ribald little gesture on someone's part. Why so? Because he is naked, and his nakedness is boundless, extending to the fact that his full tackle is on display. And what better a place to put it on show than Cock Lane? Yet the boy is also here in deadly earnest because he marks an event that was very sombre indeed. In fact, it was the second of two very sombre events that have remained unforgotten for almost 400 years. I am referring to the Great Plague and the Great Fire of London, which struck the city in 1665 and 1666 respectively. The positioning of this boy on relatively high ground, a good three-quarters of a mile uphill and to the west of Pudding Lane, marks the point where the fire was stayed – which means that by the time it reached here, its progress was halted.

Let us now consider the boy himself, and what he tells us about what many believed regarding the Great Fire in the 17th century. He is a chubby little gilded thing, both fat and squat, stomach hugely distended. He is fat because he is an emblem of gluttony. There was a belief held by many then that the fire was a mark of God's disapproval, visited upon Londoners for their widespread indulgence in the sin of gluttony. As with many works of art in the capital, the golden boy once lived above a pub called The Fortune of War, which was demolished in 1910.

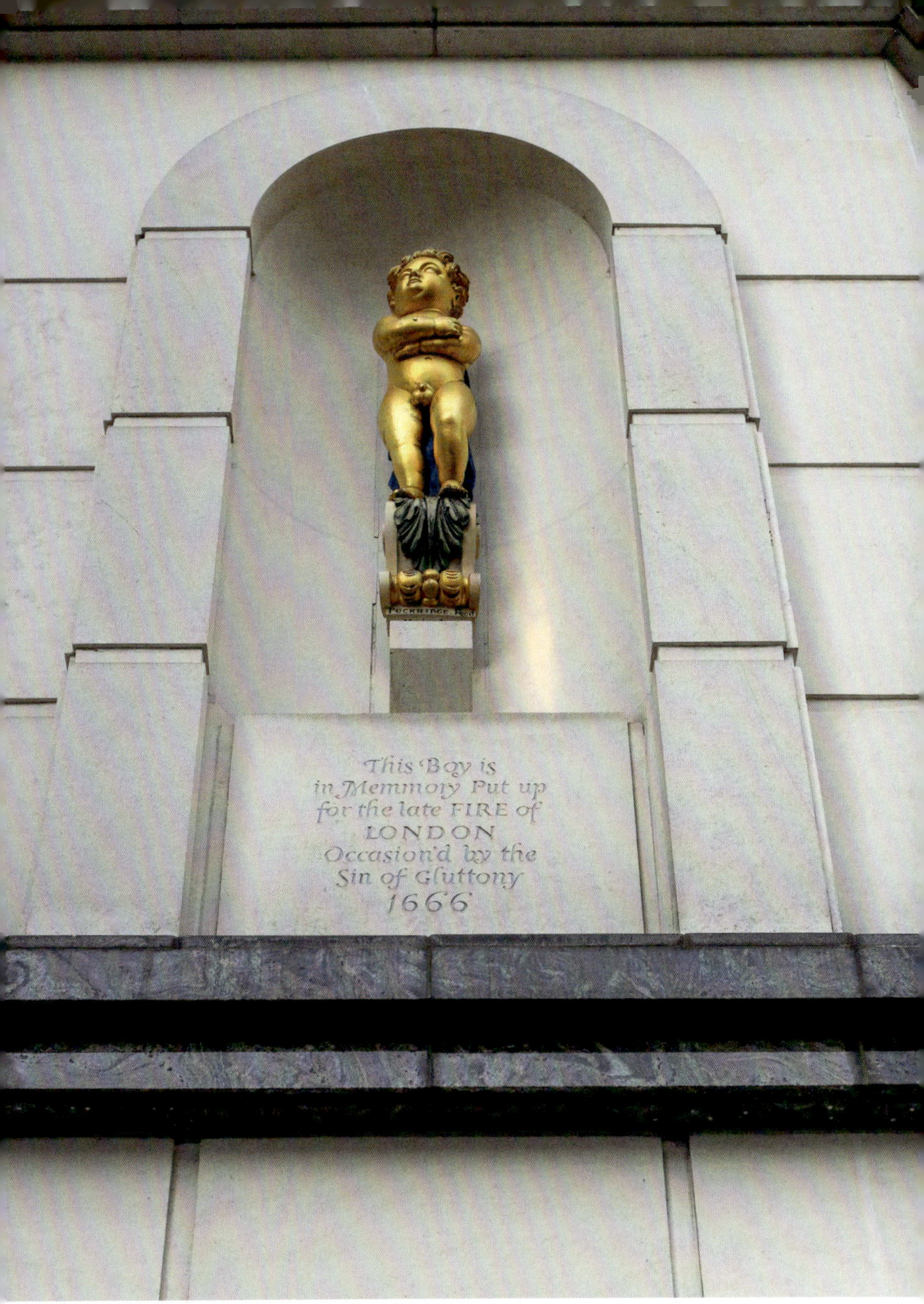

Address Giltspur Street, London EC1A 9DD | Getting there Underground to Barbican (Circle, Hammersmith and City and Metropolitan Lines), then a five-minute walk | Hours Accessible 24 hours | Tip A few minutes away is Holy Sepulchre Church, whose bells are 'the Bells of Old Bailey' in the nursery rhyme 'Oranges and Lemons'.

38 Grinling Gibbons' Font

Adam and Eve encircle the Tree of Life

Churches can have hidden corners that seem dedicated to the twin arts of sculpture and poetry. One such is St James', Piccadilly, a small jewel of a church by Sir Christopher Wren, which was badly damaged during World War II, and then, decades later, restored to miraculous life. Much of the interior, thankfully, remained undamaged.

To find that hidden corner, enter the body of the church by its only door and then, having reached the central aisle of the nave, turn left towards its north-west corner. Here you will find a memorial plaque to William Blake, the greatest poet of London (he was baptised in this church, the plaque informs us) and just beneath that plaque, behind the last row of pews on the north side of the church, a font made out of pale marble exquisitely carved with the story of Adam and Eve by an artist called Grinling Gibbons, who is much better known for his carvings in wood of swags of fruits and flowers. There are exquisite examples of those in this church too, above the wooden reredos at the back of the high altar. Doves, fruits and flowers in abundance garland the space above the cross in a great thrown wreath.

The font at the north-east corner is a scene from the Book of Genesis, when Adam and Eve stand beneath the Tree of Life itself. The font is that tree: its base is a spreading of the roots; vines encircle it as it rises.

The tree culminates in the bowl of the font itself. Adam and Eve, who both stand proud of the trunk of the tree, and hold on to it as they walk around its perimeter, seem to be playing a game of peek-a-boo with each other. Eve is already holding the apple that will lead her into temptation; Adam's hand is clasping his chest. Foliage, by some miracle, seems to be reaching out to cover his nakedness. It is a moment of high drama. The fat serpent encircles the tree and stares right into Eve's face.

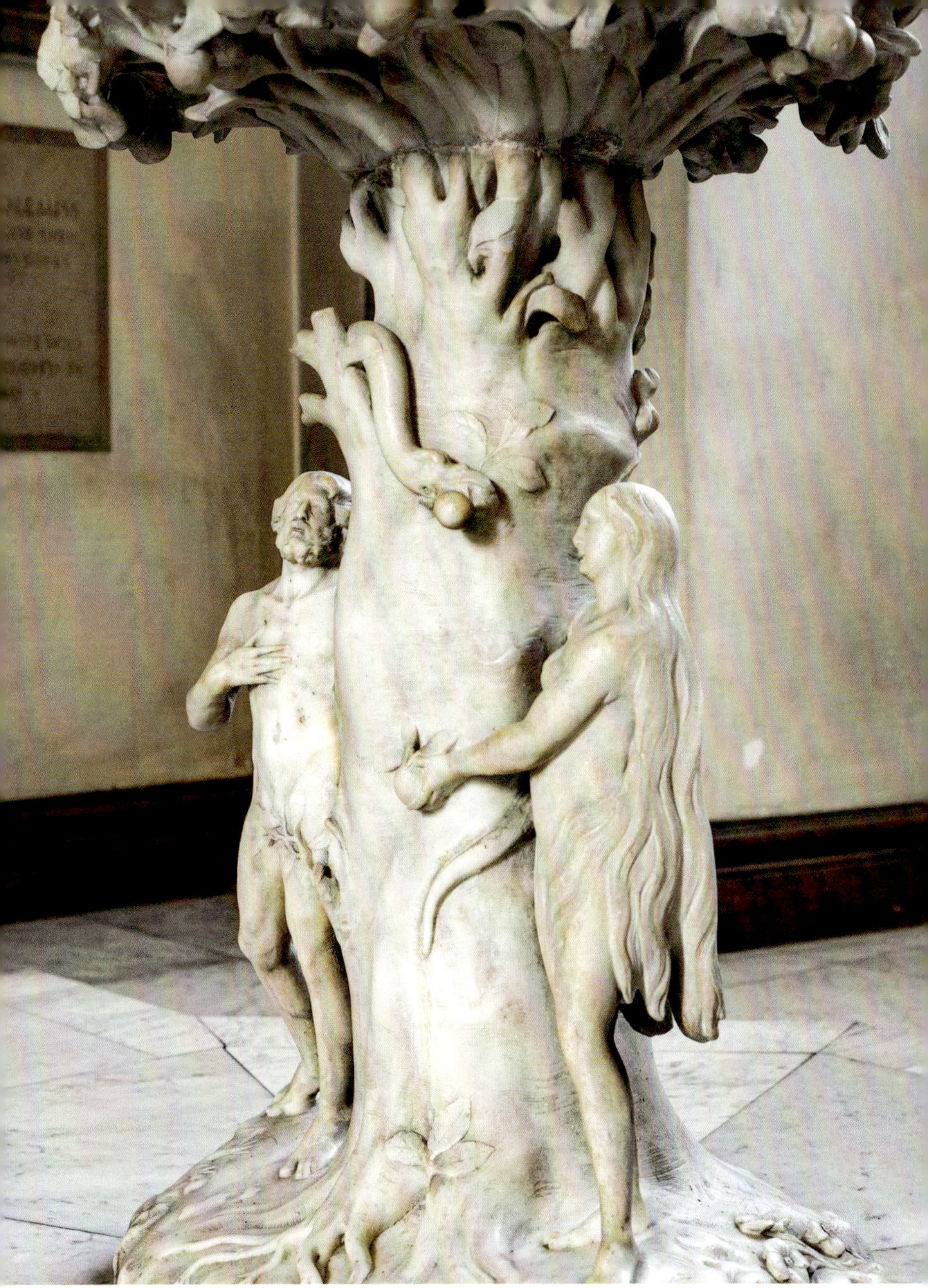

Address 197 Piccadilly, St James', London W1J 9LL, +44 (0)207 734 4511, www.sjp.org.uk | Getting there Underground to Piccadilly Circus (Piccadilly and Bakerloo Lines), then a five-minute walk | Hours Mon–Sat 10am–4pm and often later for events and concerts (see website for details) | Tip Hatchards, the oldest bookshop in London – and possibly the whole of the UK – is just two minutes away, so pop in and buy a book.

39 Heartfelt Memories

A sombre token of national mourning

The National Covid Memorial Wall is a very intimate piece of work, created by many hands. Made in memory of those who died from Covid-19 from March 2020, it engulfs a long section of the handsome stone wall on the south side of the Thames facing the Houses of Parliament. That wall marks the northern boundary of two great hospitals, the Evelina Children's Hospital, and the much more ancient foundation of St Thomas' directly to its west.

The siting of this impromptu memorial, we feel, is very particular. Its presence here, marking so many deaths, is a kind of giant question mark held up in public to all those who rule over us in that agglomeration of great historic buildings on the north side of the Thames. Were all these deaths really necessary? Could you have done more? Why did we all feel so helpless?

This wall is very much a gathering of individual voices, and it is still in the making and the re-making. As you pass by, you see a child here or a man there adding a few words, busy naming a lost relative or friend. The entire wall is a swarm of painted red hearts (some are pink) against grey, gritty stone which, in the distance, could be a swarm of butterflies recently settled.

It is here not because official donations brought it into existence but because many people, from all over this country, wanted, needed, it to be here as a collective marker of individual grief and private mourning.

As art, it is amateurish and rag-bag, a clot of hearts here, another there, all come together in order to comfort each another, to give one another the succour that proximity always creates. Such a gathering of so many makes for a powerful feeling of solidarity. The hearts are named and their relationship to the heart-maker usually mentioned: *Brenda Blair, mother for ever 05/04/2020; Gareth Jones, teacher, leader, friend xxx.* There are dates, private messages, kisses.

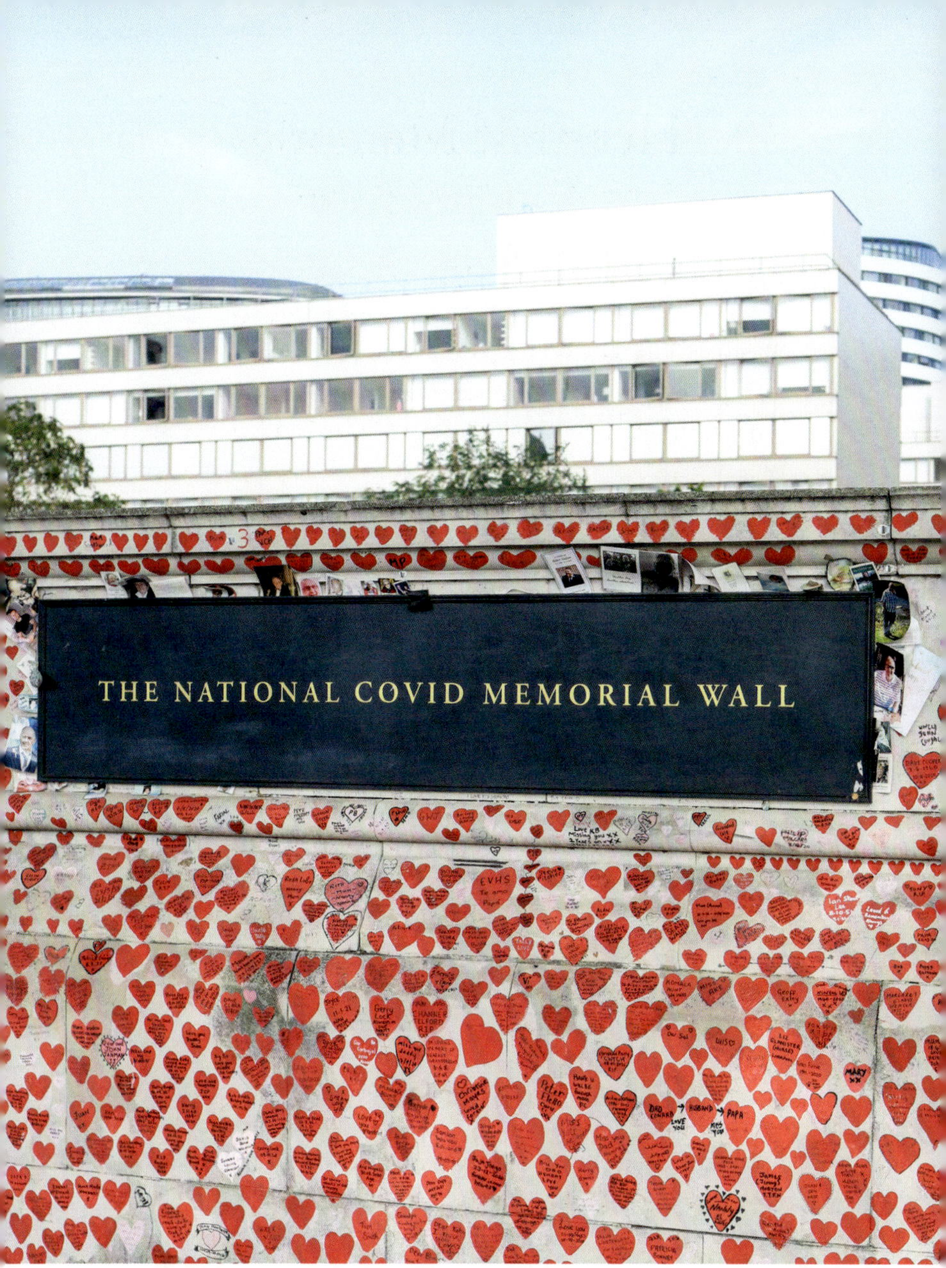

Address Embankment, London SE1 7EH, Friends of the Wall can be contacted on Twitter at @CovidMemorialUK | Getting there Underground to Waterloo (Northern, Jubilee, Bakerloo and Waterloo and City Lines), then a five-minute walk | Hours Accessible 24 hours | Tip Visit the little park inside the Westminster Bridge entrance to St Thomas' Hospital to see the statue to Mary Seacole, a nurse during the Crimean War, and voted first in a poll of 100 Great Black Britons.

40_Henry Moore and Much More

Sculpture bedded down at the riverside

Riverside Walk Gardens is a tiny, part-hidden park at the north-east corner of Vauxhall Bridge, overlooking the Thames. It is also home to a number of sculptures – including a significant post-war bronze by Henry Moore called *Locking Piece* (1968), which looks like a cross between rock and bone, one element bearing down powerfully upon the other – Moore drew inspiration from both throughout his long career as a sculptor. The two pieces do indeed appear loosely locked together, as if they might have been twisted into position. Or they could be two conjoined human or animal bones in a near perfect state of articulation – like a shoulder in its socket.

The Moore is at one end of this sliver of parkland beside the river, and the park's shape and contouring skilfully remind us of its positioning here. It is gently, rhythmically, fluidly stepped, which puts us in mind of the tidal movement we can watch just beyond the wall. The tide is out this morning. There are other sculptures here too – a recently installed piece called *Folly* by Nathaniel Rackowe shows us two wooden huts balanced precariously upon each other at their apexes – a humorously miraculous feat. This is a whimsical nod in the direction of the kinds of workaday timber structures that you would once have seen here, when the Thames was lined by wharves.

If you walk a little further along, in the direction of an equally sinuous residential block called Riverwalk, you will spot a bench by Pablo Reinoso called *We Watch You Too Bench*. It seems to be in the throes of unravelling – or perhaps it is a sculpture that decided, at the very last minute, to put itself to good use by proposing itself as a seat. Now climb the steps up to the corner of the bridge itself until you reach a little viewing terrace that is a perfect sun-trap for Peter Randall-Page's sculpture in the form of an arrested cloud.

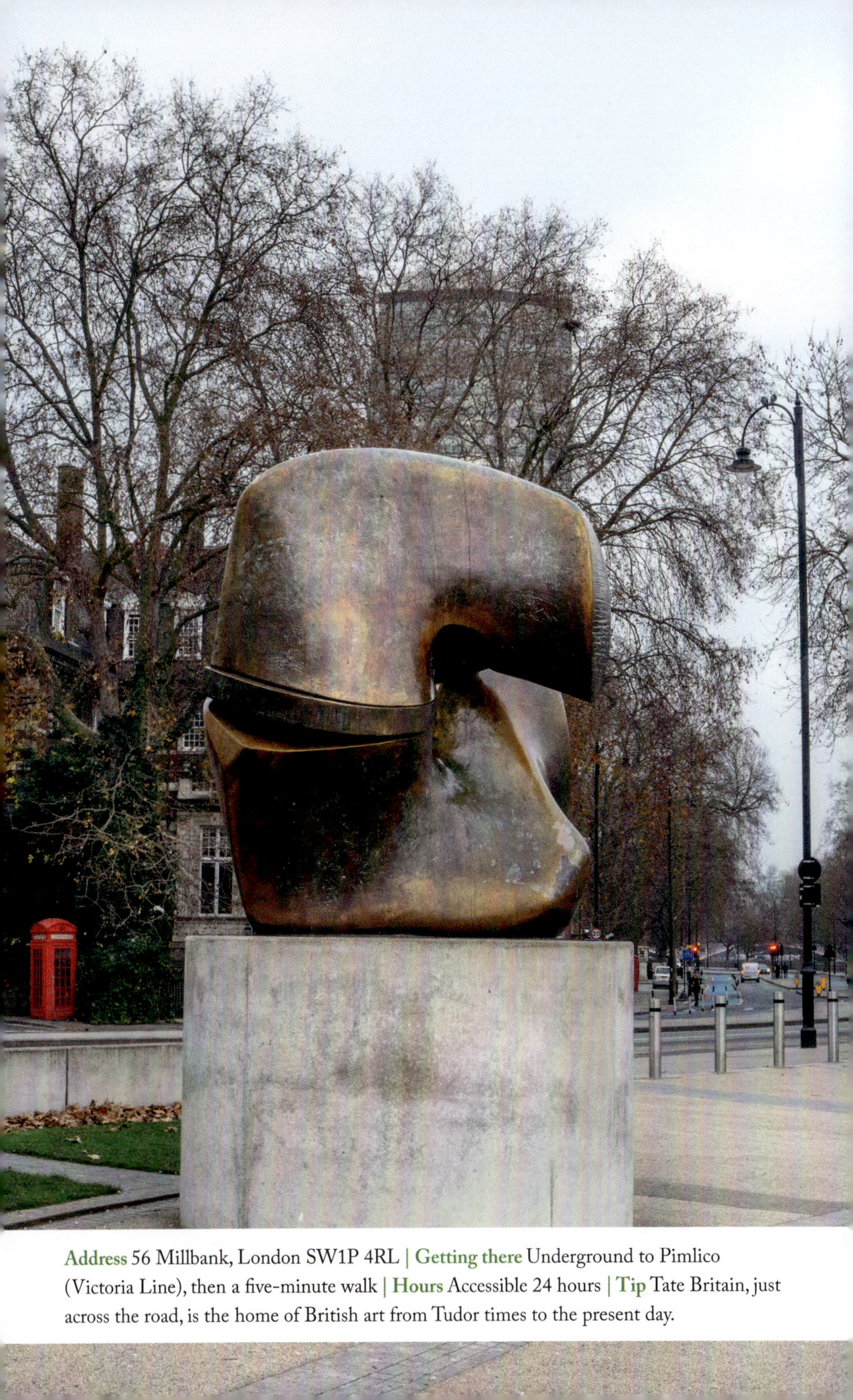

Address 56 Millbank, London SW1P 4RL | Getting there Underground to Pimlico (Victoria Line), then a five-minute walk | Hours Accessible 24 hours | Tip Tate Britain, just across the road, is the home of British art from Tudor times to the present day.

41 Hercules

The Neapolitan muscle-man

London's Royal Academy, which opened its doors in 1768, has always had its own art school, and supported free art education for a limited body of students. But how were they taught? And what were their study aids? To answer that question, you have to seek a brick-walled, barrel-vaulted corridor at basement level, which links Burlington House in Piccadilly with its second building on Burlington Gardens.

Here you will find not only the casts that were used by students of drawing, which include the flayed bodies that were employed to teach human anatomy, but also copies of some of the greatest sculptures from antiquity, such as the Venus de Milo and a recumbent figure of Christ from Michelangelo's great *Pietà*. But the greatest of them all, the original of which you can see to this day at the Naples National Archaeological Museum, is the enormous, if not nigh on overwhelming, presence of the Farnese Hercules, a looming giant of a sculpture that rises many feet into the air, and is set, dramatically lit, into its own wonderful recess.

Hercules was discovered – in bits, it has to be said (that is perfectly evident when you stare, awe-struck, up at him) – in the Baths of the Emperor Caracalla during the 16th century, and it was displayed in a courtyard of the Palazzo Farnese for much of its life. The Farnese trove was one of the greatest archaeological discoveries of all time. This cast was made especially for the Royal Academy, and it was sent over from Rome in 1790. So much about it fascinates – its extraordinary muscularity, for example, which some weedy critics averse to extreme workouts have found a bit over-egged. Hercules, that hero of mythology, has recently killed the Nemean Lion (you see how its skin hangs over his club), and he is currently resting from his 12 labours. A-bristle with virility, he seems almost nonchalant in his pose...

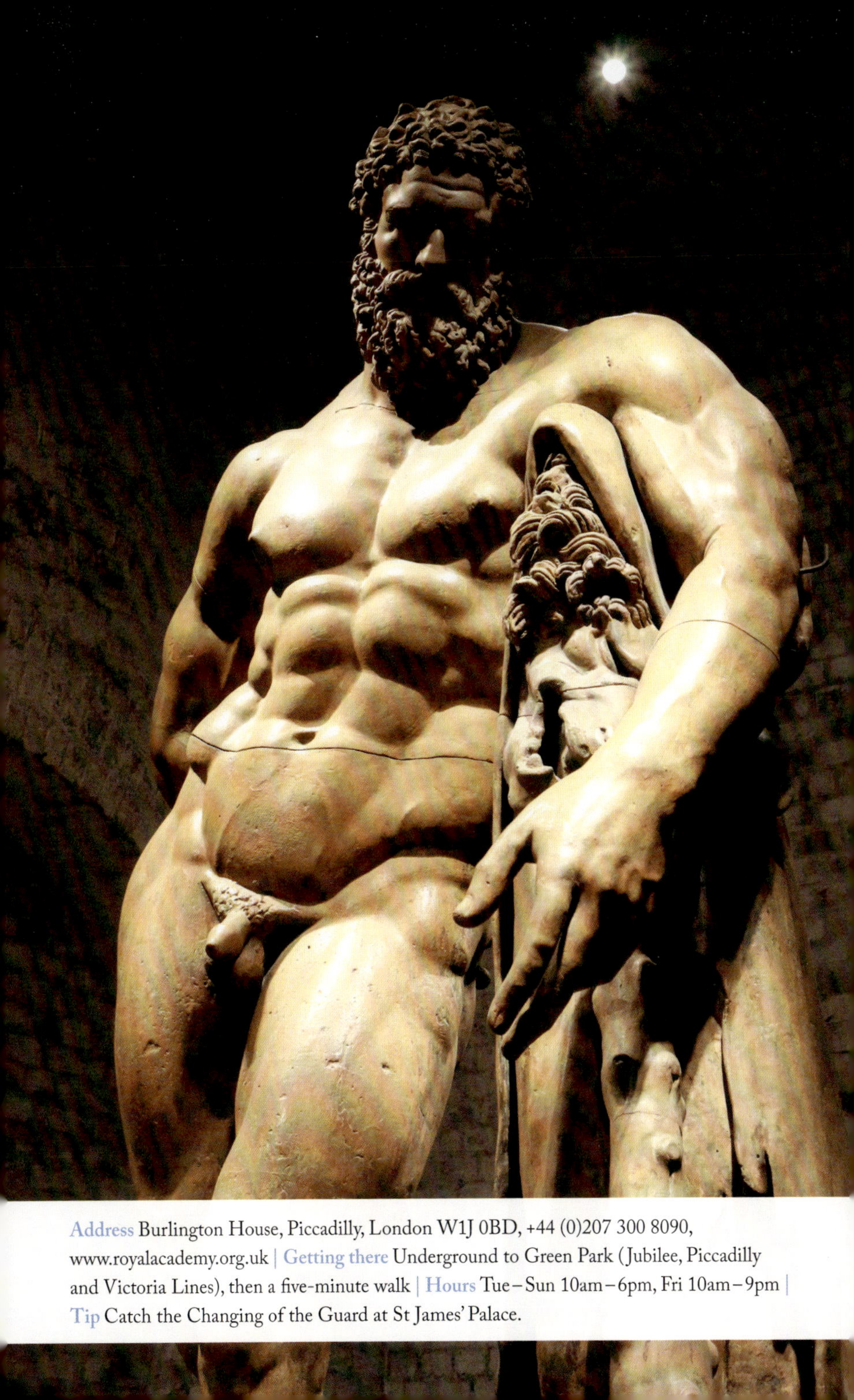

Address Burlington House, Piccadilly, London W1J 0BD, +44 (0)207 300 8090, www.royalacademy.org.uk | Getting there Underground to Green Park (Jubilee, Piccadilly and Victoria Lines), then a five-minute walk | Hours Tue–Sun 10am–6pm, Fri 10am–9pm | Tip Catch the Changing of the Guard at St James' Palace.

42 The Hidden Combatant

The poet who served in the Royal Welch Fusiliers

An official memorial to combatants in war can often conceal as much as it reveals. This close-packed formation of young soldiers in south London's Battersea Park is a tribute to all those who fought in France during the Great War of 1914–18. There are just three of them on this oval, drum-like plinth, all booted, gaitered, tommy-hatted, rifle-toting, and kitted to the nines. Look at the weight of those packs on their backs! See how their chins are constrained by those chin straps! Their movement is a briskly dutiful lock-step. They are all of exactly the same height. Their colour, in that uniform, reminds us of the hue of dirty sand. They are models of discipline, fortitude, of that spirit of keeping-on-keeping-on-ness.

The memorial is neatly contained within a well-trimmed, circular hedge, out of which they rise up, as if to surprise us by their presence here. So close is their camaraderie that they look almost squeezed together. One of them is much better known than the other two, and we can recognise him by one particular facial detail, which reveals the identity of a famous poet who did indeed fight as an officer in the Royal Welch Fusiliers. How to spot him though? Look at them all side-on, and examine their three noses in particular. Pay most attention to the young soldier on the extreme left.

The question to ask is this: how regular are these noses? One of them, you will surely notice – it belongs to the soldier with sloping arms – is damaged, oddly broken and angled down, the result of a conflict that happened not on the field of battle, but in peace time, in a boxing ring, when he was a boy at Rugby School. This is the broken nose of the poet Robert Graves. Robert Graves was one of the greatest poets of the 20th century, best known by the wider world for the televised adaptations of his cycle of novels about the Roman emperor Claudius.

Address Battersea Park, London SW11 4NJ, +44 (0)208 871 7530, www.wandsworth.gov.uk | **Getting there** Train to Queenstown Road (Battersea), then a five-minute walk | **Hours** Daily 6.30am–10.30pm | **Tip** Across the road from the park is the refurbished Battersea Power Station with its glamorous central shopping mall.

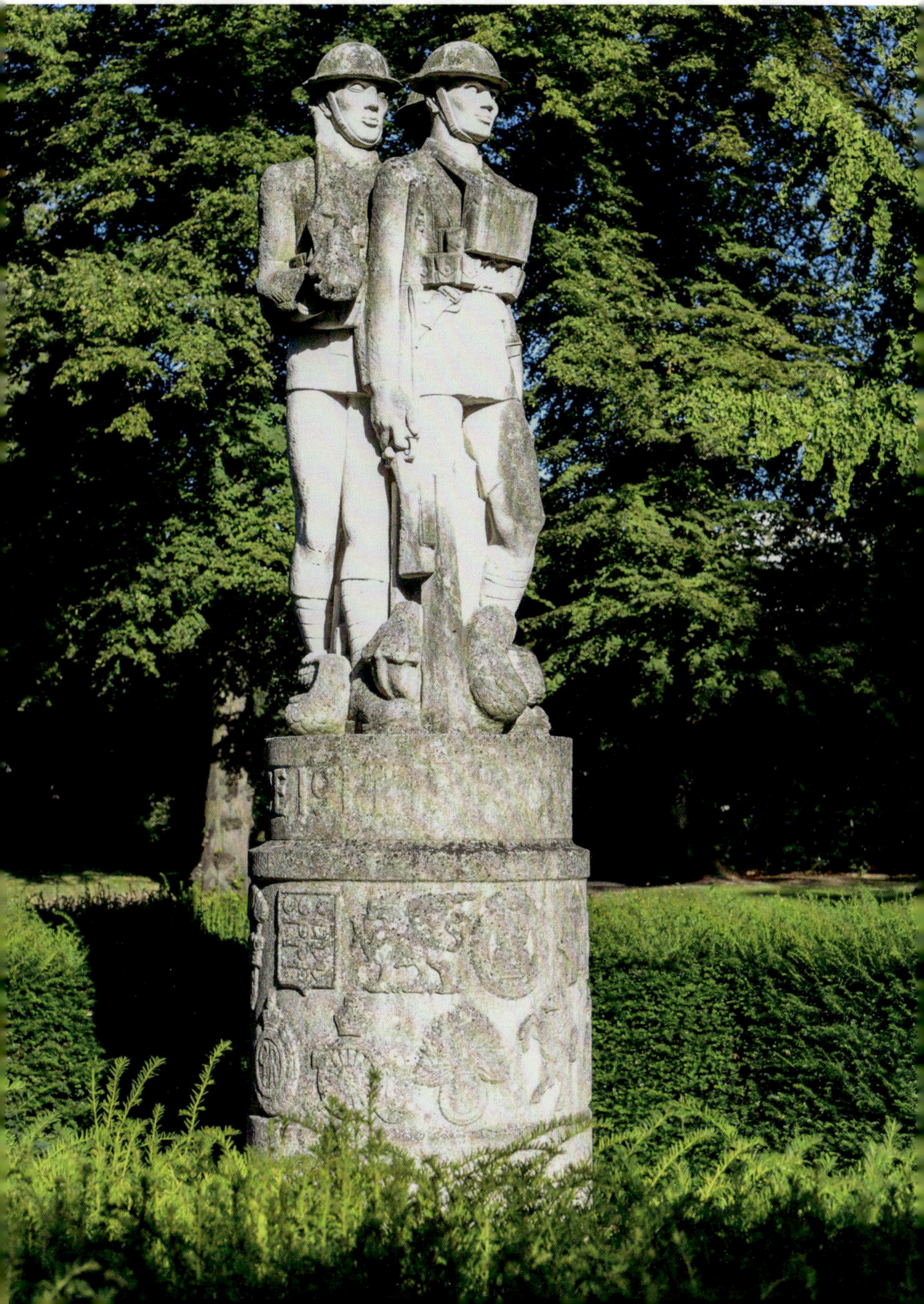

43 Hodge

Dr Johnson's most famous cat

Individual cats have seldom been raised up in bronze in the Western tradition. They are more often likely to be seen in the likes of Dutch genre paintings of the 17th century, rampaging around the kitchen, playing bit parts in the excitable company of other equally lowly creatures, as a rakishly behatted young blade tries to pull the not-so-innocent kitchen maid. In Ancient Egypt things were quite otherwise, of course. Cats often had a near godly status – they were guardians and protectors, in this life and perhaps even the one after that. Mummified cats were often buried with their owners. In ancient Rome cats were regarded as sacred to Diana, goddess of the moon.

In London, there is one particularly exalted cat sculpted in bronze, and he lives at the bottom of a small square, on a stone plinth, in the old City of London. He sits contentedly, back hunched, looking up in the general direction of the house of his master, Dr Samuel Johnson, poet, journalist, and most famous for his *Dictionary of the English Language*. He is called Hodge, and Gough Square is a very fitting place for a scribbler and his cat to have lived. It is just off Fleet Street, once the home of almost all the great newspapers ever fit to print. Now if you look up the definition of a cat in Johnson's dictionary, you will find that it reads as follows: 'A domestic animal, reckoned by naturalists the lowest order of the leonine species.'

In life, Dr Johnson seems to have disagreed with himself. There were few things, animal or human, that he cherished more than Hodge, and this is why beside the cat on that handsome stone plinth, there is the empty, opened out shell of an oyster. Much to the irritation of Johnson's great biographer, a Scot called James Boswell, Johnson indulged Hodge to a ridiculous degree, which went so far as to buy him oysters and other fishy favourites every afternoon.

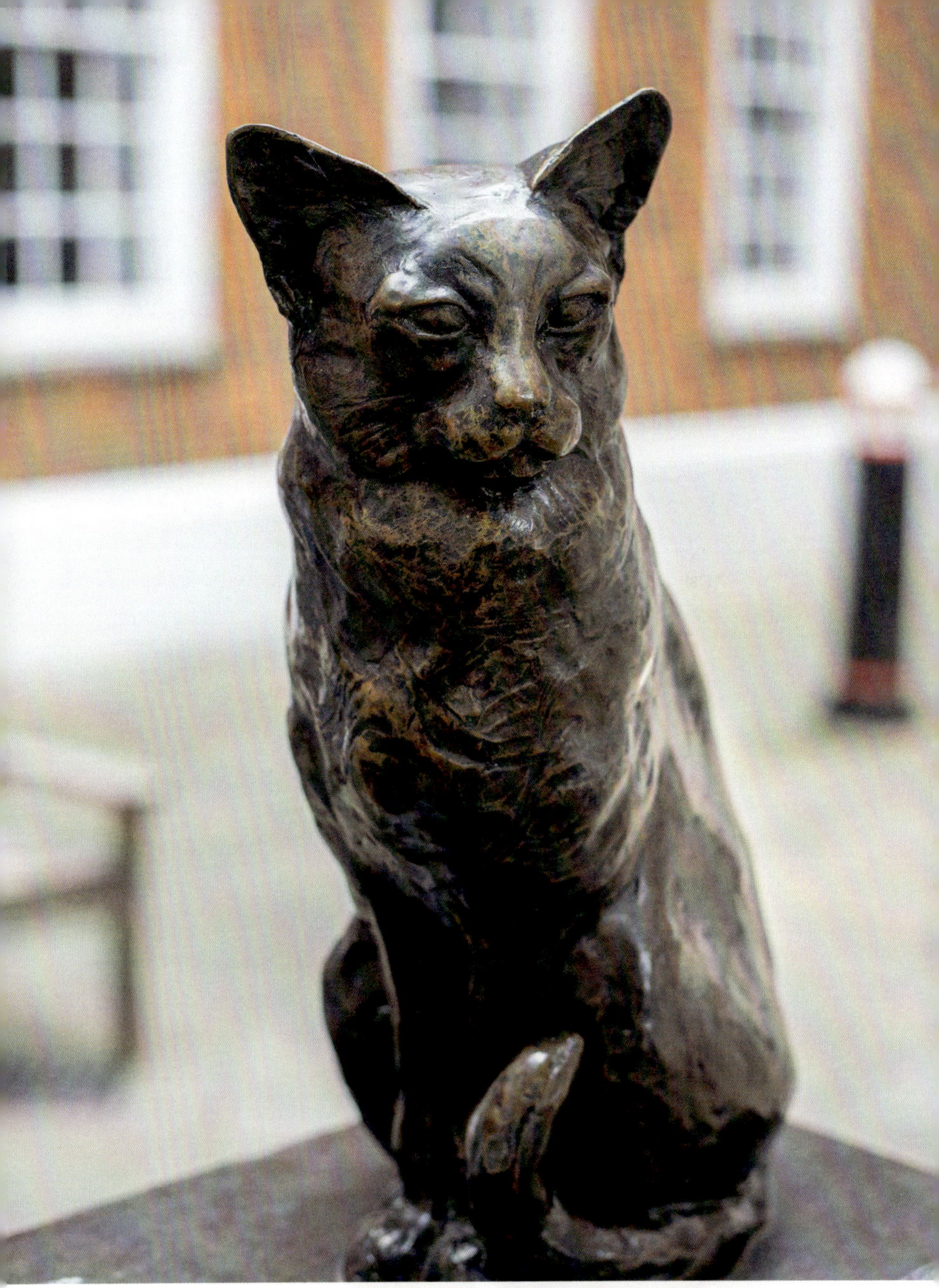

Address 2 Gough Square, London EC4A 3DE, www.talkingstatues.london.com | Getting there Underground to Chancery Lane (Central Line), then a 13-minute walk | Hours Hodge is accessible 24 hours; Dr Johnson's House open Mon, Thu, Fri & Sat 11am–5pm | Tip Ye Olde Cheshire Cheese, an ancient hostelry known for its literary connections, is two minutes from here at 145 Fleet Street.

44 Horse and Rider

'An ageless symbol of man and horse'

Do kings, queens, dukes, police personnel and members of the Household Cavalry positively enjoy being seen on horseback? The jury is still out on that one. It can certainly work greatly to the advantage of a king or any other sort of eminence to be seen on a horse in a painting or a sculpture. London is full of such representations. Just think of King Charles I, and how Van Dyke's great painting of him on horseback in the collection of the National Portrait Gallery completely distracts us from thinking about the fact that the poor man is a woefully thin-shanked dwarf. Being on horseback aggrandizes, impresses and, in the case of the police force, intimidates.

But what of this oddly androgynous being on horseback in Mayfair, sited these days at the junction of Burlington Gardens and New Bond Street? It was made by Dame Elisabeth Frink. It has not always been in this choicest of locations – the space surrounding it really sets it off. It is highly photogenic too, as anyone who travels to see it will notice because there will be many other people nearby with cameras at the ready.

It was not always so fortunately sited. Until relatively recently it sat outside a coffee shop at the Piccadilly end of Dover Street, with the horse's flanks jammed up against happy street coffee-quaffers. Now it has galloped east to a new location directly outside Ralph Lauren's flagship store, and almost directly beneath the languid float of a large Union Jack. But it is a rather strange statue of a horse and rider. He is naked for a start, and he carries no mace or sword. He does not even hold on to the horse's reins. His arms hang loose and a little helpless. It is as if his horse will bear him away to wherever it chooses. What can this mean? That he is a symbol of a helpless consumer, about to be sucked into the dangerous world of some of the most expensive brands in the world?

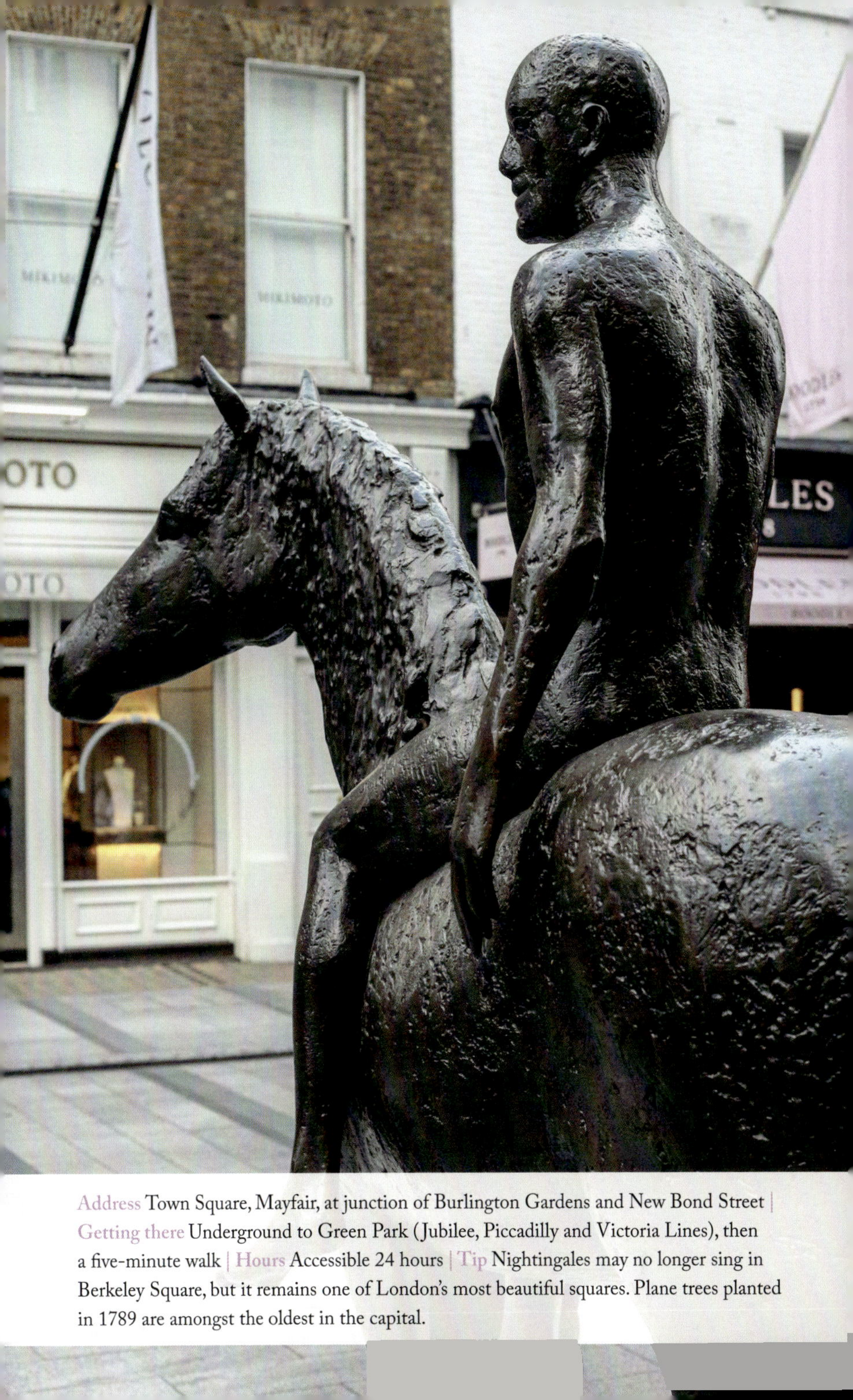

Address Town Square, Mayfair, at junction of Burlington Gardens and New Bond Street | Getting there Underground to Green Park (Jubilee, Piccadilly and Victoria Lines), then a five-minute walk | Hours Accessible 24 hours | Tip Nightingales may no longer sing in Berkeley Square, but it remains one of London's most beautiful squares. Plane trees planted in 1789 are amongst the oldest in the capital.

45 *If Not, Not*

The tapestry swooning beside the staircase

You spot this gorgeous tapestry as you enter the British Library. Raise your eyes up, and then to the right. Yes, it is hanging in the lee of the staircase. It's a giant of an affair, the largest of its kind ever to be woven in England when it was made in 2009. What makes it so unusual is that it is a story-telling tapestry of sorts.

In fact, it is the re-presentation (in tapestry form) of a large painting called *If Not, Not* by an American painter long resident in London called Ron Kitaj. Kitaj's painting, which is a dreamscape, has its antecedent, which means that we think we half recognise it when we greet it beside this staircase. Yes, it is something of a take on a famous Italian Renaissance painting called *The Tempest* by Giorgione, which lives in Venice. That was made around 1506, and it is tiny in comparison with this one.

If Not, Not was woven at Dovecot Studios from Kitaj's painting in 1996–97. It was so large that the loom on which it was woven had to be set up in a swimming pool. The tapestry feels much softer and more yielding to the eye than the original painting. The tapestry has a pink border, and within that border there is a multiplicity of fragmentary floating figures who seem to be trying to save themselves from drowning, even as they are carried across these boiling, shifting planes of colour. One of them is the poet T. S. Eliot, easily recognisable by his spectacles. He is being beckoned into a world of seduction by a mythical temptress who looks a little like a figure out of a painting by Paul Gauguin. An ominous brown tower – perhaps people are being exterminated in there – rears up at the back.

The tapestry shows us an amalgam of partially defined landscapes. Images seem to float away from us even as we stare at them. The colours are very alluring too, almost sweet enough to suck on – such pinks and yellows! Everything feels hot.

Address The British Library, 99 Euston Road, London NW1 2DB, +44 (0)330 333 1144, www.bl.uk | **Getting there** Underground to Euston (Northern and Victoria Lines) or King's Cross (Circle, Piccadilly, Hammersmith and City, Northern, Metropolitan and Victoria Lines), then a five-minute walk from both | **Hours** Mon–Thu 9.30am–8pm, Fri 9.30am–6pm, Sat 9.30am–5pm, Sun 11am–5pm | **Tip** Drop into St Pancras Station and visit the stunning Champagne bar, the longest in Europe.

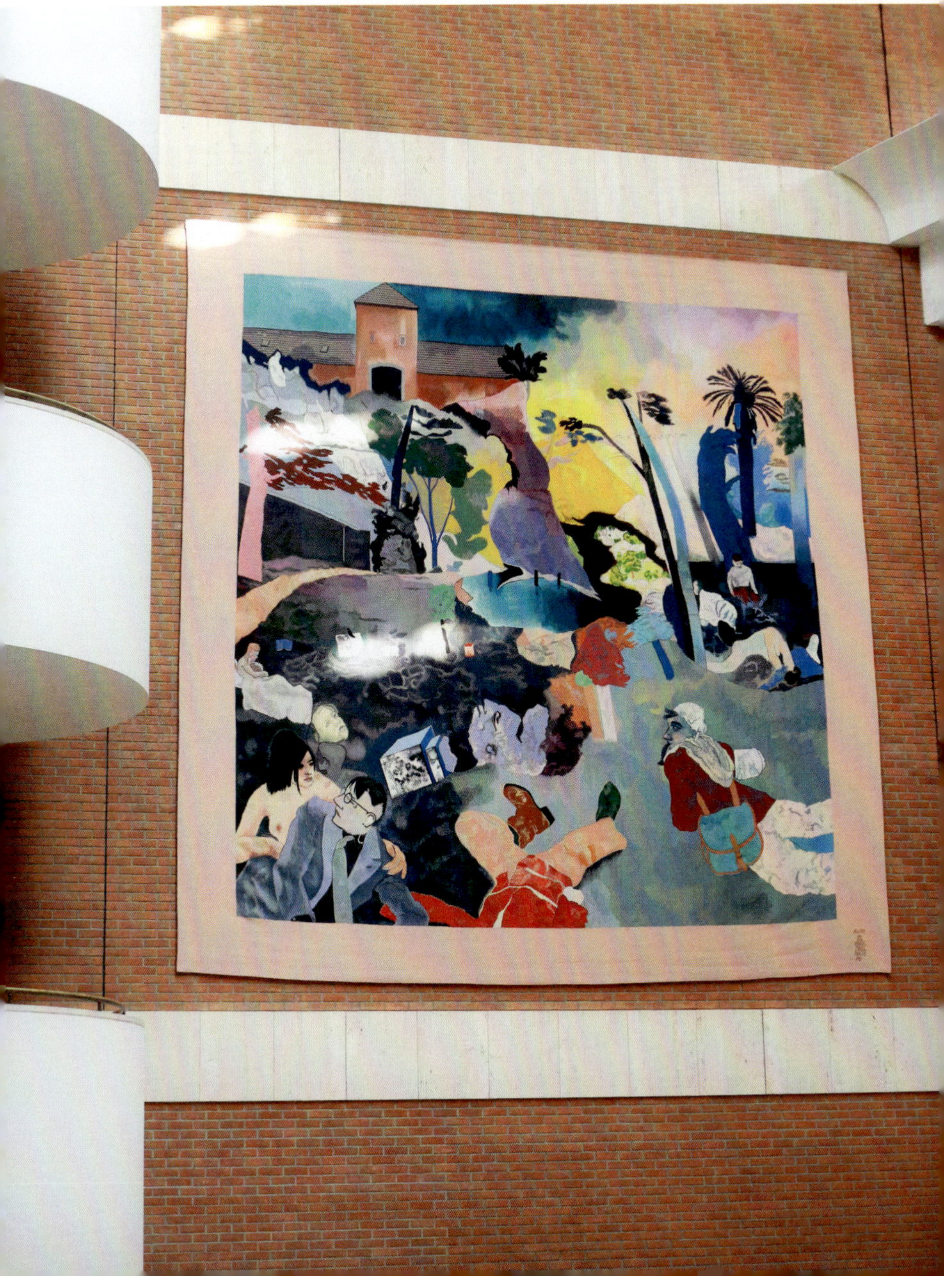

46 The Isokon Building

An artful exercise in urban living

This block of flats was designed to be a new, modernist adventure in urban living, and the elegant, white Isokon building of 1934 at Belsize Park in dramatically hilly north London still looks revolutionary in the way that it seems to slide downhill like a sleek liner easing out of its berth... Its creators were a couple called Jack and Molly Pritchard, together with architect Wells Coates, and its design was influenced by a passion for the achievements of the Bauhaus.

The building, in its simplicity and its shapeliness, is an artwork in itself. Some of the interior furnishings, which were minimal, even spartan, and involved the use of a new material called plywood, could be described as works of art too. The chairs and bookcases are made of it, for example. But why plywood? Because Jack Pritchard was the UK representative of Venesta, an Estonian company that manufactured the material. Everything in each of the building's tiny apartments – which consisted of a studio room (with bed) and a tiny kitchen – needed to be compact and unfussy. The direct opposite of Victorian clutter.

Two examples of these works in plywood, both by the designer Marcel Breuer (who also lived here), are on display in a little, two-room gallery on the ground floor, which has been carved out of a space that was once a garage. Breuer's sinuous Isokon Long Chair (1936), so mellow in colour, flows through the space that it occupies like water.

Beside it there is a bookcase that looks like a single piece of folded and squeezed material. The Penguin Donkey was designed to fit entire, colour-coded sets of Penguin paperbacks, which were the newest of the new in 1938. Left-of-centre artists, writers and intellectuals – its famous residents included Agatha Christie and László Moholy-Nagy – flocked here to admire, or to inhabit, like the gulls that wheel around in the air outside to this day.

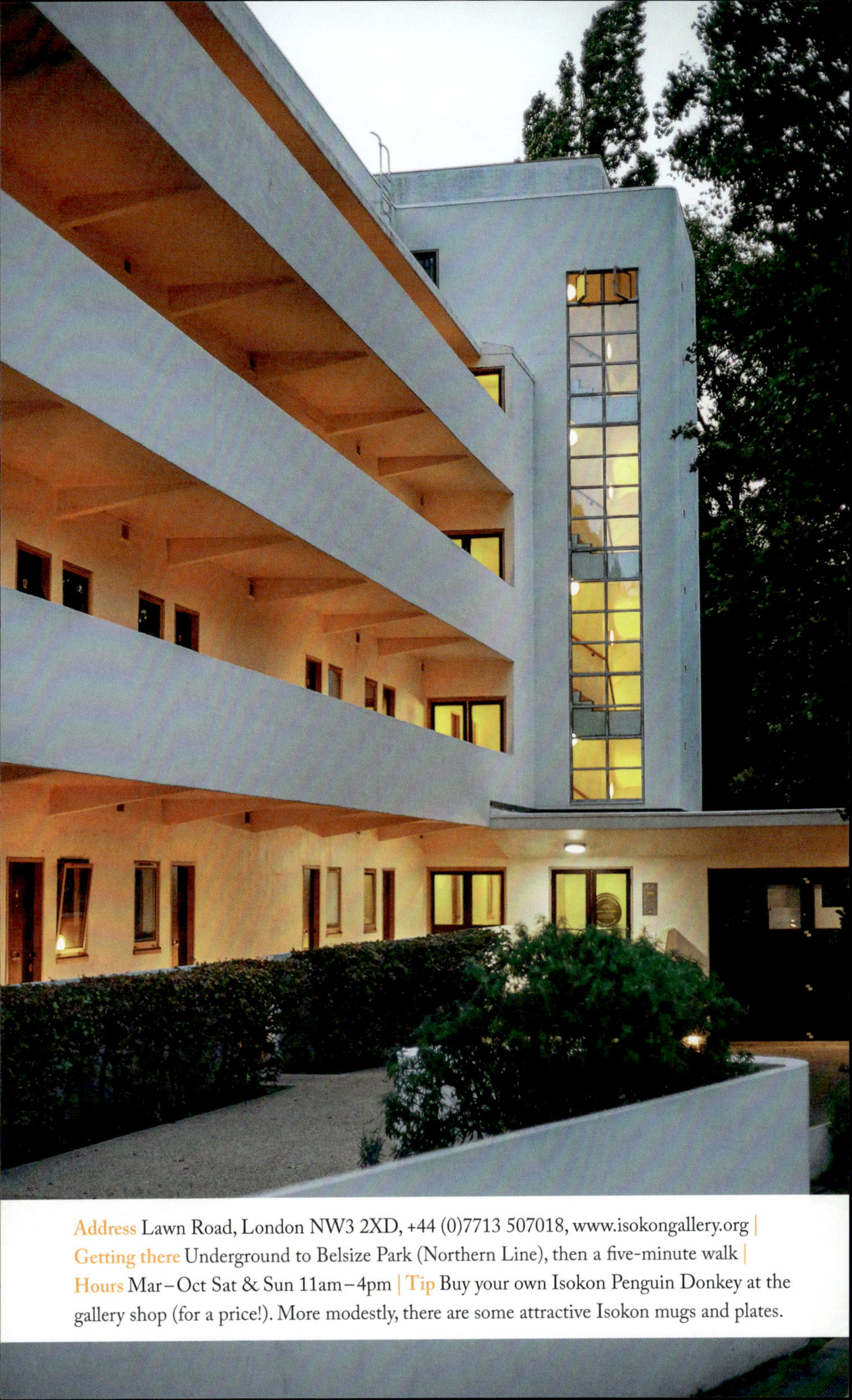

Address Lawn Road, London NW3 2XD, +44 (0)7713 507018, www.isokongallery.org | Getting there Underground to Belsize Park (Northern Line), then a five-minute walk | Hours Mar–Oct Sat & Sun 11am–4pm | Tip Buy your own Isokon Penguin Donkey at the gallery shop (for a price!). More modestly, there are some attractive Isokon mugs and plates.

47 Ivon Hitchens' Mural

Folk traditions doing a merry dance

Cecil Sharp House, which opened in 1930, is home to both the English Folk Dance and Song Society and the Vaughan Williams Memorial Library. Its Great Hall lost its lovely Musicians' Gallery to bomb damage during World War II, but the loss meant that greater wall space became available to create a work of art that would celebrate the spirit of the entire enterprise.

These days, the building plays host to a dizzying variety of movers and crooners, from ribbon-shaking, bell-jingling, high-stepping Morris Dancers to excitable conventions of belly dancers in their clingy gold lurex. And all this frenzied activity is overlooked by an extravagantly ambitious mural completed in 1954, after three years of labour, by Ivon Hitchens, one of England's greatest post-war painters of the natural world. At its unveiling, it was described as the largest public mural in the whole of England.

The work, which surges in a single, uninterrupted sweep across the length of the Great Hall's longest wall, celebrates the primitive energy of folk dance and the enduring pull of folk traditions. How to make a work of such a size cohere though? Hitchens divides the work into individual episodes, and then loosely contains each one within bulging, circular sweepings of paint. The mythical, the animal and the human all interweave, dancing in and out of a dream-suffused woodland setting. A trio of musicians pipe the music. Figures and forms, from the definite to the relatively indefinite, seem to be poised between appearance and disappearance. No figure overwhelms. A hobby horse is lured into dance mood by its teaser. The Queen of the May swims into view on horseback. There's chain-dancing through the bracken. The colours range through sandy yellows to pallid greens and greys, but it is blue that holds everything together, and gives the onlooker a sense of buoyancy and free-floatingness.

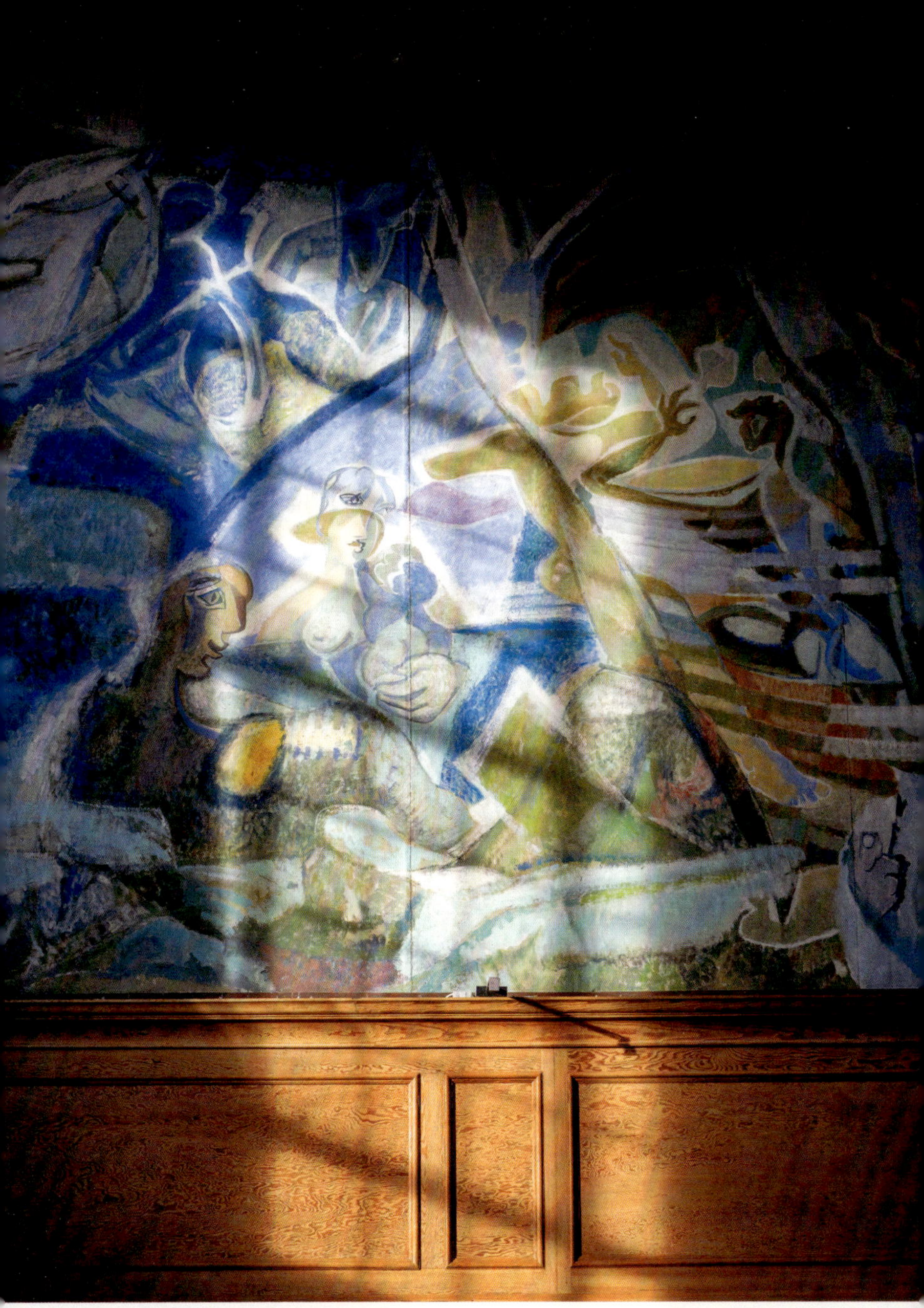

Address 2 Regent's Park Road, London NW1 7AY, +44 (0)207 485 2206, www.efdss.org | Getting there Underground to Camden Town (Northern Line), then a 10-minute walk | Hours Daily 9am–11pm | Tip Walk towards the Outer Circle of Regent's Park and visit London Zoo, the world's oldest scientific zoo.

48 The Iznik Corner

Where the Victorians smoked and canoodled

Hertford House, home to the Wallace Collection, contains the great amassing of paintings, furnishings, armour and much else once bought by a rather unpleasant Victorian aristocrat called Sir Richard Wallace. This is the man who made the little-known Frans Hals very famous by buying his work and talking about it to all and sundry, and gave what became Hals' most celebrated painting, *The Laughing Cavalier*, its name. One of the house's most hidden nooks tells the story of the extraordinary Victorian tiles that once covered all the walls of the Smoking Room. That great ground-floor room is now itself divided into two, and occupied by the low-lit 15th and 16th-century galleries.

How to find it though? The place itself is such a fascinatingly over-stuffed warren of objects. When you enter the house, take a sharp right turn into the Front State Room. Walk through that towards a wonderful painting of St Catherine of Alexandria by the great Venetian painter Cima da Conegliano. Now you are standing in part of what was once the old Smoking Room. Walk right through the two galleries until you spot, on the extreme right-hand side at the very back, what looks like a well-lit, tiled, cupboard-like corner, with a statue at its centre. It is the walls that deserve our attention, and the floor mosaics too.

This remnant of the walls of the Old Smoking Room is covered in tiles – all the better for cleaning off tobacco fug. These Victorian tiles are based on a Turkish style that was very popular from the 16th century onwards, and is closely associated with the town of Iznik. (Elsewhere in the gallery you can see examples of Iznik ceramic ware.) There is always an abundant interweaving of stylised foliage. The Victorians, passionate Orientalists, yearned to bring back to their smoking rooms some savour of the exoticism of the Far East as they smoked and canoodled.

Address The Wallace Collection, Hertford House, Manchester Square, London W1U 3BN, +44 (0)207 563 9500, www.wallacecollection.org | **Getting there** Underground to Bond Street (Central, Elizabeth and Jubilee Lines), then a 10-minute walk | **Hours** Daily 10am–5pm | **Tip** The house where Simón Bolívar (the Venezuelan soldier and revolutionary) lived is at 4 Duke Street, off the far side of the square.

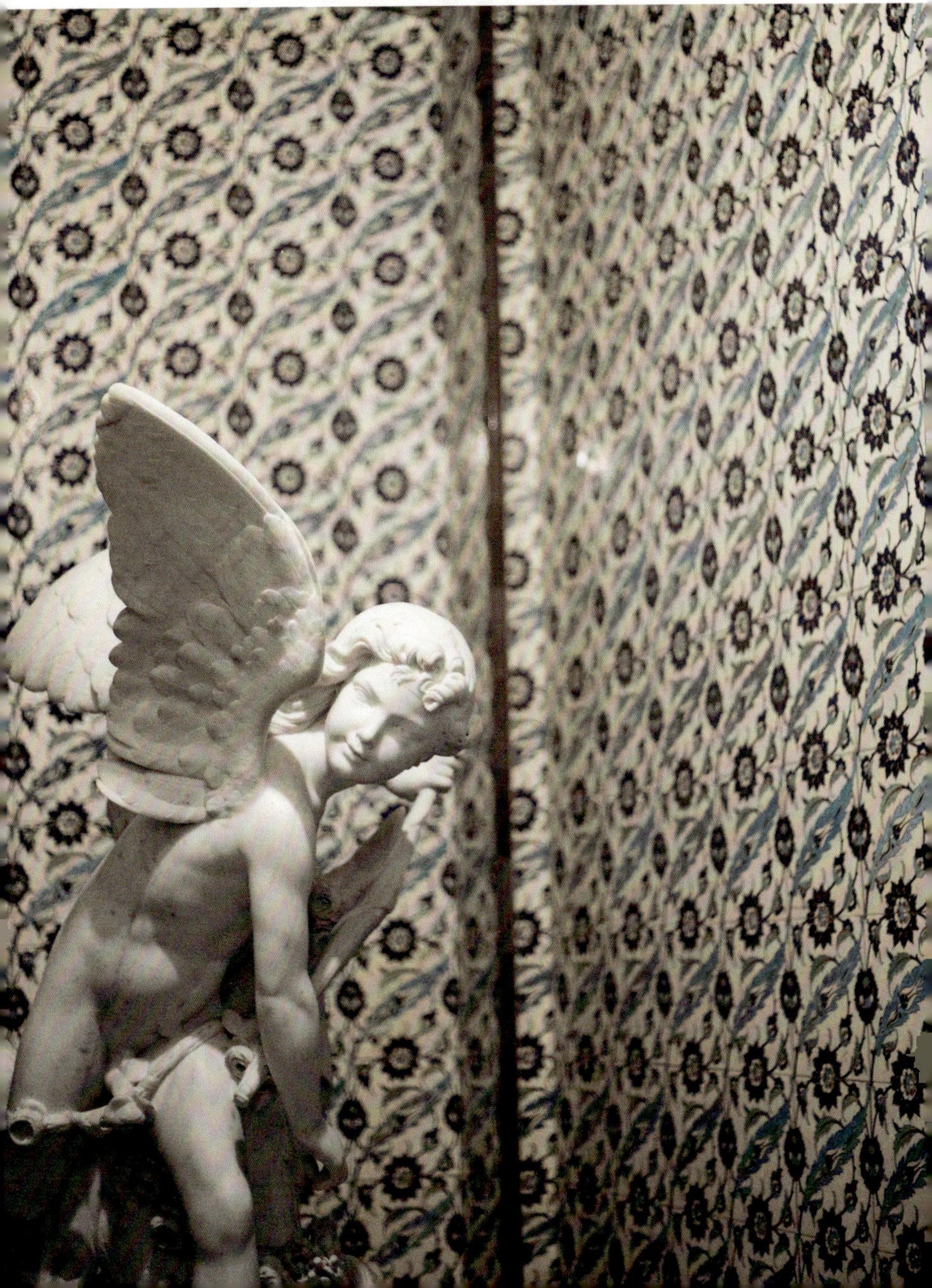

49_Jeremy Bentham

The philosopher who never sleeps

Long before the artist Marc Quinn decided to make a cast of his own head in blood, an important English thinker had beaten him to it. The great social reformer and philosopher Jeremy Bentham (1748–1832) thought long and hard about what should happen to his body after his death. His wish was that it should be transformed into an auto-icon (or self-image) as an inspiration to others. His wishes were duly carried out, and his presence at University College London has been part haunting and part inspiring that great institution ever since (it is still, almost 200 years after his death, one of the world's highest-ranking universities).

The wax and mummified body has spent much of its time in a large wooden structure resembling a giant wardrobe, which is still prominently displayed in the Wilkins Building, the oldest part of the university. There is no mistaking who was inhabiting this beautiful upended box of a wardrobe. His name is prominently displayed in gold lettering. The mummified head, somewhat ghoulish and shrunken, has lived a fairly peripatetic, freelance life, often quite separately from the rest of the body. Does it amuse or unnerve? The cheeks certainly look strangely shrunken. Its silver-grey eyebrows still bristle alarmingly. It has been on display in Ripley's Believe It or Not! Museum. It has occupied its own shelf in an exhibition display called 'What is it to be human?' beneath the university's famous octagonal dome.

It even used to be the case that its presence was required at the head of the table during significant meetings of the university professors. This was not a religious gesture by any means because UCL was and remains a proudly secular institution. And where is Jeremy Bentham now then? These days his body, fully clothed, can be seen seated, observing all who approach, in a display case at the UCL Student Centre.

Address UCL Student Centre, University College, 27–28 Gordon Square, London WC1H 0AH, +44 (0)203 108 9782, www.ucl.ac.uk | **Getting there** Underground to Euston Square (Circle, Hammersmith and City and Metropolitan Lines), then a seven-minute walk | **Hours** Accessible 24 hours | **Tip** Head for the Wellcome Collection in Euston Road, a fascinating museum of science and medicine.

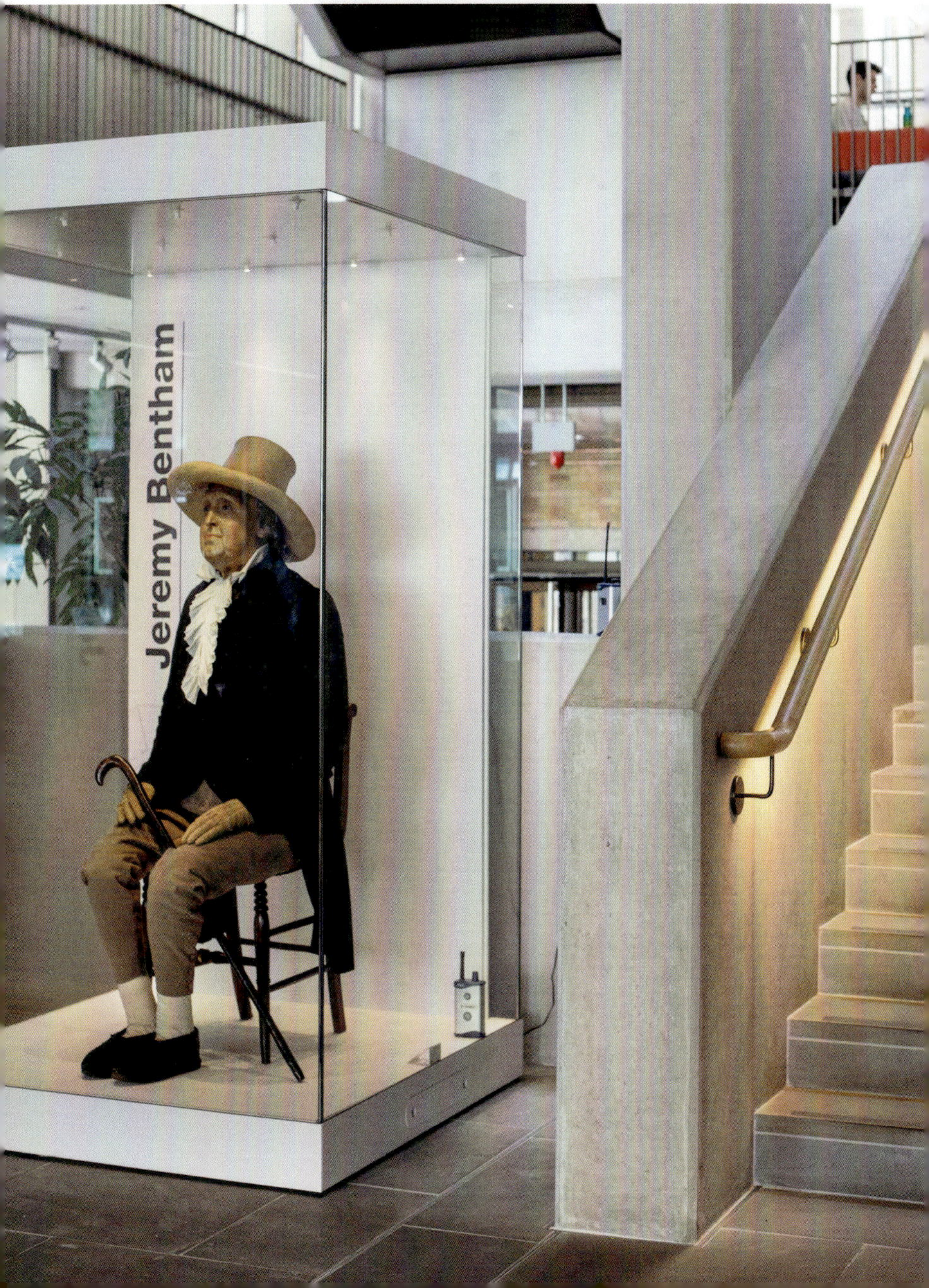

50_John Henry Greathead

Tunneller of London's Underground

Unlike so many of the statues that are raised up high on plinths in the heart of London, this one does not honour a duke, a king or a political eminence.

It is a tribute to John Henry Greathead (1844–96), a mere commoner, and chief engineer of the City and South London Railway. The bold inscription on the handsomely elevated, round-cornered plinth informs us that it was Greathead's brilliant invention of 'the travelling shield that made possible the cutting of the tunnels of London's deep level tube system', in the 19th century and on. What is more, Greathead looks every inch the working man. He stares down, and not across – he is not inclined to be distracted by the admiration of onlookers – at the portfolio of drawings that he is holding. Casually stepping forward, his trousers look stretched and well worn, as do his boots. In short, he is not a poser, on foot or on horseback. Compare how he looks with the representation of the Duke of Wellington, mounted on his horse, just yards away. Greathead is neither suave nor proud. His hat partly conceals his tilted head, with its heavy beard. He carries a raincoat, casually, on his right arm. He is merely getting on with the job. The statue itself could scarcely be positioned at a more symbolically important place in the City of London, at the very point where three of London's most symbolically important buildings practically face each other: Lutyens' Bank of England, the Mansion House and the Royal Exchange, at the bottom of Queen Victoria Street.

The siting of the statue itself, rudely blocking the road at the tail end of Lombard Street, is magnificently intrusive, as is its plinth, with a huge roundel on its side showing the labouring men of London at their dangerous work beneath these intersecting roads at the very centre of the old City of London. The trains rumble on incessantly beneath his feet.

Address Cornhill, London EC3 | **Getting there** Underground to Bank (Central, Northern and Waterloo and City Lines) | **Hours** Accessible 24 hours | **Tip** St Peter Upon Cornhill, a church rebuilt by Christopher Wren after it was destroyed in the Great Fire of London, is just up the street, and well deserves a visit.

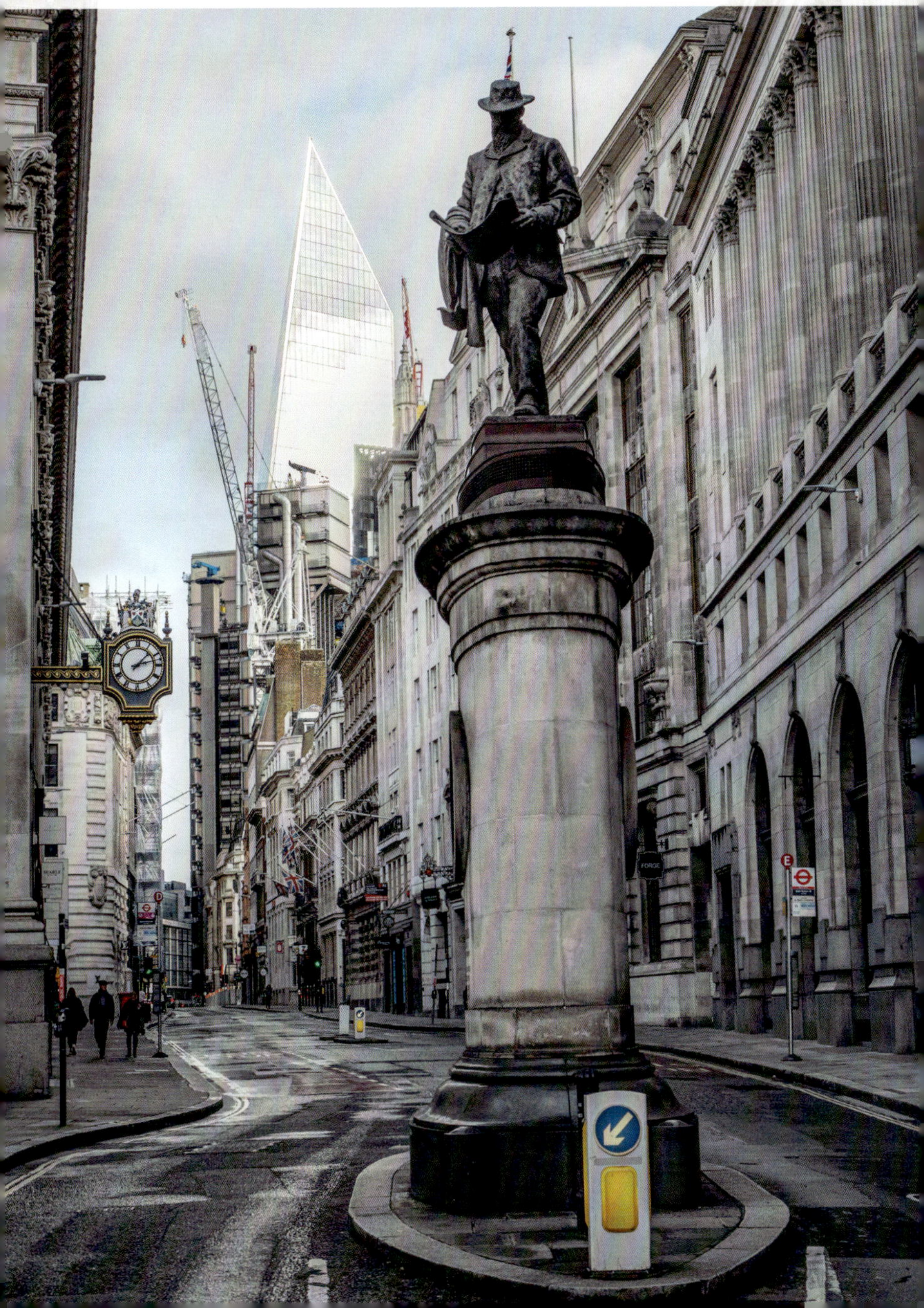

51 John Keats

The poet with blood on his hands

The pose of the young man is a very artful one. He is seated at the very outer edge of a semi-circular bench beneath a protective, 18th-century stone alcove, as if wishing to keep himself to himself. You notice that his head is averted. This morning, on the other end of that same bench, two nurses are sitting, having a smoking break. They are both human beings. The young man, on the other hand, is in fact a bronze sculpture by Stuart Williamson of John Keats, one of the most celebrated of English Romantic poets, who died tragically young, of tuberculosis, in 1821. He was just 25 years old.

The young poet looks small and delicately formed. He is formally dressed in waistcoat and bow tie. His hair is parted down the middle. His feet are crossed. His hand rests, rather reverentially, on a small book. Of his own poems? He found some fame as a published poet during the last four years of his life.

The alcove in which he sits is in the middle of a small square. Look up directly into the sky and you will see The Shard, London's tallest building, rising up like an extraordinarily dangerous sliver of glass. Here is the old in violent confrontation with the new. The stone alcove is surrounded by grass littered with daisies and a few cigarette butts.

This is the inner courtyard of Guy's House, which was built by Thomas Guy in 1725. It is now a campus of King's College, London, and it is next to Guy's Hospital. Why is the presence of Keats marked here?

Because there was another, more mettlesome, side to the delicate Romantic poet that is less well known. At the age of 14 he trained at Guy's Hospital as a surgeon apothecary. If you walk a little way along to 9 St Thomas Street, you will find the Georgian house where he lodged when he was in training. The work was tough – as a 'dresser' to a surgeon his work included the disposal of amputated limbs.

Address Guy's Courtyard, St Thomas Street, London SE1 9RT, +44 (0)207 848 6004, www.kcl.ac.uk | Getting there Underground to London Bridge (Jubilee and Northern Lines) | Hours During daylight hours | Tip In this same courtyard, look out for the plaque to the philosopher Ludwig Wittgenstein, who worked at Guy's Hospital as a drugs porter and ointment maker from 1941 to 1942.

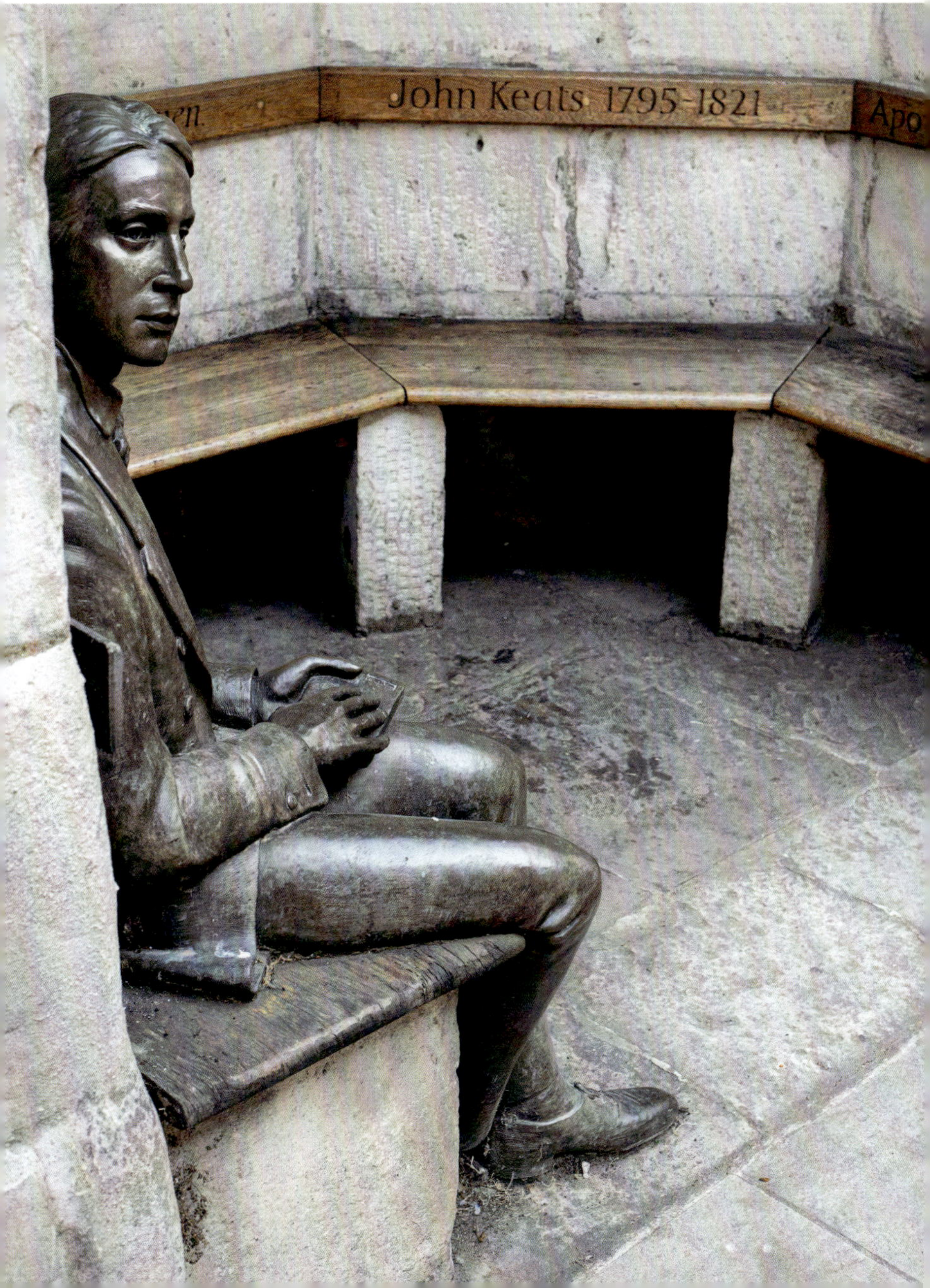

52 Johnny Haynes

Fulham FC's footballing maestro

Sculpting a footballer is no easy matter. How to represent all that swervy speed and headlong energy? In the 20th century, the Dutch painter Nicolas de Staël chose abstraction: he painted footballers on the pitch at a high vantage point, like so many blurrily moving dots, blobs and dashes. Over at Craven Cottage, Fulham FC's ground just beside the Thames in London, the sculptor Douglas Jennings has opted for a kind of heightened realism in his bronze sculpture of Johnny Haynes (1934–2005), the greatest footballer who ever played for the club. It looks and feels just right.

Haynes stands on a pleasing cylindrical drum of a pedestal – its terracotta bricks match perfectly the handsome brickwork of the club's façade. Although Haynes is not on the move, he stands as if poised for the kick-off whistle, with one foot bearing down on the ball, right leg turned out, shin pads visible beneath his socks. The figure looks animated, tense, beautifully at the ready. His shorts are rucked up, his face furrowed in concentration, hair slicked back. His short-sleeved shirt is a bit crumpled from having been jammed into these shorts. Elbows thrust out, his hands are jammed down onto his hips. Though not very tall, his body looks like a tower of strength and concentration. Just look at that muscly inner right leg. He is every inch the captain whose job it is to make things happen.

Haynes captained both club and England as an inside forward, and was a masterful passer of the ball – Pelé once described him as the best he had ever seen. In one important respect he was very lucky. In 1961, the cap on footballers' earnings was removed; no one had been allowed to earn more than £20 a week until then. Haynes' wages were immediately raised to £100 a week. Craven Cottage backs onto the very back of the Thames between Putney and Mortlake, a stretch of water most famous for the Boat Race.

Address Craven Cottage, London SW6, +44 (0)203 871 0810, www.fulhamfc.com | Getting there Underground to Putney Bridge (District Line), then a 10-minute walk | Hours Accessible 24 hours | Tip Nearby Bishop's Park on the banks of the Thames has a poolside beach, children's play area, plenty of sporting activities and a Sunday food market.

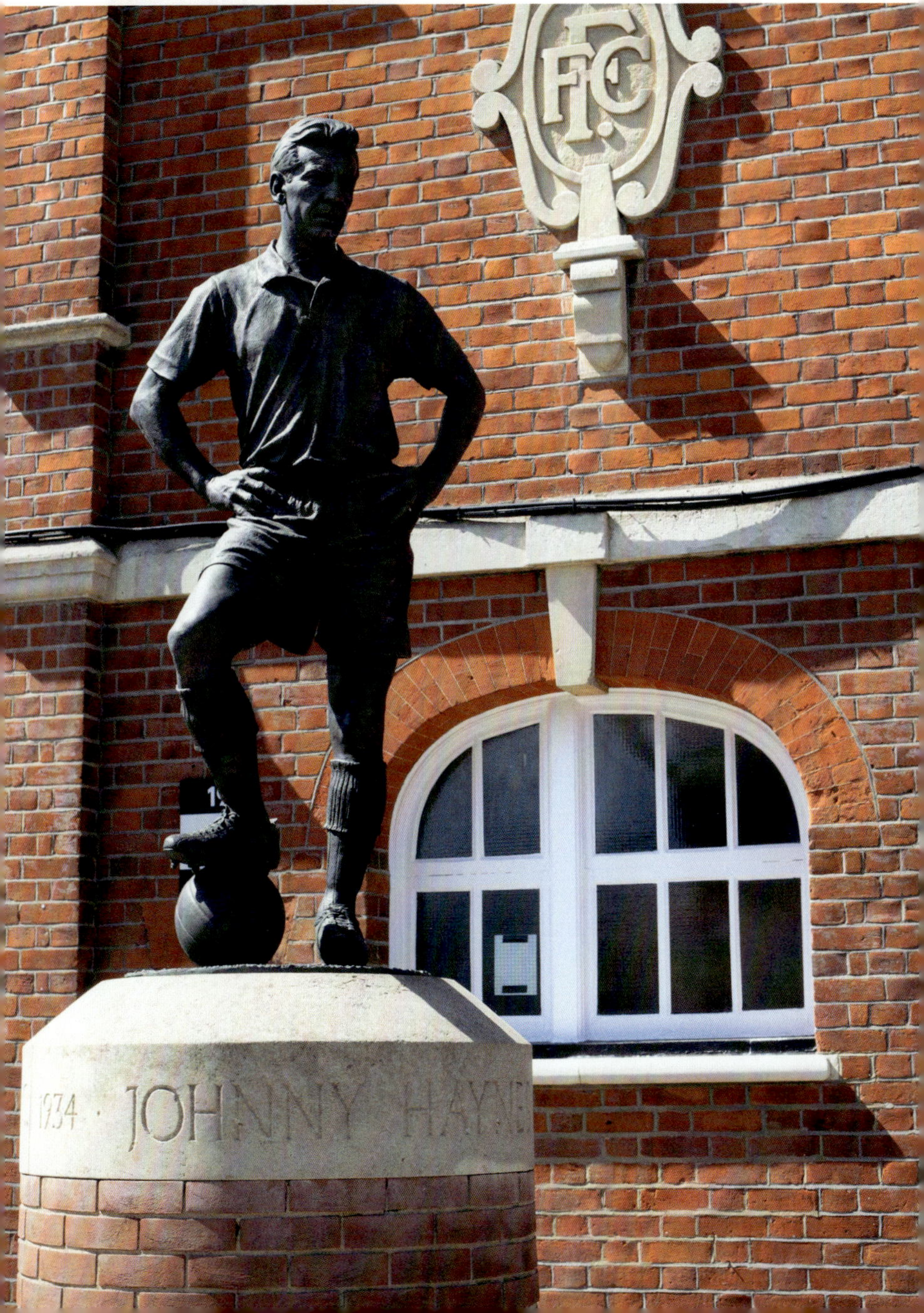

53 King's College Chapel

Where the sacred reverences the human

Hidden churches are always a source of wonderment. The chapel of King's College, London, is completely unseeable from any public vantage point. You will not encounter it at all until you find it. What is more, and unlike most churches, it is not at ground level. To arrive at King's College on the Strand is to encounter a clean-lined modernist façade that lacks even a hint of earlier architectural traditions. Then, as you walk through the building from front to back, the new begins to morph into the old, first with the appearance just off to the right of a spacious Great Court showing off statues of Socrates and Sappho and then, having gone up a double flight of well-appointed marble stairs, you will suddenly encounter an ecclesiastical blaze from the 19th century as you see through the chapel's entranceway.

The only points of public entrance or exit are at this western end. Here, like some marvel dropped in from the sky, is a tiny, perfect Christian basilica, refashioned in 1864 to look as it does now by the celebrated architect Sir Gilbert Scott. Yet its character is not quite that of other Christian basilicas. Though magnificent, it also feels less mystical, more secular, workaday and even humanist than many other chapels. After all, this great university, founded in 1819, is best known and most celebrated for its scientists, its physicians, its physicists, its doctors.

The great wooden seats topped by tall gothic arches that flank the organ at the western end, for example, are reserved for professors of the college, and not specifically for the religious fraternity. The figures in some of the stained-glass windows, but especially so in the apse, contain figures that look refreshingly human and of their moment – here is a child, for example, in the Temple at Jerusalem, looking robust and well made. There is not a whiff of sanctity about her.

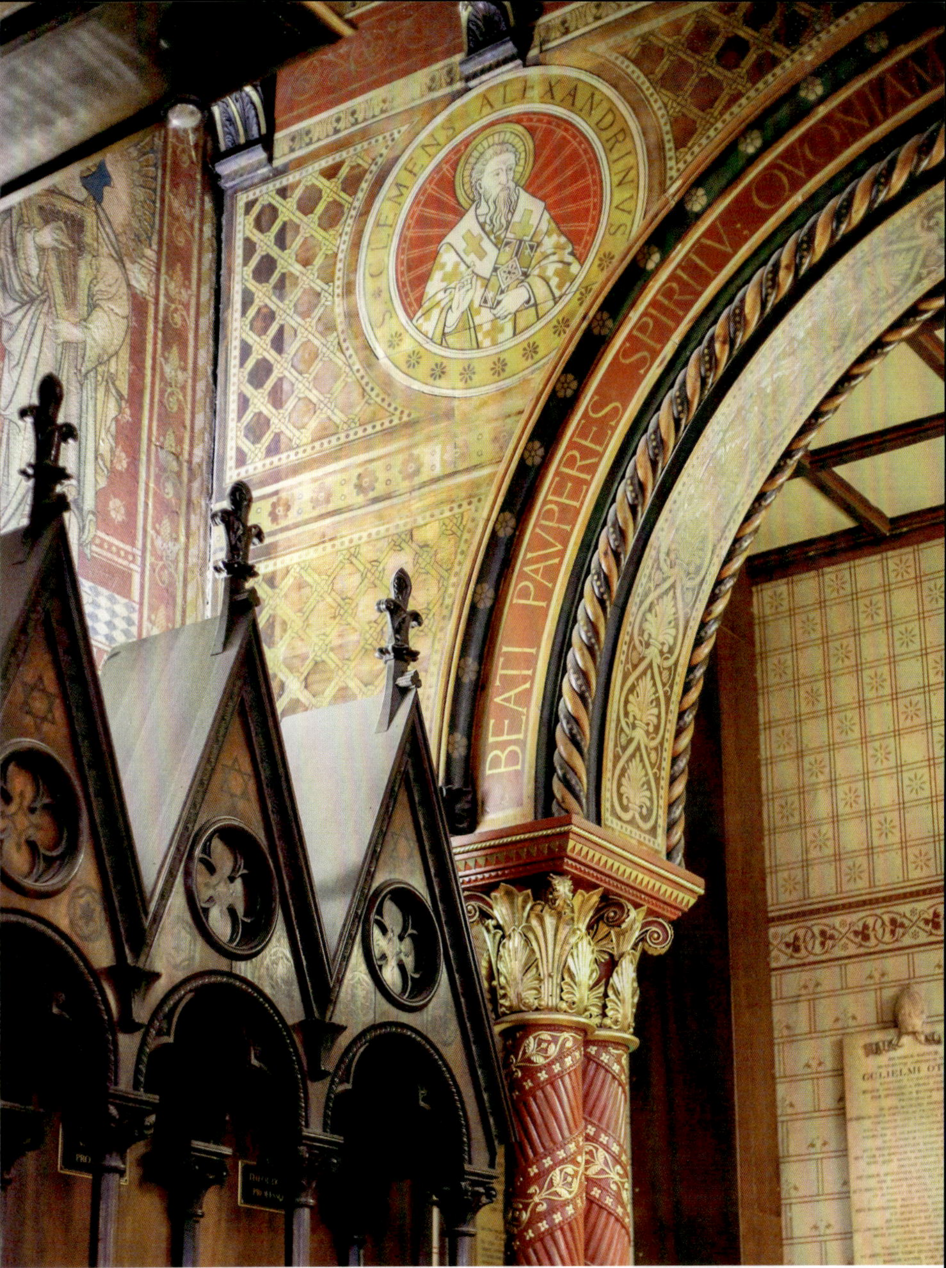

Address King's College, Strand Lane, London WC2R 2LS, +44 (0)207 848 2333, www.kcl.ac.uk | Getting there Underground to Temple (Circle and District Lines), then a five-minute walk | Hours Visitors are welcome to view the Chapel when it is not in use for a service, so either report to reception on arrival or email before visiting: dean@kcl.ac.uk | Tip The Royal Courts of Justice are a five-minute walk away on Fleet Street. On weekdays you can join a tour of this grand and historic building.

54 Langley Street Gate

Where the brewers fumed away…

When did Covent Garden first emerge as a great public market? It was during the reign of Charles II, that king who returned from over the water to re-establish the monarchy after the Cromwell years. In May 1670, a licence was issued to the fourth Earl of Bedford for the 'buying and selling' – on every day of the year except Sundays and Christmas Day – 'of all manner of fruits, flowers, roots and herbs…'. Eventually, Covent Garden became the most extensive market for the sale of fruit and vegetables in the whole of London. Now it is a place where restaurants and retail thrive, from a forever busy Apple store in a building at the perimeter of the Central Markets' building, to Marks and Spencer along Long Acre.

Those plain old red-brick warehouses, still soaring into the sky along narrow and once cobbled streets, are prettified by hanging baskets of flowers. These places, once used as storage for fresh produce, are now repurposed for such businesses as a dance studio (Pineapple on Langley Street, for example). And it is next to Pineapple Studios that you come across another kind of industry that once thrived here: a distillery. Langley Street Gate, paid for by the Mercers' Company, is as much a delightful work of symbolic art as a working gate.

This gate, in polished, forged steel, which arrived here in 2021, and guards the entrance to Old Brewers' Yard, was the work of an artist/blacksmith from Devon called Bex Simon, and it was forged and fabricated by CB Arts Ltd. To look at it is to be reminded of the processes of brewing that once went on here behind this gate. It begins at the base, where stylised barley is growing. Further up you spot details of an oak barrel or two and, at the top, round holes suggestive of effervescence. It is a very intricate piece of making, with much over-layering and hand-making – see how the steel leaves gleam in the sun!

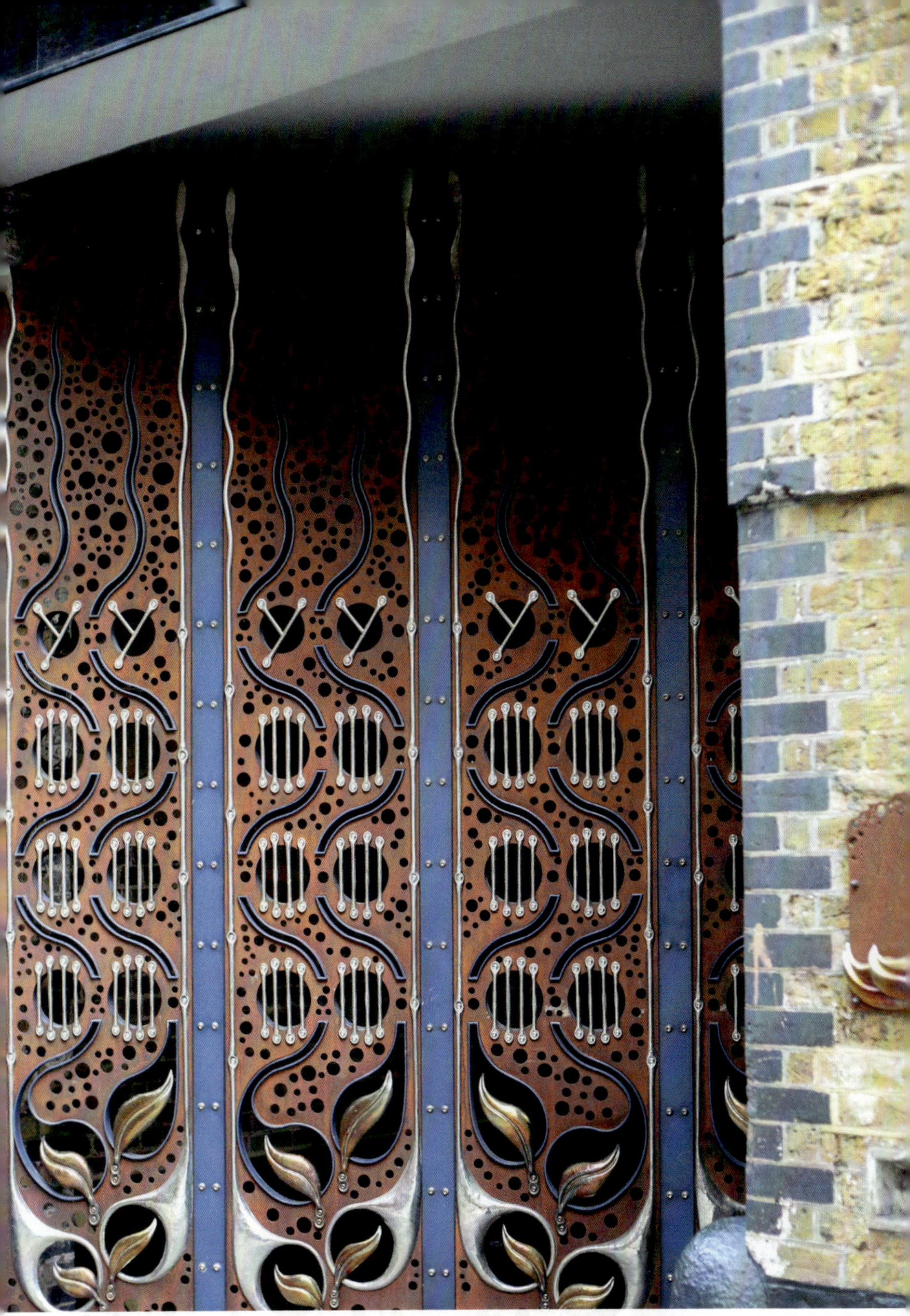

Address Langley Street, London WC2H 9JA, www.cb-arts.co.uk | Getting there Underground to Covent Garden (Piccadilly Line) | Hours Accessible 24 hours | Tip Excellent Thai meals at Busaba on Floral Street, five minutes from here.

55__Leake Street

Where the graffiti wars are waged

Graffiti does not belong within the orderly, well-categorised corridors of museums. It is untamed, impromptu, unauthorised, and of the street. For all that, there is one extraordinary location in central London where graffiti, that wild art that forever comes and goes, often overnight, reigns supreme. It is in a long, dark railway arch underneath Waterloo Station, beneath the very terminal (now closed) where the Eurostar trains once took passengers off to Paris.

The location is called Leake Street, and if you are approaching it from York Way, your path may well be part-blocked by a huge blue plastic rubbish container on wheels, heaving with coke cans, polystyrene cartons yawning open, sodden, mashed up cardboard, and whatnot. Entirely appropriate, of course. The barrel-vaulted tunnel is ill lit and relatively low-ceilinged, so overhead lighting helps to light the way.

There's a mild atmosphere of menace. The works swarm everywhere, one squeezed in beside, or even over, another – graffiti artists are no respecters of distance – engulfing the arched ceiling space, and every other surface available. There are no spaces that are authorised or unauthorised for a graffiti artist. Everything amounts to an act of rude violation. Some of the work is signed, much is not – graffiti artists often like to work anonymously or to give as much of an identity as a brief tag can ever offer.

Today – but perhaps not when you visit – TOSH WAS HERE. The paint is sprayed, spattered, flung about, across rippling metal shutters and light fittings. Here's a fiercesomely crouched over bird, a raptor, and there a giant sweet baby – the mood is forever on the move, on the lurch. There is much ferocious zigzagging, and then the bounce of bubble script. Nothing goes with anything else. Everything seems to be laid down in gleeful defiance, as if there's a war being waged in paint.

Address Leake Street, London SE1, www.leakestreetarches.london | **Getting there** Underground to Waterloo (Northern, Jubilee, Bakerloo and Waterloo and City Lines), then a five-minute walk | **Hours** Accessible 24 hours | **Tip** There are some excellent cafés in Lower Marsh at the far end of Leake Street Tunnel.

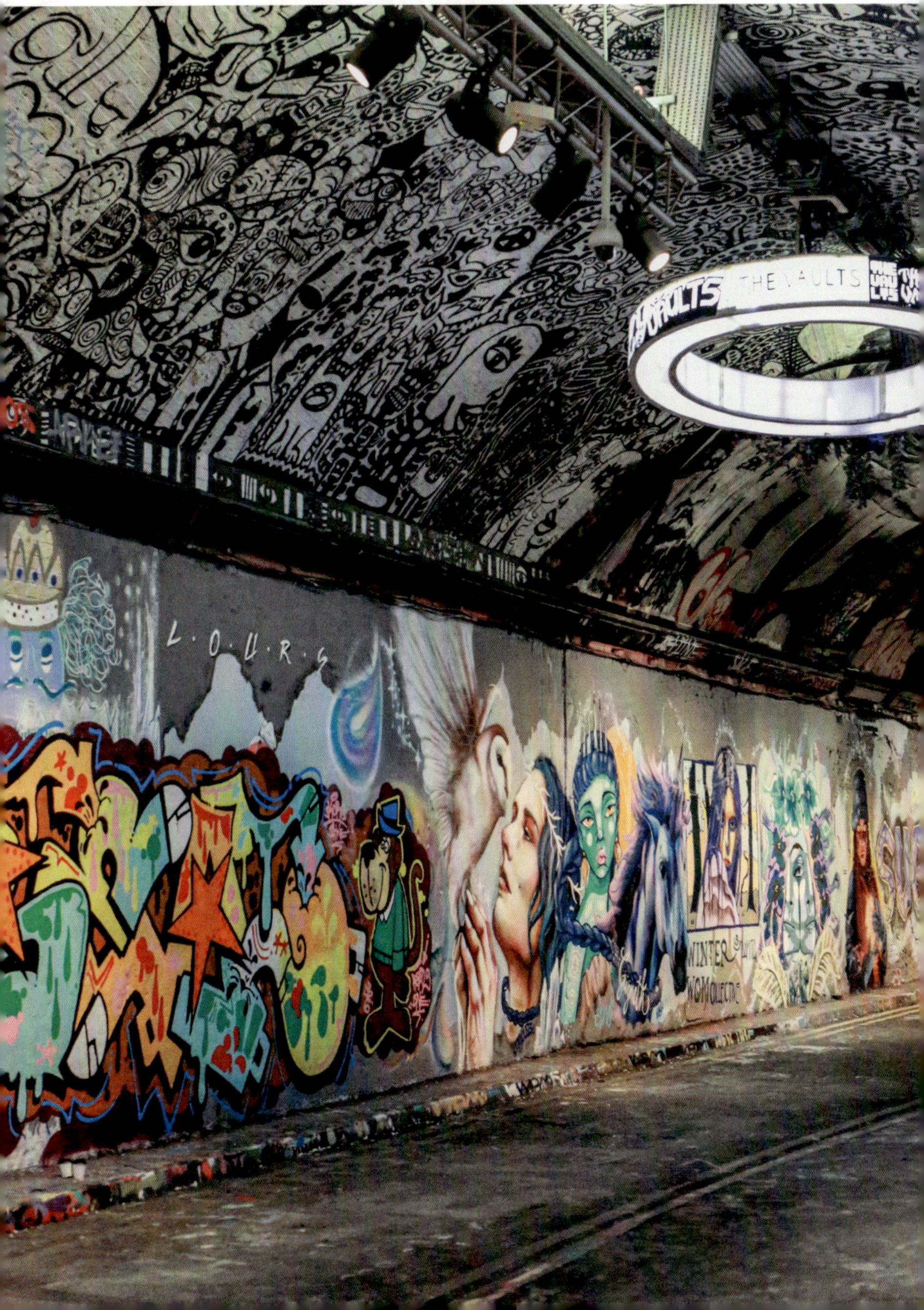

56 The Leaning Woman

Is she is hiding today or not?

Locals call her the Dancing Lady. But she has not achieved lift-off yet, not quite. She sits beside the Great West Road, which tears out of London on its way to Heathrow Airport and all points west. Blink – or accelerate, as so many do along this pitiless track of unrelieved urban dreariness – and you will miss her. So the best way is to approach her through the back streets of Hammersmith, weaving your way through almost to the road's edge, which is where she sits, on a tiny leftover scrap of land (now green). This was good for nothing else at the end of the 1950s, when she arrived here, one example amongst many of the new public art of London. She sits next to a lovely church and a tiny square that could be a rural idyll but for the road racket, which never, ever ends.

There is something odd about our lady today. She is no longer part naked and Grecian in inspiration because we cannot see her at all very much. Has Christo, the artist who made himself world famous by swathing huge public things in fabric (the Reichstag in Berlin, for example, various bridges, and even a stretch of river) been here? His was an art of concealment.

And this is exactly what has happened to our lady. She has been Christoed – but by whom? Christo's long dead. The local council, in preparation for restoration work? There is no explanation for the fact that she is currently a ghostly white form muffled and bound in very tough white plastic, and then secured by tape to keep all this feverish wrapping in place.

So, all we can currently see is a fine concrete sculpture in hiding. We cannot enjoy the fact that she is cantilevered to the right to an almost extraordinary degree, almost lifting herself off from her rather brutish brick plinth, as if yearning to flow away in the general direction of the speeding traffic. Will she still be in hiding when you turn up to seek her out?

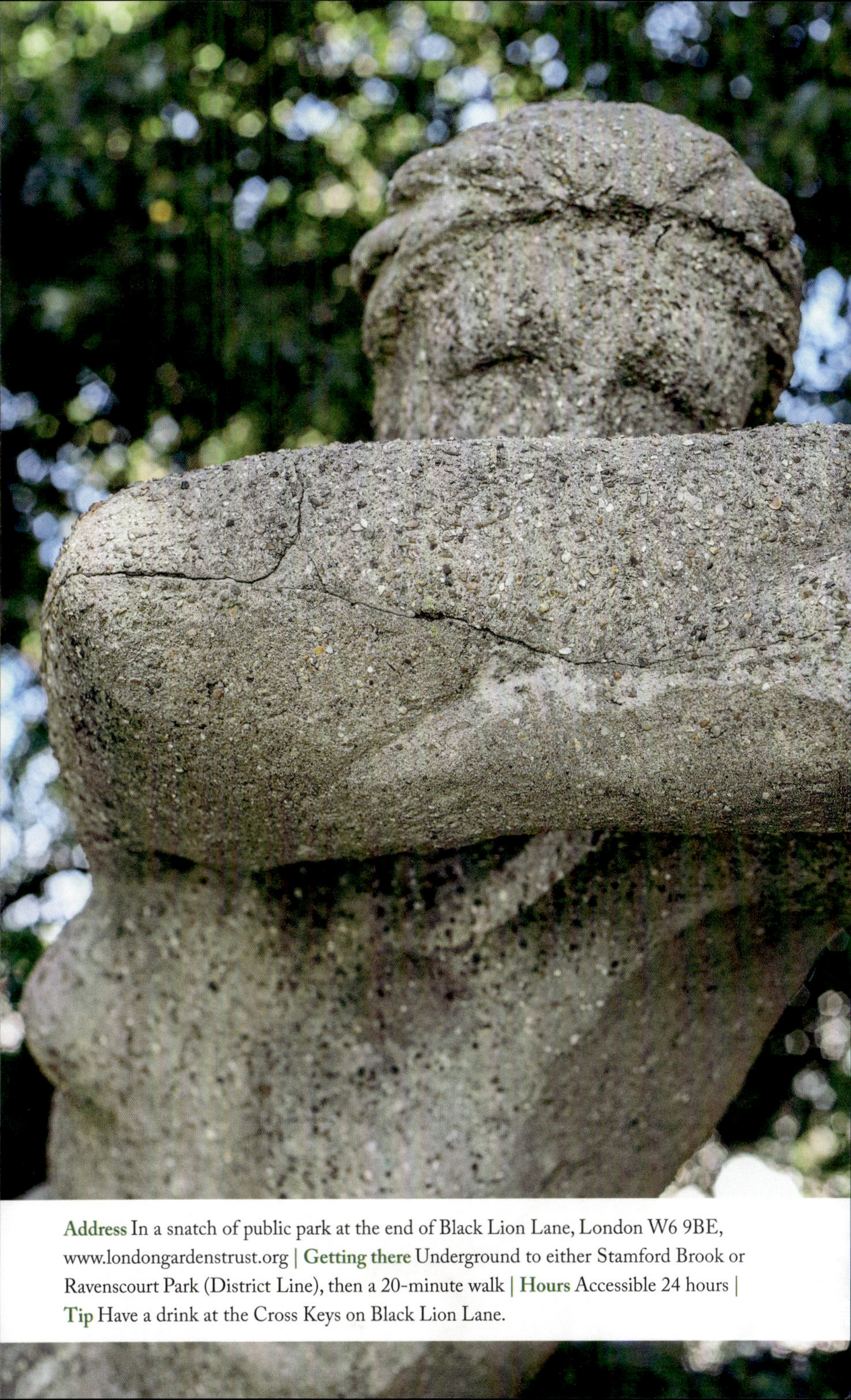

Address In a snatch of public park at the end of Black Lion Lane, London W6 9BE, www.londongardenstrust.org | **Getting there** Underground to either Stamford Brook or Ravenscourt Park (District Line), then a 20-minute walk | **Hours** Accessible 24 hours | **Tip** Have a drink at the Cross Keys on Black Lion Lane.

57 Londinium's Amphitheatre

Where much gladiatorial blood was spilled

How many people know that there was once a fine Roman amphitheatre in the City of London? And that the painstaking reconstruction of what remains of it can be seen today, entirely free of charge, deep in the basement of an art gallery in the City of London celebrated for its collection of 19th-century paintings, which is still too little celebrated? The art gallery in question sits at an angle to London's fine medieval gothic Guildhall, which was lucky to escape destruction during the Blitz, when so many of the great Wren churches of London were destroyed.

The amphitheatre was hidden from view for hundreds of years. Created in approximately A.D. 47 (the Romans had invaded in A.D. 43), and abandoned in the fourth century, the amphitheatre was used both for the execution of criminals and for traditional gladiatorial games-playing. This was a grisly spectator sport involving muscly men with short swords in contention with rampant beasts of prey, which was enjoyed by aristocrats throughout the Roman Empire.

It was not until 1988 that a team of archaeologists from the Museum of London made the discovery, and they continued until 1996. Today, having first taken the lift deep down, we can now step out into a dark and mysteriously narrow corridor and, taking a quick turn to the right, see what there is to be seen… We find ourselves standing at the amphitheatre's eastern entrance. There are remnants of the huge boundary walls (together with its footings), which superseded the original structure in timber, lengths of timber draining, and samplings of the amphitheatre's flooring, which would have been a combination of soft sand, gravel and mortar. Onto the far wall the shape of the amphitheatre – a long, curving line – is projected. About 6,000 people would have roared their hearts out, a quarter of the city's population.

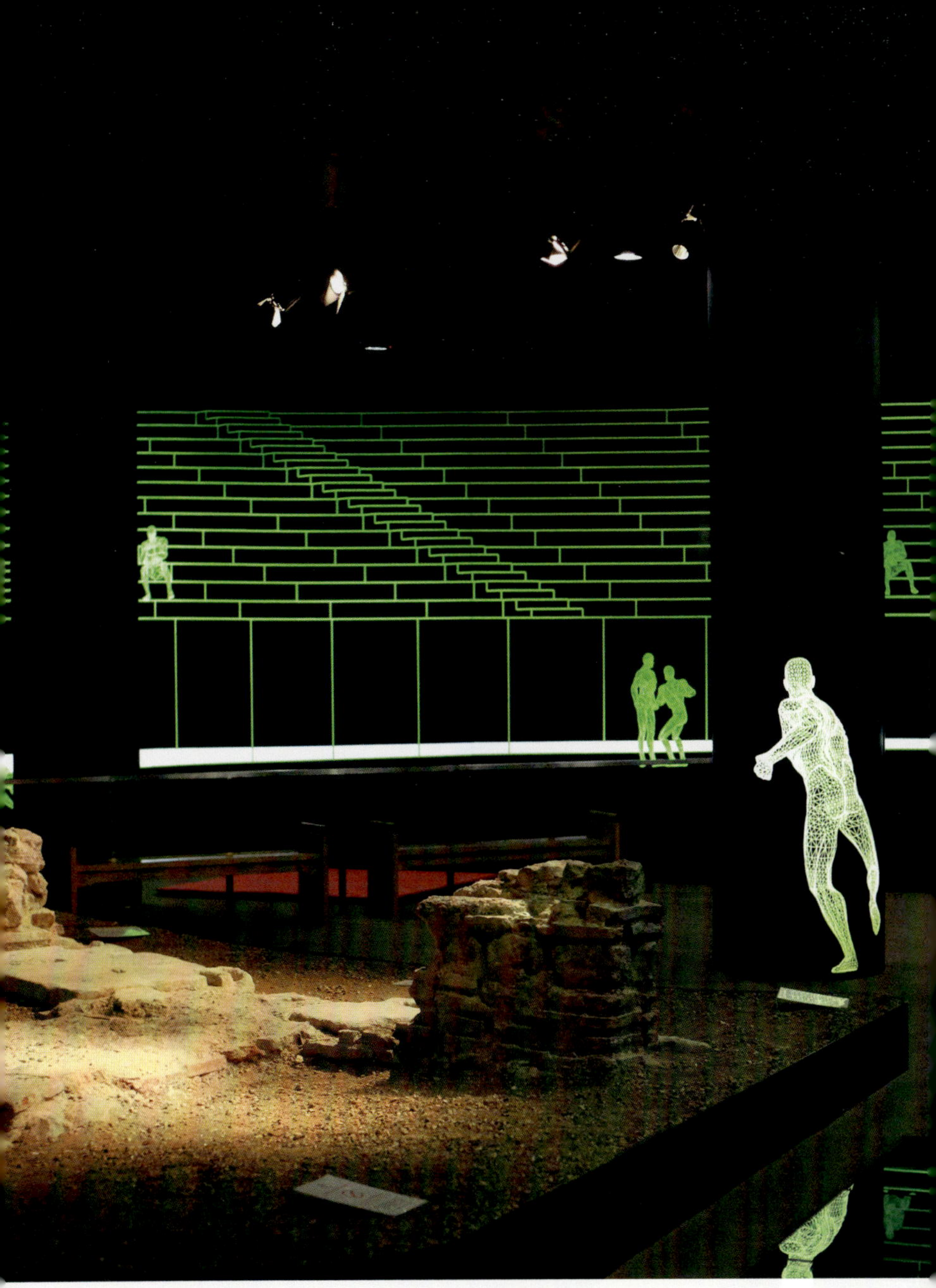

Address Guildhall Art Gallery, Basinghall Street, London EC2V 5AE, +44 (0)207 332 3700, www.cityoflondon.gov.uk | **Getting there** Underground to Bank (Central, Northern, Waterloo and City Lines and DLR), then a five-minute walk | **Hours** Daily 10.30am–4pm | **Tip** There is a first-rate collection of paintings from 1670 to the present day in the Guildhall Gallery itself. Of note are several fine Pre-Raphaelite paintings.

58 Lost Women of World War II

Coats, bags, hats and dungarees never posture

How exactly should a public sculpture commemorate momentous matters? There are two great monuments in Whitehall to those who died or served during the two great wars of the 20th century, and both are in the middle of the road. They are at a distance of about 200 yards away from each other. One of them, the Cenotaph, given that it is always at the centre of the Armistice Day celebrations, gets almost all of the attention. It was designed in a great hurry – two weeks flat – by Sir Edwin Lutyens, and later fabricated in Portland stone. It resembles a series of stacked plinths, which get smaller as they rise, and its embellishments are few: flagpoles and a stone wreath. Nor does it have any Christian symbols or any evidence whatsoever of the human presence.

The other monument is dedicated to the women of the war, and it is a simpler affair altogether – a rising black box. It is also much more humanly interesting than the Cenotaph. By that I do not mean that it shows off the human figure. Its poignancy lies in its suggestion of the human figure by the fact that it makes reference to the *absence* of the human presence. How? The monument is a kind of giant rectangular coat rack from which objects hang on all sides. It's a very sombre monument, almost an empty shell. What it shows us has nothing of the pomp and the circumstance of the warmongers we can see close by – Earl Haig for example. No, all that we see belongs to the plain, workaday stuff of life: bags, dungarees, overcoats, cases, hats, a land-mine detector. All very particular stuff, and all hung closely side by side, almost an untidy clutter you could say, as if to remind us that warfare is always a messy affair, lacking in all ceremony. These are all women whose names we do not know, who have disappeared into anonymity. All we know is that they, too, made great sacrifices. Empty coats can't posture.

Address Whitehall, London SW1A | Getting there Underground to Westminster (Jubilee, District and Circle Lines) | Hours Accessible 24 hours | Tip Just opposite is the Household Cavalry Museum, which contains many fascinating artifacts all related to the ceremonial and operational duties of the Regiments of the Household Cavalry.

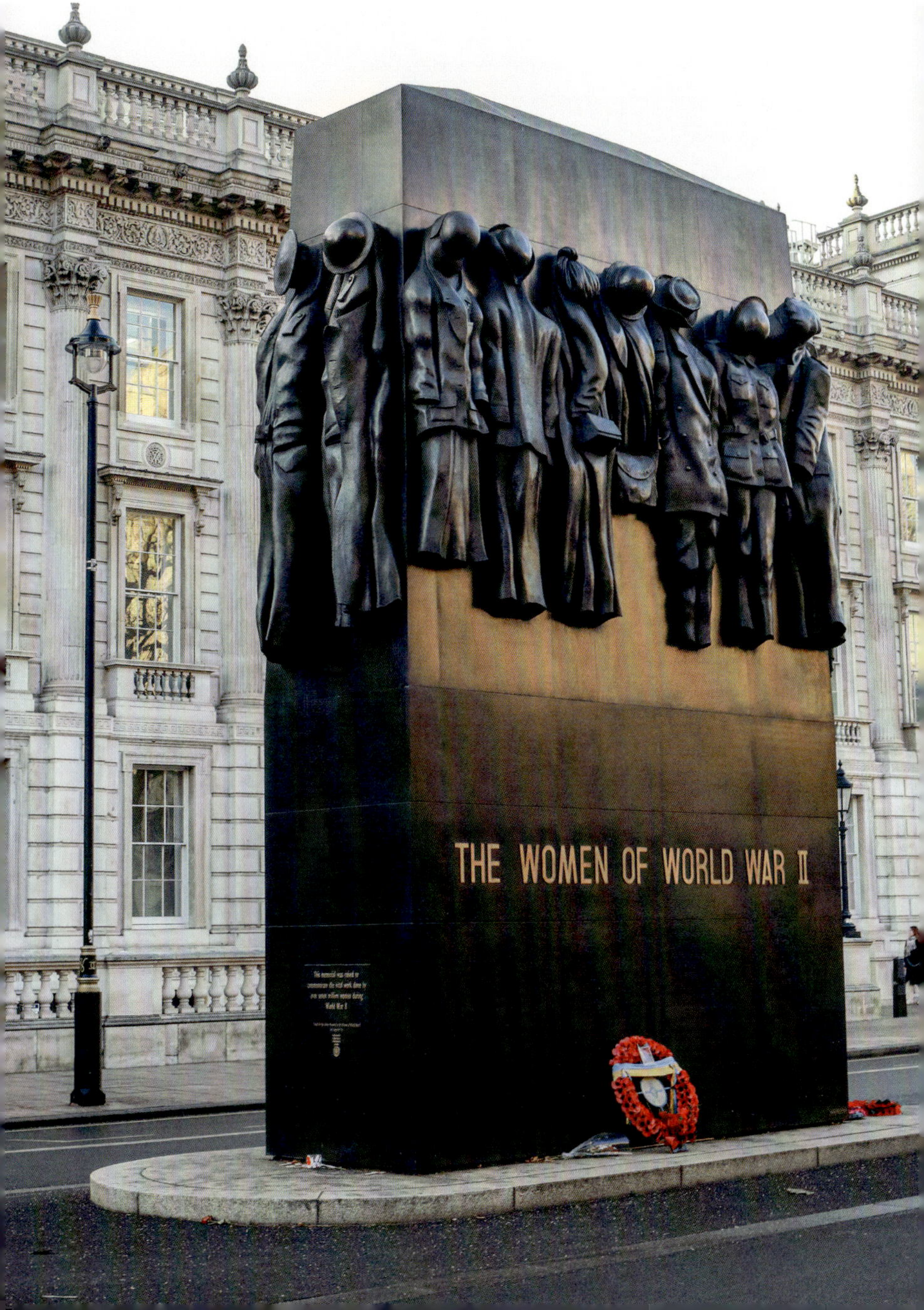

59 The Masonic Temple

A mysterious sunken chamber

The Andaz Hotel, situated as it is beside Liverpool Street Station, seems much like any other place where the weary traveller might rest his or her head after a long and arduous journey. Except that it most definitely is not. Having passed through the lobby, you then thread your way through a maze of corridors until you encounter a spiral staircase, which will spirit you down and down into a subterranean room, a magnificent sunken chamber half lost in darkness.

Welcome to the Greek Masonic Temple, created in 1912 at a cost of £50,000 by Charles Barry, the son of the man who rebuilt the Houses of Parliament after the great fire of October 1834. The Temple is built in the classical style, and only its principal features blaze, dramatically, with light (much else is lost in darkness): the chandeliers above your head, for example, and the four great, back-lit marble thrones that face each other. Marble columns, Doric and Ionic, process up the room – the temple has 12 different kinds of marble, all sourced in Italy. The signs of the zodiac – Fish, Ram, Bull, Crab and so on – flare in a burst of rays across the coffered ceiling. There are inscriptions in Latin to be read above the thrones: Audi (listen), Vidi (look), Tace (keep your counsel). A table on a chequer board marble floor in black and white is set for 12 absent guests. Heavy mahogany chairs – more like thrones than chairs – beckon.

This room was lost to view for decades. Then someone noticed a fake wall and tapped on it. It was hollow. Was this Jack the Ripper's temple? Many have alleged that he was a Mason, and this area was undoubtedly amongst his favoured stamping grounds. The first Chair of the Temple was Grand Master Duke of Connaught, seventh child (and third son) of Queen Victoria. What used to happen here? What mysterious rites? The room still keeps its counsel like any good Mason.

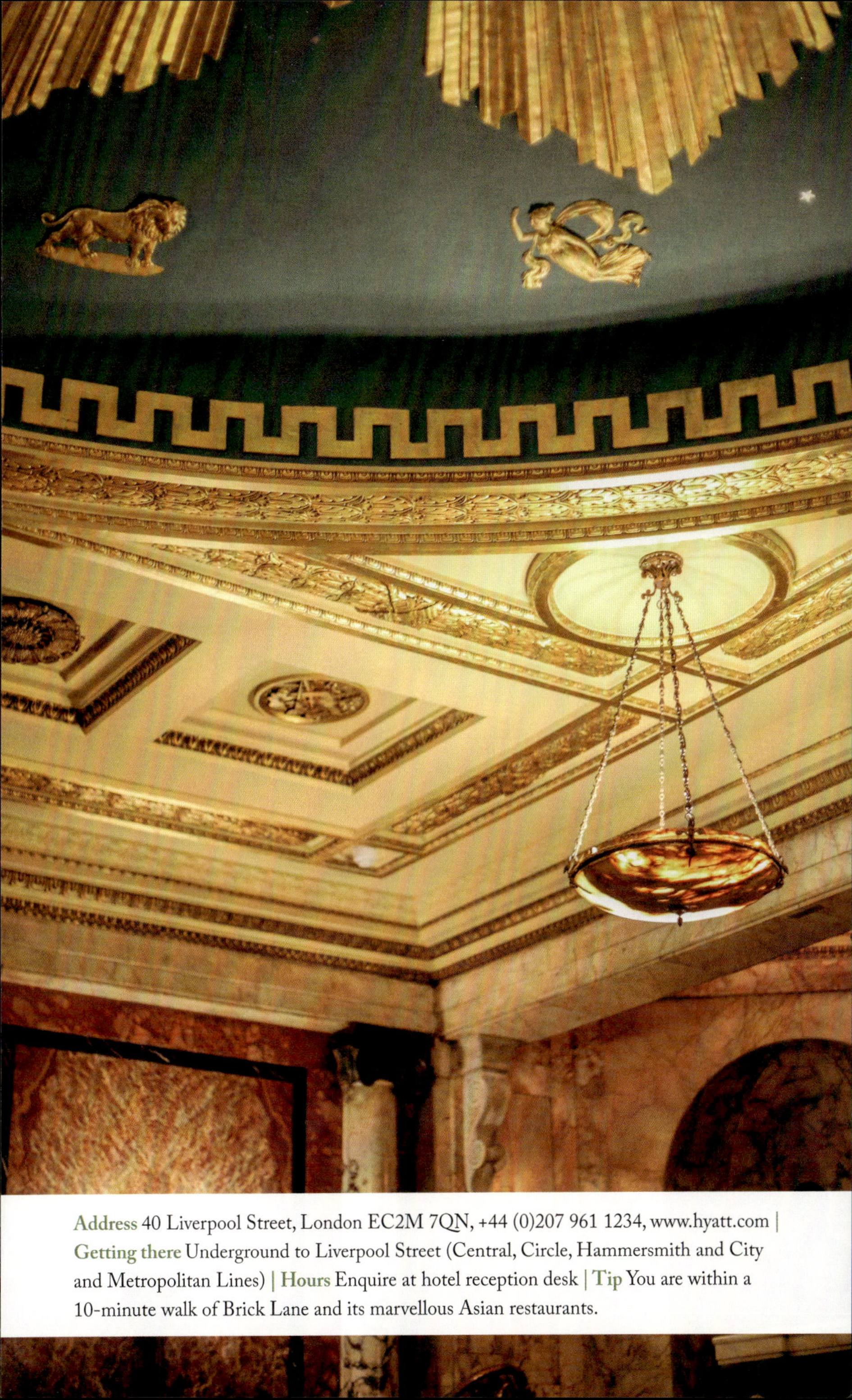

Address 40 Liverpool Street, London EC2M 7QN, +44 (0)207 961 1234, www.hyatt.com | **Getting there** Underground to Liverpool Street (Central, Circle, Hammersmith and City and Metropolitan Lines) | **Hours** Enquire at hotel reception desk | **Tip** You are within a 10-minute walk of Brick Lane and its marvellous Asian restaurants.

60 The Minotaur

Where man meets rampant bull

Twentieth-century art has had much to do with the minotaur, that fabulous creature of myth, half man, half bull, which, according to the Ancient Greeks, was trapped inside a maze, and eventually slaughtered by King Theseus.

Picasso also had much to do with minotaurs because, according to legend, he was a bit of a hard-driven, Catalan minotaur himself when it came to the ladies. The finest minotaur on the rampage within the square mile of the old Roman City of London is a sculpture in bronze by an English artist called Michael Ayrton, who was more than a touch minotaur obsessed himself. He wrote a novel around the subject, and made various sculptures and prints.

Ayrton's *Minotaur*, displayed on a square, chunky plinth, is displayed on a snatch of grass between two lovely gardens just off London Wall and in the shadow of Salters' Hall, the headquarters of one of the City's livery companies. It seems entirely appropriate that this venerable beast should be so close to various remnants of the City's Roman wall – ancientness calls out to ancientness.

Ayrton's is a fiercely rampant, take-no-prisoners sort of a beast which, when you stand facing it, looks as if it is ready to come thundering full tilt at you, and will show you no mercy. As you face it, and admire the fine bristle of its two horns, you also notice, as you tentatively lower your gaze, its enormous, pendent testicular sac. It resembles, in all its indomitable heftiness, the weights of an old clock. Seen from behind, you admire its powerful human buttocks, and the way its arms are wrenched back. It crouches, menacingly, kneeling on its left knee. Its back is powerfully humped. Its hip bones bulge. The pose suggests a runner waiting for the crack of the starting pistol to ignite all his inner fire. The pelt on either side of the prominently outlined curve of its spine looks alarmingly bristly.

Address London Wall, EC2Y 5DE | Getting there Underground to Moorgate (Metropolitan, Hammersmith and City and Circle Lines), then a five-minute walk | Hours Accessible 24 hours | Tip Admire the magnificent gates of the nearby Salters' Hall, home of the Worshipful Company of Salters, one of the City of London's livery companies.

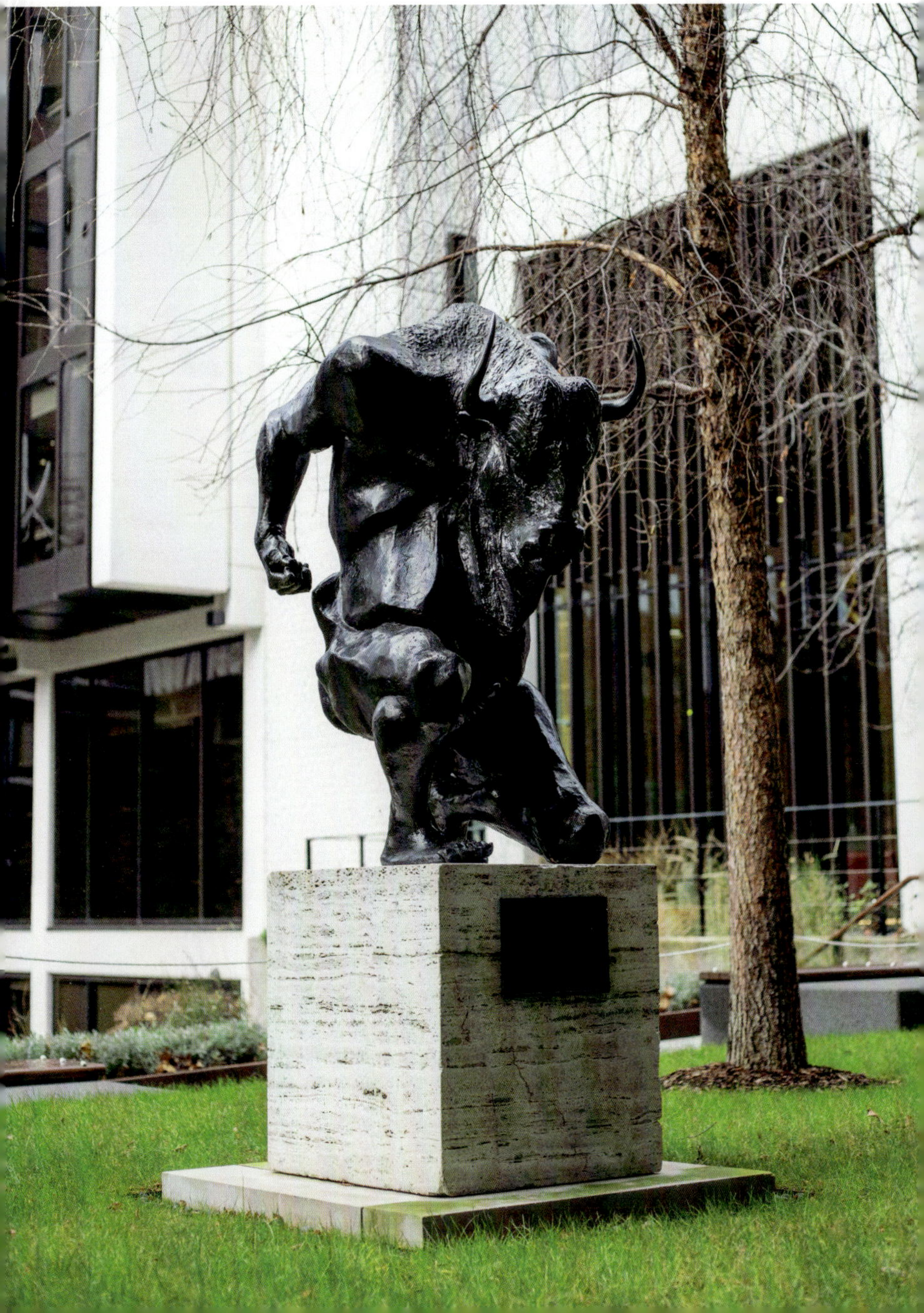

61_The Mithraeum

Digging down to Roman London

Is the best of London deep underground? Many commuters wouldn't necessarily agree. Having said that, the square mile of the City of London, the old Londinium built by the Romans after their conquest, and not finally vacated until early in the sixth century, continues to yield up marvels. In 2012, a great archaeological dig along the length of Walbrook, which is a hop and a skip from the Bank of England, was undertaken in preparation for the construction of Bloomberg's new European headquarters.

On this site, the Temple of Mithras, a male-only cult devoted to appeasing a mysterious, bull-slaying god, had been discovered in 1954. Now, after five years of deep digging and careful siftings, the temple can be seen again, at its original depth, in almost its original location – by 1066 it was already deep underground, according to the wall markings of stratigraphers that we see as we descend many flights of stairs into the creepy, half-lit, fumy darkness of the new temple experience – which comes complete with Latin chants and the ringing of newly discovered Roman bells (the very bells that are on display in the cabinet upstairs).

The Mithras experience is on three levels. On the ground floor there is a permanent display of some of the 14,000 Roman artefacts that were discovered in the course of the dig, from a personal nail grooming kit to belt buckles. On the middle floor, the significance of the cult is explained and illustrated. And, deep underground, every 20 minutes, low lights illuminate the mysterious remains of the temple itself – the foundations of its walls are still in place, as is the well at the altar end. In shape, the temple looks much like any Christian basilica. In this one, cult members – merchants and soldiers made up the majority – habitually ate chicken, archaeologists have established. There was such a preponderance of old bones down there.

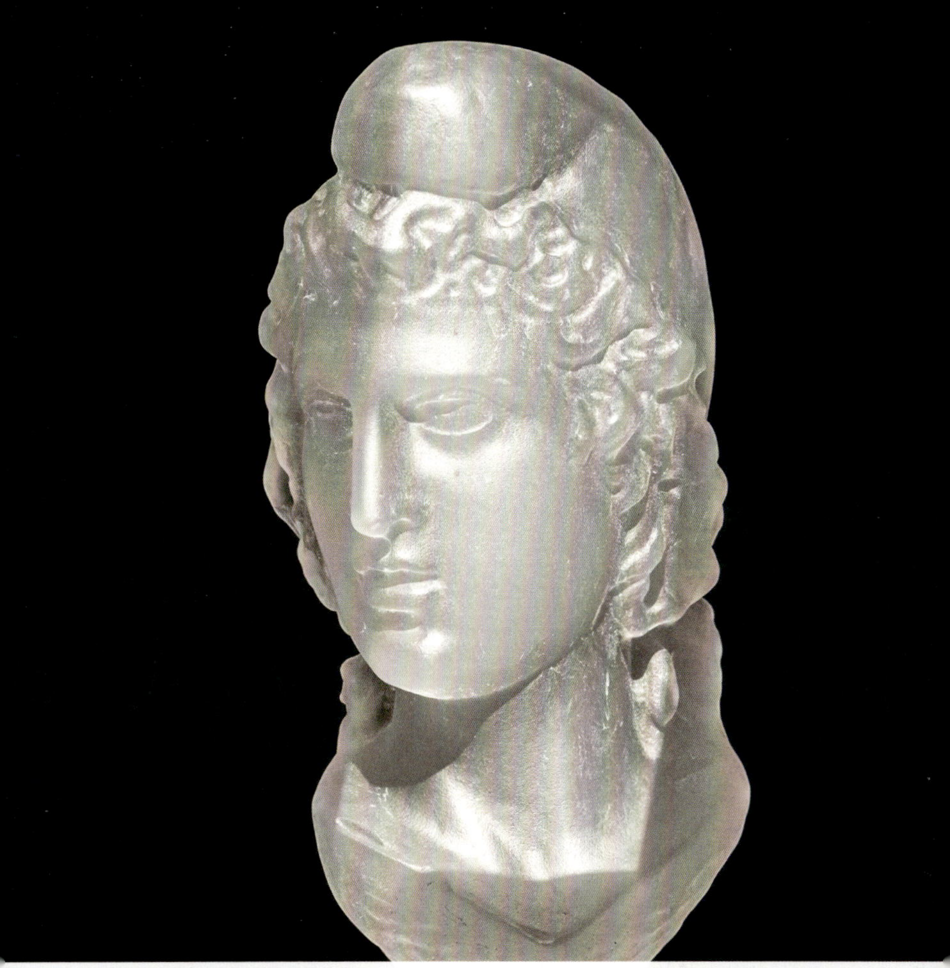

Address 12 Walbrook, London EC4N 8AA, www.londonmithraeum.com | **Getting there** Underground to Bank (Central, Northern and Waterloo and City Lines) or Mansion House (Circle and District Lines) | **Hours** Tue–Sat 10am–6pm, Sun noon–5pm, first Thu of the month 10am–8pm | **Tip** Mansion House, the home and office of the Lord Mayor of London, is open to the public every Tuesday afternoon (pre-booked tickets).

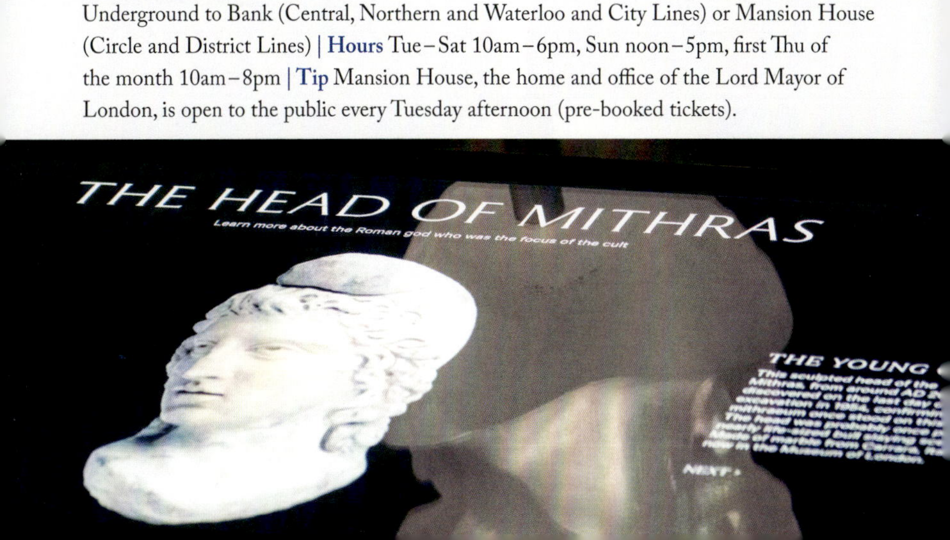

62 Morris & Co.

Arts & Crafts for the Common Man (and Woman)

Where best to go in London to be reminded of the achievements of that great Victorian polymath and entrepreneur William Morris, whose talents bestraddled art, literature and design? He was a prolific and best-selling poet, printer, publisher, essayist, pamphleteer, visionary fabulist – and maker of objects for Everyman. Try Walthamstow, one of the city's northern suburbs. Here, at the William Morris Gallery, you can enjoy meandering through the telling, in room after room, of Morris' own story.

Morris lived his childhood and teenage years (he was the third of nine children, and the family downsized to this three-storey Georgian villa after the death of his father), from 1848–56, in this delightful 18th-century house.

It was built around 1750 for Squire Woodford, and is still set down in 50 acres of parkland (now public, of course) and it is a wonderful surprise to come upon it in the midst of this seething conurbation – and also enjoy many fine examples of work by Morris' circle of many friends and collaborators.

Morris was an inflammatory socialist, through and through. He believed art existed to be a part of everyone's everyday life. He also hated Victorian clutter. This was not mere theory. He strove to make it happen. The common man deserved the best of everything, from the finest of hand-crafted chairs to quality wallpaper and stained-glass windows (the last is represented here with some stunning work by Edward Burne-Jones) – courtesy of a pioneering interior design company called Morris & Co. which, by 1877, had opened a store at 449 Oxford Street, and survived as a business until the 1940s. The house itself is quite as much to be savoured as the story and the art of Morris and his circle, starting perhaps with the fine staircase, crafted from Spanish sweet chestnut, which sweeps you up from the ground floor to the first-floor rooms.

Address Lloyd Park, Forest Road, London E17 4PP, +44 (0)208 496 4390, www.wmgallery.org.uk | Getting there Underground to Walthamstow Central (Victoria Line), then a 15-minute walk | Hours Tue–Sun 10am–5pm | Tip Take a walk around Lloyd Park, the garden surrounding Morris' childhood home. There's a nature area, moat, the original terraced garden and a café.

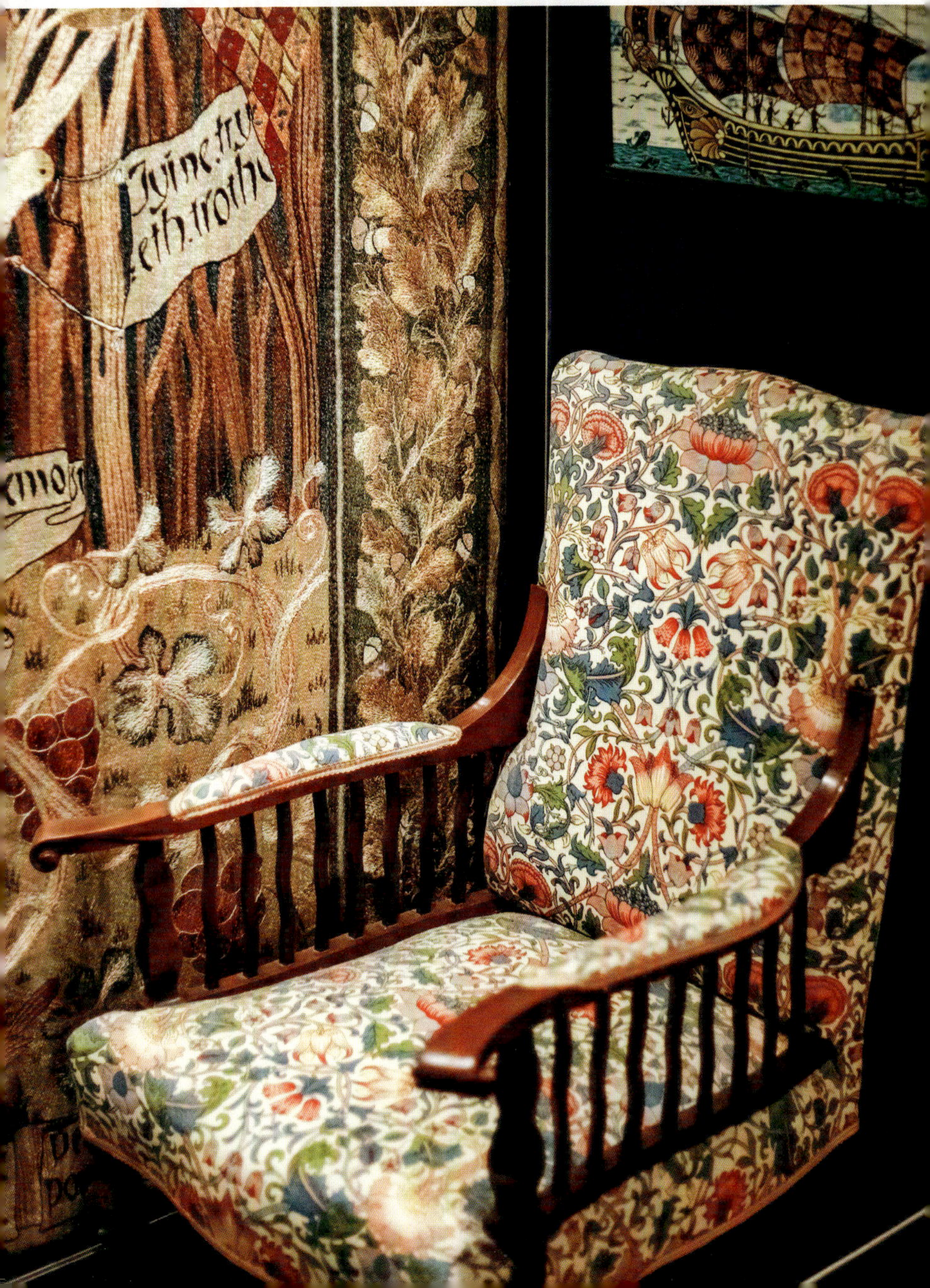

63 Mother and Child

Jacob Epstein's homage

The Jewish sculptor Jacob Epstein was much criticised as an artist during his lifetime. His large-scale sculptures were thought fit for nothing but the fairground. A suite of sculptural reliefs embellishing what is now Zimbabwe House in the Strand were mutilated because their sexual explicitness caused offence to the public eye, the moralists boomed.

This lovely sculpture of a mother and child, hidden away in a narrow, cobbled mews just off Cavendish Square to the north of Oxford Street, suffered no such fate. What exactly is it doing here anyway? It does not hang from the wall of any recognisable place of worship these days. It feels like a touchingly rootless religious symbol, hovering, slightly adrift, above an arched entranceway. The scrawny child with eyes sunk deep into their sockets and stick-thin legs, is nestled into the virgin's stomach, as if about to emerge from her body. Her eyes are downcast; the babe looks directly ahead. His arms are outspread, as if referring both to his birth and to his future fate, splayed on a cross. The thin vestments look rather like a bandage. Somewhat comically, a piece of street furniture standing in front of the sculpture at the entrance to the mews and attached to an old gas lamp – indicating that the road is a dead end – seems to echo its overall shape and significance. The figure is flanked, rather trumpetingly, by pilasters with Corinthian capitals.

In fact, this building, now owned by the King's Fund, was once the Convent of the Holy Child of Jesus. It was bombed during World War II, and then rebuilt, with a new bridge thrown across the mews. A sculptor needed to be commissioned to create a religious symbol, and Epstein was proposed. The choice proved controversial – was a Jew a fit choice for such a task? The statue made its appearance in 1953. Epstein was never more than a whisper away from controversy.

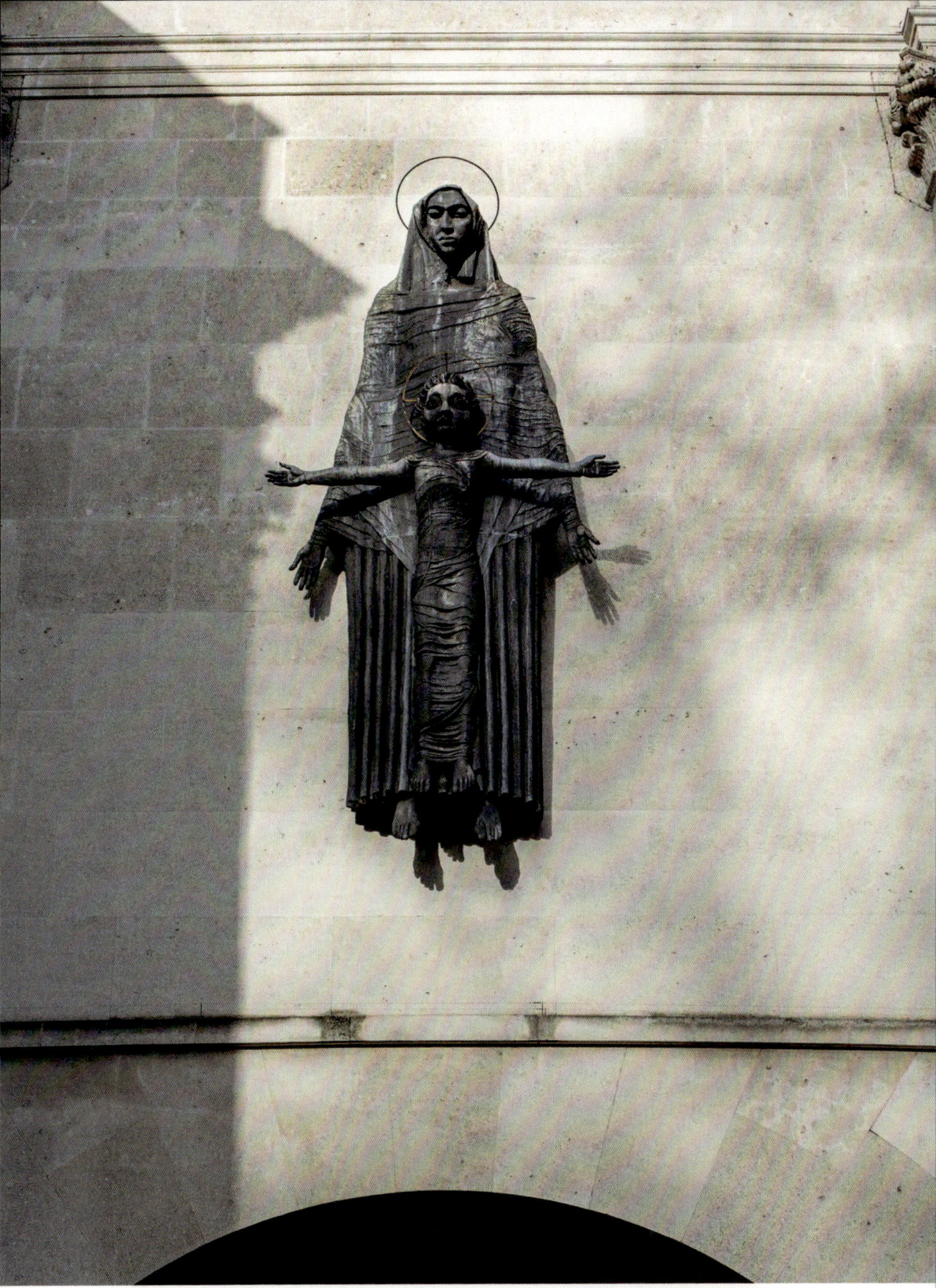

Address 7 Dean's Mews, London W1G 9EF | Getting there Underground to Oxford Street (Bakerloo, Central and Victoria Lines), then a seven-minute walk | Hours Accessible 24 hours | Tip Just across the road is Cavendish Square (confusingly, a circular park). Surrounded by blue plaques, and featuring an imposing statue of politician and racehorse owner Lord George Bentinck, it's an attractive calm oasis to relax in.

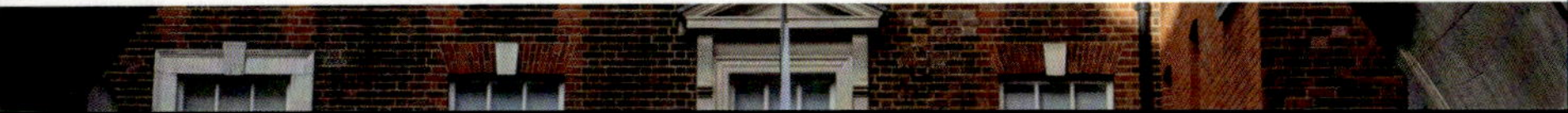

64 Murillo – or Not?

Copying the old masters

St Patrick's Church, Soho, is on the east side of Soho Square, not far from the fine, 18th-century building (No. 1) which for the past (almost) 50 years has housed MPL Communications, Paul McCartney's music publishing company. Soho itself has often been regarded as popular music's natural home – the street popularly known as Tin Pan Alley (actually Denmark Street, and still the best place to browse for a new or a second-hand guitar) is just five minutes on foot from here. In fact, the area has changed and changed again down the centuries – this part of London was once a place where the aristocracy hunted. We can still hear the huntsman's old hue and cry in the very name of the place: *So! Ho!* Much later, poor Irish eked out a meagre living here, and there was much slum clearance.

And then, towards the end of the 18th century, a place of worship was created in Soho Square for Catholics to worship in, which, by the end of the 19th century, was on the way to becoming the very handsome, red-brick basilica, complete with tall, barrel-vaulted and coffered ceiling, which you can see when you enter it today.

In common with so many Italian churches, St Patrick's has many paintings above its altars, but there is one that surprises us when we find it. We come upon it almost immediately, on our right, when we are about to enter the nave, having first acknowledged the presence of two huge standing angels that seem to threaten to block our way – it is on the wall to our right, on its own. The name of the painter, when we read it, rather amazes us too: Murillo. Murillo was one of the great Spanish devotional painters of the 17th century, a master renowned for the tenderness, if not the sweetness, of his work. Can this work be authentic? No, it is in fact a fake or – to put it more gently – a copy, made some 50 years ago. The signature was added then. To titillate?

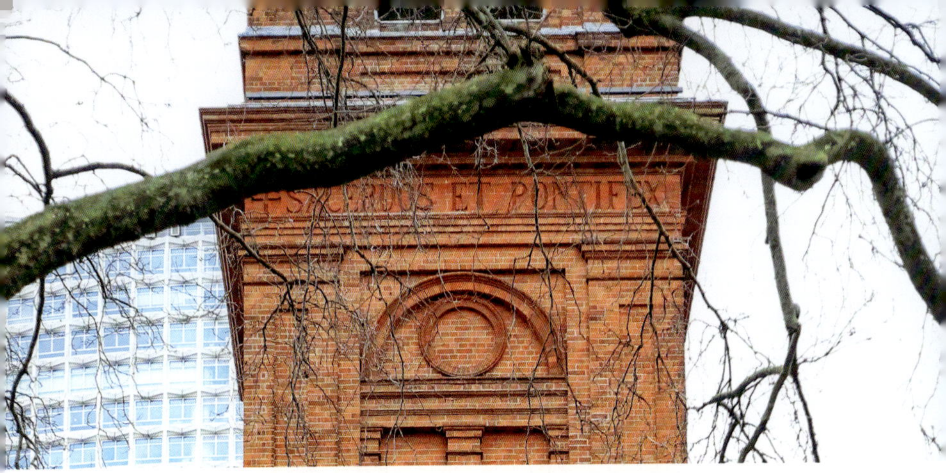

Address 21a Soho Square, London W1D 4NR, +44 (0)207 437 2010, www.stpatricksoho.org | Getting there Underground to Tottenham Court Road (Central, Northern and Elizabeth Lines) | Hours Mon–Fri 7am–7pm, Sat & Sun 9am–7pm | Tip A 10-minute walk away on Ramillies Street is the Photographers' Gallery, the first public gallery in the UK devoted solely to photographs and photographers.

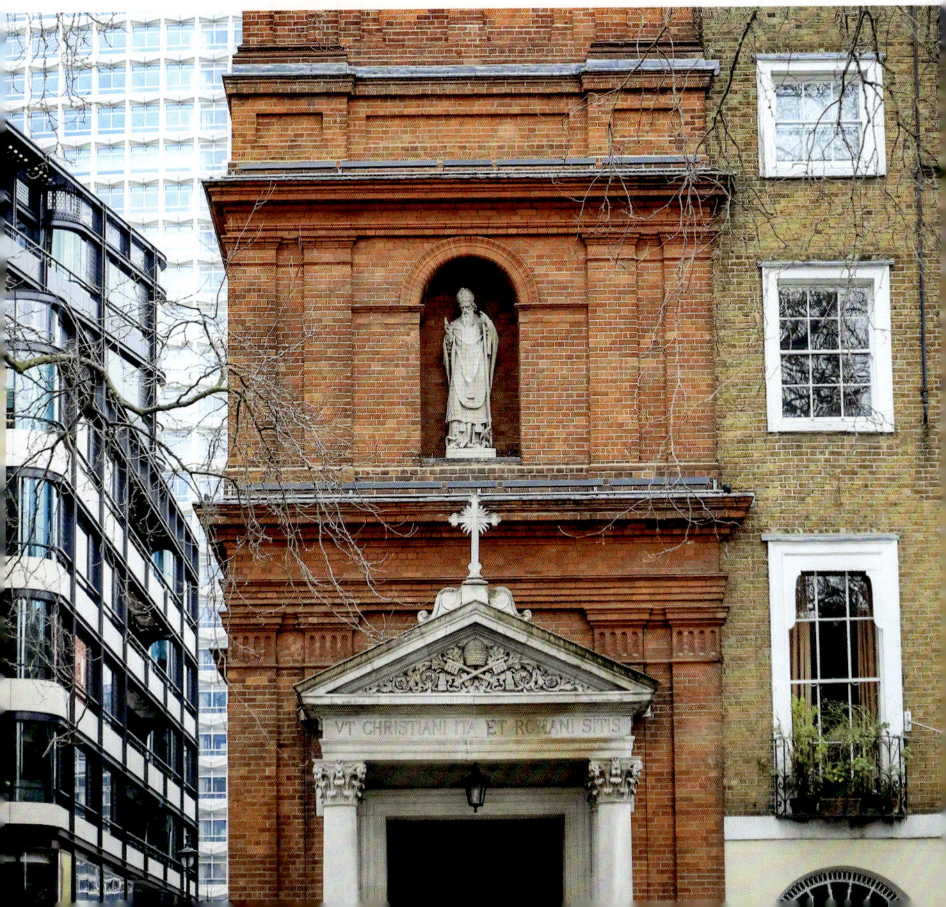

65 The Neasden Temple

The elephant god of north London

Amongst the glitzy shopping arcades, the drive-through car-wash facilities, and the 1930s housing developments of the north London Borough of Brent, there are two great cultural centres, one secular and the other sacred. They are both places where thousands regularly gather to pay homage to their gods. One is Wembley Stadium, home of English football, visible from miles around by its soaring arc. The other one is the Shri Swaminarayan Mandir, better known as the Neasden Temple, one of the largest and most magnificent traditional religious structures sacred to the many gods of Hinduism outside India itself.

The temple was opened in 1995, although in appearance it could have manifested itself visually in this way at any time over the past 200 years. Built with 5,000 tons of limestone and of marble mined in India, Bulgaria and Italy, it was carved in sections by craftsmen in India itself, and then transported to England, where it was assembled by thousands of volunteers over a period of two and a half years, as if this were no more difficult a task than creating a child's house out of Lego bricks.

Now, white as the driven snow, and with its many flags flying over the multiplicity of domes that mark its most sacred places, it is open for all to see and to marvel at.

To enter those most sacred shrines and see the gods as Hindus wish them to be seen, in their gilded niches, it is best to approach by the long marble staircase that you will see as you enter the site. Next to it there is the giant gilded figure of His Holiness Pramukh Swami Maharaja (1921–2016), the revered religious teacher who is the creator of this temple. He sits cross-legged, with a string of beads trailing from the fingers of his right hand. Beside him there is an elephant, representing Ganesha, the elephant god, whose presence is also upstairs in that sacred heart of the building.

Address 105–119 Brentfield Road, Neasden, London NW10 8LD, +44 (0)208 965 2651, www.londonmandir.baps.org | Getting there Underground to Wembley Park (Metropolitan and Jubilee Lines), then 206 bus to the temple | Hours Daily 9am–6pm; visit the website for details of the dress code before visiting | Tip There's good veggie food at the Shayona Café in the temple car park.

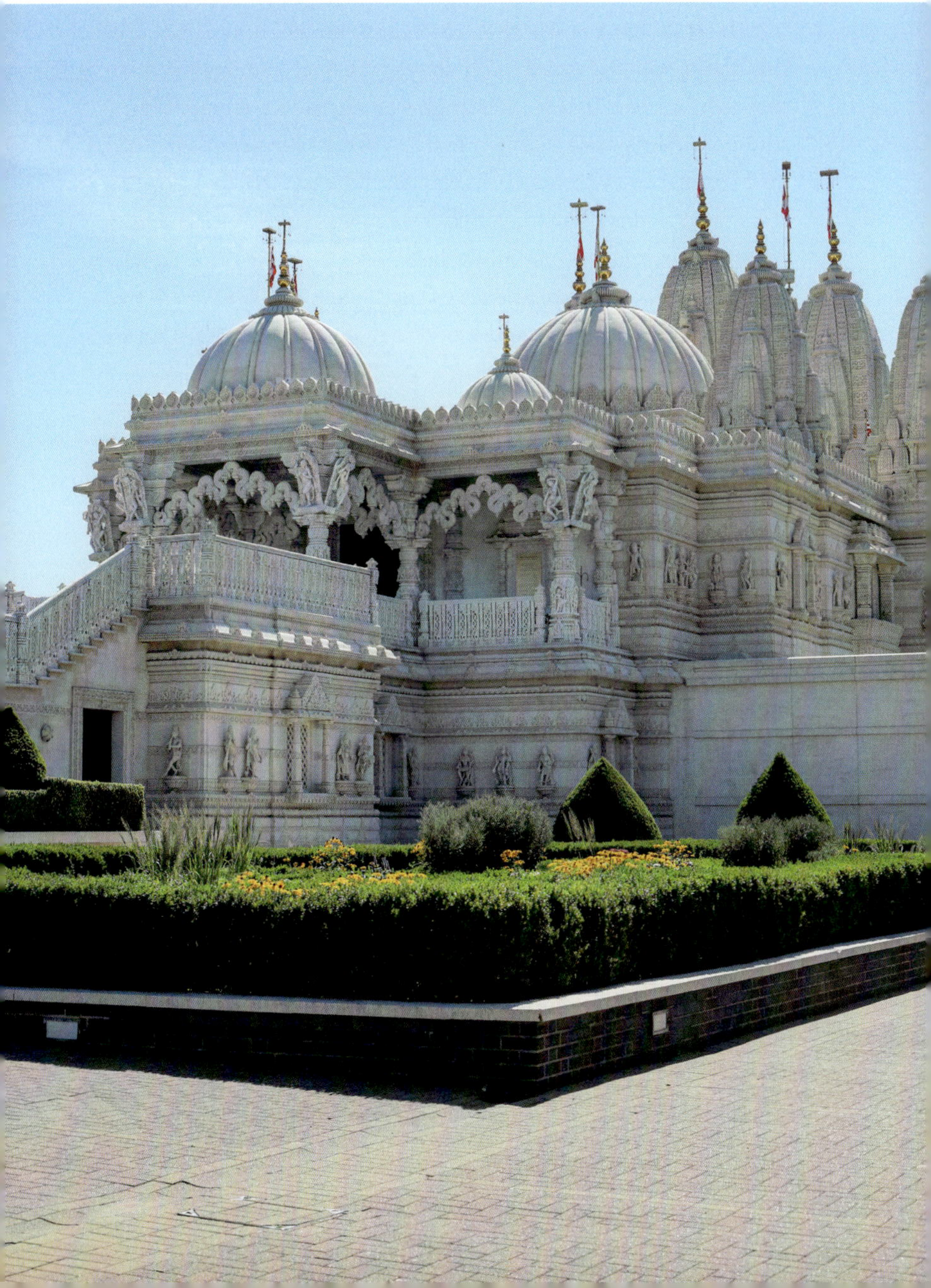

66 The Nelson Stair

Where the Navy's needs were served

Somerset House, one of London's finest neo-classical buildings, sits high on the north bank of the Thames, just a little to the east of London Bridge. The Thames is a swift-moving, mood-changing, tidal river, and there is much that links Sir William Chambers' imperious and ostentatious building to seafaring and the sea. Walk through the great inner courtyard where ice skaters do their daring leaps and turns in the winter months, and you will see what I mean.

It was in the wing that overlooks the Thames that the Navy Board was once headquartered, and it is here that you will find a staircase that deserves to be re-categorised as a well-hidden, magnificent work of art in its own right.

It is called the Nelson Stair. To find it, turn right off the Seaman's Waiting Hall, and just keep walking, past the entrances to a restaurant and a café or two. It will be facing you as you walk ahead. Each section of the staircase is slightly different. At the top of the staircase, you would once have found the Navy Board Room, from where much of the administration of the Navy would have been managed, from the repair of ships to the needs of seamen. Nelson would have been a frequent visitor.

As an aid to reflection upon the ingeniousness of this staircase, which twists and spirals up through all six floors, from the basement up, of this building, have a good look at something on the wall to the left of you just before you reach the foot of the staircase. It is a drawing of 1950 by F. S. Samuels, showing what the staircase looks like seen from above, as if you could magically peer right through the roof, and down into its spiralling movement. This drawing was made because the staircase was badly damaged during World War II, and it needed to be restored to its former glory. Its ingenious upward movement makes it look a bit like an artwork by M. C. Escher.

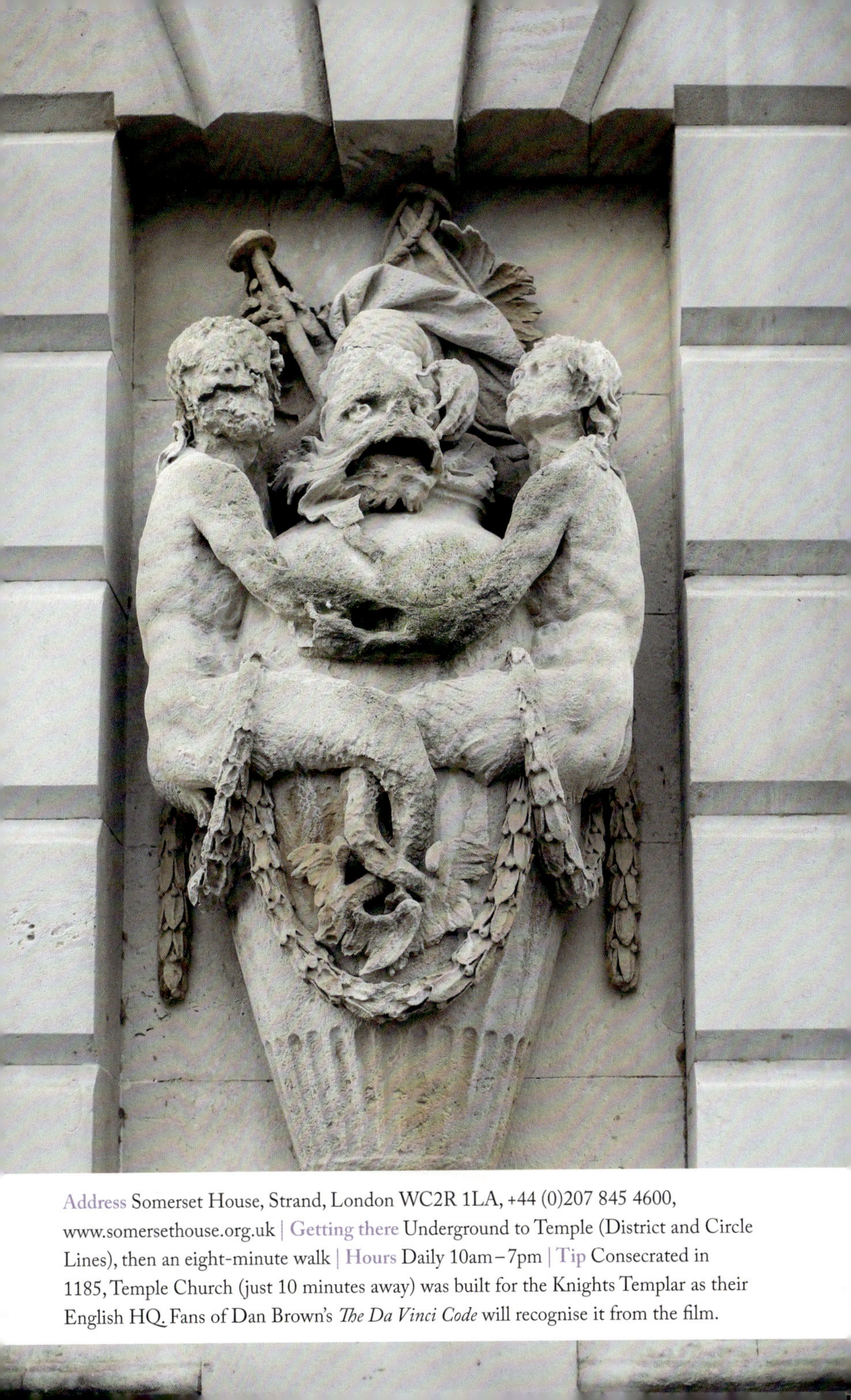

Address Somerset House, Strand, London WC2R 1LA, +44 (0)207 845 4600, www.somersethouse.org.uk | Getting there Underground to Temple (District and Circle Lines), then an eight-minute walk | Hours Daily 10am–7pm | Tip Consecrated in 1185, Temple Church (just 10 minutes away) was built for the Knights Templar as their English HQ. Fans of Dan Brown's *The Da Vinci Code* will recognise it from the film.

67 Networking

Thomas J. Price's black Londoner

How, and where, we place a sculpture in a public place is of great importance, and especially so if it is a representation of a human figure. Other factors matter too. How tall? On horseback or not? Standing still, gesticulating, walking? In Parliament Square, Churchill impresses by his hugeness and bulk, and the fact that he is walking forward, leaning on his stick – the indomitability of the spirit of a great war leader is the resounding message.

Many military men are displayed on horseback, and raised tall on plinths. A horse suggests a man of action. A plinth aggrandises, as does upscaling the human form. A sculpture of monumental proportions also needs to sit well, centrally in its space, not askew or off to the side. You could say that these decisions are political ones. They are about talking up the significance of the man or woman – it is all too seldom a woman in London's greatest and most visible public spaces – in question.

All these issues crowd in when we happen upon this over-sized representation of a young black man staring down at his phone in a small, recently created public space – part courtyard, part striplet of park overhung by handsome young trees in the shape of a stick of candyfloss, just yards from Exit One of Old Street Underground station. There is no grand point of entry. You slip in beside various newish buildings, part retail, part domestic, part commercial. When you enter the square, you notice a pasta restaurant, which faces side on to a gym. And you also see him, a young black man on the extreme outer edge of a strip of grass, and standing on that grass without the aid of any plinth. He is staring down at his phone, in an utterly casual pose. His trousers ruck up at the ankles. He wears a puffa jacket, belling out at the back. He is the very epitome of someone caught in the act of being himself. This is the real London, now.

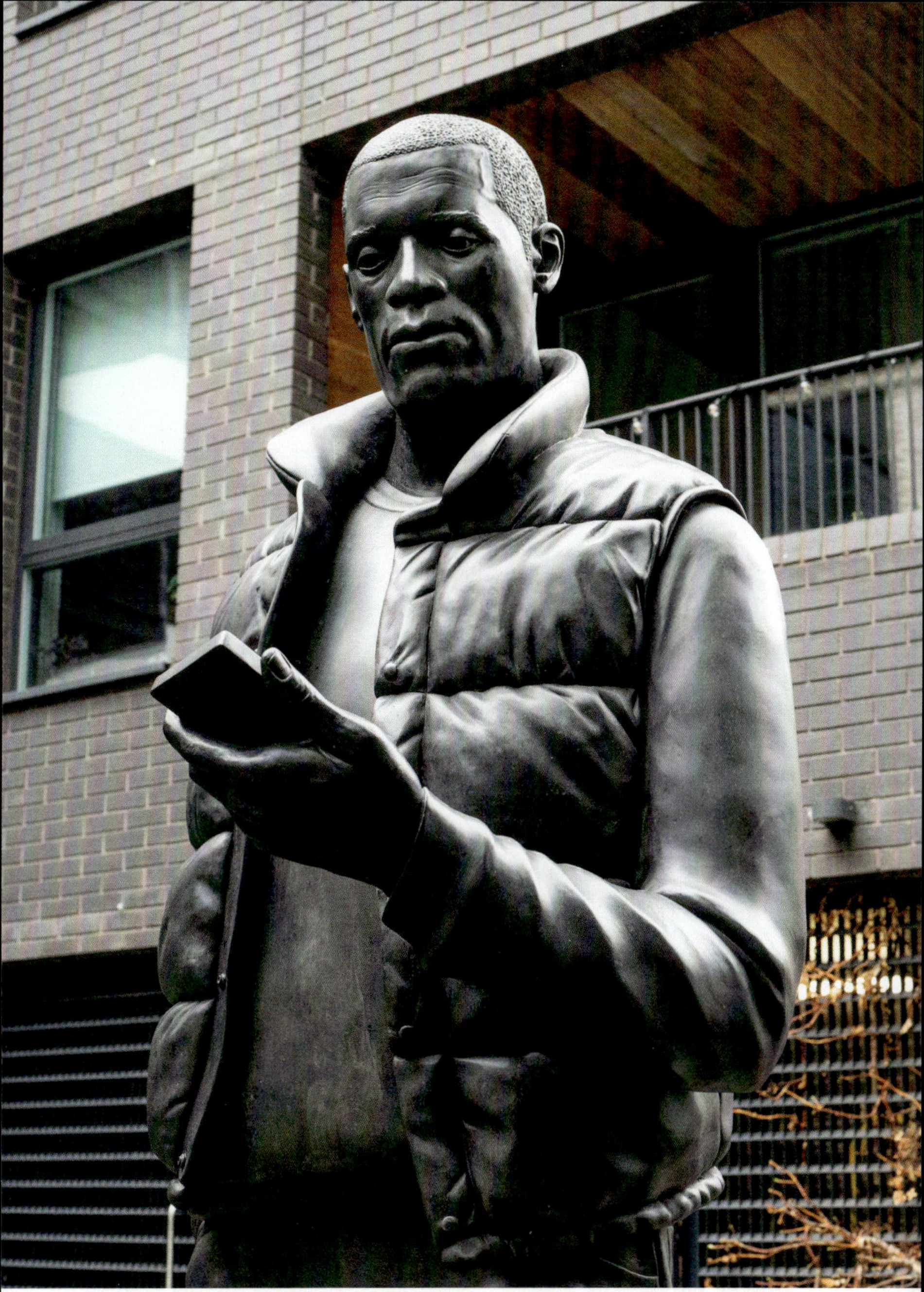

Address Outside White Collar Factory, Old Street Yard, London EC1Y 8AF | Getting there Underground to Old Street (Northern Line) | Hours Accessible 24 hours | Tip Take your picnic to the wonderful Bunhill Fields Burial Ground five minutes from here at 38 City Road, where Daniel Defoe and William Blake are buried.

68 A New Dawn

Fighting for women's rights

The British Houses of Parliament have been much buffeted in their time – comprehensively destroyed by fire in the 19th century, and then pummelled by bombs during the Blitz of 1940. And yet one magnificent part of that complex of buildings has survived for more than 700 years.

I am referring to Westminster Hall, which dates from the 11th century, and proudly shows off the oldest wooden roof in Europe. Towering characters have strutted across its stage, from Simon de Montfort to Charles I, and on to Nelson Mandela, who addressed both Houses of Parliament in this room in 1996. It is here that Churchill lay in state, and it was here that, as a sobering brass plaque set into the floor records, in scrupulous detail, that Charles I stood and listened to the pronouncement of his own death sentence in 1649, having been tried for high treason on this spot by the High Court of Justice established by the Commons, sentenced to death on Saturday 27 January, and executed in front of the Banqueting House.

Less somber, and much more cheering in its message, is the very innovative artwork you will see if you ascend the great flight of stone stairs towards the two chambers, and then look up and to your left at the arch that leads into St Stephen's Hall. The Parliamentary Estate is overflowing with statues and paintings of the worthies who have strutted through these lobbies, but there is nothing else quite like Mary Branson's *New Dawn*, which exists to commemorate in a most unusual way the achievements of the suffragette movement. What we see are circles of light that fade and intensify even as we look at them – they are responding to the tidal movements of the Thames. Each circle of light represents a single scroll of legislation on that slow, forever onward march to do justice to the rights of women in this country – the Equality Act, the Equal Pay Act…

Address London SW1A 0AA, +44 (0)207 219 3000, www.parliament.uk | Getting there Underground to Westminster (Jubilee, District and Circle Lines) | Hours A range of tours is available, all bookable through the website | Tip Hobnob with a politician or two at The Clarence, 53 Whitehall, a traditional pub bursting with character.

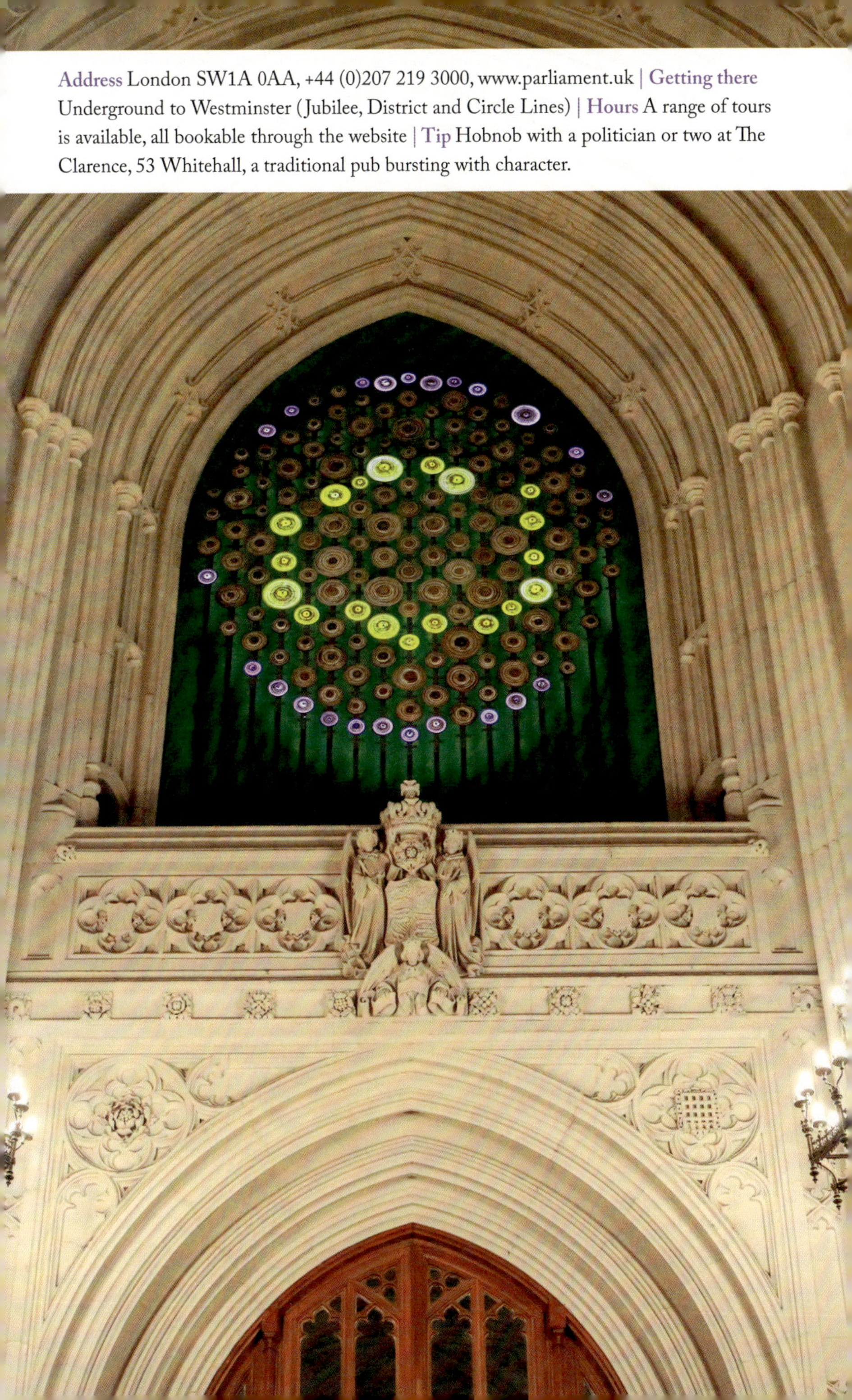

69 Offering the Host

The sacred statuary of Theatreland

Eager little children, chaperoned by anxious parents, stream through the streets of Covent Garden dressed up in all their finery – long, gauzy dresses, magic wands held aloft. They are off to see *The Lion King*! Just minutes from here, a hidden church tells a very different story. The Church of Corpus Christi in Maiden Lane – yet another street busy with bars, restaurants and the excitably noisy overspill of Theatreland – was created towards the end of the 19th century to cater for the needs of the families of the Catholic costers who lived and worked in this great market.

To reach this church you take several stone steps down from the street, and then turn right to reach a place of utter quiet whose small yet sumptuous interior quite takes you aback. This is not the pared back simplicity of Protestantism. Thomas Cromwell would have smashed this interior to bits. There are glittering, painted statues. A crucifixion scene shows Christ bleeding from his wounds, quite graphically.

This place is more akin to an 18th-century church you would see in Spain, full of polychromatic statues that provoke awe, fascination and even a little fear – and especially those such as St Patrick, which are life-size and seem to be striding forth, or just about to, in order to greet or warn or admonish.

A remarkable figure of a priest resembles the work of an Australian contemporary of ours called Ron Mueck, who creates works so hyper-realistic, and yet so oddly scaled, that they utterly unnerve us. As does this priest, who holds up in his right hand the disc of the consecrated host, Christ's body, given for all. The disc is over-sized, extraordinarily so. He might be holding out the sun. He is miniaturised, perhaps one-third of his usual size, and he makes this dramatic gesture of outreach amongst the pews where we all sit. His name is Padre Pio, also known as St Pio of Pietrelcina.

Address Corpus Christi Catholic Church, 1–5 Maiden Lane, Covent Garden, London WC2E 7NB, +44 (0)207 836 4700, www.corpuschristimaidenlane.org.uk | Getting there Underground to Covent Garden (Piccadilly Line), then a five-minute walk | Hours Mass times Mon–Fri 1.05pm, Sat (vigil) 6pm, Sun 9.30 am & 11.30am | Tip Enjoy a display of historic costumes in the café of the Royal Opera House just five minutes from the church.

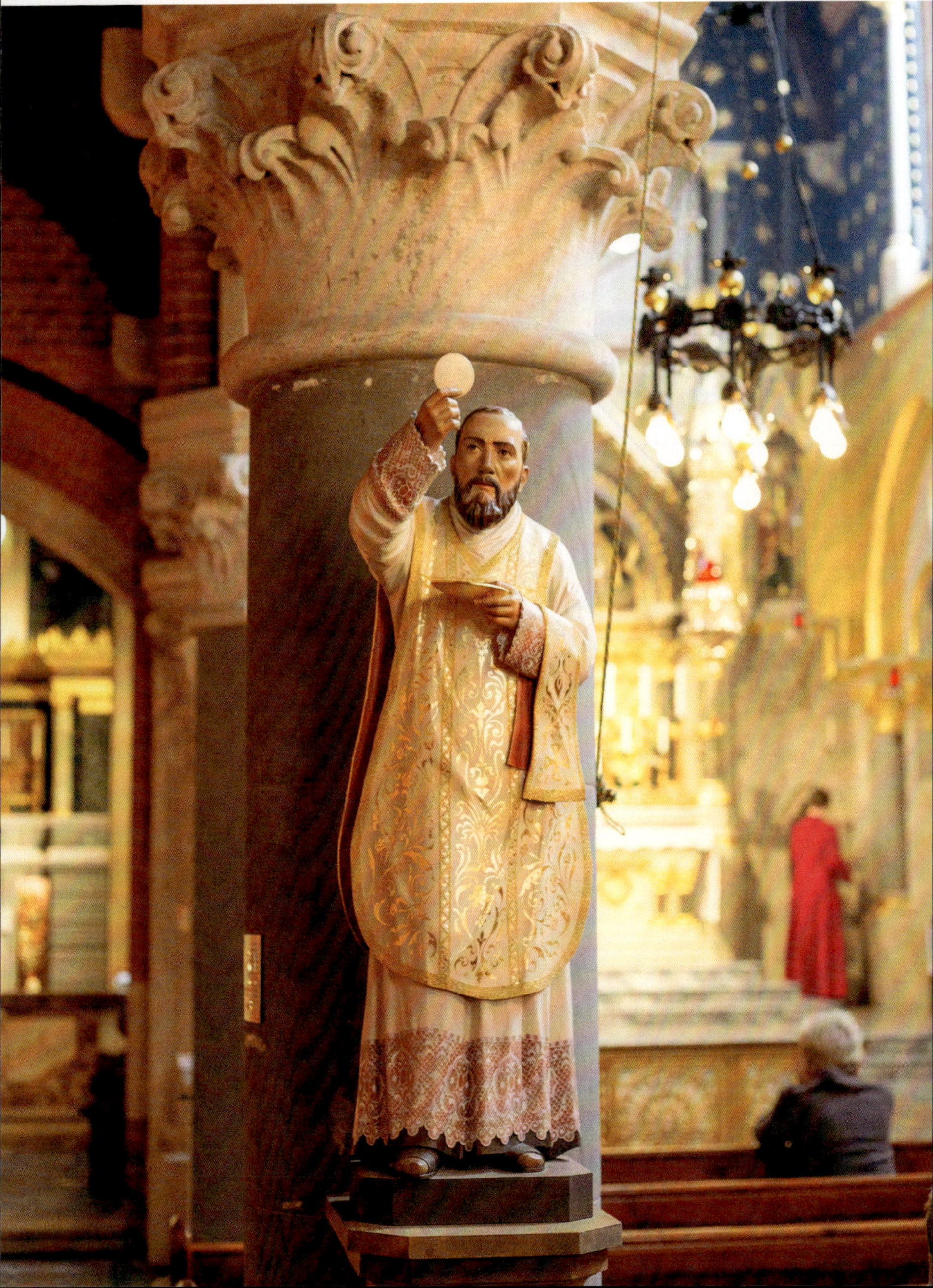

70_The Painted Ceiling

Showing off the Royal Navy in some style

To get an almost overpowering whiff of England's great naval heritage, you need to take a boat downriver from Westminster to Greenwich, and visit the splendours of the Painted Hall of the Old Royal Naval College, which these days is the principal campus of the University of Greenwich and a UNESCO World Heritage Site. This building is yet another creation by Sir Christopher Wren, and the magnificent painted ceiling of its Hall is the work of Sir James Thornhill. It was painted over a period of almost 20 years, from 1707 to 1726. You reach it by walking up a great flight of marble stairs from the level of the vestibule. Here you may also see Wren's hand-written letter of 11 October, 1700, ordering a supply of 2,000 tons of Portland Stone from Dorset for the building of the Old Royal Naval College.

It is a piece of wonderful, overblown royal propaganda, which begins at the very centre of the great painted ceiling oval that hangs over you as you walk the length of this magnificent, light-flooded 17th-century room (Wren was a great believer in the importance of much light), with its processional of brown pilasters topped by the flourish of gilded Corinthian capitals. This is the room where Admiral Nelson once lay in state. (Visit the Nelson Room adjacent to read of Nelson himself, and also to see a maquette of the statue that has dominated his column in Trafalgar Square for almost two centuries.)

Fortunately, there are mirrors on tables in the Central Hall to enable you to scrutinise what is above you without causing too much pain to your neck. At the centre of the ceiling there is William III of the House of Orange and his consort Queen Mary II, both enthroned languidly amongst clouds, dressed up to the nines in their coronation outfits, and being paid much attention by the gods of antiquity. Bad Louis XIV of France holds a broken sword in his hand. Good.

Address Romney Road, London SE10 9NN, +44 (0)208 269 4799, www.ornc.org | **Getting there** Underground to Canary Wharf (Jubilee Line), and then change to DLR (stop Cutty Sark), then a short walk to Old Royal Naval College | **Hours** Daily 10am–5pm, grounds open 8am–11pm | **Tip** The National Maritime Museum is just a couple of minutes away.

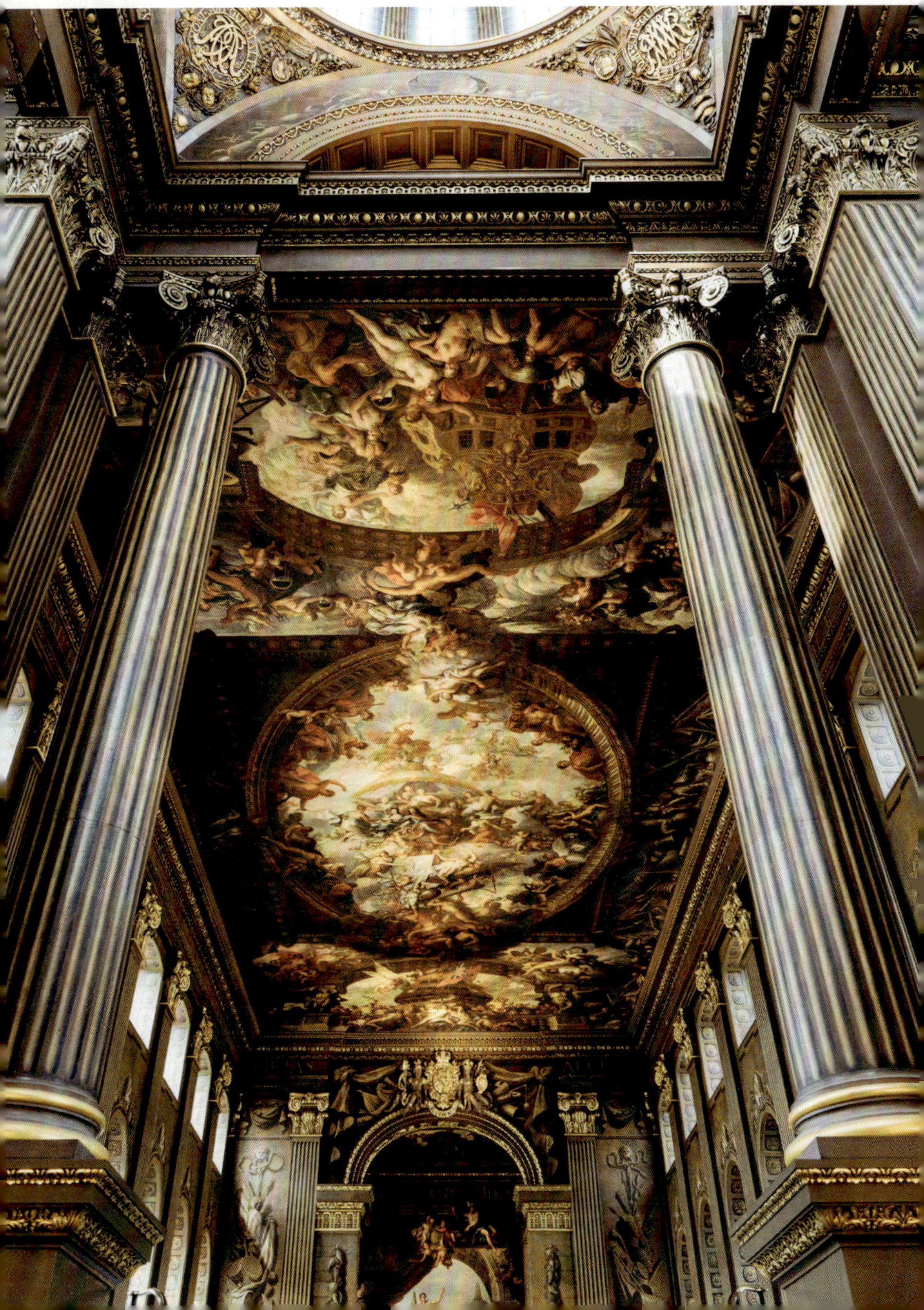

71 Paolozzi's Newton

William Blake turned robotic

It seems entirely fitting that Eduardo Paolozzi's sculpture of Newton should preside, ominously, broodingly, on its huge, triple-stepped plinth, over the courtyard of the British Library in Euston Road, that powerhouse of intellectual endeavour. The work itself, made in 1995, is both a tribute to and a radical reinterpretation of a great watercolour by William Blake, which shows Newton in exactly this posture, a muscular giant of a man straight out of Michelangelo's copybook, hair a tight nest of golden curls, leaning over, compass pinched beneath his fingers, fiercely attentive to the work in hand.

There is a terrible ambivalence at the heart of Blake's characterisation of the great scientist. Blake was no lover of Newton's mechanistic view of the universe. He regarded it as barren, abstract, an enemy of the boundlessness of human experience, which led directly to the enslavement of man within those dark satanic mills.

And yet Blake's great work of 1795 – exactly 200 years before – is a magnificent, even hallowed, evocation of Newton's quest for scientific knowledge. Its colours astonish – the brilliant blue of the sweep of universal sky tones at his back; the pinky glow of his flesh tones; the astonishing merging of blues, greens and oranges in the rocky outcrop on which he sits, which looks as if it might be submerged in water.

By comparison, Paolozzi's bronze is dour and fiercely austere – as bronze can often be. Blake's representation of the muscles of the naked Newton are decidedly odd. They proceed up from buttocks to the top of his back in regular symmetrical bands, unlike any muscles known to an anatomist. Paolozzi has taken this strange regularity and given it greater emphasis by adding what look like rivets at key pivotal points – at thigh, elbow and ankle, for example. He has turned Newton into a robotic, almost metal-plated version of himself.

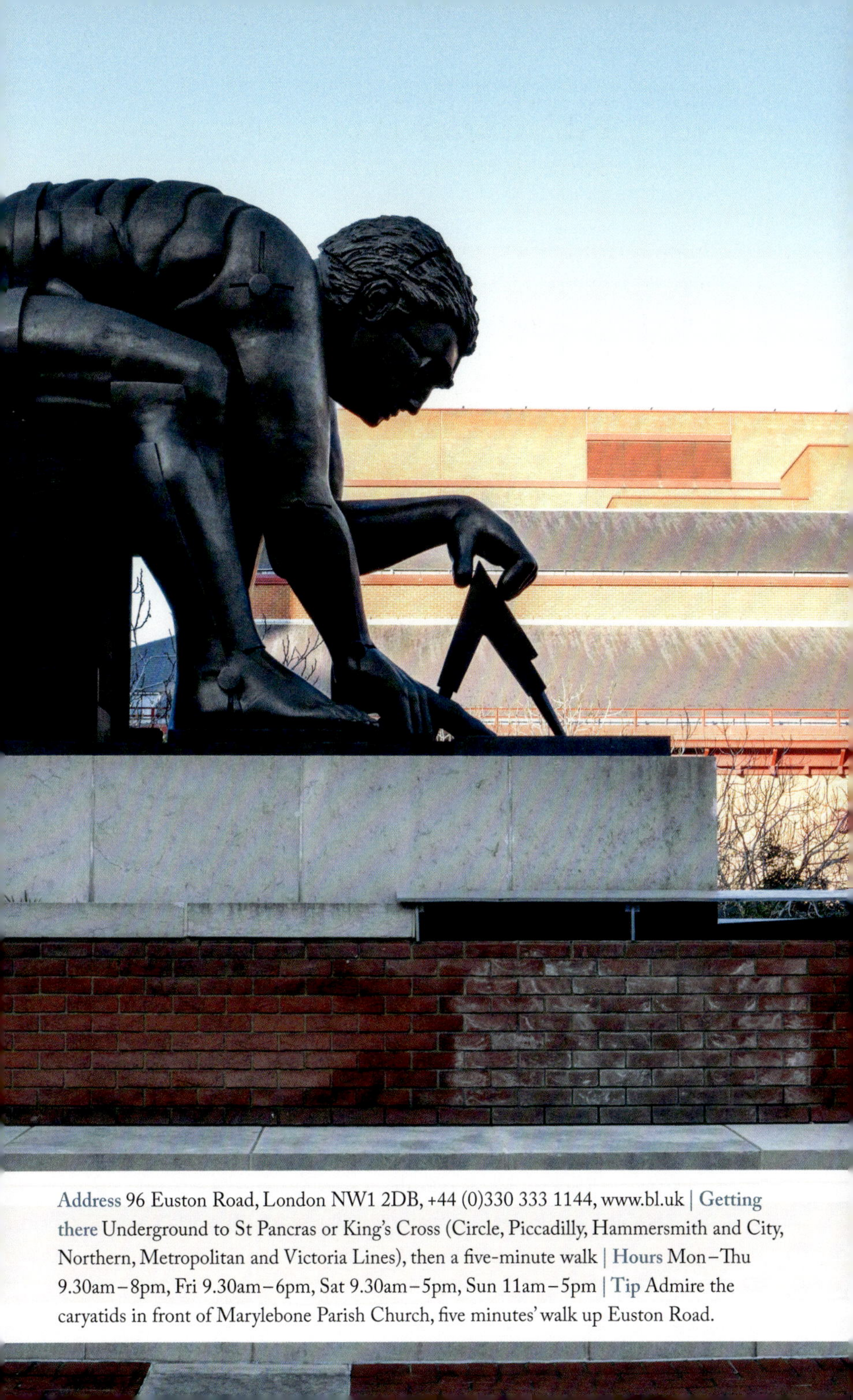

Address 96 Euston Road, London NW1 2DB, +44 (0)330 333 1144, www.bl.uk | **Getting there** Underground to St Pancras or King's Cross (Circle, Piccadilly, Hammersmith and City, Northern, Metropolitan and Victoria Lines), then a five-minute walk | **Hours** Mon–Thu 9.30am–8pm, Fri 9.30am–6pm, Sat 9.30am–5pm, Sun 11am–5pm | **Tip** Admire the caryatids in front of Marylebone Parish Church, five minutes' walk up Euston Road.

72 Paradigm

The scientific spirit in the ascendant

Leave by the west door out of St Pancras International Terminal, and you will be confronted, directly across the road, by the wonderful, cantilevered, over-and-sideways swoop (it looks a little like a steel comb-over) of the roof of the Francis Crick Institute, named after the Nobel-Prize-winning English scientist who discovered the structure of DNA. This is a building devoted entirely to scientific endeavour, and as if in acknowledgement of that fact, there is a 46-foot-high sculpture in the piazza outside its front entrance called *Paradigm* by Conrad Shawcross. Fabricated out of weathering Corten steel, which goes an ever more dense and gritty chocolatey brown as it matures, it consists of a stacking of tetrahedra (triangular sheets of steel that lean and lock onto each other, creating three dimensional facets), one perched upon another, which grow and grow in size the higher they rise. The smallest is at its base.

The sculpture makes a deft, showy little twist as it rises, as if to woo the audience just that little bit more. To look at it is to wonder about such issues as balance and precariousness, and how things of such weight and massiveness are capable of holding themselves up in the air with such seeming ease.

It is almost a balletic movement that we are staring at – the ability to stand perfectly still on one leg. This sculpture seems made to honour the scientific spirit as defined by Thomas Kuhn. Discovery is more than a mere succession of incremental and collaborative endeavours, he argued.

There are moments when great breakthroughs occur that redefine the very nature not only of the physical structure of the world in which we live, but of these bodies we are pleased to call home.

Kuhn called it a 'paradigm shift'. Crick's famous diagram of the double helix would have been one such great breakthrough. *Paradigm* shows a similar bursting forth.

Address 1 Midland Road, London NW1 1AT, +44 (0)203 796 0000, www.crick.ac.uk | Getting there Underground to King's Cross (Northern, Victoria, Circle and Hammersmith and City Lines), just across the road from the side entrance to the international terminal of St Pancras Station | Hours Accessible 24 hours | Tip Go into the institute itself to admire its attractive light-filled atrium and visit the gallery.

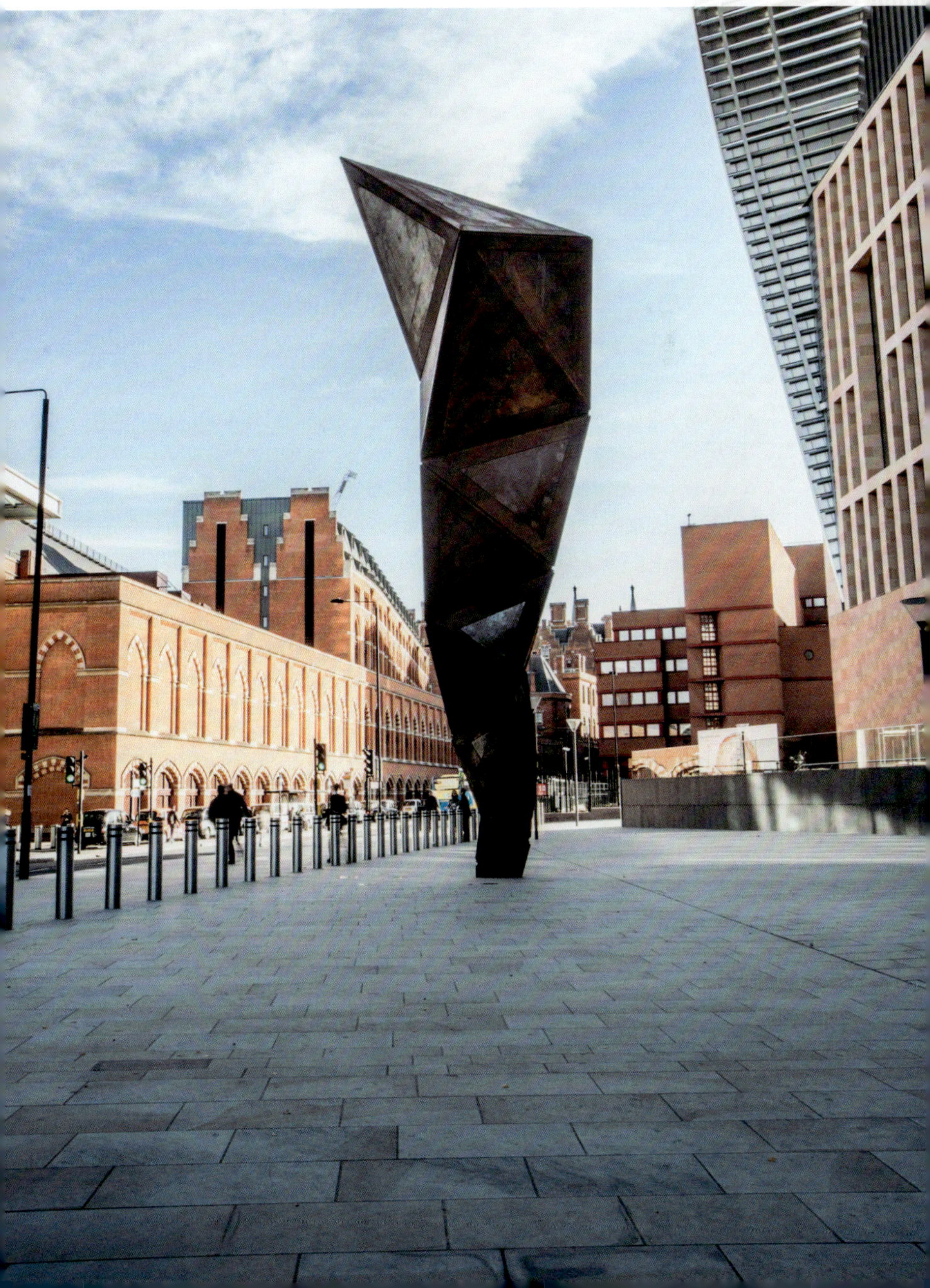

73 Paternoster

The shepherd with his docile flock

The height at which we see a sculptural grouping has a huge impact upon our response to it. This rather slow-moving formation of a shepherd urging his five sheep along in front of him is exactly level with our eyeline when we come across it, almost by accident, it seems.

You might expect it to be placed in the centre of the square, as so many sculptures tend to be. Not so here. It is close to one of the entry points to this lovely spot much used by office workers, which is adjacent to London's largest and most magnificent church, St Paul's Cathedral, that great survivor of the London Blitz. It is as if the shepherd and his docile, biddable sheep have drifted into our ken from a nearby dream.

Is it not a little odd to have this small flock of sheep, astray on a raised plinth, in central London, we ask ourselves? Yes, it is. But it also is not, for two reasons, one religious and the other secular. The title of this group by Elisabeth Frink is *Paternoster*. As is the square it inhabits. This means Our Father, in Latin, and it is the first two words of the Lord's Prayer. But sheep are important to the Christian message in other ways too. Sheep, like humans, are often inclined to go astray. They need a shepherd to guide them back onto the right track, with the aid of a crook perhaps – our shepherd has such a crook. But sheep have other religious meanings too. They can also be foolish, and too easily led. How to save them from themselves? By sacrificing a sheep in the form of the Paschal Lamb, who has to die on a cross to save them from their sins.

That sheep is Jesus himself, and there is something of this hinted at here. The shepherd is near naked (apart from a bit of fudged concealment at the genital area), and his arms are flung out wide as if to say: take me, hang me, I am ready. There is something else too. There was once a meat market here.

Address Paternoster Square, London EC4M 7BP, www.paternostersquare.info | Getting there Underground to St Paul's (Central Line) | Hours Accessible 24 hours | Tip Fortify yourself at one of the great stalls selling street food in the square, then head for St Paul's Cathedral.

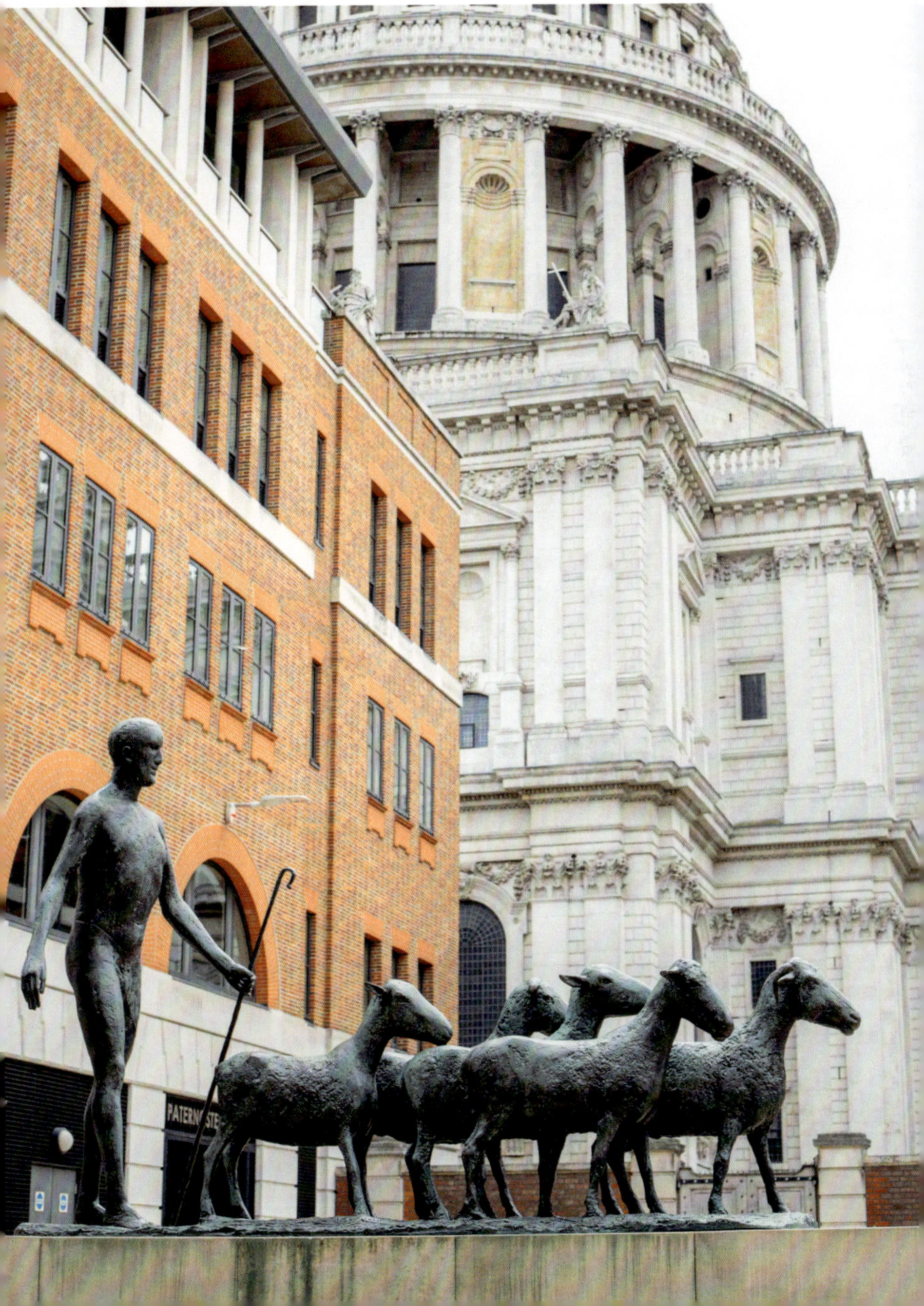

74 Pecking Bird in Action

Gary Hume invites the jungle into town

The annual Turner Prize for art is known for stirring controversy, getting our backs up. It has also brought to our attention young and unknown artists of remarkable talent who have gone on to become household names. One of these is the painter Gary Hume. One of his most eye-catching works is displayed for us all to see, in the open air, close to a ferociously contested, inner-London road junction. At the point where once louche and down-at-heel Fitzrovia ends and Camden begins, there is a wildly busy and fiercely traffic-contested intersection where Euston Road and Hampstead Road cross swords at brutal speed.

You spot this intersection as you leave Warren Street Underground Station at the northern end of Tottenham Court Road. Turn your head to the left. There it is. But immediately you spot something else too, something much more gentle on the eye, and quietly humorous too. Pinned to the side of a multi-storey development known as Regent's Place, there is a glossy looking panel painting raised up high in the air. It looks like the only exhibit in the gallery, and it seems to be lifting off from the wall on which it sits in a sort of sideways motion, as if just about to please itself.

The bottom of it is carefully positioned up (just) above a line of fairly newly planted trees, which are processing up the street in the general direction of Camden. The trees add to the illusion that raised above this stretch of relentless urbanity, there might just be a jungle of sorts. Hume has painted a parrot in an extraordinarily vivid and glossy yellow. Its beak is reaching down to feed off a succulent leaf to which it has taken a fancy. The making is highly characteristic of Hume – crisply outlined, smooth surface, with a high and almost glossy sheen. The layering of its feathers is clearly shown – the painting is almost in low relief, like a shallow sculpture.

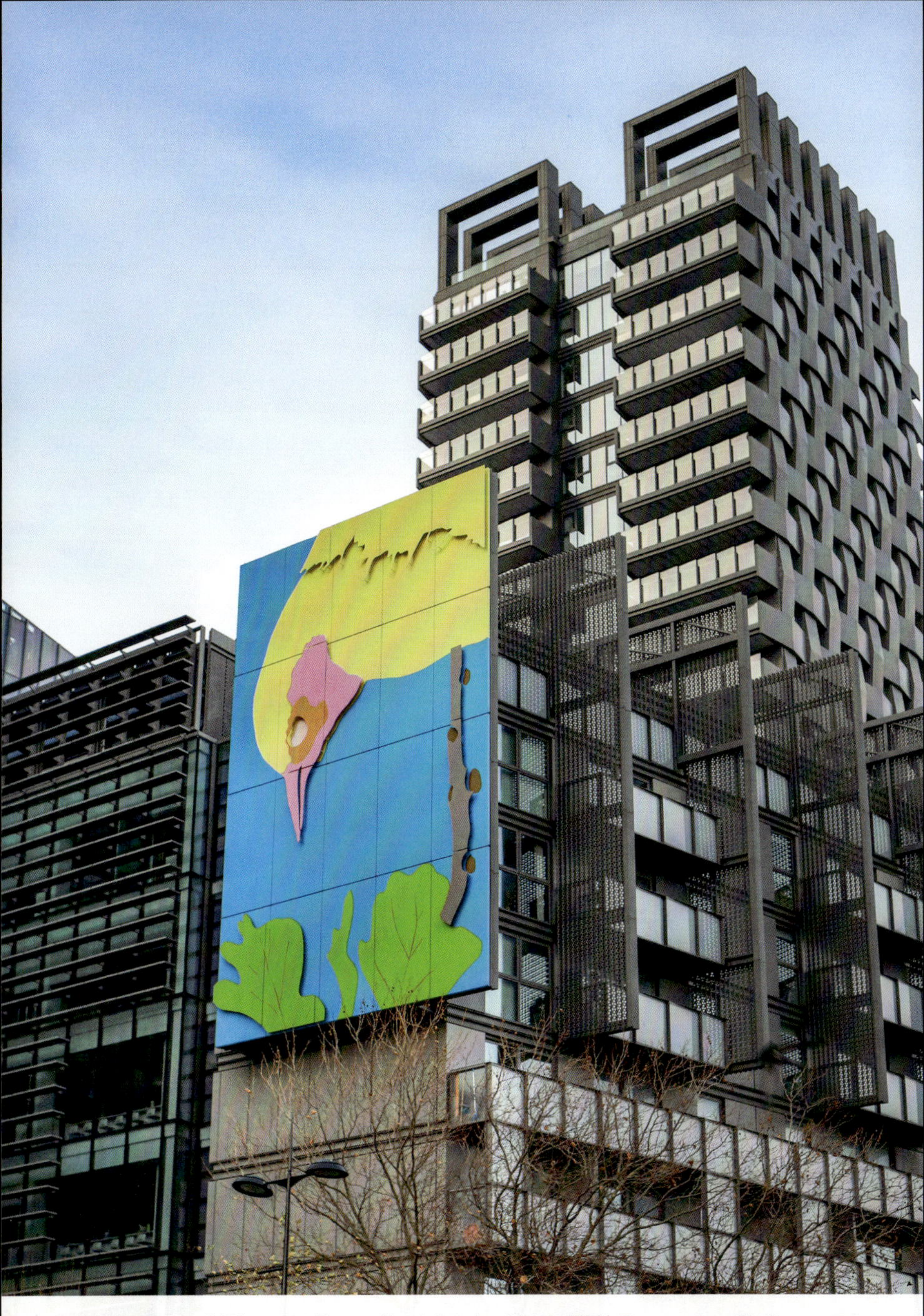

Address Regent's Place, 338 Euston Road, London NW1 3BT | Getting there Underground to Warren Street (Northern Line) | Hours Accessible 24 hours | Tip A five-minute walk away, at the top of Great Portland Street, is The Albany, a splendid Victorian pub that hosts all manner of comedy nights, gigs and the popular Ukulele Wednesday jam.

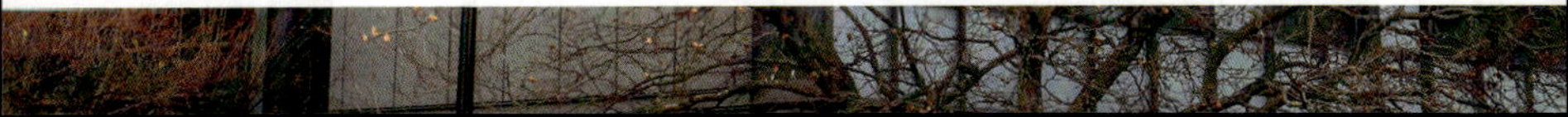

75 Periwigged Hans Sloane

A Chelsea garden to do us all good

Dr Hans Sloane, standing tall and proud on a plinth in his high piled periwig and stacked heels, commands the ground at the very centre of the Chelsea Physic Garden. You can see him from the café, as you enjoy your tomato soup and salad – all grown here. This is the Dutchman who once owned vast swathes of Chelsea, and whose name is memorialised in famous street signage – Sloane Street and Sloane Square, for example – and who was the direct begetter, two centuries on, of a sleekly fashionable kind of young female once called the Sloane Ranger.

He is also the man who, in the early 18th century, leased this piece of land to the Society of Apothecaries, and in it they created this very special garden of plants that exist to do us good, whether as food, drugs or medicines. Some cure us of ills or send us sky-high with pleasure. The vegetables certainly nourish us. Everything is neatly categorised and lovingly tended. This garden is also a poignant meeting place.

It was on a bench in the shadow of Sloane's statue (which is a fine copy of an original by a Dutchman called John Rysbrack), that in 1918 the poet Wilfred Owen had his last conversation with his friend the fashionable portrait painter John Singer Sargent, who lived in nearby Rule Street, before Owen returned to the battlefields of the Western Front and met his death. From his monument Sloane keeps a close eye on this small place (it is about four acres in all these days). The river gate by which royalty traditionally entered the garden – it is called the King's Gate – is not so close to the River Thames as it would have been in the 18th century. An embankment was added later, and a noisy road thrust through. This is the very gate through which plants and herbs would have been carried, to be transported downriver by barge to those apothecaries, who would have dried them and ground them to powder.

Address 66 Royal Hospital Road, London SW3 4HS, +44 (0)207 352 5646, www.chelseaphysicgarden.co.uk | **Getting there** Underground to Sloane Square (District and Circle Lines), then a 12-minute walk | **Hours** Sun–Fri 11am–5pm | **Tip** Stroll along to Cheyne Walk and see if you can spot all 10 of the plaques to the rich and famous who have been drawn to the street's beautiful and historic mansions.

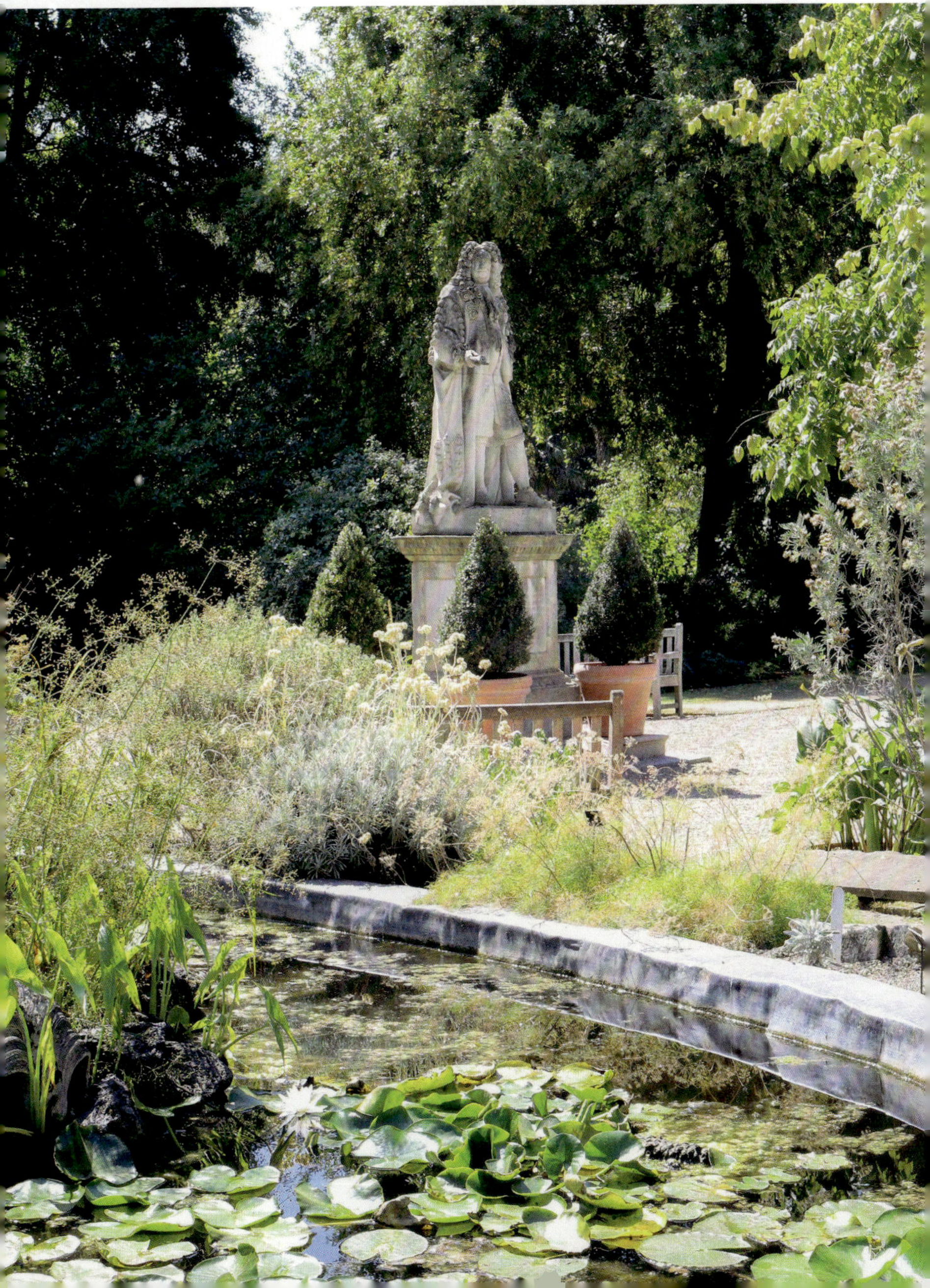

76 The Petrie Museum

The beautiful and the useful of Ancient Egypt

The Petrie Museum of Egyptian Archaeology is a small jewel of a place well off the beaten track in a mews in Bloomsbury. You approach it up a flight or two of rather unprepossessing concrete stairs. William Matthews Flinders Petrie was himself a pioneering archaeologist who numbered Lawrence of Arabia amongst his friends. A good part of the museum, which is tightly packed with his collection of the fruits of his archaeological digs, is displayed in old, lovingly cared-for wooden cabinets, some of them pyramidal cases at exactly the right height for close scrutiny. Its labels are hand-written.

The best objects include a Roman tomb portrait of the head and shoulders of a young woman from the Hawara Cemetery. It is an extraordinarily affecting likeness (and all the more affecting for the fact that she is so young), painted on a very thin panel of lime wood, bonded with beeswax. It is propped up, as if expecting admiration. Willingly. She has dark hair, and is dressed in a brown robe. We admire her gold earrings, and the simple necklace that hangs around her neck. There is a single word, Isarous, written in Greek across the background. This is typical of the breathing-close intimacy of the museum.

Equally to be admired is the Tarkhan Dress, a woman's garment that is probably one of the oldest of its kind in the world to have survived and the oldest known piece of clothing from Egypt – it may be as much as 5,000 years old.

Made of fine linen and delicately pleated, it was definitely once worn by its sometime owner – when first found, it was turned inside out, which suggests that she had taken it off and flung it aside. It is creased at the elbows and the armpits. Petrie and his team found it during a dig in 1913, in a cemetery dating from the First Dynasty (3,000 B.C.). It was hidden in a pile of linen. Other treasures here include 14 cats' heads.

Address Malet Place, London WC1E 6BT, +44 (0)203 108 9000, www.ucl.ac.uk/culture/petrie-museum | **Getting there** Underground to Euston Square (Metropolitan, Hammersmith and City and Circle Lines), then a five-minute walk | **Hours** Tue–Fri 1–5pm, Sat 11am–5pm | **Tip** Take a picnic to nearby Russell Square. Once fortified, you could visit the British Museum, which is really close.

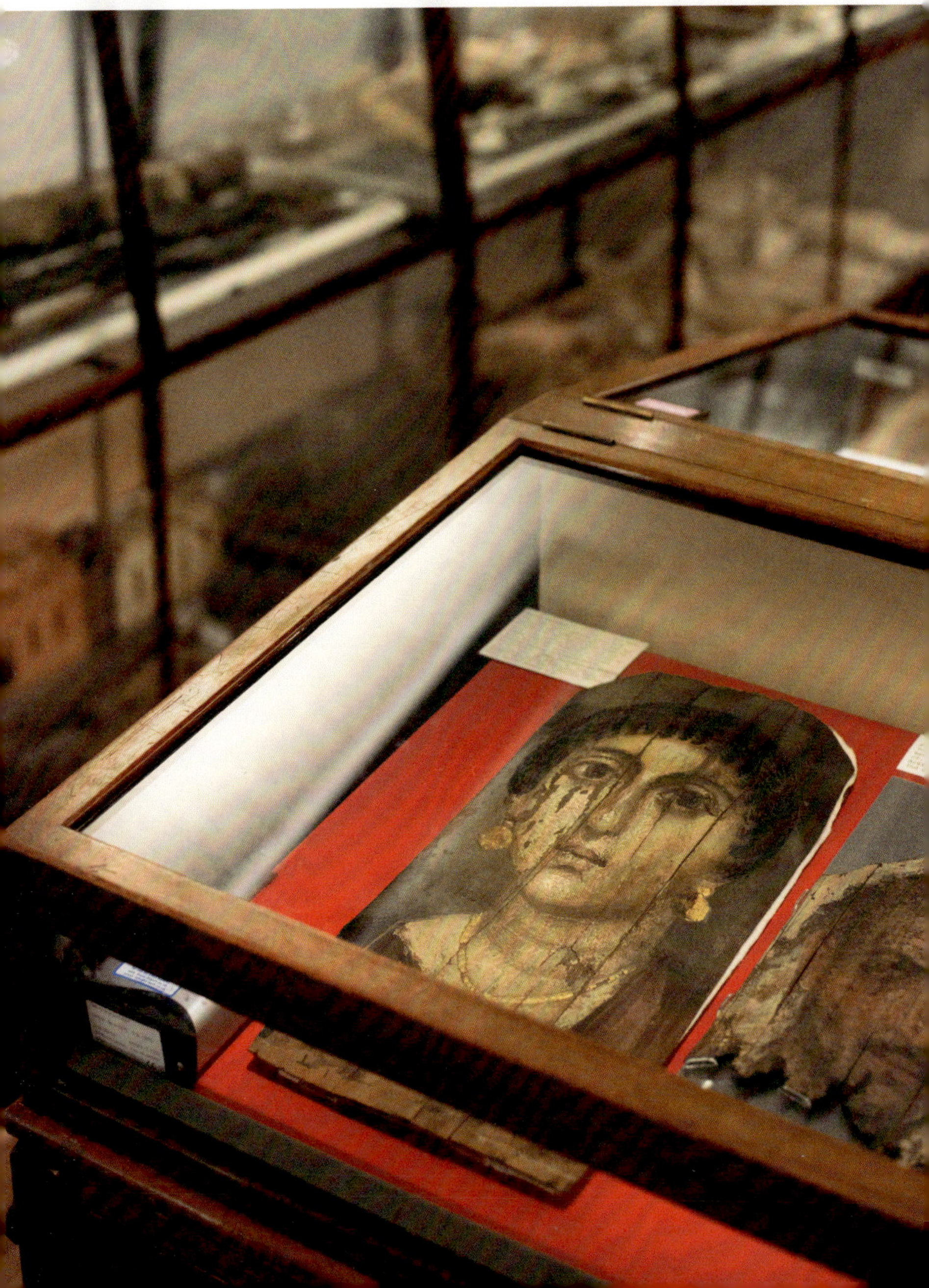

77 Pitzhanger Manor

A great architect's country retreat

Any great architect needs a place to hide. At the beginning of the 19th century, Sir John Soane, architect and surveyor of the Bank of England, built a country retreat for himself (complete with an estate – now a park – which the house overlooks from its conservatory) in Ealing, West London, a rural fastness in those days. Filthy, crowded London wasn't too far away – he regularly did the eight miles on foot. The house was called Pitzhanger Manor, and it has recently been refurbished.

Unlike the house, which became his museum in Lincoln's Inn Fields, it is not overwhelmingly cluttered with his collections of Greek and Roman antiquities, though individual pieces do sing out from time to time as you make your way through the house. There's the helmeted statue of Minerva, complete with spear and shield (that goddess who, appropriately enough, presides over the arts and crafts) on the turn of the stairs, for example, with the twin bulls to the left and right of her feet, and the marvellous Chinese wallpaper in the Upper Drawing Room. Soane was a great and nifty re-cycler – this Minerva was acquired from the Bank of England, as were the bulls' heads.

It does not really matter that the house lacks much art because that very lack enables us to spend more time contemplating the wonderful detailing that beautifies the building itself, and especially the eight caryatids – female figures that usually serve as supports – that line up across its façade, topping off the four Ionic columns. Soane had used the same design at the Bank of England. This is perhaps a gentle reminder...

So don't forget to look straight up before you enter the building. They are marvels of gracefulness and fine craftsmanship – a very close examination of their exposed feet, for example (you may have to take this on trust), will enable you to spot the modelling of their raised toe nails.

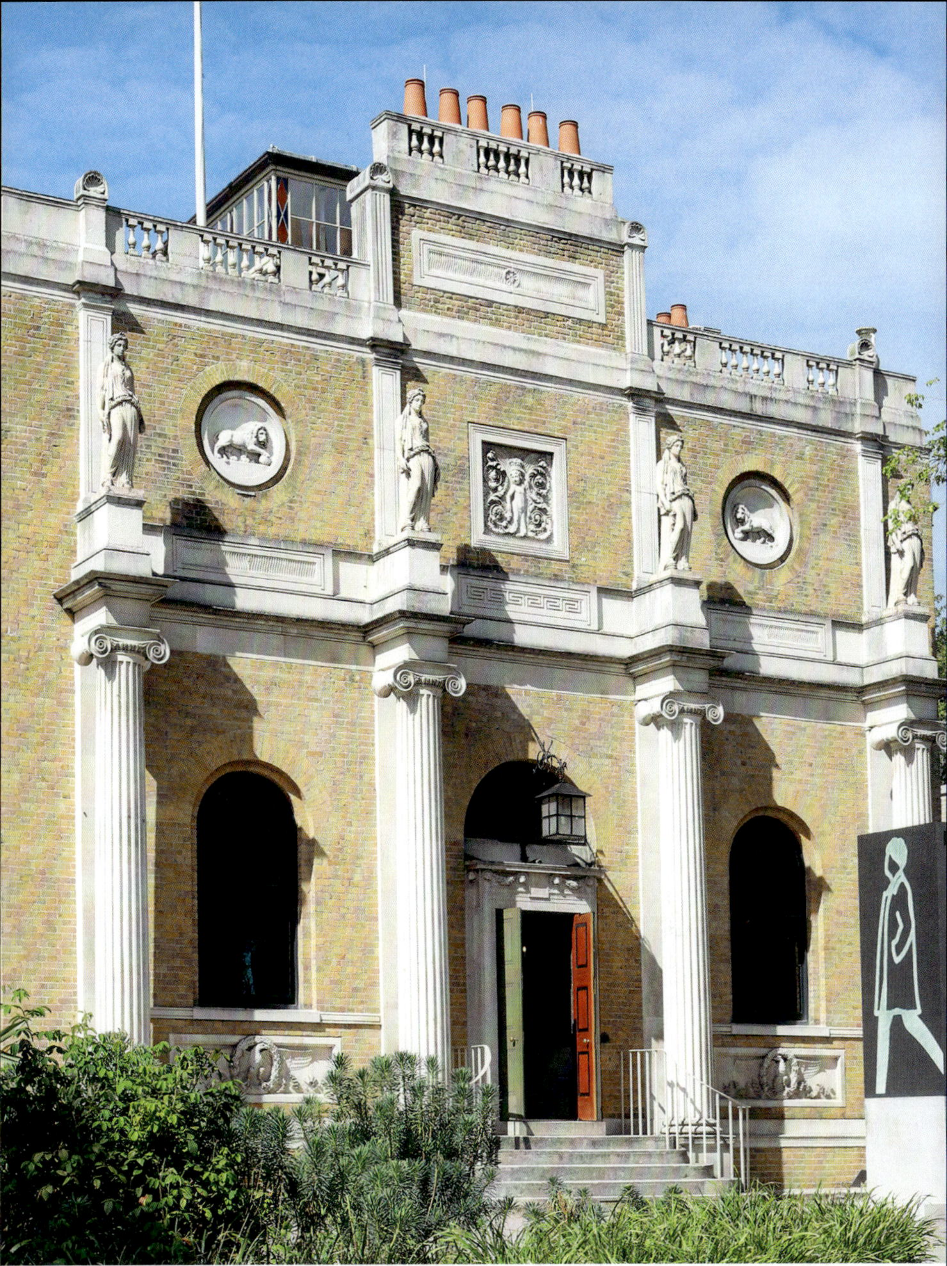

Address Ealing Green, London W5 5EQ, +44 (0)203 985 8888, www.pitzhanger.org.uk | Getting there Underground to Ealing Broadway (Central, District and Elizabeth Lines), then an eight-minute walk | Hours Wed, Fri – Sun 10am – 5pm, Thu 10am – 8pm | Tip Nearby is Walpole Park, now restored to how it would have looked in Soane's time. There is a walled kitchen garden, a fishpond and Regency-planted beds. For children, there is a playground.

78 Postman's Park

A memorial to heroic self-sacrifice

The narrow, beautifully gated entrance, spanned by a metal arch to contain a lantern that is missing, leads you a few steps up and into this shady, sequestered spot, a tiny snatch of parkland, shaded by giant London plane trees, within a stone's throw of St Paul's Cathedral. This garden was created in 1880, and it is an amalgamation of several ancient churchyards.

Ahead of you there is a circle of stout benches with a weakly sputtering fountain bordered by grass at their centre. On this fountain a fat pigeon sometimes sits, directly over the jet, even on a cold winter's day.

To the right is the entrance to an 18th-century church, and directly ahead of you as you continue to walk ahead, a remarkable monument in the form of a wall of hand-made Victorian tiles telling stories of local acts of heroism. The display is protected by a long canopy overhead, which means that you can sit beneath it when the rain comes on. This monument of hand-crafted tiles, all ranged in several rows, one above another, against the back of a single long wall, was the brainchild of a painter called George Frederick Watts, who lived on the cusp of the 20th century. It is called the G. F. Watts' *Memorial to Heroic Self-Sacrifice*, and was unveiled in 1900.

Each tale tells its own story of bravery – they look almost as if hand-written, with floral embellishments. The names of all these heroes and heroines, many of them mere children, are intensely poignant. Here is one that remembers William Donald of Bayswater, a railway clerk who died at the age of 19 on 16 July, 1876 in the River Lea trying to save a lad from a 'dangerous entanglement of weed'. Or one that tells us of Amelia Kennedy, also aged 19, who died trying to save her sister from their burning house in Edward's Lane, Stoke Newington on 18 October, 1871. All were such models of 'exemplary behaviour and character'.

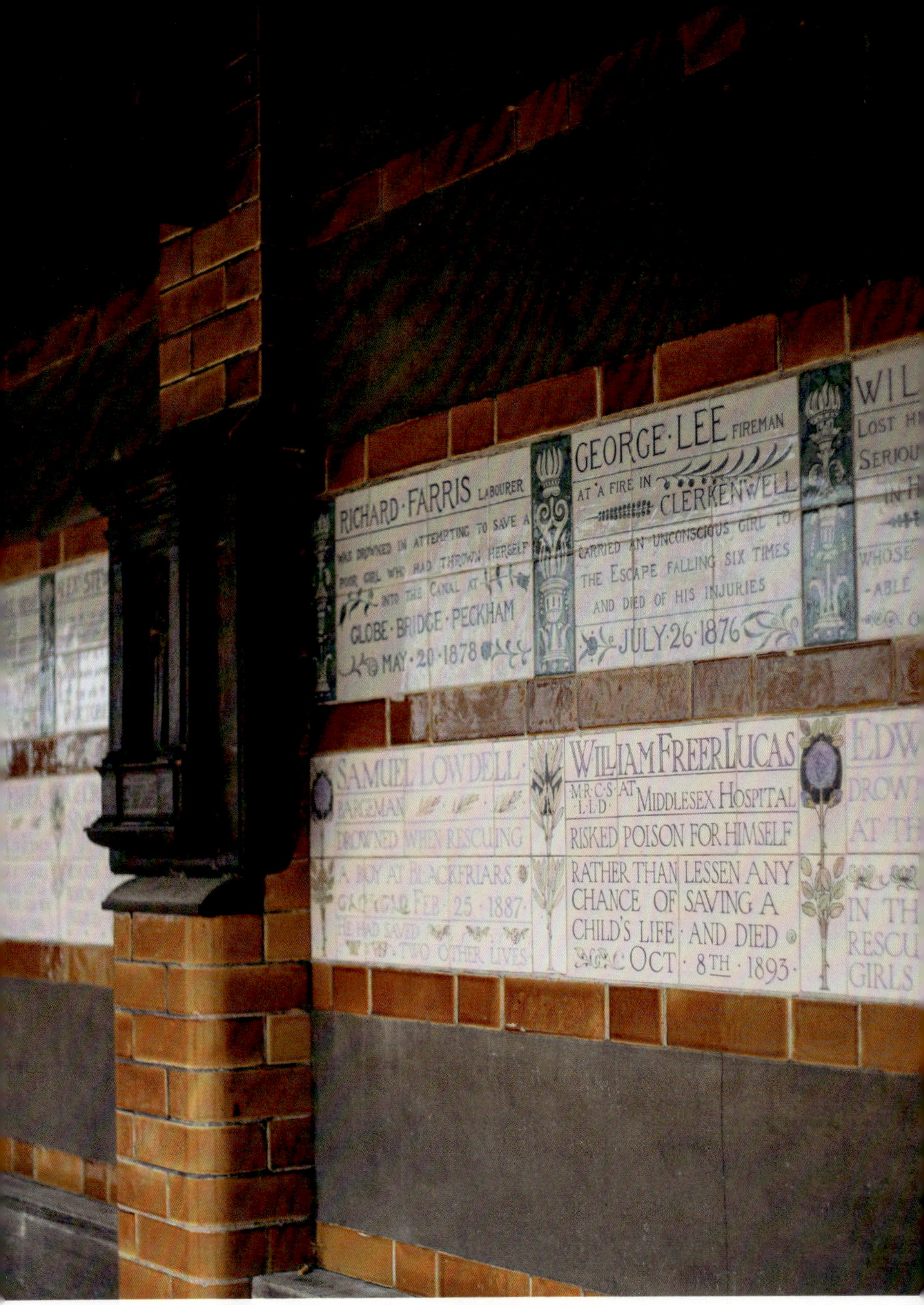

Address King Edward Street, London EC1A 7BT, +44 (0)207 374 4127, www.cityoflondon.gov.uk | **Getting there** Underground to St Paul's (Central Line) | **Hours** Daily 8am–7pm or dusk, whichever is earlier | **Tip** Admire the interior of St Botolph-without-Aldgate, which is also inside this little park.

79 Racing Against Time

The unstoppable art of the Elizabeth Line

Whether of a philosophical bent or not, every traveller on London's vast and ever-further-sprawling Underground network reflects, day in, day out, upon the nature of Time: will I catch it? Will I be late? When will the next one arrive? And, as it happens, Time's never ending and forever headlong race into the future matches perfectly the life-long preoccupations of an English artist called Darren Almond. The number of times that his work has featured multiple clock faces is almost uncountable.

And so, the appearance of three new abstract works by Almond at the Davies Street entrance of the new Western Ticket Hall of Bond Street station to serve the newly opened Elizabeth Line looks like a good and timely decision. The first of the three you encounter is arguably the most eye catching. You see it facing you on the wall in the form of a great, steely-grey reflective panel showing a grid of numbers and part-numbers that seem to flicker and change even as you stare at them, which is just as you are about to be sucked down and down onto the escalators. This new line is very deep indeed, and requires two long, steeply diving journeys to reach the edge of the tracks.

These numbers, and the way that they jitter and even seem to part-disappear – only the zero (0 is a perfect and unchangeable whole) – matches perfectly that sudden, unstoppable onrush of nerves that travellers always experience when they are pressing ever onward with so many others who are equally feverish. Between the two escalators, you pause for breath on level ground, and Almond's other works become visible. One of them faces you on the wall as you prepare to descend again. Another is above your head as you rise again to street level: From Under the Glacier, it reads. A descent to such depths is also a plumbing of geological time, is its timely reminder.

Address Bond Street Underground, Oxford Street, London W1R 1FE | Getting there Underground to Bond Street (Central and Elizabeth Lines), Western Ticket Hall, Davies Street | Hours Variable (check at station) | Tip Browse the fashionable clothes shops of South Molton Street, where William Blake once lived.

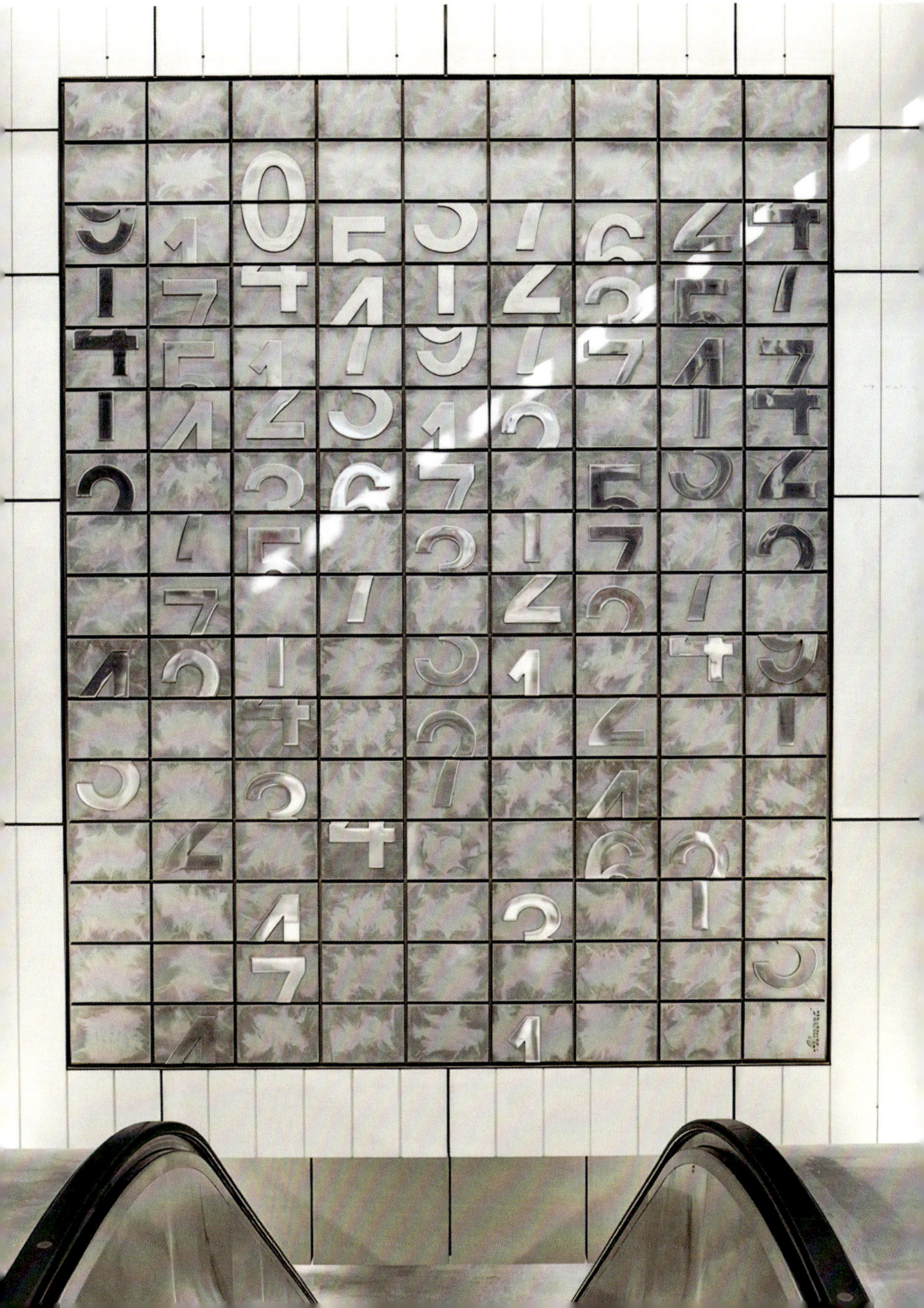

80 The Rarest of Vermeers…

A Dutch masterpiece in its north London home

Johannes Vermeer (d. 1675) is one of the greatest artists of the past. But his known output is very small: just 34 paintings by him are known to exist. How many of these are on regular public display in London? Two, of which one is in the National Gallery. The other one is hidden away in Kenwood House, which abuts Hampstead Heath in north London. This house, built in the 18th century, was once the country home of the first Earl of Mansfield, and its art collection is magnificent – the Vermeer lives in the dining room alongside a great, late self-portrait by Rembrandt, one of the finest portraits ever painted by Frans Hals, and a towering Van Eyck above the fireplace.

Last year, there was a great show of 27 Vermeers at the Rijksmuseum in Amsterdam. The one at Kenwood House was spared the stresses and the strains of travel – it was said to be too fragile to be moved. What is more, it is the only Vermeer in existence that is still on its original stretcher.

Like many another Vermeer, it is an intimate, domestic scene that focuses all its attention on one sitter, a young woman, who is playing the guitar. As with other females by Vermeer, this girl is just a touch coquettish, although not exaggeratedly so. Vermeer is too subtle for that. But as she leans over her instrument, we also register the fact that she is looking askance at someone else, whose presence we cannot see, and her smile suggests that it might just be a suitor. We will never know. She is interrupted in her playing, but her glance, and the colour of her cheeks, suggest that she is also being *playful* – they are positively hectic. Otherwise, she is boxed into a small room, within a thoroughly bourgeois setting; these were paintings made for the homes of prosperous merchants, not for aristocrats or kings. The great Dutch Republic, newly emancipated from Spain, was on the rise.

Address Kenwood House, Hampstead Lane, London NW3 7JR, +44 (0)370 333 1181, www.english-heritage.org.uk | **Getting there** Underground to Golders Green or Archway (both on Northern Line), then bus 210 | **Hours** Daily 10am–5pm (grounds open longer) | **Tip** Explore the sprawling wonders of Hampstead Heath just outside the door.

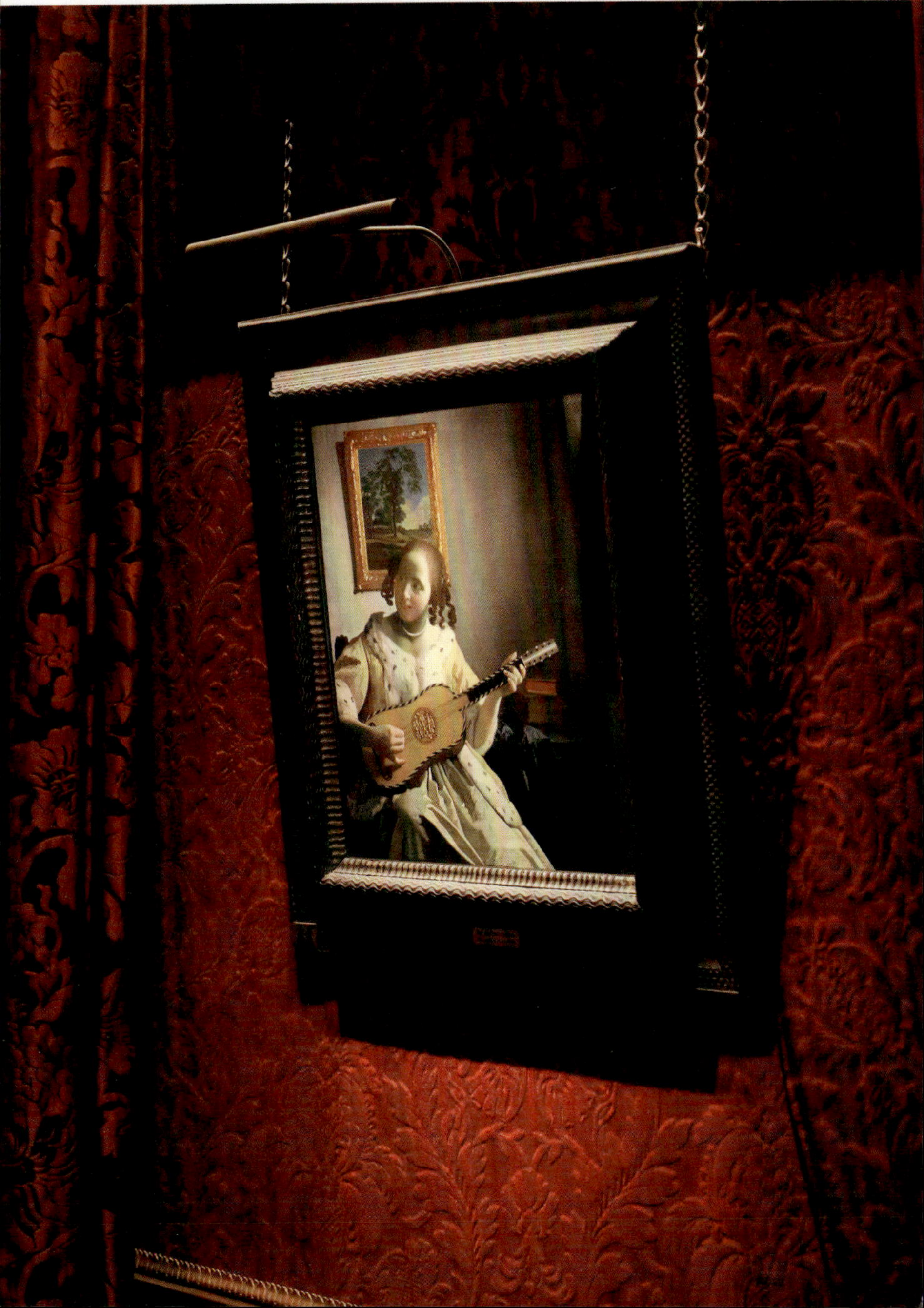

81 Rodin's Sculptural Gesture

How war prompted a great gift

It is amongst the greatest gifts ever made by a sculptor to a major museum, but you may struggle to find it. What is more, there is no announcement that it is here at all until you happen upon it, almost by chance. And, stranger still, it is by chance that it is here anyway.

We are talking about the gift of a large group of sculptures that Auguste Rodin made to the Victoria and Albert Museum in London in 1914. They had been on display at an exhibition of modern French art in the Grosvenor Gallery, staged in the capital in July of that year, when war broke out, and they were trapped by the sudden flare-up of conflict. They could not be returned. They were stranded. What to do with them? Rodin made a gift of them to the nation, in perpetuity.

But where exactly to find them? If you enter by the main doors on the Cromwell Road, you will have to thread your way right back through the shop, and then take a few steps down to the long, narrow sculpture court that overlooks the museum's inner garden. No sign of works by Auguste Rodin here though, not immediately. What you do see is a long line of marble portrait busts on plinths facing each other across the corridor, many from the 18th century. All of them are interesting, a few are great. There is wall-mounted sculpture too. In order to find Rodin's great bequest, you have to turn left and walk in the direction of the Exhibition Road entrance. And there you will at last find them, with the bronze of Rodin's *John the Baptist* imploring your attention in the centre of the corridor. Yes, the rather dull rhythm of the corridor has been broken at last. Statues of differing sizes are now commanding the ground. And there are smaller works in cabinets against the wall to marvel at too, some tiny.

Why did Rodin behave with such generosity? Because when his native country of France was unsure of him, England embraced him as a master.

Address Victoria and Albert Museum, Cromwell Road, London SW7 2RL, +44 (0)207 942 2000, www.vam.ac.uk | Getting there Underground to South Kensington (District, Circle and Piccadilly Lines), then a five-minute walk | Hours Sat–Thu 10am–5.45 pm, Fri 10am–10pm | Tip Enjoy the lavish décor (and good food) of the V & A café.

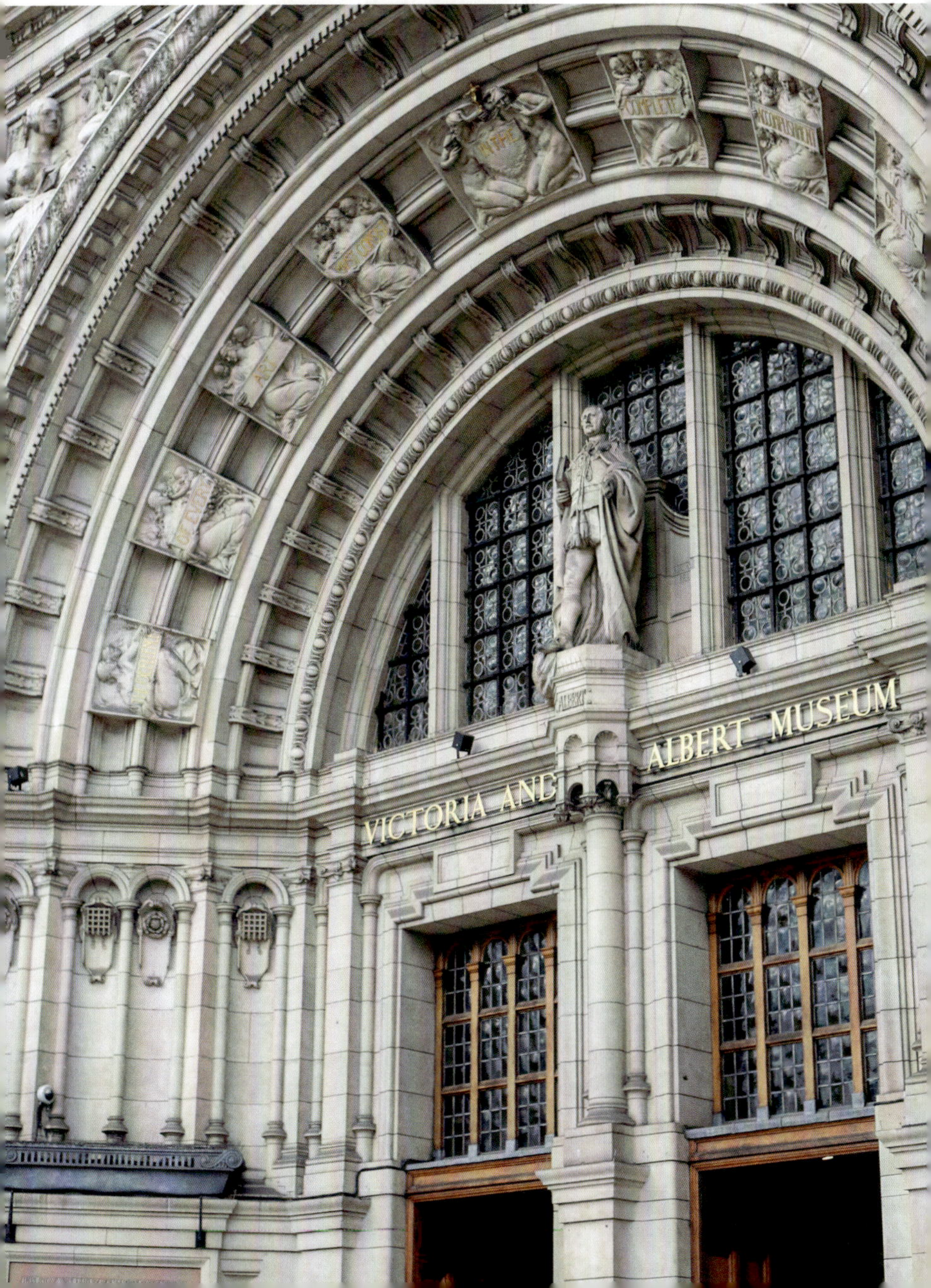

82_St George Rides High

The eccentricities of a church-builder

That innovative 18th-century churchbuilder Nicholas Hawksmoor often opted for obelisks rather than spires. Something, often, of rather fattish proportions, rather than the wistful, heaven-aspiring slenderness of the spire. In the case of the church of St George's, Bloomsbury, he pushed the idea of the extravagantly muscular obelisk to its limits, to such an extent that Walpole, the prime minister of the day, speaking in Parliament so that the whole world of informed male opinion might hear and take heed, condemned his experiment, in thunderous terms, as a species of recklessness, if not insanity.

And even now, Hawksmoor's stepped obelisk, which you can easily spot soaring high into the sky directly above Chang's Noodle Bar, at the point where New Oxford Street meets Coptic Street, is an eccentric wonder. For it is not only the obelisk itself that Hawksmoor has treated so extravagantly. It is also the structures at its base that appear to be supporting it, the pedimented façades of four classical temples, one on each side, complete with columns, as if it were desirable, and even necessary, to set off the figure of England's patron saint at the pinnacle of not one building but five, albeit four are miniaturised versions of themselves.

But the real surprise is what happens above that drumroll of preparation. To the sides of the obelisk itself, one at each corner, a unicorn and a lion are clinging for dear life.

Each one is the size of a mature horse. Neither one is looking up in wonder at the figure of St George himself. The unicorn, with his twisty gilded horn, stares out into space. The lion is awkwardly face-down, and appears to be wrestling with an invisible antagonist. Will he fall?

The obelisk is topped by a decorated urn on which stands the saint, showing off his fine pair of powerful knees. The whole ingenious display is a comic wonder.

Address Bloomsbury Way, London WC1A 2SA, +44 (0)207 242 1979, www.stgeorgesbloomsbury.org.uk | **Getting there** Underground to Tottenham Court Road (Central, Elizabeth and Northern Lines), then a five-minute walk | **Hours** Accessible 24 hours | **Tip** The Monmouth Coffee Company, a five-minute walk away, sells the best whole bean and ground coffee in London.

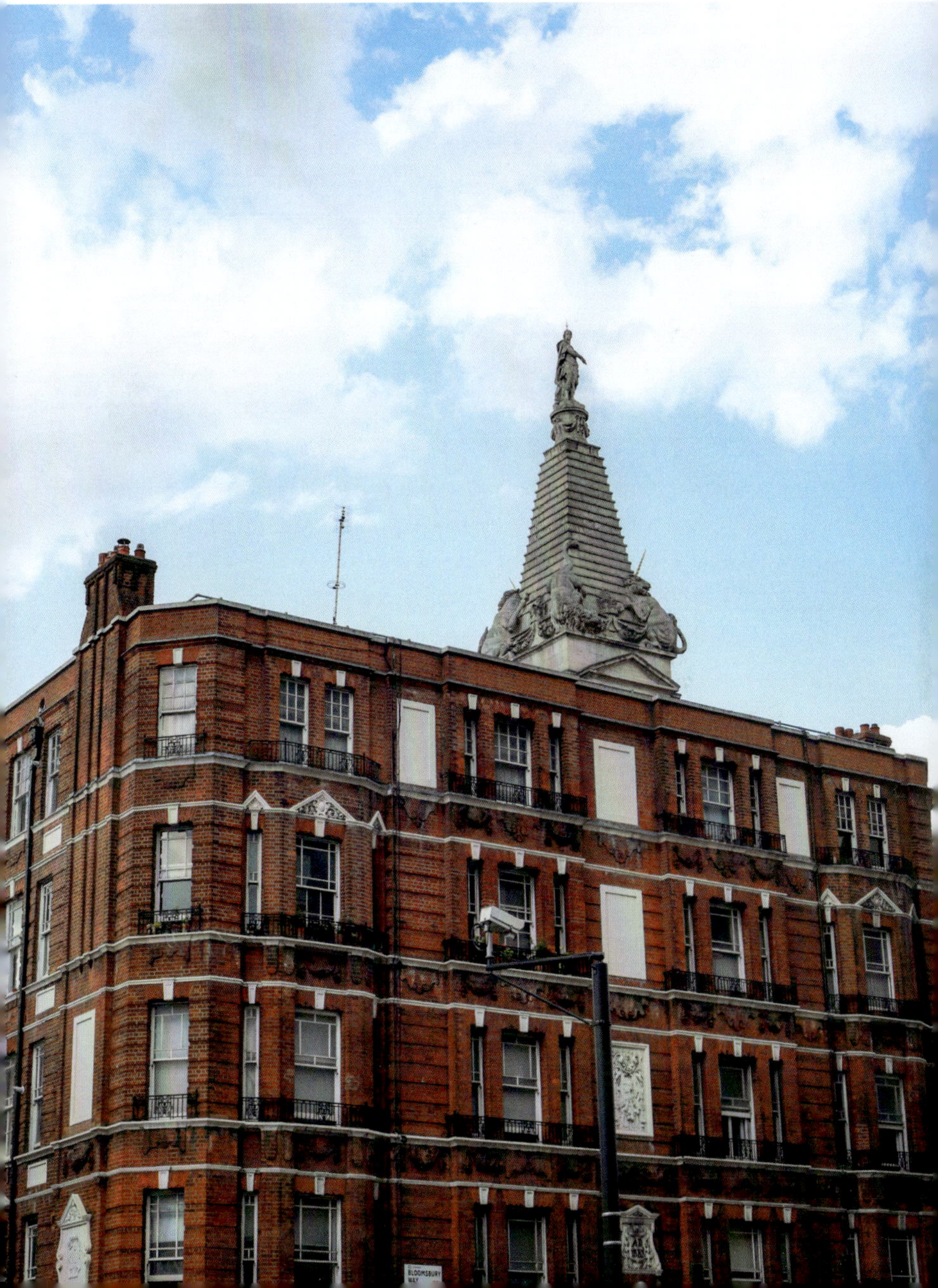

83 St Odilia

She who attends to our ocular needs

The street feels, as you walk up it from Northumberland Avenue to the Strand, to be amongst the least visited in central London, so quiet and set apart it seems – and this in spite of the fact that Craven Street is just around the corner from Charing Cross Station, and one minute's walk from Trafalgar Square at its top end. What is more, as you pass its long terrace of wonderful 18th-century houses, you notice how many famous people have lived here, from the polymath and American Founding Father Benjamin Franklin to Herman Melville, American author of *Moby-Dick*, or the great German poet Heinrich Heine.

Right at the top of the street on the right, you will find one of London's most precious small museums. It lives in fairly straitened circumstances in the basement, and it is called The British Optical Association Museum. It first opened to the public in 1915, the year after World War I broke out.

What a teeming wealth of objects is on display in these small rooms, from eye glasses of the most intriguingly primitive kind to a series of fine portraits, including one of Sir Joshua Reynolds, founder of the Royal Academy, in his own pair of fashionably handsome eye glasses. But the object that is most arresting to our own eyes is a small statue of a saint on her own little decorated wooden bracket. This is St Odilia, who carries her own giant eyes, at chest height, on a Bible. Before there were health-care professionals to attend to our ocular needs, who would you pray to for relief from suffering? A sympathetic saint of course. St Odilia was amongst the chosen few – another was St Lucia, who transported *her* eyes on a plate. This statue, middle-European in origin, and magnificently gilded, possibly dates from the 15th century, and is the jewel of the collection. She looks towards us with befitting concern, pity and humility.

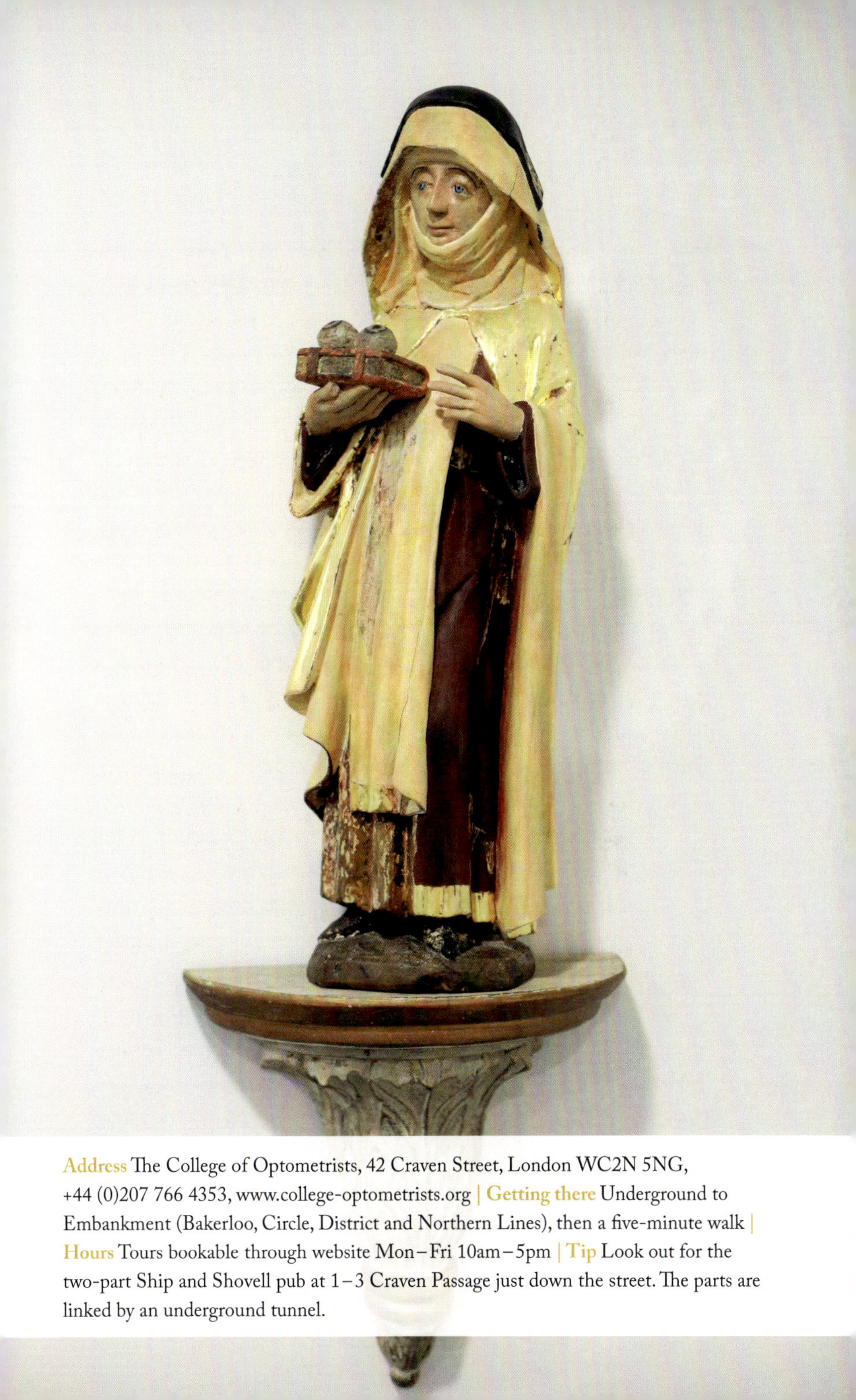

Address The College of Optometrists, 42 Craven Street, London WC2N 5NG, +44 (0)207 766 4353, www.college-optometrists.org | Getting there Underground to Embankment (Bakerloo, Circle, District and Northern Lines), then a five-minute walk | Hours Tours bookable through website Mon–Fri 10am–5pm | Tip Look out for the two-part Ship and Shovell pub at 1–3 Craven Passage just down the street. The parts are linked by an underground tunnel.

84 Sayer's Sanctum

At home with the collection

Take a modest Victorian terraced house in Islington, north London, and then fill every inch of it with art – paintings, prints, drawings, sculptures, photographs, ceramics, antiquities, tribal art – until the very walls almost groan and buckle beneath the sheer visual stimulation of it all. That is the exciting challenge that a man of relatively modest means called Tim Sayer, formerly a writer of the BBC Radio News, has eagerly risen to over the past half century.

Sayer's passion for collecting began early. First it was Dinky Toys and books, and then, at the tender age of 17 (1962) he spotted a tatty portfolio of prints in a junk shop in Richmond and was offered them for a song. Ten bob (in the old currency), if you really must know. That created an intolerable itch to collect and collect and collect, which has never left him. Not that he has ever had much money. He always only had almost just enough – to buy on the instalment plan for the most part, and most decent, fair-minded dealers were happy to oblige.

Now his three-storey house of nine rooms, a hallway, a staircase complete with generous wall space and, oh yes, a loft, is full of everything that pleases him. In the downstairs kitchen, there are walls that face each other, hung with paintings and prints. One wall is for the abstract, the others for the figurative works. Mostly. He plucks a small one down. 'By Max Bill,' he says. 'Tectonic Plates' is the description, though not exactly the title. Yes, its two intersecting shapes do look rather like the way those tectonic plates shift, far beneath the world's feet. We flit about, taking it all in. Henry Moore. Picasso. Hockney. Bert Irvin. Prunella Clough. David Nash. It is all a very personal passion, whatever gripped him at particular moments in an ongoing quest – he has always been a rapid decision maker. And aided, always, by his wife, Annemarie Norton.

Address In a quiet street just off Highbury Fields | Getting there Underground to Highbury and Islington (Victoria Line) or Overground, then a 10-minute walk | Hours Feb, Apr, June, Aug, Oct & Dec Sat 2–5pm, groups of up to 12 welcome; to book your visit, write to: tjtsayer@yahoo.com | Tip Nearby Upper Street has got it all – pub theatres, cafés, restaurants and bars exist alongside an unrivalled assortment of independent shops.

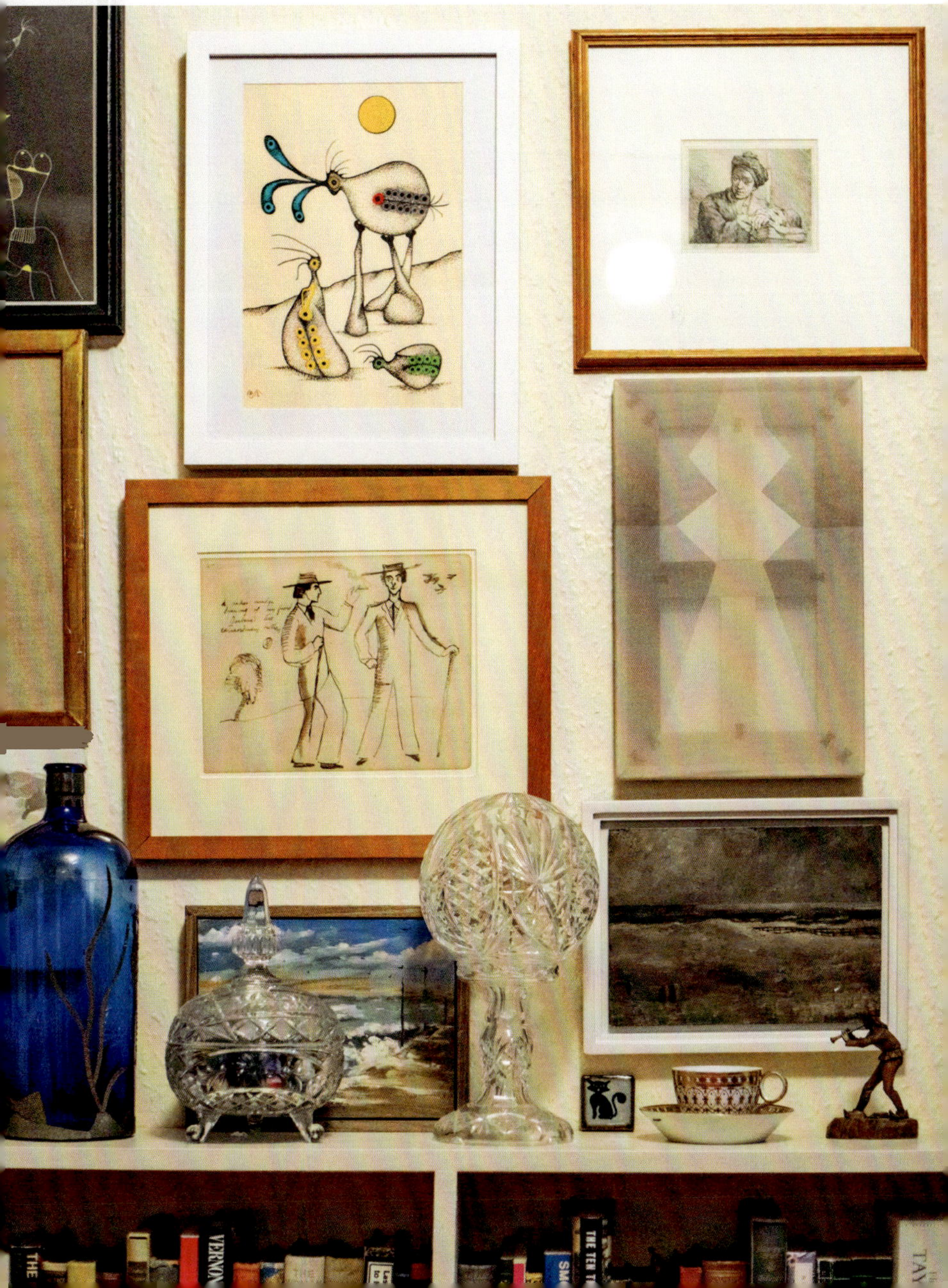

85 The Sea Wallower

A strange tribute to Sir Edwin Lutyens

Between Jermyn Street (where the toffs buy their expensive suits, silver cufflinks and straw boaters) and Pall Mall, on a gentle downward slope towards the Thames, is London's clubland in the heart of the West End.

Much of this nexus of fine buildings and private squares, all within the City of Westminster, was created in the latter part of the 17th century under the inspiration of Henry Jermyn, Earl of St Albans, a diplomat who also happened to be a favourite of Queen Henrietta Maria, wife of King Charles I, that Stuart king who lost his head in 1649. Henry Jermyn was called 'Founder of the West End'. A plaque at the bottom of Duke of York Street marks the site of the house where he was born. Further up that same street – St James' Church is at the top of it – and very easily missed if you are toiling up it on its fairly steep incline, and find yourself visually seduced by the beauty of Wren's magnificent church, there is a small and easily missable and abrupt turn off to the right, sweetly misnamed Appletree Yard.

Perhaps apple trees once flourished here. No longer. Turn into the yard and look at the building to your right, and at the long commemorative text set into a low wall in front it. That text informs us that it was in a building on this site that the great architect Sir Edwin Lutyens, creator not only of New Delhi, but also of many great country houses back in his homeland, once worked as an architect. There is more than the inscription to look at though. Raised up on a wall to the right of that long and handsomely carved inscription there is a mysterious low-relief sculpture, in stone, set within a recessed panel, of a naked human form that looks as if it is both part disappearing into and part emerging from the sea. Its legs taper to a point. Face featureless, its arms are stumps. It is called *Figure Emerging*, and was made by Stephen Cox, RA.

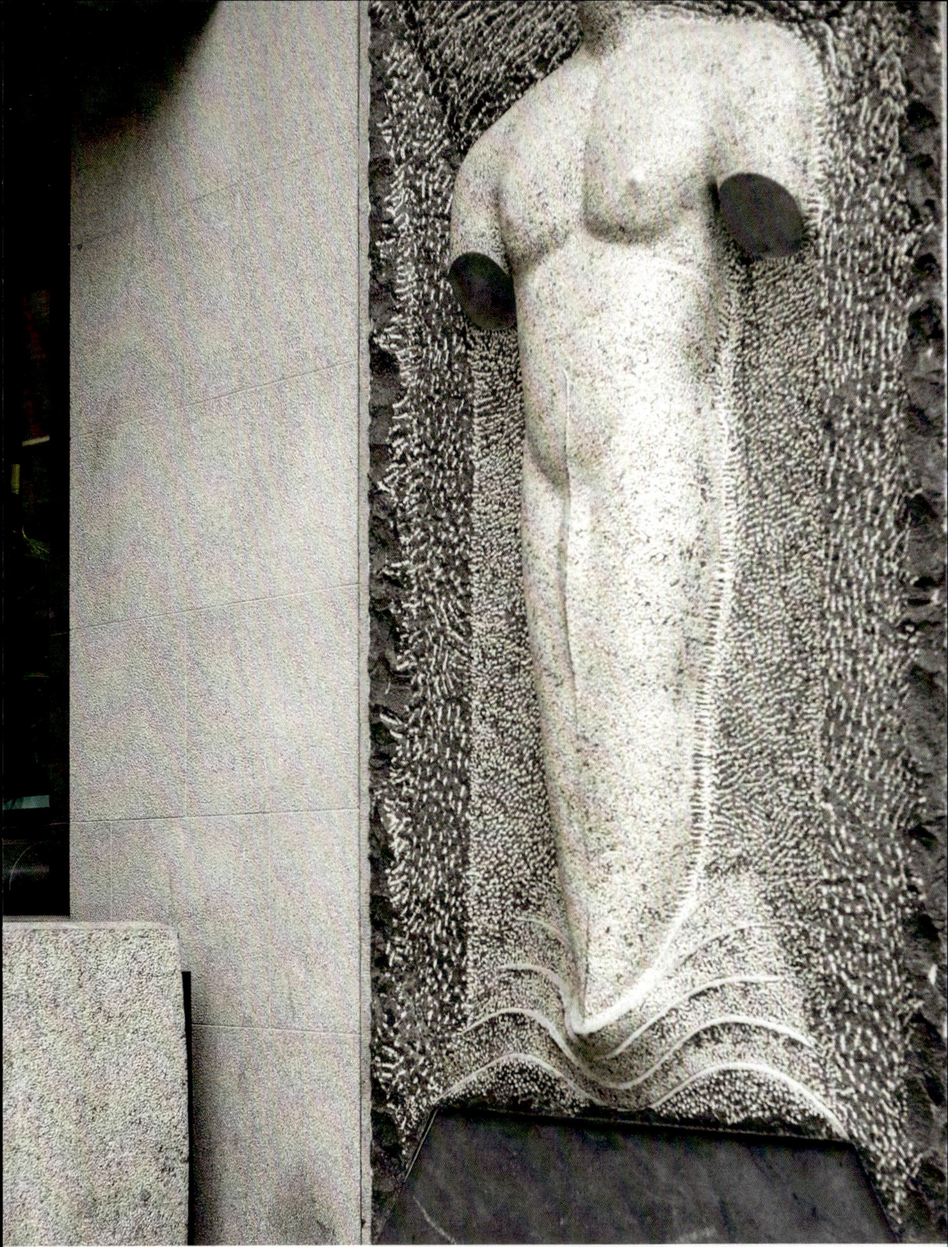

Address Apple Tree Yard, Duke of York's Street, London SW1 6AE, www.lutyenstrust.org.uk | Getting there Underground to Piccadilly Circus (Piccadilly Line), then a six-minute walk | Hours Accessible 24 hours | Tip Have a pint in the tiny Red Lion, 2 Duke of York Street, former gin palace and one of London's finest Victorian pubs.

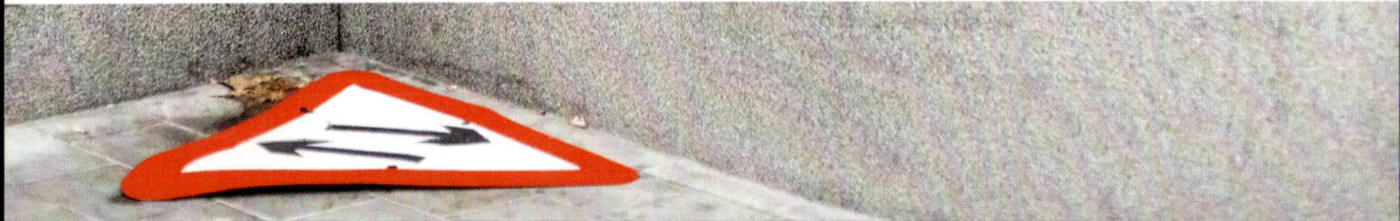

86 The Seasons in Mosaic

Where the shepherdesses once gambolled

An unexpected break in the terrace of handsome Georgian houses – between nos. 135 and 137 Shepherdess Walk, to be precise – finds you staring down a flight of steep stone steps, and into the opening of a very dark, damp and narrow passageway. There's a sign in mosaic above its entrance, which thankfully gives the slightly fearful hope of a good outcome: *To the Mosaics*, it reads. Roman or what?

Having passed through that narrow chill, you emerge, after a steep climb once again, into the sequestered corner of a small and delightful public park named after the street itself. In order to find those promised mosaics, you turn sharply to the right, and double back on yourself. Here they are, in a sun-splashed corner, three large panels grafted onto red-brick walls, with others underfoot: two large, square mosaic carpets of the kind you might find in any Roman villa.

Except that these mosaics are not 2,000 years old. They were created by mosaicist Tessa Hunkin and the local people of the Borough of Hackney in 2012, as a celebration of this particular locale in north London, a delightful, broad-brush look at its history – what it was then; what it is now. On stone posts you read a list of the many makers – this was a collaborative, community effort. Two of the wall panels take for their themes the four seasons, mingling past and present with carefree ease: birds of the air flit about; beasts of the field leap and romp; and a solitary swimmer, in goggles, wearing a bikini, frolics about in the local lido. On the far wall, the name Shepherdess Walk is celebrated, and what that name harks back to: the presence here, once, of shepherdesses herding sheep through fields. And underfoot, on those ceramic carpets, we admire stylised local flora, all interweaving and intermeshing. The names of flowers, as you murmur them over, are so transporting: traveller's joy, pimpernel…

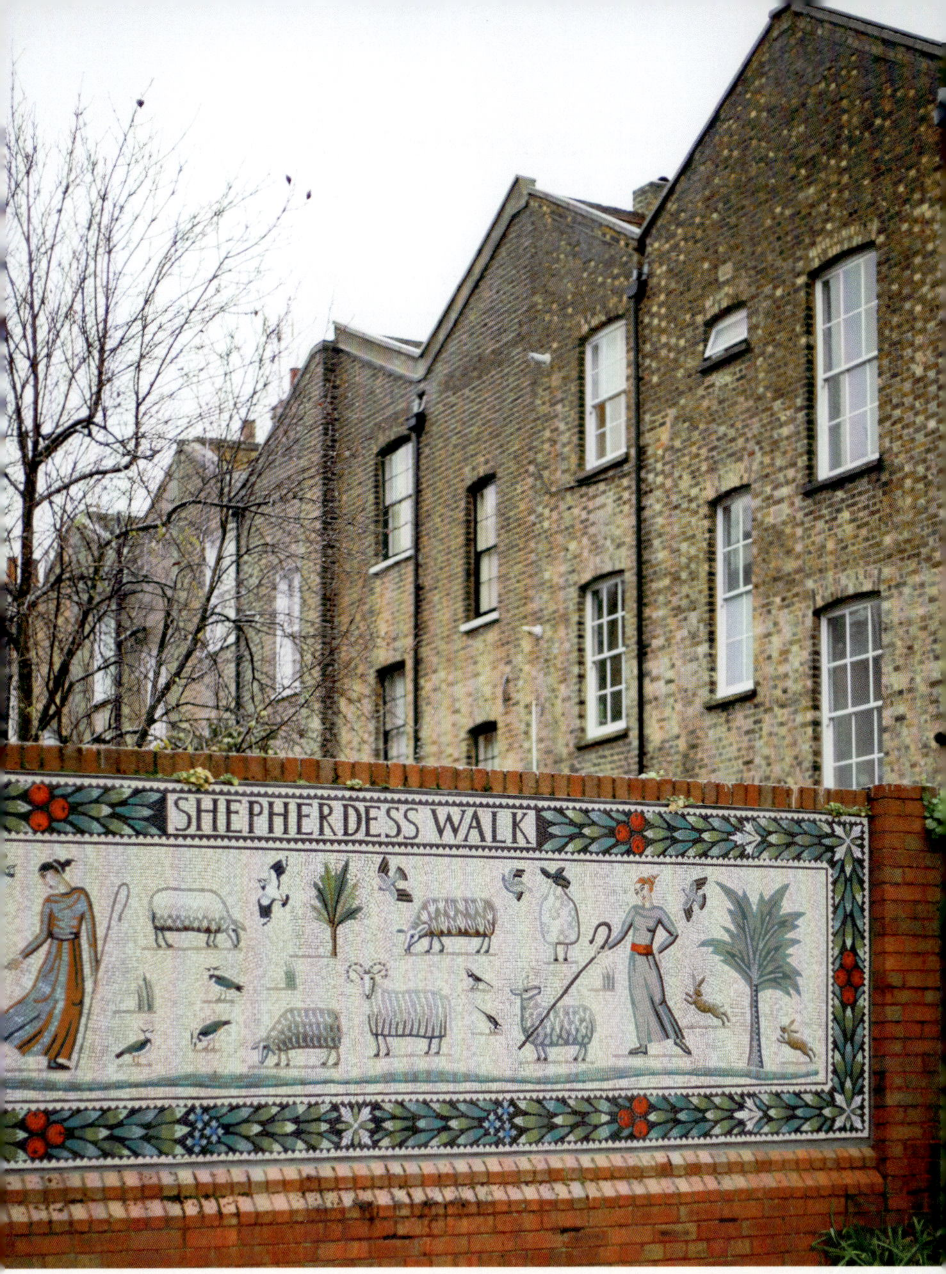

Address Between 135–137 Shepherdess Walk, London N1 7QA, www.livinglondonhistory.com | Getting there Underground to Old Street (Northern Line), then a 10-minute walk | Hours Accessible 24 hours (when gates closed, enter by park to your left) | Tip Go for a drink at The Eagle. Once known as the Grecian music hall, local workers would 'pop' (pawn) their 'weasels' (tools) to raise the price of a drink, which inspired the children's nursery rhyme 'Pop Goes the Weasel'.

87 Sekhmet, the Lion-Goddess

Sotheby's ancient Egyptian mascot

What's happening in New Bond Street today? A fresh spring wind is stirring the banners outside Dior and Jimmy Choo. Burberry's flagship store is getting a facelift. The orange blinds are down outside Louis Vuitton to protect the rich from the morning sun. Meanwhile, over at Sotheby's, London's oldest auction house (it opened its doors in this beautiful Georgian town house in 1742), the black statue of an ancient Egyptian lion-goddess called Sekhmet (she dates from the 18th dynasty or 1320 B.C., which means that Tutankhamun could have paid her reverence) is sitting regally over the main entrance, just behind the flagpole, as she has done for over 100 years.

The security guard who is hovering just beneath him invites me in to sample Japanese and Korean antiquities, but I tell him I'm more interested in how this bit of ancient Egypt above our heads got to be here. A collector bought it at the end of the 19th century, he tells me, but he never collected it, so it was eventually put on display above the main entrance as the company's mascot. Another story tells us that it was an unsold lot that just hung around. Does this mean that Sekhmet is the oldest sculpture on public view in London? Probably. An older one has never come forward to challenge her claim at least.

Sekhmet sits on a narrow white plinth at the apex of the door frame, clocking all the visitors, this gleaming, snub-nosed goddess, with her stylised mane, and the smooth, stubby remains of human arms. The breasts are well defined too. Her name is picked out in a regal gold. Her eyes are heavy-lidded. She looks serenely inscrutable.

The Sotheby's banner, which juts out from the end of its flagpole at a magnificently provocative angle directly in front of her, gold lettering against a royal blue ground, wipes the lion goddess' broad snout from time to time. She doesn't even blink. She's seen it all.

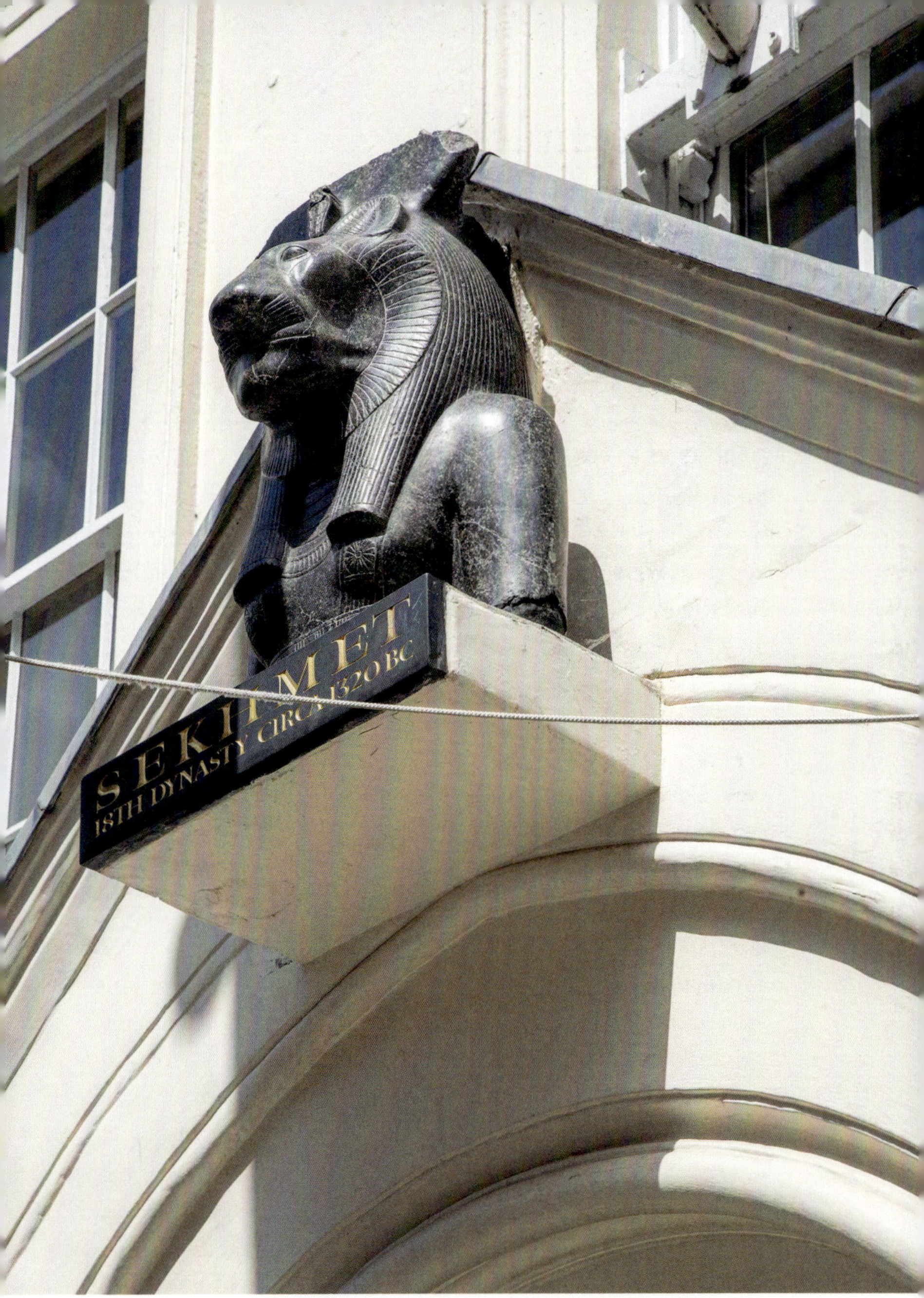

Address 34–35 New Bond Street, London W1A 2AA, +44 (0)207 293 5000, www.southebys.com | Getting there Underground to Bond Street (Central and Elizabeth Lines), then a five-minute walk | Hours Accessible 24 hours | Tip Go and see an exhibition at Annely Juda Fine Art, a contemporary art gallery at 23 Dering Street.

88_Single Form

One eye for the water

Do you perhaps experience some sense of *déjà vu* when you see this monumental abstract sculpture by Dame Barbara Hepworth? It lives just off a tree-embowered avenue, beside a small lake populated by teals, ducks, swans, moorhens, Canada geese – and even the odd heron – on the south side of Battersea Park, which fits in snugly beside the Thames, directly across from the swank of Chelsea. The park itself is a humanly fabricated landscape that was created from swampland in the 19th century, so it is full of delightful moments of unexpectedness – little dells, avenues, hillsides. So much variousness. And this lake too, which you can sit beside. Seldom can a lake have been supplied with quite so many comfortable wooden benches on which to take one's ease.

Why that sense of *déjà vu* though? Because this sculpture (fabricated in 1964), sited in this sequestered spot in a riverside park in south London, has an identical sibling in New York, in a much more prominent place: beside the UN building. In New York, fountains play nearby. A little plaque at ground level will give you the reason for its placement in New York too. It is dedicated to Dag Hammarskjöld, the second Secretary-General of the UN. Hepworth was a friend of Hammarskjöld's. They were both idealists, people who believed that art could heal and elevate and inspire – in short, have a positive influence upon human lives. Hammarskjöld's own life ended in tragedy when he died in a plane crash. This sculpture is a tribute to him. It is an irregularly shaped disc, pierced by a single hole, and it rings when you tap it.

Standing upright to attention on a low, grassy mound, it looks a little like a cross between a shell and a shield. Greeny-grey in colour, its surface is pitted, scored, as if by inscrutable hieroglyphics. The side facing the water bulges out, thickens. It also looks lighter and more lustrous.

Address Battersea Park, London SW11 | **Getting there** Underground to Battersea Park (Northern Line), then an eight-minute walk | **Hours** Accessible 24 hours | **Tip** Visit the Promontory, a landscaped garden created to enhance the riverside views from both sides of the Thames.

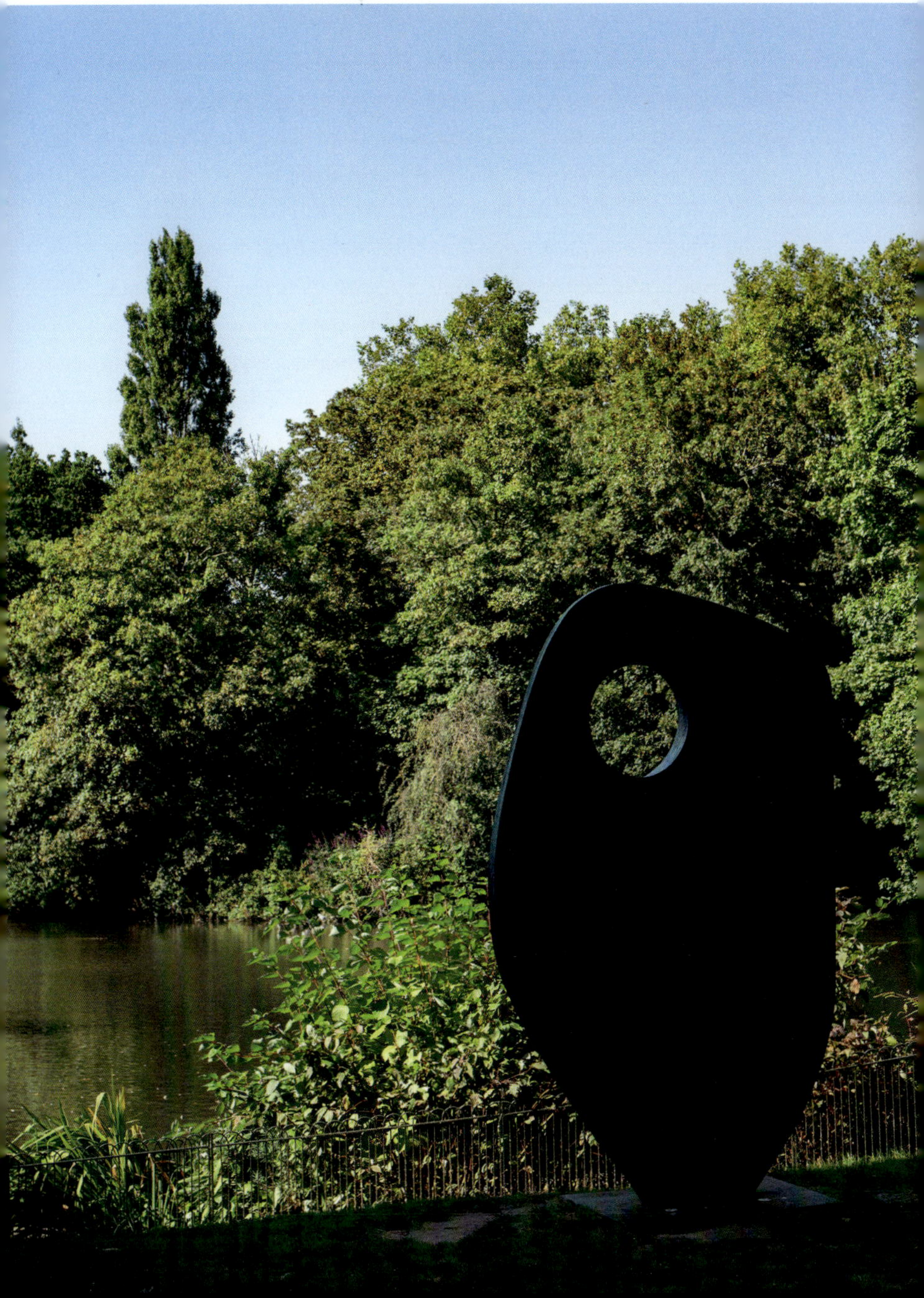

89 Sir John Soane's House

Antiquities from every angle

Visiting the Sir John Soane Museum is not so much an encounter with an institution, as an act of eavesdropping upon one of the most extraordinarily art-and-object-cluttered private residences of the 18th century that you are likely to encounter.

Soane was a great architect: the Bank of England was his work (now demolished), as was the Dulwich Picture Gallery (still surviving), which was the very first public building of its kind in England. He was also a pedagogue, who wished to show off to his students some of the finest examples of the art of ancient Rome and ancient Egypt that he could possibly muster. So he had casts of antiquities made (of hands, feet, portrait busts, death masks and much else), many of them fragmentary, and they are everywhere.

The house itself is a warren of rooms large, medium and small, corridors, and niche-like spaces, many of them quite dark, which only adds to our sense of surprise and discovery when we turn the very next corner. We weave in and out, back and forth, upstairs and down, as if the house is a three-dimensional game of snakes and ladders. One of the most enticing spaces of all is the Picture Gallery, which we see approaching us from the other end of a dark corridor.

Facing us as we enter is one of the prizes of Soane's collection, a painting by the prolific Venetian painter Antonio Canal (better known as Canaletto). It is a view, made at a high vantage point, of the Riva degli Schiavoni, and it was painted in 1734–35, 60 years before the Republic was to lose its independence to the forces of Napoleon. Soane bought it 10 years after its fall. In this painting, which is much larger than many others by Canaletto, we see both the daily bustle of a working port, and evidence that the city is now mainly a pleasure garden for the idling rich, who take evening walks dressed in all their finery, to see and to be seen.

Address 13 Lincoln's Inn Fields, London WC2A 3BP, +44 (0)207 405 2107, www.soane.org | Getting there Underground to Holborn (Central and Piccadilly Lines), then a five-minute walk | Hours Wed–Sun 10am–5pm | Tip Take a picnic into Lincoln's Inn Fields, London's largest public square, directly opposite the house. For the more energetic, there are several public-access tennis courts.

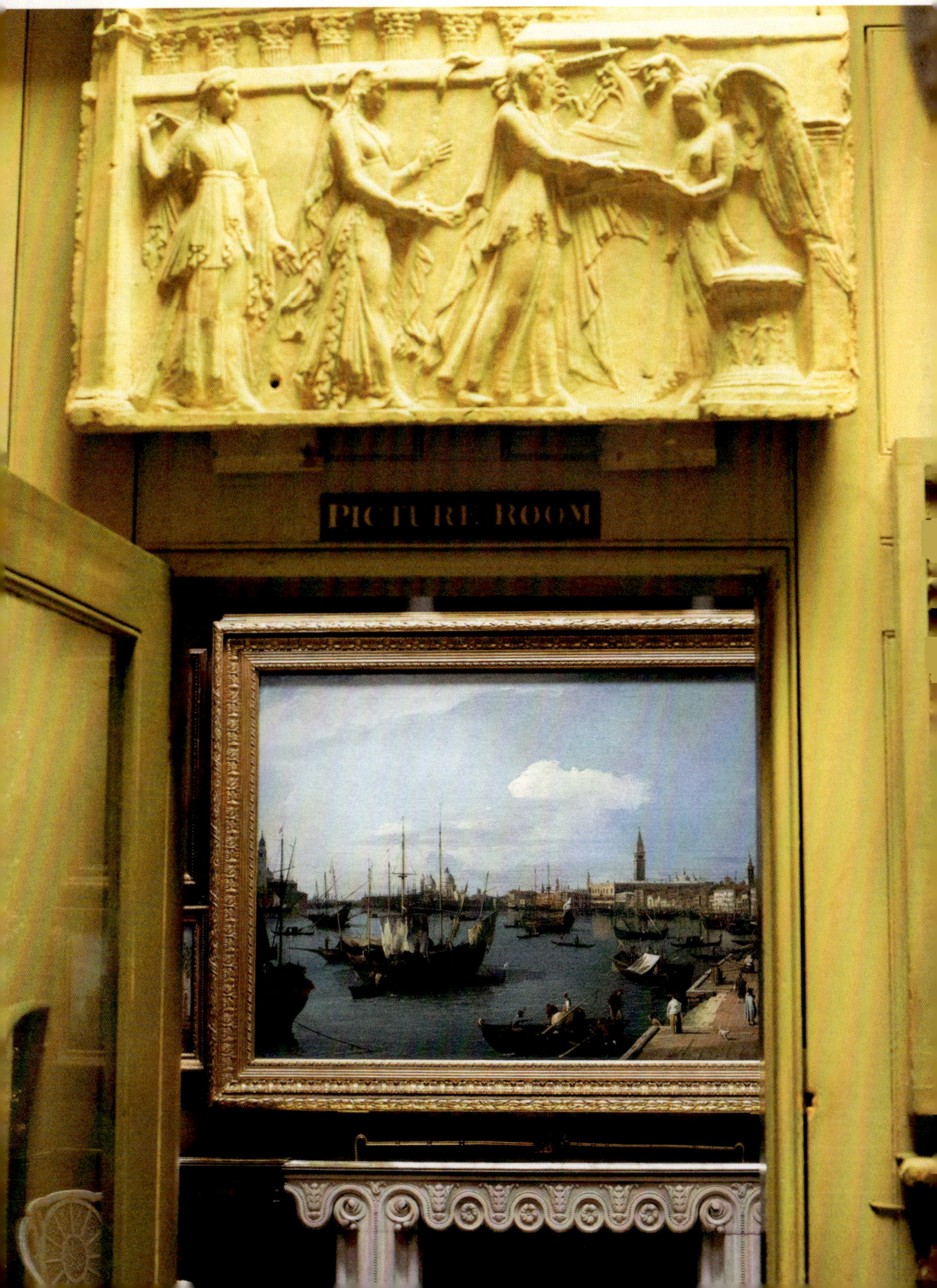

90 Sir Richard's Tent-Tomb

The great Victorian explorer remembered

Deep in the heart of somnolent Mortlake in south London, just five minutes' walk from a stretch of the Thames made famous for its hosting of the annual Oxford-Cambridge boat race, there is one of the most bizarre and delightful memorials to the dead ever created by the hand of a woman. Her name was Lady Isabel Burton. This is the stone tomb commissioned by her in the shape of a Bedouin tent to house the body of her husband, Sir Francis Richard Burton, Victorian explorer of the source of the Nile, linguist, diplomat and translator of *The Arabian Nights*, who died in Trieste in 1890. She outlived him by six years.

The Bedouin tent-tomb lives in the cemetery of St Mary Magdalen Roman Catholic Church, set close to a tall brick wall beyond which you can see a street of Victorian cottages. Seagulls mew in the air. The voices of excitable young children rise from the nearby Montessori nursery school. A sculpture of our crucified lord, willingly taking upon himself the sins of the world, flings out its arms on the nearby tomb of Emily Paynter. The tent-tomb itself, an appropriately dusty looking dunnish grey in colour, looks like fabric rippled by a North African wind. Moss grows across its roof. Suspended across its façade there is an open stone book, which records his name and hers, and beneath that a piece of free-flowing stone faux fabric reminding us that the tomb was paid for by public subscription.

The tomb looks closed, impregnable. It was not always so. At the back of the tomb there is a very strong metal ladder that can be climbed up as far as a window of plain glass. Peer in, and you will see that the tomb is filled with objects – the sepulchre, hanging lamps, a swag of metal bells, an image of the Virgin, a crucifixion scene. This was once a window of Victorian stained glass, but sadly it was vandalised in the 1970s. Money is being raised to replace it.

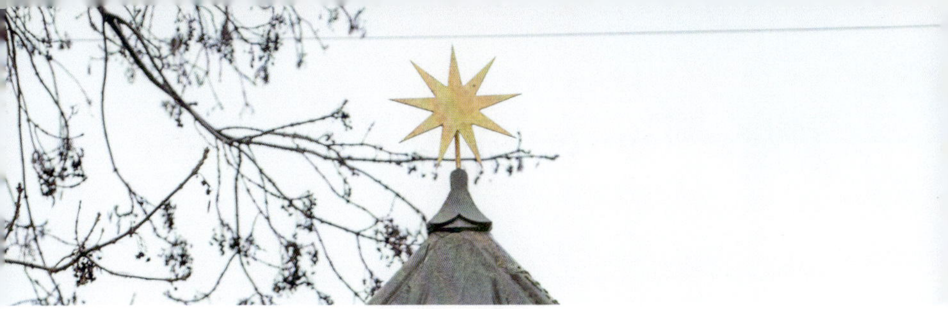

Address 61 North Worple Way, London SW14 8PR, +44 (0)208 761 3265 | Getting there Train to Mortlake, then a 10-minute walk | Hours Cemetery open 9am–3pm, but advisable to check with the church first | Tip As you leave the cemetery, look out for a blue notice above a circular hole in the wall. This is part of the Barnes Hedgehog Highway.

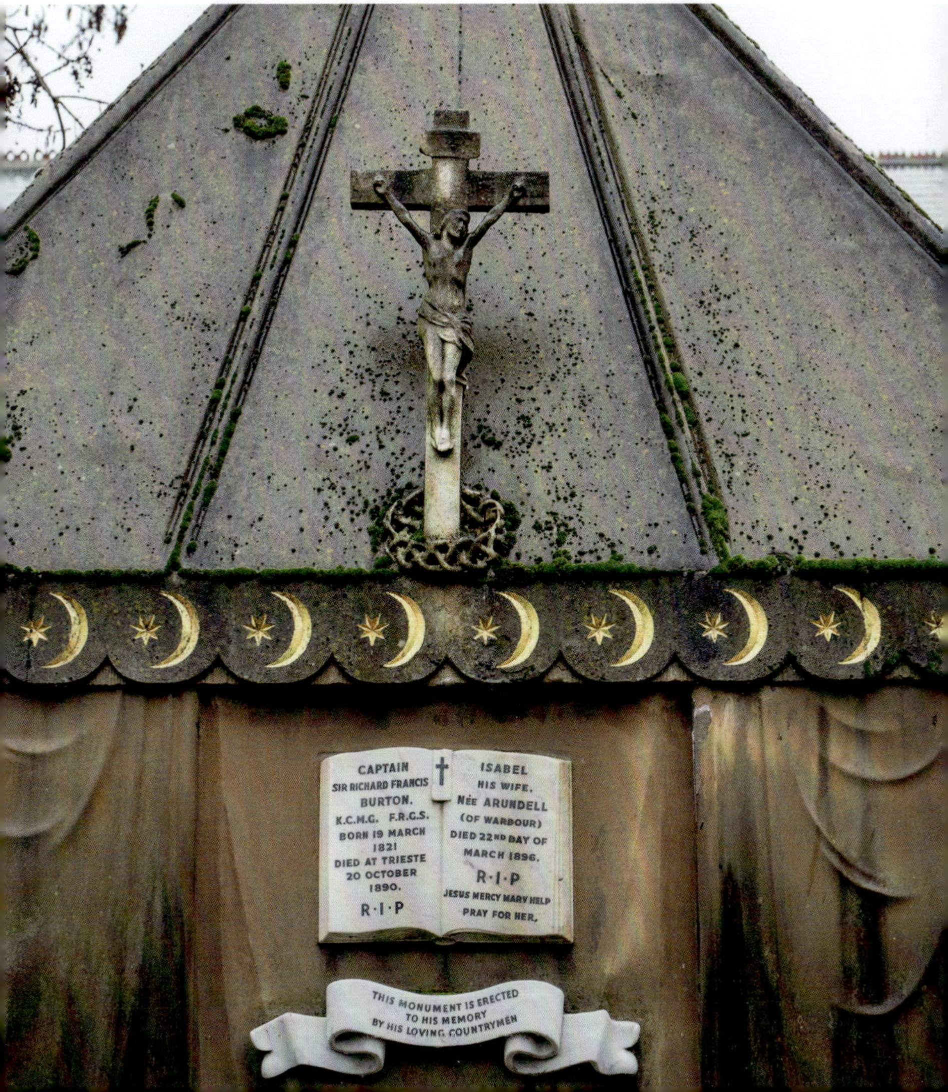

91 The Spanish Volunteers

No pasarán!

Jubilee Gardens on the south bank of the Thames, once the site of 1951's Festival of Britain, and overshadowed these days by the ever-slow-wheeling London Eye, plays host to a magnificent adventure playground for children and, just yards away, a remarkable memorial to those members of the International Brigade, all volunteers, who fought against Fascism during the Spanish Civil War of 1936–39. Of the 2,100 men and women who volunteered to fight side by side with the republicans of Spain, 526 were killed.

Ian Walters' bronze sculpture, which was unveiled in 1985 in the presence of Michael Foot, the then leader of the Labour Party, thrusts itself up into the air from a black granite base. It shows a single, semi-abstracted, helmet-headed human form out of which other figures seem to be emerging in an organic, plant-like fashion. The torso of the figure, which is kneeling, lunges forward alarmingly, stretching its head back as it goes, so that the body bows back and upwards, yearningly.

Arms seem to reach around and catch it, cradling it, as its head rises, so that the whole group appears to be arrested in a kind of intricately balletic rocking motion. They all cleave together as one. All the other faces are blank and featureless. One arm is raised in a tense fist of defiance. Another sweeps back and over, palm pushing up towards the sky, as if protecting the group from certain harm. The whole ensemble seems to amount to a gesture of defiance mixed with a wail of lamentation.

This is war, and the pity and the tragedy of war. From time to time, flocks of local pigeons gust by, like some overflight of aircraft, as if adding their own snatch of commentary to the occasion. County Hall, once the seat of a democratically elected London government, and now reduced to the lesser status of a luxury hotel, is at the memorial's back.

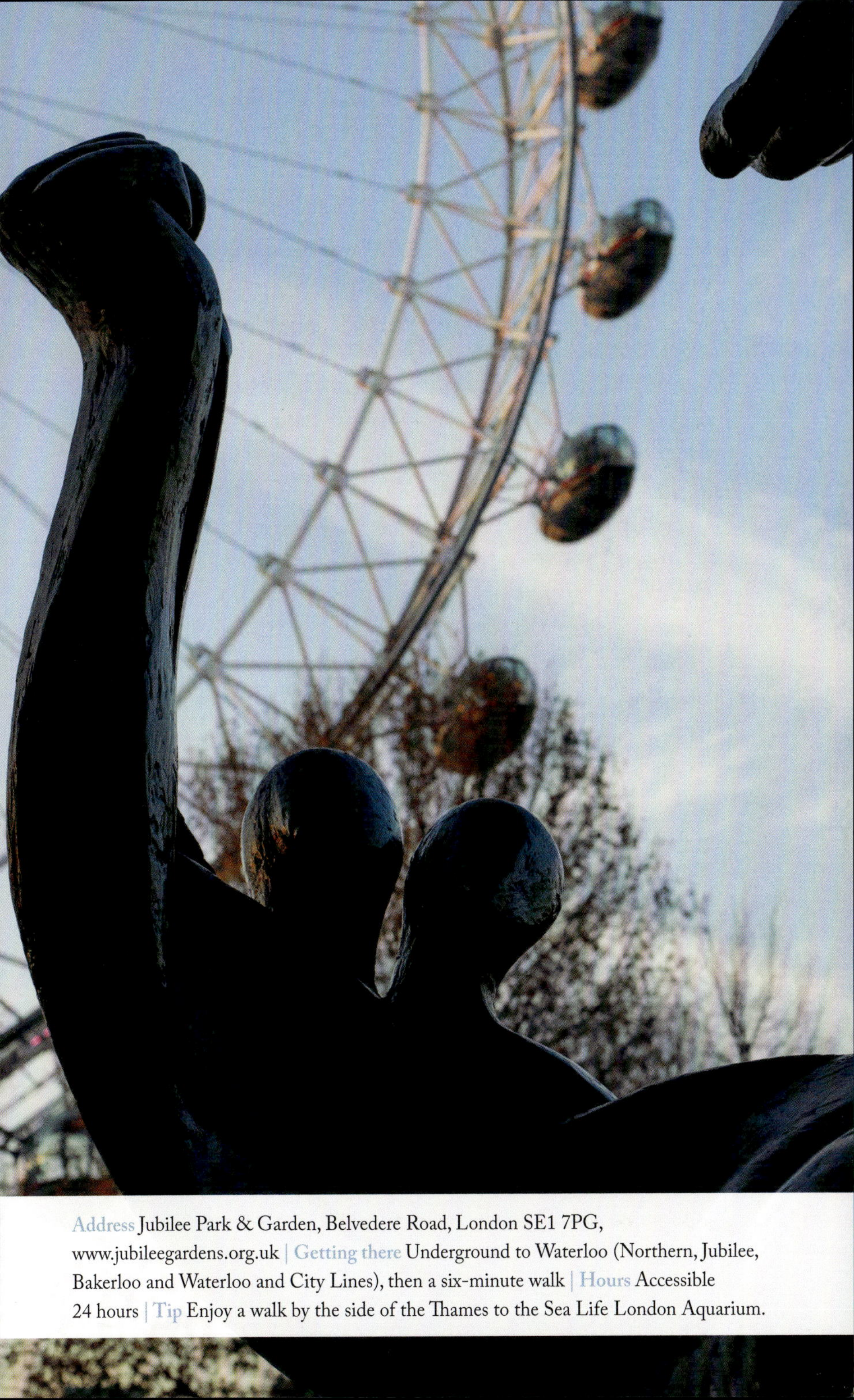

Address Jubilee Park & Garden, Belvedere Road, London SE1 7PG, www.jubileegardens.org.uk | Getting there Underground to Waterloo (Northern, Jubilee, Bakerloo and Waterloo and City Lines), then a six-minute walk | Hours Accessible 24 hours | Tip Enjoy a walk by the side of the Thames to the Sea Life London Aquarium.

92 The Spencer Family

A most theatrical send off

How does a great family memorialise itself? In the past, the devout have often chosen to pay their way to immortality by creating great and extravagant monuments in churches. Some of the finest of these are in the medieval church of St Helen's, Bishopsgate, a sequestered spot with its own green surround, set back at a pleasing angle to Bishopsgate itself, one of the busiest of the great and noisy arterial roads that push through the City of London, and then onto fashionable Shoreditch and all points north.

Here, the monuments crowd the walls, far too many to count. The greatest of them, which is in praise of the overwhelming importance of the Spencer family, looks like a great theatre set, which is divided into two distinct halves. The upper half sets off a coat of arms to indicate the nobility of the dead, a skull flanked by a pair of gilded wings, topped by an hour glass to indicate how quickly life has drained away. It is almost as if this upper half of the monument sits on display on a mantelpiece.

The lavish memorial at ground level, an arched tabernacle that is protected by iron railings, takes in an entire scene. It is as if you are staring down from the balcony onto a stage set, complete with players. It feels surprisingly intimate too, as if you are privy to a scene set in a private residence.

Here, to the left, you admire a devout, kneeling woman vested all in red, who prays, her hands raised in prayer, for the souls of the dead before a small altar. Behind her lie the dead who are being remembered by the living – fully stretched out. What is unusual is that it looks as if they are resting not on a slab of stone, but on a bed because what they lie on seems of be rucked, as would have happened if this were indeed a bedchamber. Their hands are also raised in prayer. The male Spencer is in full armour, as if ready to spring up into action.

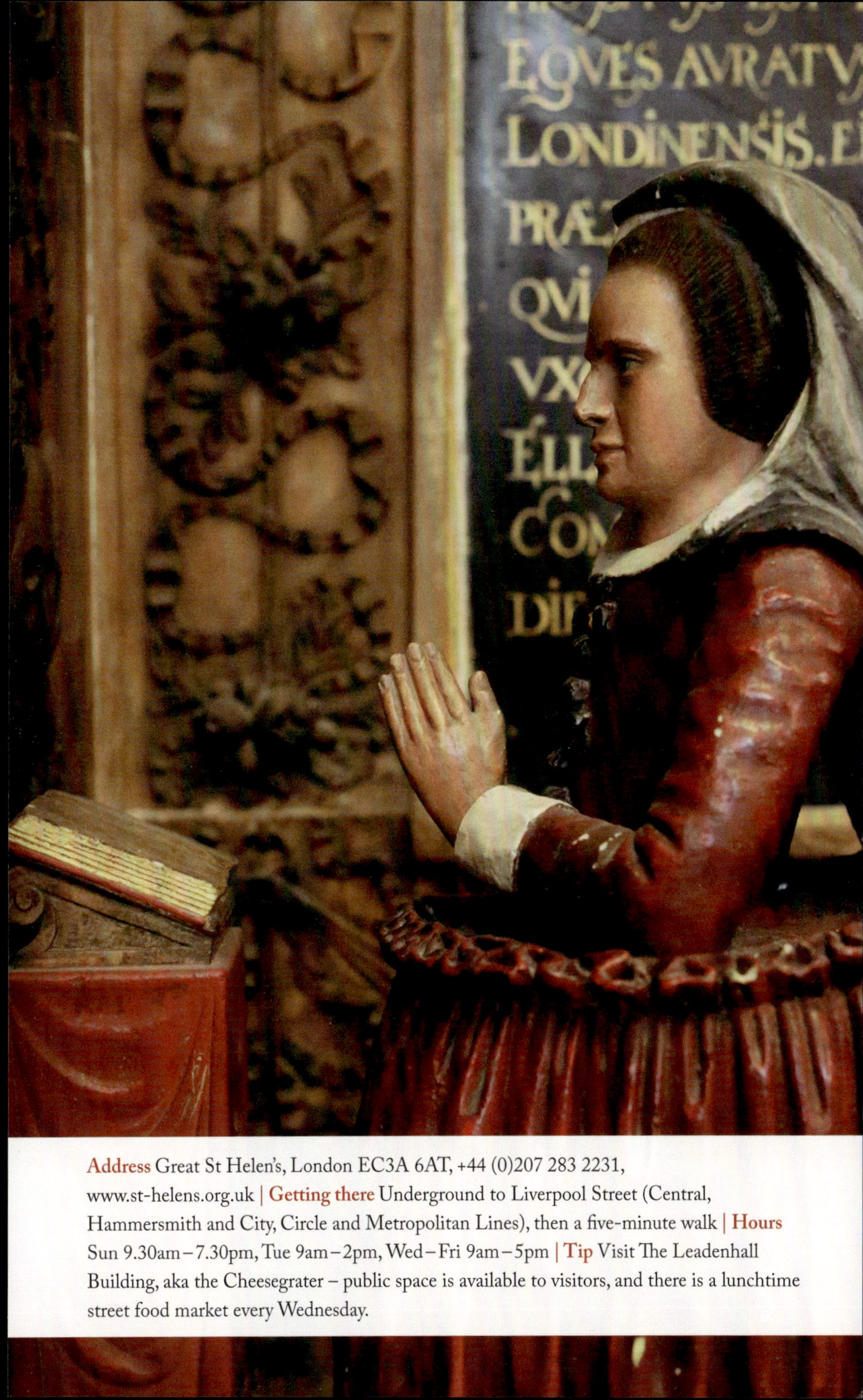

Address Great St Helen's, London EC3A 6AT, +44 (0)207 283 2231, www.st-helens.org.uk | **Getting there** Underground to Liverpool Street (Central, Hammersmith and City, Circle and Metropolitan Lines), then a five-minute walk | **Hours** Sun 9.30am–7.30pm, Tue 9am–2pm, Wed–Fri 9am–5pm | **Tip** Visit The Leadenhall Building, aka the Cheesegrater – public space is available to visitors, and there is a lunchtime street food market every Wednesday.

93 Square the Block

Kingsway's forever falling corner

Where do we go in London to find some rough visual equivalent of an elegantly broad, 19th-century Parisian boulevard? Try Kingsway, which sweeps down in a single, arrow-straight line from Holborn until you reach the long curve of the Aldwych, with Bush House, long time the headquarters of the BBC World Service, at its southern end. And it's in Kingsway, at the point where Sardinia Street feeds in from the left, that you will find a work of art by a man who has often given buildings extraordinarily violent makeovers.

Richard Wilson likes to crush things and then pull them back into their original shape – something as handily biddable as an aeroplane, for example. His most celebrated early work, *20:50*, a mesmerising pond of oil onto which you are perhaps being beckoned to venture at your peril, was once on permanent display at the Saatchi Gallery in Chelsea.

Most of all, he likes to pretend to do violence to built structures, and so it is here in Kingsway, at the junction with Sardinia Street, where he has done something alarming with the corner of the LSE's New Academic Building. The building's smooth elegance has been ripped to shreds. It is as if, at this corner, the entire structure is in the throes of exploding outwards, unmaking itself in a kind of gesture of defiance of the fact that it was ever made in the first place. Could this be a symbol for the headlong unruliness of the creative impulse? Blocks of stone are falling, cascading, spewing forwards, huge and rugged, dusty and untidy lumps of the stuff, hefty, and seemingly heavy enough to kill us, should we be injudicious enough to shelter from the rain in their shade. But no, it does not quite happen after all. The shattered corner remains poised, frozen, leaving it mysteriously, if not magically, arrested there in the air, as if it has changed its mind at the very moment that it decided to fall.

Address Corner of Kingsway and Sardinia Street, London WC2B 6LH | Getting there Underground to Holborn (Piccadilly and Central Lines), then a five-minute walk | Hours Accessible 24 hours | Tip Have a drink at the Princess Louise on High Holborn, one of London's most ornate Victorian pubs, 10 minutes from here.

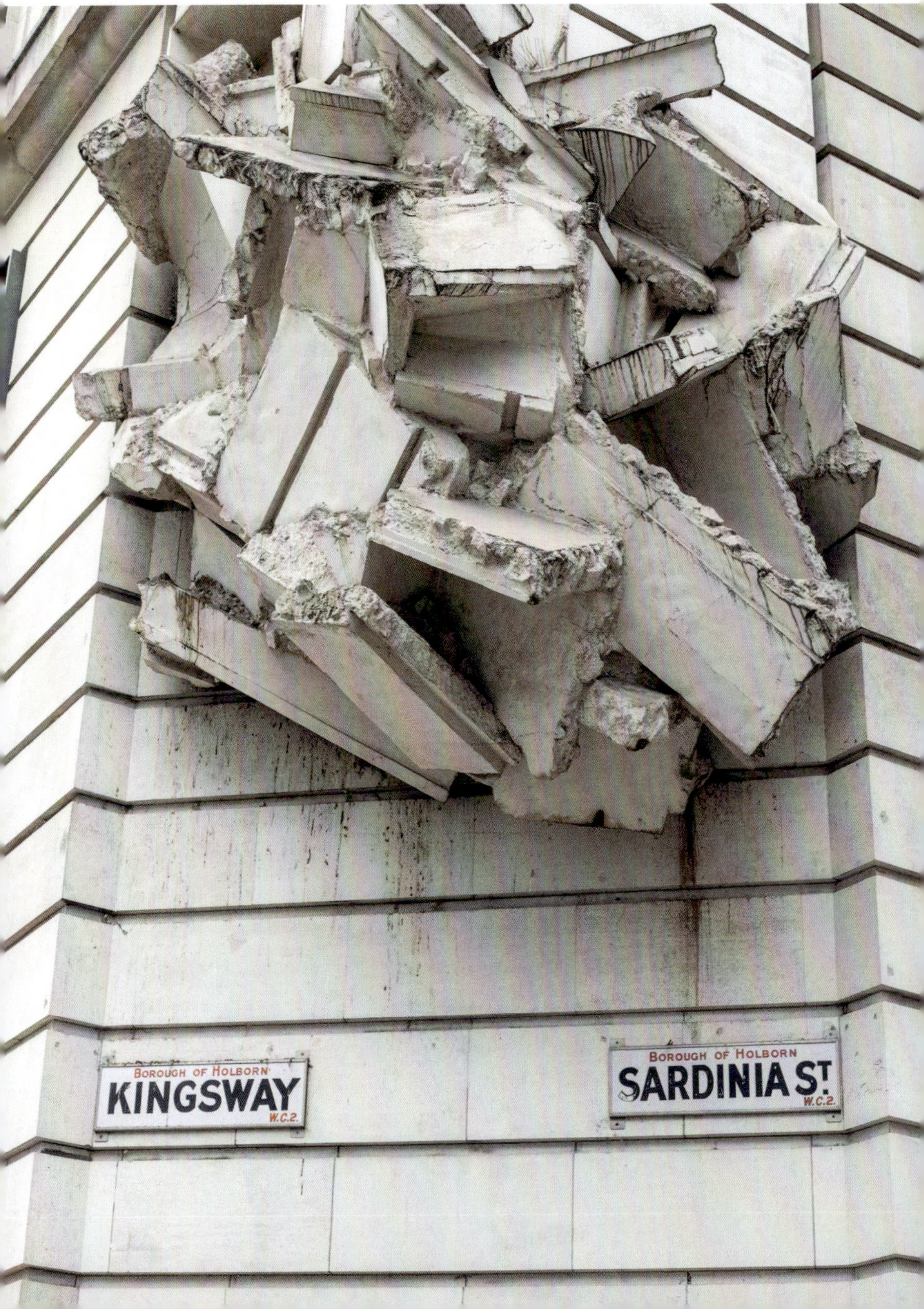

94__St Martin-in-the-Fields

The great church sings out

St Martin-in-the-Fields, at the north-east corner of Trafalgar Square, James Gibbs' masterwork of 1726, is a church of live music-making. In fact, its very walls seem impregnated by the music of the 18th century (Bach, Vivaldi, Albinoni and others), the epoch of the church itself. For all that, its greatest wonder dates from our own times: an East Window created by the Iranian artist Shirazeh Houshiary.

The church itself has a gorgeous opulence about it, from the six chandeliers that process up the nave, almost grazing the heads of the worshippers, to the plaster work of the barrel-vaulted ceiling, the lavish use of gilding and its great ceiling-scraper of an organ at the west end. By contrast, the East Window shocks by its very plainness and subtle simplicity. Here we see colourless glass – the church was badly war-pummelled – contained within a tall arch, criss-crossed by leading. But that leading, at its very centre, is interrupted by an oval shape, slightly fogged, and gently on the cant. It could be a pebble. It could be an almond. It could be a suckable boiled sweetie. It could even be a pearl of great price. That oval, by some miracle of making, has a ripple effect on the leading that surrounds it, pulling it out of shape, warping it, you might say. The effect of such a tiny gesture is extraordinary. We begin to read that oval shape, and the leading upon which it impinges, as the head of a suspended human form, somewhat abstracted, but powerfully present all the same. This is an image of the crucifixion in all but name. And its gentle canting seems to more than hint in the direction of the Man of Sorrows.

This is a very welcoming church, as much a safe haven for the ragged few who may wish to do little other than snore almost inaudibly in a warm back pew, as for those who find themselves in the grip of architectural fervour.

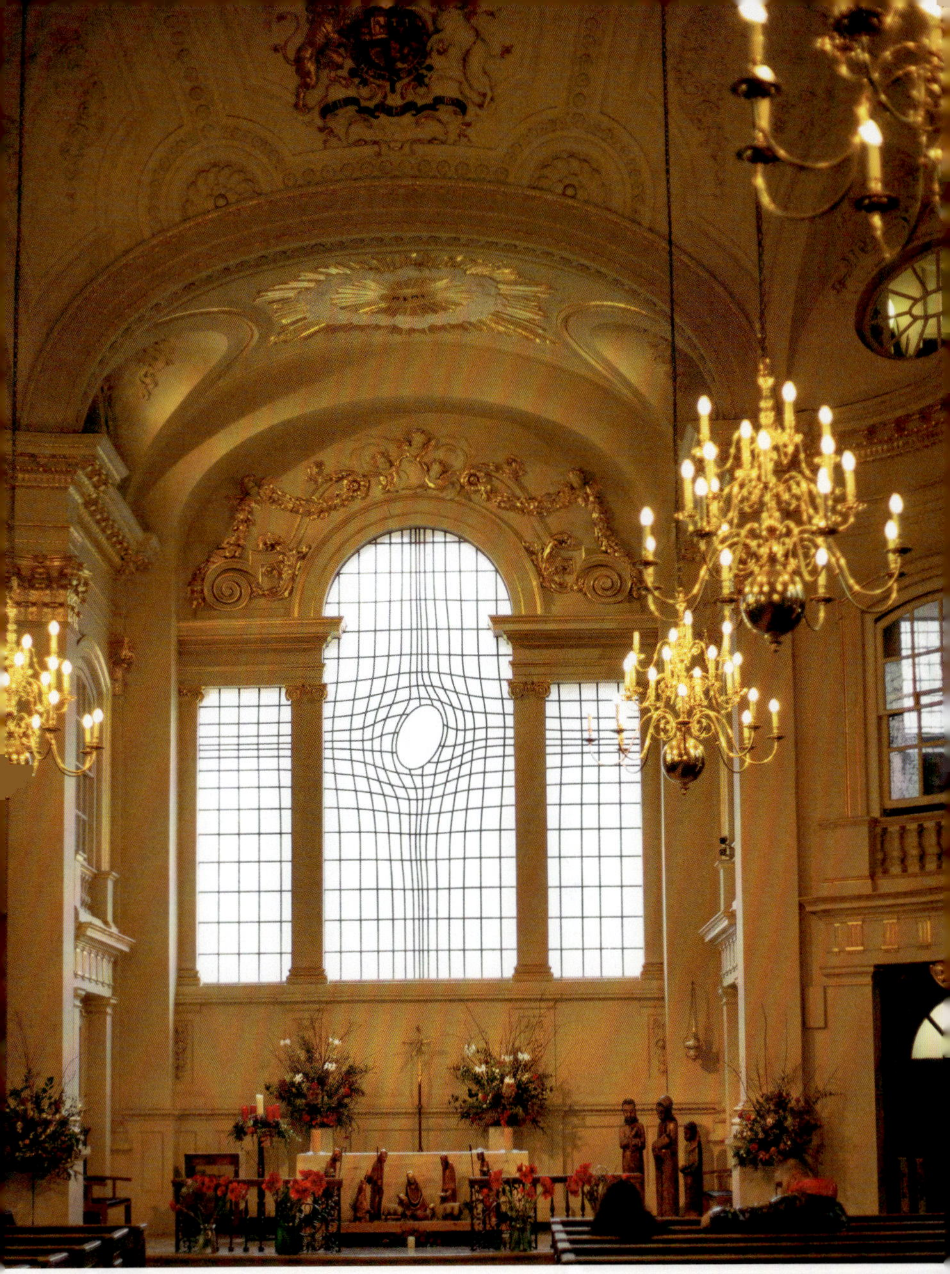

Address Trafalgar Square, London WC2N 4JJ, +44 (0)207 766 1100, www.stmartininthefields.org | Getting there Underground to Charing Cross (Bakerloo and Northern Lines) | Hours Daily 9am–5pm, but see website for extended hours | Tip Try a reasonably priced lunch or coffee in the church crypt, or, during the summer months, the café in the courtyard. Then enjoy one of the outstanding concerts (check website for the full programme).

95_St Stephen, Walbrook

Moore's great stone altar in the midst of it all

After the twin tragedies of the Plague (1665) and the Great Fire (1666), the City of London called on Sir Christopher Wren to rebuild its churches. He created 50 of them, including St Paul's Cathedral. Many think that his masterpiece was the little church of St Stephen, Walbrook. That too suffered terrible damage during World War II, and it was not fully restored until 1979.

The restoration included some remarkable new art by the sculptor Henry Moore and the painter Patrick Heron. Moore was commissioned to create a new High Altar, and Heron to provide colourful painterly patterning for the kneelers – they resemble a sequence of abstract paintings – which surround that altar. Yes, the altar sits at the dead centre of the church, beneath its dome, and beyond it, rippling onwards, row upon row of them, are carved wooden benches, all made on the curve.

St Stephen's is a very pleasingly dramatic church to enter. You climb up to it by a broad flight of steep stone stairs – an inscription on the left-hand wall reminds you (in Latin) that Wren was its fabricator. The fact that it has double glass entrance doors means that you can see into its extraordinarily light-filled interior even before you reach it. It is not divided into nave and side aisles. The whole is a single high, square space, with clusters of soaring columns capped by Corinthian capitals at its corners. There are memorials on the walls, but not a cluttering amount. About the whole interior, there is such a pleasingly airy and light-filled simplicity. The glass is all plain, with no stained glass to darken one's mood. And over it all dominates Moore's high altar, which looks like some great elemental stone that has landed here from on high. It is in the round, and it ripples slightly. It has dimples and recesses, which seem almost to become the shapes of doors and windows, but never quite…

Address 39 Walbrook, London EC4N 8BN, +44 (0)207 626 9000, www.ststephenwalbrook.net | **Getting there** Underground to Bank (Central and Northern Lines) | **Hours** Mon–Fri 10.30am–3.30pm | **Tip** Enjoy a coffee at Fortnum and Mason's café in Wren's Royal Exchange building just over the road.

96 Stepping on Virginia

Quirky mosaics at the National Gallery

When did you last knowingly and brazenly walk across the face of Virginia Woolf? To enjoy that pleasure, you need to hurry over to London's National Gallery in Trafalgar Square. She is at the top of the first flight of stairs you will need to climb if you are allowed to go in by the old, grandly porticoed main entrance directly beneath the dome. If you can't get in that way, you will have to ask someone and then find your way back to it. Yes, that's where you will find Virginia, together with one or two of her pals from the Bloomsbury Group, striking a fairly languid pose, as if comfortably reclining on a *chaise longue*, and holding up her hand in a way that suggests a cigarette might just be dangling from her fingers.

Yes, it really *ought* to be a cigarette, we feel, but it is in fact a quill because she is a most celebrated writer, and she is posing as Clio, the muse of history. And you are treading on her because she is on the floor, as part of a huge mosaic which, in its shape, looks like a carpet.

This is one of several mosaics created in and around this space by an associate of the Bloomsbury Group called Boris Anrep. This one was made in the 1930s. Others were a little later. The mosaic has a name: *The Pleasures of Life*. Bacchus, god of wine and revelry, presides over the scene, and Bacchus himself has the face of Roger Fry, another famous Bloomsbury. Fry introduced a shocked and repulsed English public to the hitherto unknown delights of Post-Impressionism in 1911. You would expect Bacchus to be red-faced and roaringly bibulous, but in fact Fry posed as that dissolute god looks rather solemn. Perhaps that's because the first Post-Impressionist show had not been a raging success with the English public. Another mosaic up the stairs is a delight too. Spot Winston Churchill in fatigues and a Tommy's hat seeing off a fanged monster.

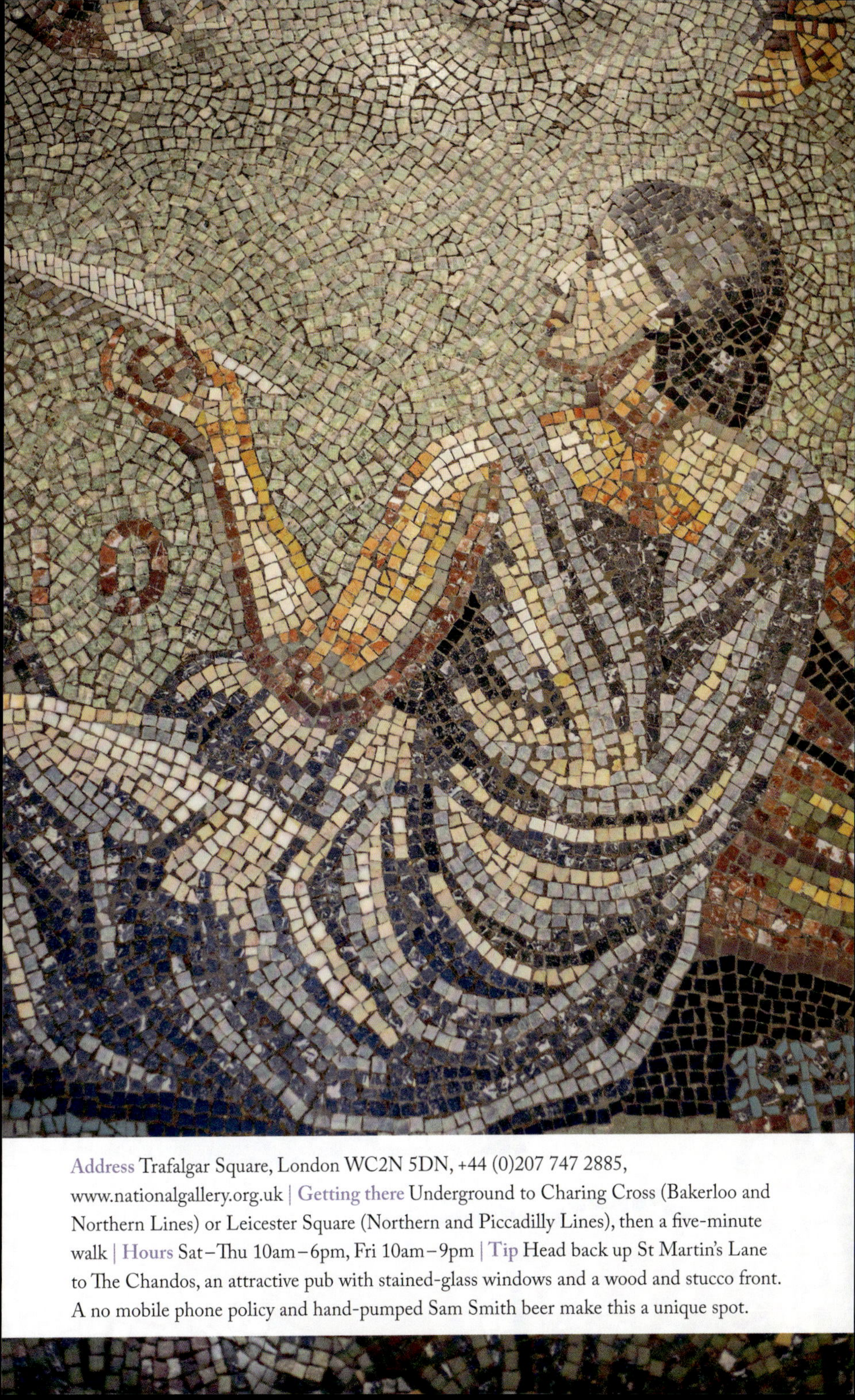

Address Trafalgar Square, London WC2N 5DN, +44 (0)207 747 2885, www.nationalgallery.org.uk | Getting there Underground to Charing Cross (Bakerloo and Northern Lines) or Leicester Square (Northern and Piccadilly Lines), then a five-minute walk | Hours Sat–Thu 10am–6pm, Fri 10am–9pm | Tip Head back up St Martin's Lane to The Chandos, an attractive pub with stained-glass windows and a wood and stucco front. A no mobile phone policy and hand-pumped Sam Smith beer make this a unique spot.

97 Sullivan (Sans Gilbert)

Choice Edwardian erotica

Being the back end of a pantomime horse means that you, as the rump, do not enjoy quite the same degree of street recognition as the horse's proud head. And so it is (and was) with Arthur Sullivan, theatre impresario, and the man even better known as a collaborator with Sir William Schwenck Gilbert to form a duo that enjoyed huge fame in Victorian England and on as Gilbert & Sullivan (their twinned surnames were more than enough to know them by). As creators of a string of comic operettas, such as *H.M.S. Pinafore*, *The Gondoliers* and *The Mikado*, they wowed and delighted audiences by their pomp and extravagant buffoonery.

Some years after the death of Sullivan, during the reign of a suitably sybaritic king called Edward VII, Sullivan was memorialised at last with the aggrandised and erotically enhanced portrait bust still on display in Victoria Embankment Gardens, a long sliver of parkland that begins at the point where the railway surges in across the Thames at Hungerford Bridge into Charing Cross Station, and continues east as far as Aldwych. This delightful, stop-start fragment of planted parkland, with its serpentining paths, its benches, and its welter of interesting public statuary, is a delight to stroll through – and the fact that it exists at all reminds you that it was once part of the Thames itself until the river was embanked to make it deeper and therefore more navigable.

The monument to Sullivan is appropriately close to the Savoy Hotel – the hotel in fact looms over it – because it was at the Savoy Theatre that many of the most famous of their operatic collaborations were first staged.

Arthur's portrait bust looks quite demure. The comedy and the outrage is in the female figure that seems to be slithering up towards him, clothes falling away as she rises, seriously or unseriously lamenting the fact that he is no longer with us.

Address Victoria Embankment Gardens, London WC2R 0BP | **Getting there** Underground to Embankment (District, Circle, Bakerloo and Northern Lines) | **Hours** Accessible 24 hours | **Tip** Look out for the magnificent York Watergate, five minutes' walk away in Watergate Walk.

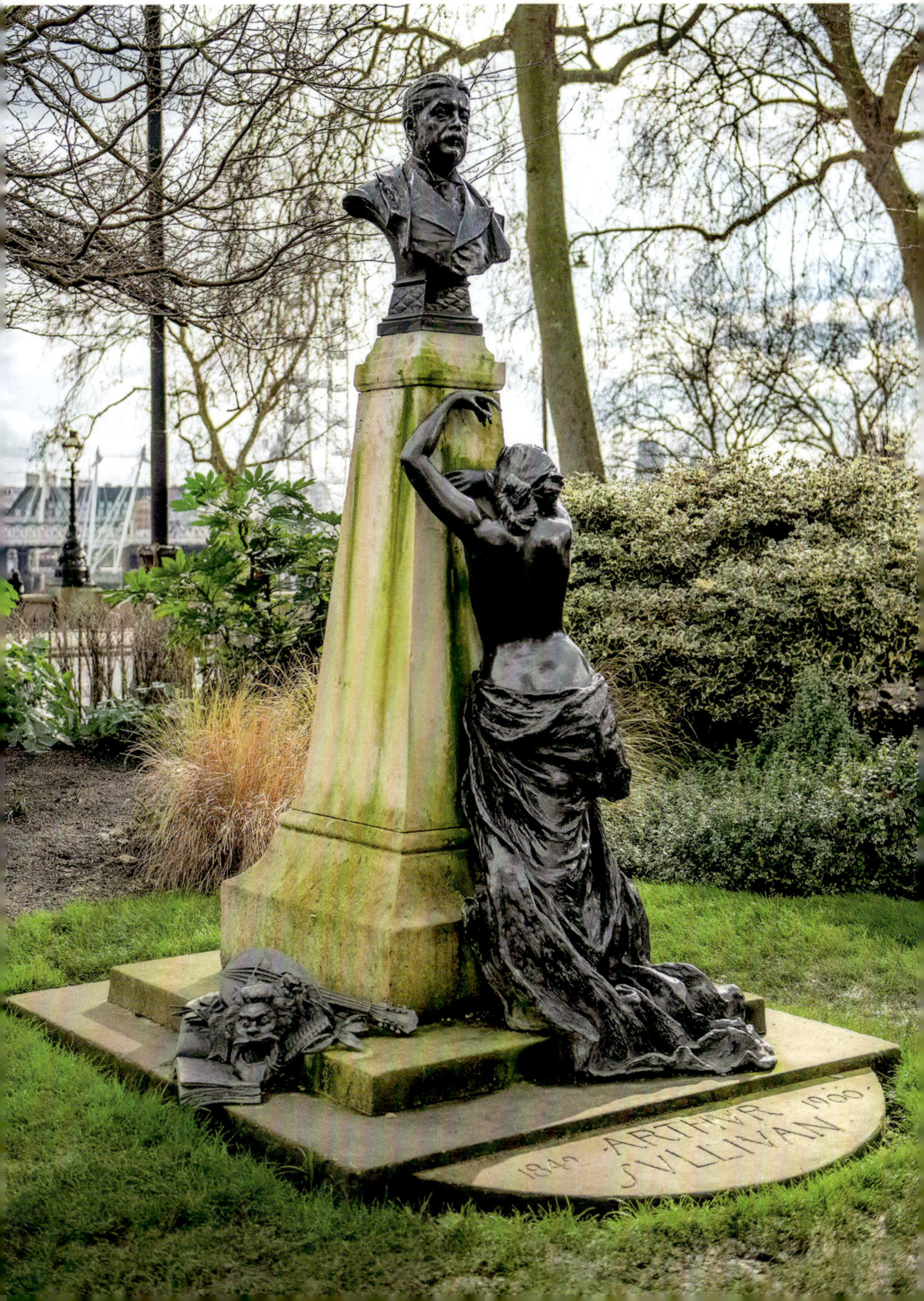

98 Sword Fish Masquerade

Summoning the water spirits

Even a bit of graffiti sprayed down her left side doesn't seem to daunt or dismay her. Steely-grey in colour on even the sunniest of East London afternoons, she stands proud on her own drum-like plinth at the junction of Hanover Park and Clayton Road, arms raised towards the traffic roundabout that speeds cars into the centre of Peckham past a Morrison's supermarket and a car wash. A relatively new apartment block – as grey as she is grey – part encircles her at her back. A few spindly trees punctuate the concrete courtyard whose centre she commands. Is she a goddess then? *Sword Fish Masquerade* is the name of this piece, though no plaque tells us that.

Her maker is the Nigerian sculptor Sokari Douglas Camp, and the sculpture has lived here in this relentlessly urban setting – there is a strew of gin, beer and coke bottles at her feet – mysteriously summoning up the spirits of the water, for almost a quarter of a century. Is she a tribute then to the fact that so many of London's rivers flow underground, and therefore need calling from the depths? Her legs are widespread and her girth enormous. She tapers to a kind of frittery, frivolously gauzy metal train at the back that someone, we feel, should be holding in homage to her presence here. It is her head and her headgear that are the most formidable elements of her character. The head seems to be enshrouded by a giant upturned bucket of a fierce metal helmet, above which rises a great outspraying of feathers topped by a swordfish, which swims off her head as if released from the launch pad of an aircraft carrier. Her garments fall away from her in thin, riveted folds of steel.

Is she an outlandish creature of carnival? Almost certainly. And is she also here to remind us of the fact that so many Nigerians live fairly locally, and that their vitalising presence deserves to be celebrated? Almost certainly.

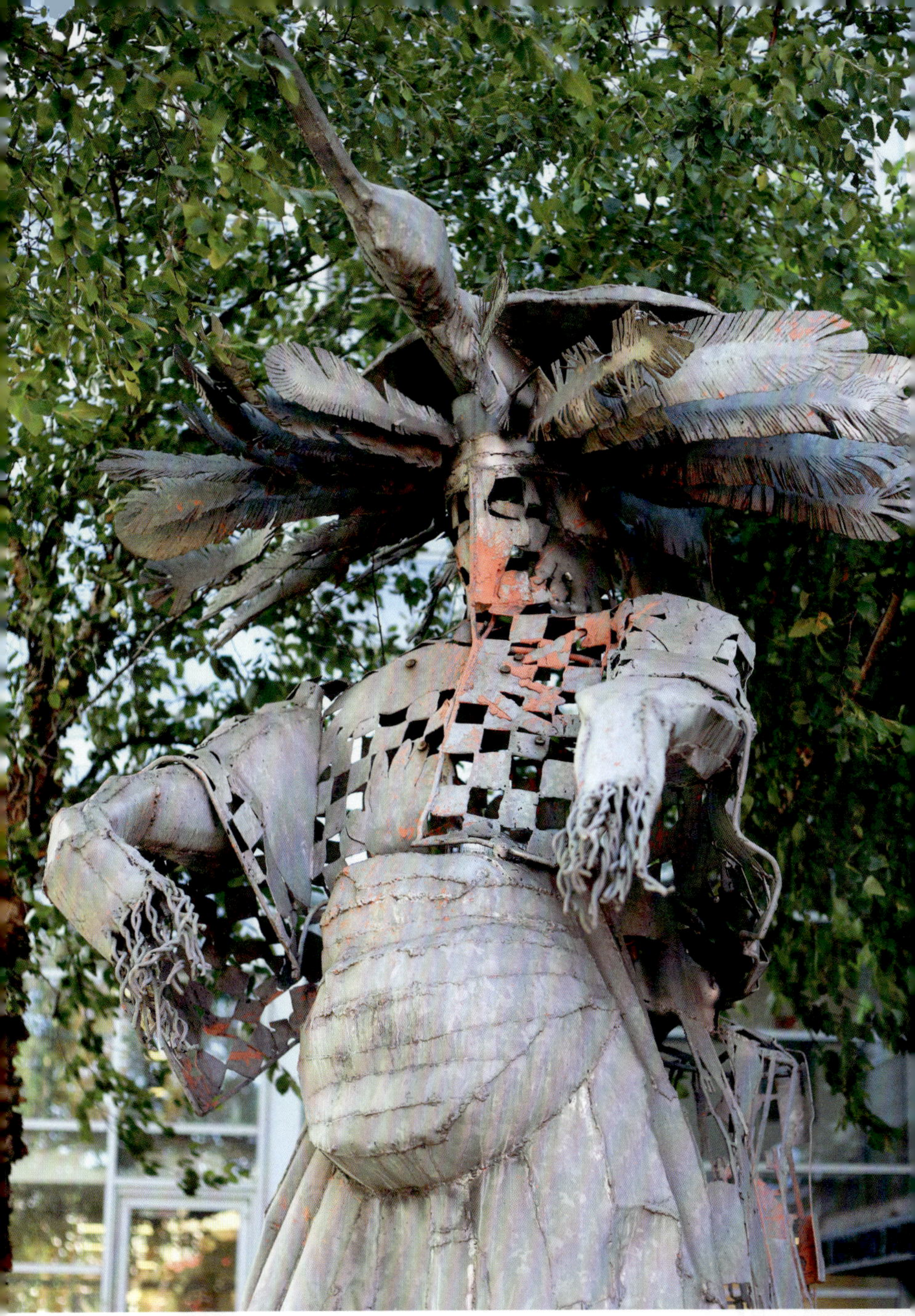

Address Hanover Park, London SE15 5HD | Getting there Overground to Peckham Rye, then an eight-minute walk | Hours Accessible 24 hours | Tip Go veggie shopping on Rye Lane – it's bustling with shops and stalls from all over the world.

99_ The Taddei Tondo

Michelangelo in all his greatness

Until three years ago, the Royal Academy in Piccadilly was generally regarded as a rather expensive place to visit. Not quite so any more, not since it expanded to take in a magnificent building along Burlington Gardens. Look out for the marvellous array of full-length statues of British worthies in their niches, which once housed the British Museum's anthropological collection.

Now many more spaces have been opened up to the public, which cost nothing to enter. One of the least known is blandly described as the Collection Gallery, which is at the back of the building, on the Burlington Gardens side, at the top of a magnificent razzmatazz of a marble staircase. This is the room in which you can see a changing display of many of the works that have been gifted to the Royal Academy since it was founded a quarter of a millennium ago, works by the Royal Academicians themselves, and those left to the RA by benefactors.

It is in here that you can see a magnificent self-portrait of a be-hatted Sir Joshua Reynolds, the Academy's first president, pretending to look like – and therefore be at least the equal of – Rembrandt. It is in this room that you will see a brilliant copy of a painting by Leonardo of *The Last Supper*, made during his own lifetime – the original is in far worse condition than this copy. But the artwork that deserves most attention is the most important work by Michelangelo in the country, the *Taddei Tondo*, which for years was hidden away behind the back of a staircase. This circular sculpture looks both smooth and rough because it is unfinished and shows Michelangelo's own chisel marks. Parts of it are refined – the babe who lies across its mother's lap, for example, and the face of Mary herself. It thrills us in part because this is so evidently a work of great art in the making, sculpture being wrested from a raw chunk of quarried material.

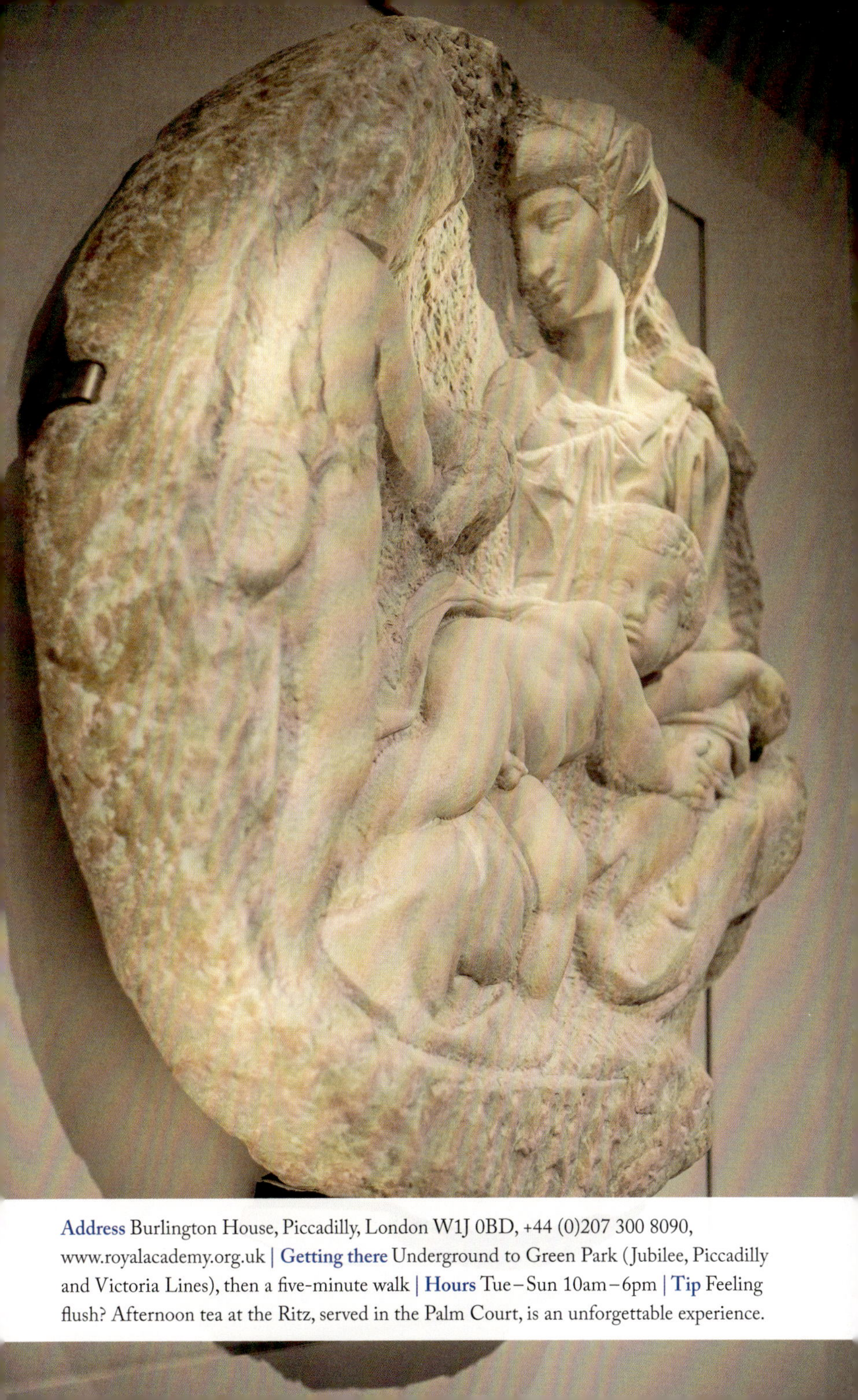

Address Burlington House, Piccadilly, London W1J 0BD, +44 (0)207 300 8090, www.royalacademy.org.uk | **Getting there** Underground to Green Park (Jubilee, Piccadilly and Victoria Lines), then a five-minute walk | **Hours** Tue–Sun 10am–6pm | **Tip** Feeling flush? Afternoon tea at the Ritz, served in the Palm Court, is an unforgettable experience.

100_ The Take-Away Rembrandt

How great art can come and go…

The Dulwich Picture Gallery, the first public art gallery ever to open in England, is a *bijou* affair created by an architect called Sir John Soane, and it lives in a part of London that looks and feels like a village. The gallery is surrounded by parkland and school playing fields, and it even has the odd wooden finger post to point the way elsewhere, should you ever wish to leave this charming rural fastness. The gallery was the brain-child of two French art dealers who had been commissioned to create a first-class collection of Old Masters for the king of Poland. Unfortunately, the king abdicated, and the deal melted away. What to do with all this marvellous stuff? There were Rembrandts, Tiepolos, Murillos, Watteaus and much else in the collection. The dealers wanted to keep it together, and so Soane was commissioned to create a building, which opened to the public in 1817.

The Rembrandts are unusually small, and this smallness has helped to cause a problem for one of them in particular. Imagine stealing one of the National Gallery's Rembrandts. Their size, even when rolled, would make it a challenge for any thief. Not so the portrait of a young man called Jacob de Gheyn III, which can be seen (if you are lucky) in Gallery Five. I urge caution because this painting, unlike any other Rembrandt in England, has been stolen on no fewer than four occasions since the 1960s.

Luckily it has always been re-found in the end, unharmed – once beneath a bench, and on another occasion on a luggage rack in Germany. Its very smallness has favoured the thieves, of course. It is one of what was once a pair of portraits of notable young men of Amsterdam, and Rembrandt painted this youthful effort in 1632, just after he had moved to the city from Leiden. It is a very refined painting, undramatic. It also looks like a very good likeness of its sitter.

Address Gallery Road, London SE21 7AD, +44 (0)208 693 5254, www.dulwichpicturegallery.org.uk | **Getting there** Underground to Brixton (Victoria Line), then take the P4 bus | **Hours** Tue–Sun 10am–5pm | **Tip** Take a walk around the three acres of gardens then have a sandwich or a coffee at the gallery's excellent café.

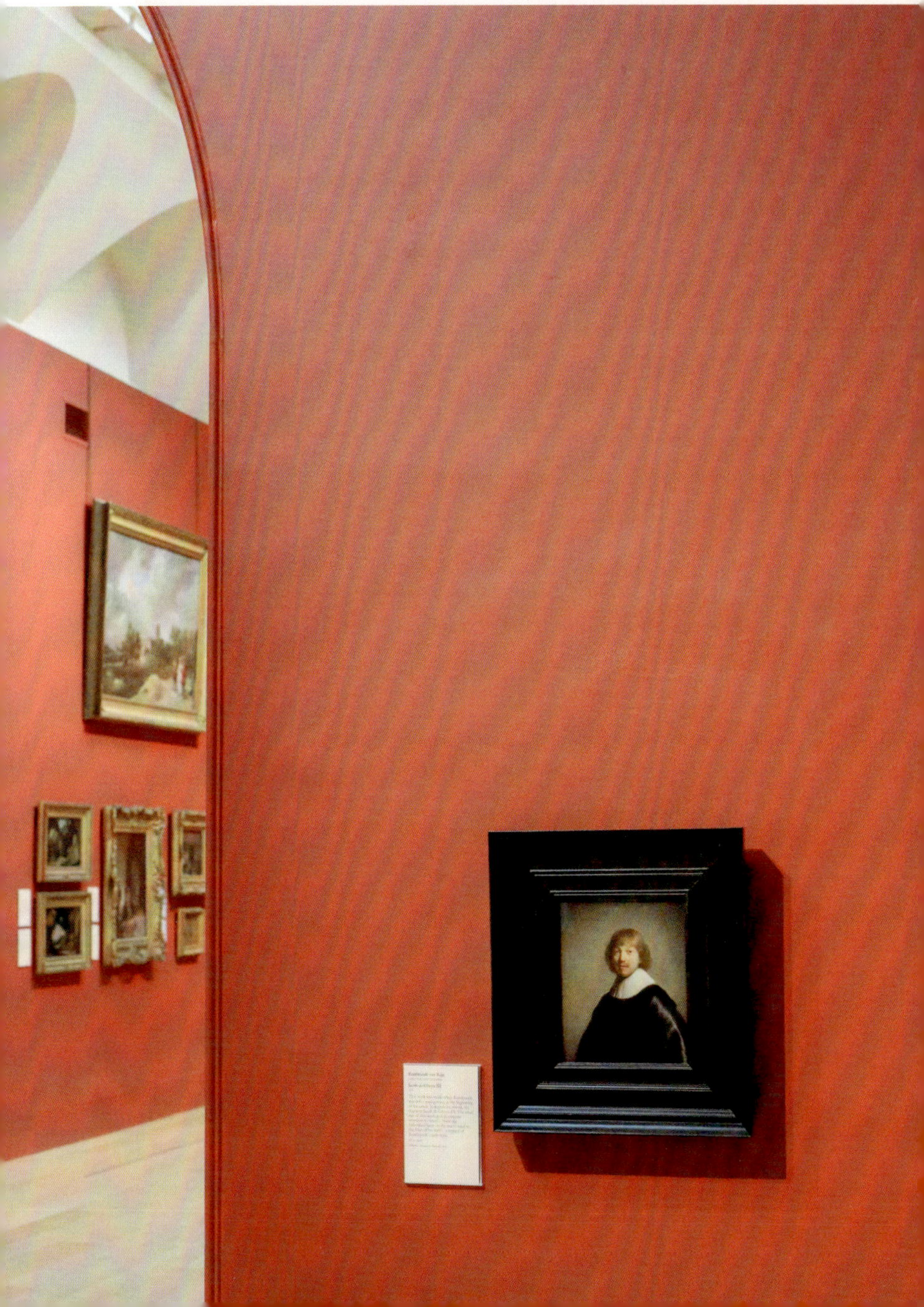

101 Temple Bar

Wren's masterpiece in motion

Great city gates often hide away in museums when they are no longer useful. Temple Bar, Sir Christopher Wren's stone gateway to the City of London, has taken a more interesting and serendipitous journey. Once upon a time – before the Royal Courts of Justice were created in the middle of the 19th century – it stood at the head of Fleet Street, marking the place where the old Roman city of Londinium began. (There is a huge silver dragon on a plinth marking that spot now.) Unfortunately, horse-drawn traffic being what it was in Victorian times, it eventually became a public nuisance, too small and too narrow for traffic to move easily in either direction, and the huge blocks of stone from which it was created were removed to a field in the countryside, where it languished, partially dismantled, for decades.

Now, cleaned and refurbished, it is back in town again, guarding the approach to the relatively young Paternoster Square at the top of Ludgate Hill. It is a little hidden away, so you will need to walk part way across St Paul's Churchyard to find it. Its position here could not be more fitting. It faces towards the west flank of St Paul's Cathedral, Wren's masterpiece. Temple Bar glows honey coloured when the sun shines, and its massy presence has a great swagger about it, from its statues in niches, to its fluted pilasters crowned with Corinthian capitals, and its magnificent wooden doors, ferociously spiked at the top against interlopers.

The two statues in their niches facing St Paul's show us two Stuart monarchs, Charles I on the left and Charles II on the right. This is a cunning sleight of hand. It seems to suggest that England moved seamlessly from one Stuart to another. Not at all. A terrible, divisive war separated the one from the other, and a man called Oliver Cromwell was head of a short-lived republic. All conveniently fudged away.

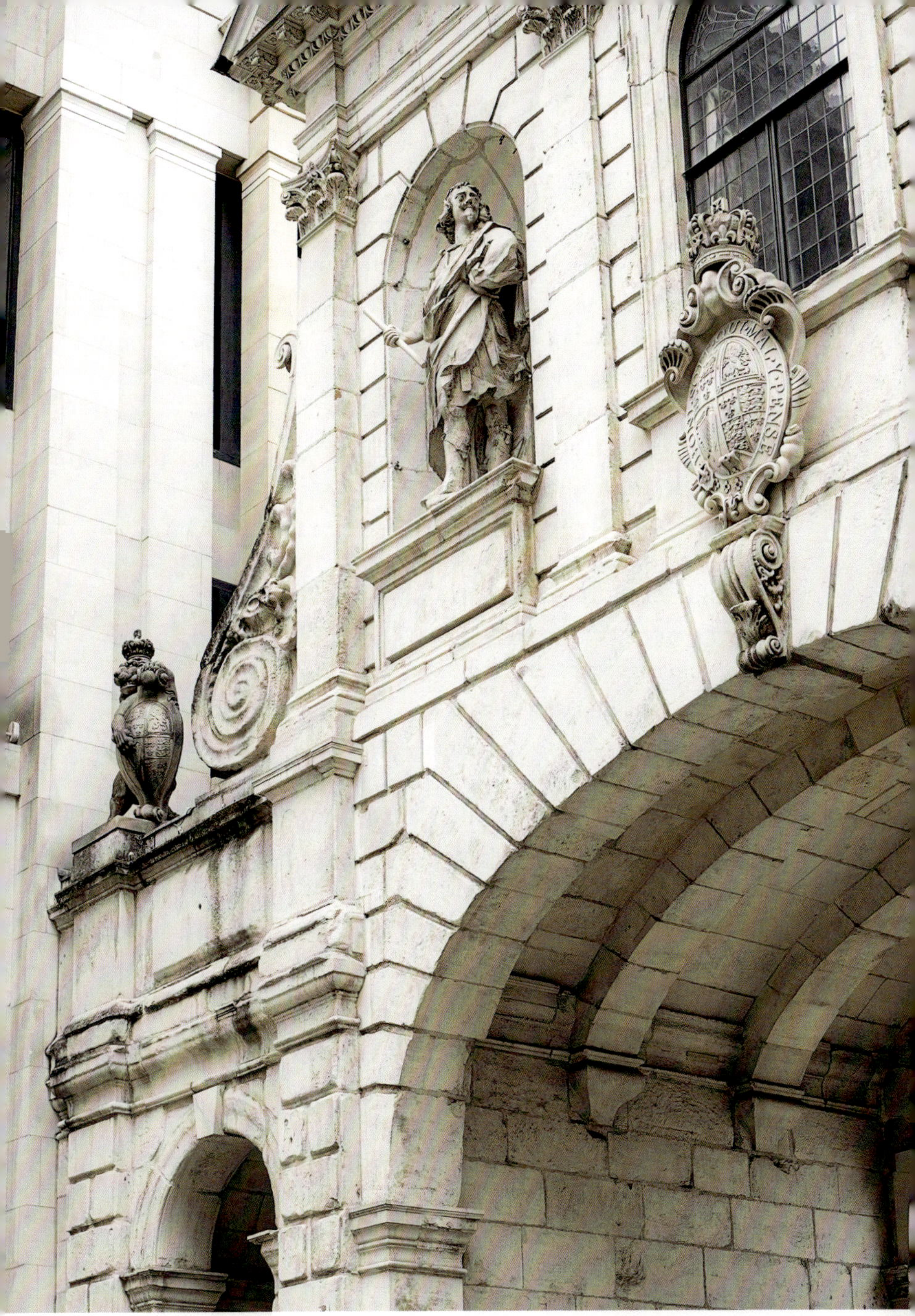

Address 1 Paternoster Row, London EC4M 7DX, www.thetemplebar.info | Getting there Underground to St Paul's (Central Line) | Hours Accessible 24 hours | Tip Enjoy a coffee in St Paul's Churchyard.

102 Tolpuddle Martyrs' Mural

Fighting for workers' rights

Prosperity has come at last to the post-industrial no man's land that was once to the north of King's Cross Station. A new, giant headquarters for Google is in the rising. Tourists idle in the sun beside the canal near Coal Drop Yard. The old gasometers, those giant, cast-iron, circular Victorian storage facilities beside the railway tracks, have been converted into odd, cheese-slice-shaped luxury apartments from which you can look down on the Eurostar (destination Brussels or Paris) easing in and out noiselessly, such is the quality of the sliding doors' insulation.

But if you walk 10 minutes to the east along Copenhagen Street in the direction of the centre of Islington, you will once again find yourself in the midst of a much poorer, scruffier, and more stricken London altogether – an old woman is hacking at the weeds in the pocket-sized front garden of her council flat with the aid of a kitchen knife as one passes by. Walk a little further still and you will come across, on the gable-end wall of a block called Rambler Building (no. 183), a remarkable mural, 40 years old now, which is fading a little due to overmuch sunlight, but still very visible. It has been signed too, so we know who made it: Dave Bangs. His telephone number no longer works.

Follow the little brown sign to Edward Square, and turn off, down a cobbled path, into a patch of scrubby park that is slowly becoming overwhelmed by its mature trees, and sit down on one of the seven stout wooden seats. Now you will get a very good view of some of that crowd of 100,000 Victorian people – there are quite a few top hats to be seen – processing in the general direction of Parliament. Several carry banners. These working folk are marching in support of the six Tolpuddle Martyrs, Dorset farm labourers who were threatened with deportation to Australia for having joined a trade union. The date is 1834.

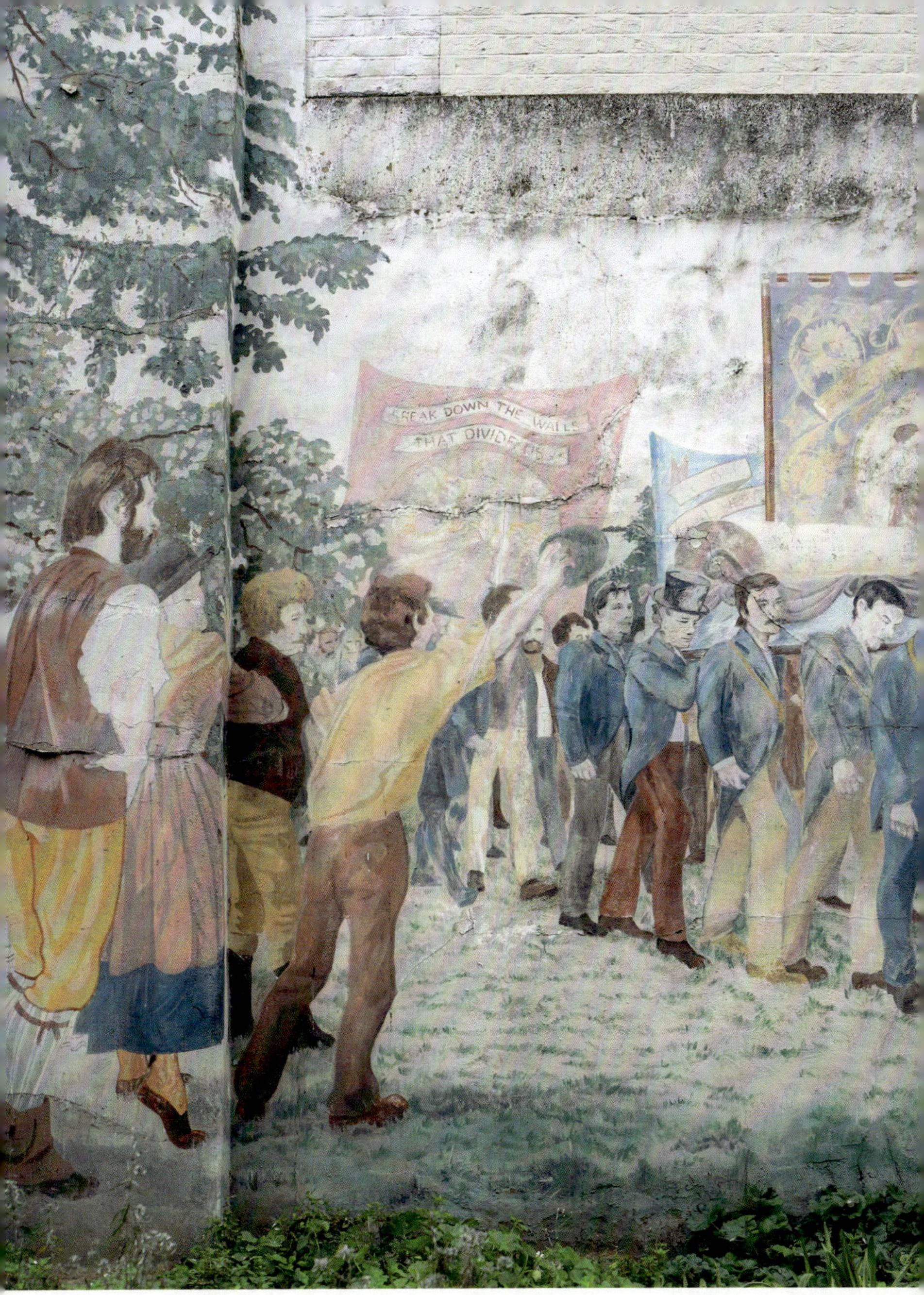

Address 183 Copenhagen Street, London N1 0SR | Getting there Underground to King's Cross (Circle, Piccadilly, Hammersmith and City, Northern, Metropolitan and Victoria Lines), then a 10-minute walk | Hours Accessible 24 hours | Tip Take a short walk to York Way and visit Kings Place, a concert hall and exhibition space that also has an excellent café and bar.

103 Trajan's Column

How a masterpiece took root elsewhere

Now, thanks to digitisation, the world-in-the-round can be brought to our door within a millisecond. We can do virtual tours of many great institutions and public monuments. Not so once. How could the past be brought closer in earlier times? What means were available to the ingenious?

There are two great galleries hidden inside the maze of one of London's greatest museums that demonstrate, with great panache and drama, how the Victorians, those visionary innovators, brought the world of remote places to our very door in London. These are the two great Cast Courts of the Victoria and Albert Museum, immense and soaringly tall lumber rooms that contain physical copies of some of the world's greatest sculptures and monuments, from giant city gates to Michelangelo's *David*; from delicate Renaissance portrait busts on plinths, to sculpted, low-relief wall panels.

The greatest and most surprising jewel of the collection is a copy of Trajan's Column in Rome. Why should we value this copy so much? Because since the copy was taken about 150 years ago, there has been much damage suffered by the great column as a consequence of a multiplicity of factors such as traffic, general air pollution and careless custodianship. What we see in London, though a copy, is better preserved and much richer in fine detail.

The column itself is in two halves, because otherwise it would have been taller than the museum's tallest ceiling. The narrative of the column is told in a spiral of scenes that swarm with eventful happenings such as the waging of wars – we witness the clash of armies, the hurrying of high-stepping horses, the sprawl of the dead and dying. The emperor had the column created in order to celebrate his conquest of what is now Romania. The copies themselves were first made in metal, from a plaster mould, at the instigation of Napoleon III of France.

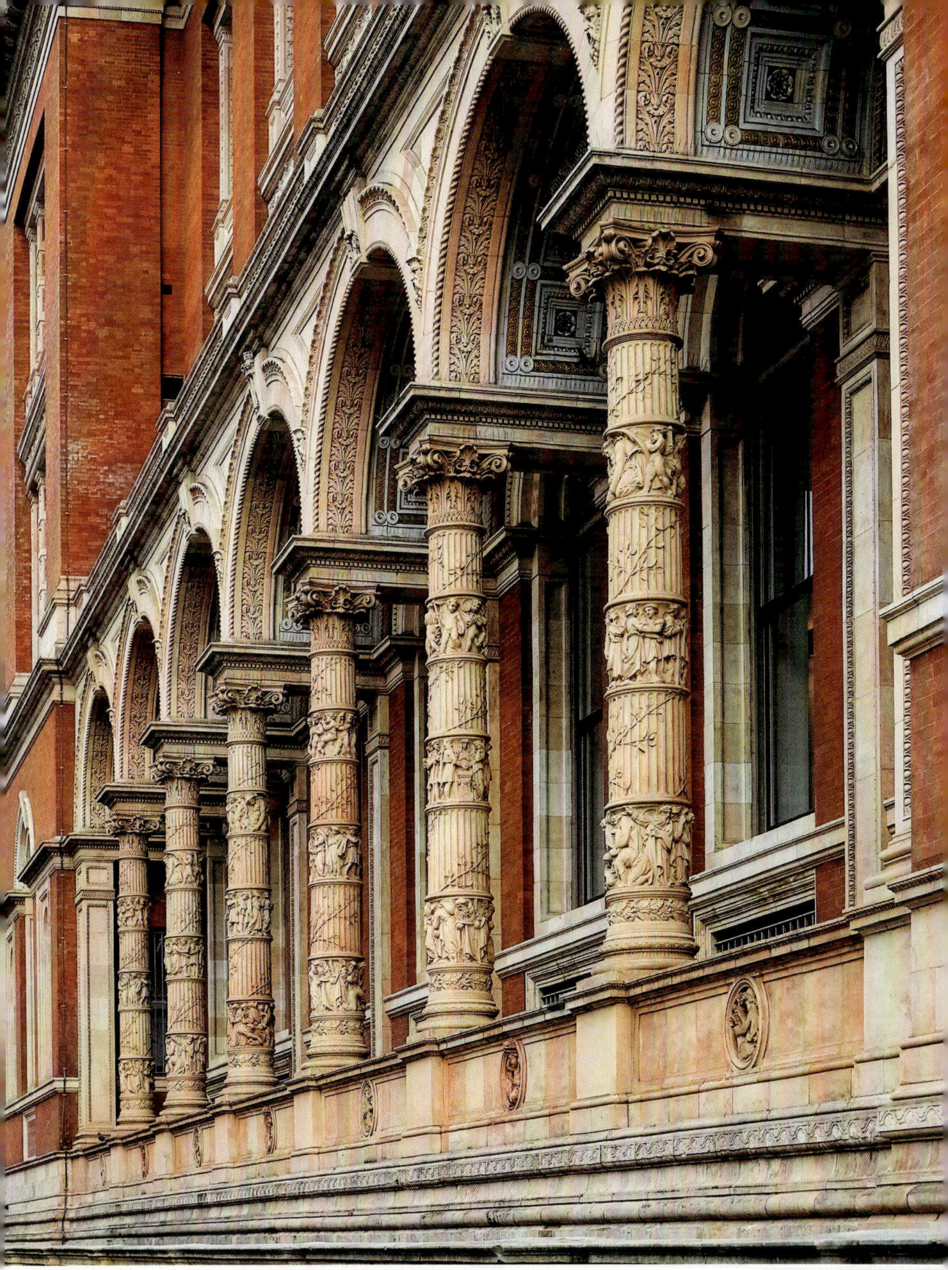

Address V&A, Cromwell Road, London SW7 2RL, +44 (0)207 942 2000, www.vam.ac.uk | Getting there Underground to South Kensington (Piccadilly, District and Circle Lines), then a five-minute walk, or Gloucester Road (Piccadilly, District and Circle Lines), then a 10-minute walk | Hours Daily 10am–5.45pm, Fri to 10pm in selected galleries | Tip Once you've seen all you want to of the V&A, you can choose between the Science Museum and the Natural History Museum – both just along the road.

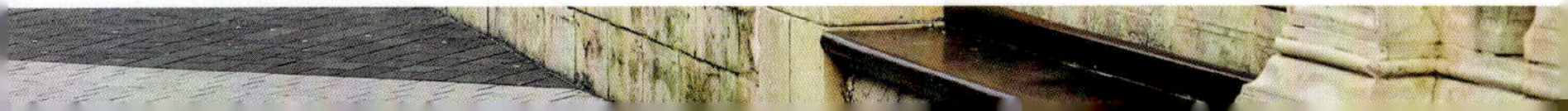

104 Trinity Buoy Wharf

A remnant of maritime London

The most interesting way to reach this wonderfully revitalised Thameside remnant of old London and its maritime industries, is to travel intrepidly on foot from Canning Town Overground Station. Following signs to Bow Creek as you leave the station, cross a brilliant red bridge and then walk beside twisty Bow Creek itself – which looks like a deep, muddy and almost waterless channel until the Thames, towards which you are foot-slogging, rises a full 23 feet and floods the creek with water and bobbing water birds at high tide.

You are journeying towards Trinity Buoy Wharf in London's Docklands, where remnants of old industries – there was an ironworks just up river from here once – meet modern innovation and much art. The Royal Drawing School has an important outpost here. It was at this spot, in 1864, on the south bank of the Thames directly opposite what was once known as the Millennium Dome (now better known as the O2 Arena), that the great Victorian inventor Michael Faraday created London's sole experimental lighthouse where he tested various new forms of lighting equipment.

There are other historic buildings here too, all of them tough, red brick and made to last. The largest of these is the Chain and Buoy Store, for example, where iron mooring chains were once kept, or the Proving House, where chains that would be needed to tether the buoys to the river bed were tested for their water worthiness. This building is now artists' studios – you may even spot a sculpture hanging from a wall. In fact, it is on and around and inside such buildings as these that art is flourishing now. If you fancy a challenging climb, try the first floor of the lighthouse itself where you can listen to Jem Finer's *Longplayer*, a musical experiment that promises never to end. Or stare up at the taxi that seems to have a tree sprouting out of the top. This is called *The Knowledge*.

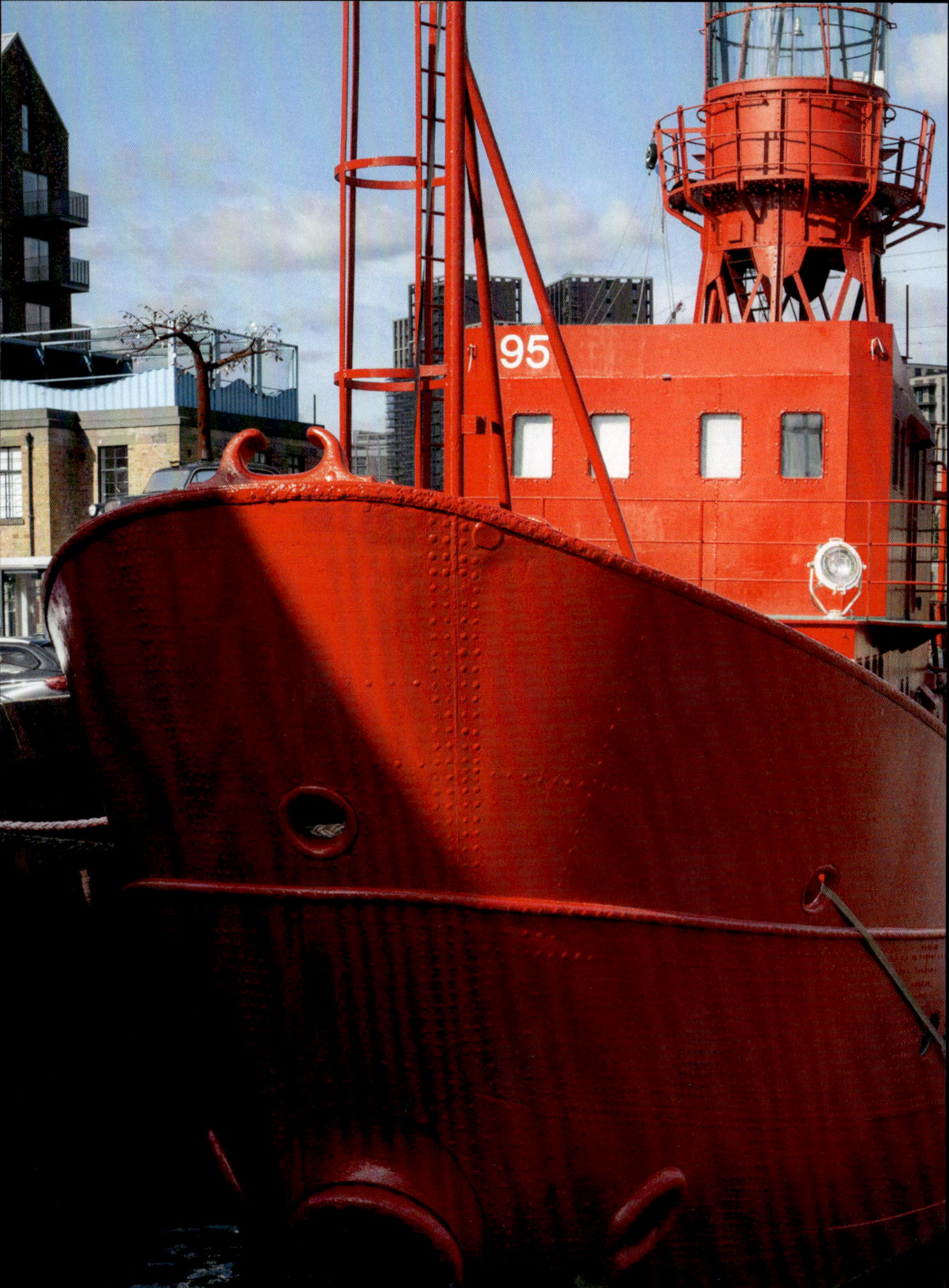

Address 64 Orchard Place, London E14 0JW, +44 (0)207 515 7153, www.trinitybuoywharf.com | **Getting there** Overground to Canning Town, then a 14-minute walk from there beside Bow Creek | **Hours** Wharf open daily 7am–7pm; Lighthouse open Sat & Sun 11am–4pm | **Tip** Have a drink and a bite at the Orchard Café, housed in a shipping container.

105 Two Old Boys Showing Off

Welcome to the Gilbert & George Centre

Gilbert & George, that famous duo of living sculptures who have always dressed to look as much alike as possible, have been making art out of themselves and their image for more than half a century. The Gilbert & George Centre in East London is a small museum created by them, and paid for with their own money, to show off their achievements. Sited in a part of East London popularly known as Banglatown because of the sheer number and quality of its Asian restaurants, it is housed in a newly converted 19th-century brewery, off a cobbled courtyard, with a pretty garden to set it all off. The duo's home is in Fournier Street, just a short walk away. These two gays, who are now in their 80s, and still making art just as furiously as ever, are the stuff of local legend. Every day, you can spot them walking the streets of Spitalfields, probably on their way to their favourite restaurant.

The museum consists of three galleries, a reception area and a film room, in the last of which you can watch them being interviewed about their long life in art. According to a recent interview, when they were first setting out in the 1960s, Andy Warhol had cooked them eggs for breakfast during a visit to New York. Or was it perhaps Robert Rauschenberg? One or the other.

The artworks in the galleries, digitally manipulated images that are often almost as big as a small cinema screen, almost always show us Gilbert and George themselves, two eternally rebellious pranksters, as the centres of attention, playing hide and seek amongst strangely creepy vegetation, whirling through the galaxies, snoozing on benches, presiding over street trash, and always smartly be-suited in time-honoured fashion. The colours of their artworks are often wildly psychedelic, and the boys themselves change in colour too, from cobalt blue to emerald green to pink. They just go on and on.

Address 5a Heneage Street, London E1 5LJ, +44 (0)207 477 2484, www.gilbertandgeorgecentre.org | Getting there Underground to Aldgate East (District, Hammersmith and City Lines), then a five-minute walk | Hours Thu–Sun 10am–5pm | Tip Have a pint next door in The Pride of Spitalfields, a 'proper boozer'.

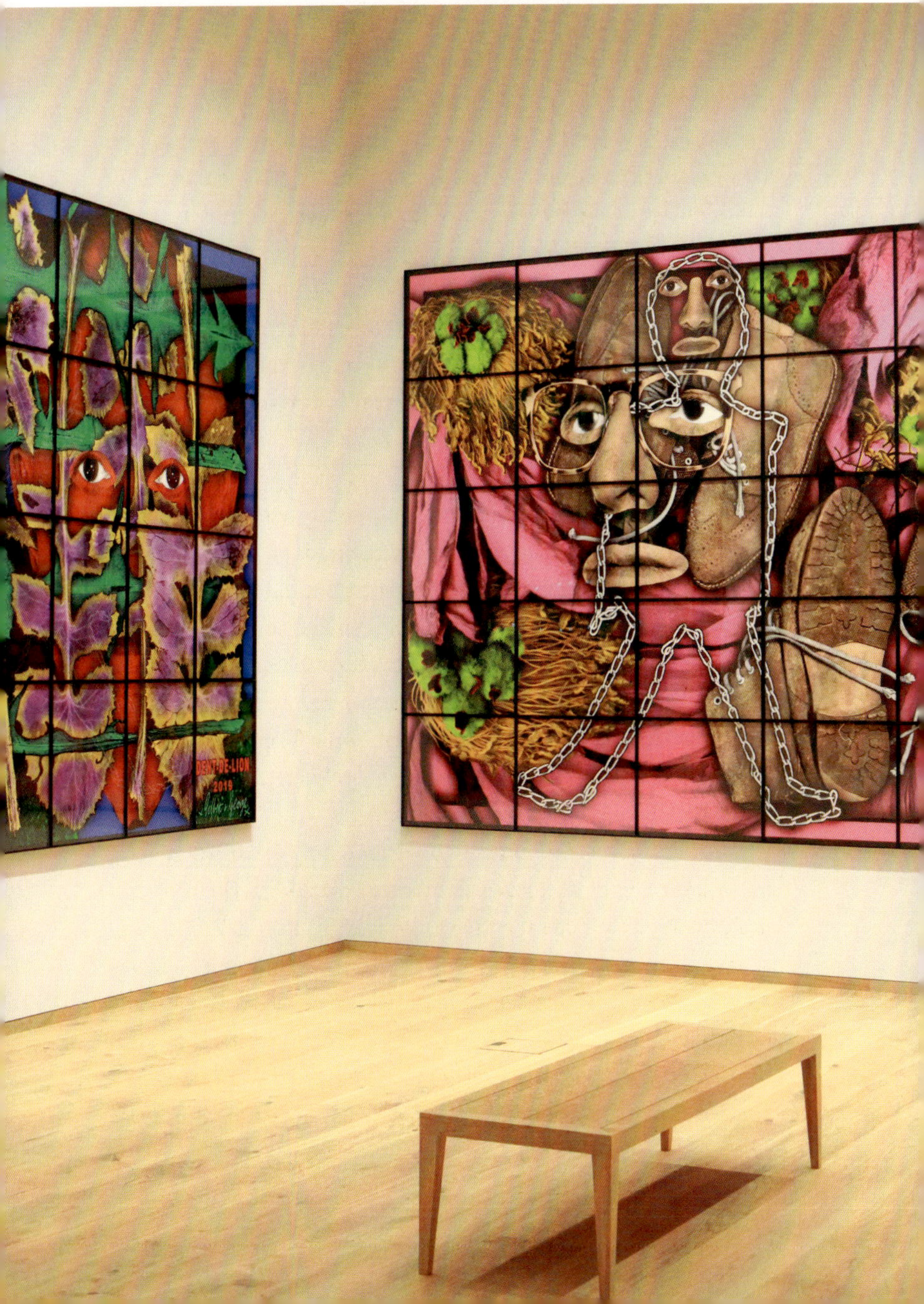

106 Veronese Triumphant

The healing power of art on the march

Can art help to heal us and soothe us and distract us from all bodily ills? The Chelsea and Westminster Hospital, with its building-wide, permanent display of prints, paintings, mobiles and sculptures, certainly seems to think so.

From the strangely robotic (though it also happens to be barefoot and pork-pie hatted) Eduardo Paolozzi full-length bronze figure, which doubles, delightfully, as a collection box, aptly entitled *The Healing Arts*, which greets us at its entrance, through its various atria and corridors, there is enlivening art everywhere in this building. It thrills you. It engulfs you. It distracts and delights. It helps to shape and define the very experience of being a visitor or a patient.

Most of the art is modern, and it is often playful and stridently colourful – think of Allen Jones' balletic *Acrobat* of 1993, for example, tricked out in bendy, curvaceous gelato stripes of green and yellow, balancing a red ball in the air in one corner of the double height atrium, while simultaneously wildly striding and tumbling along, or of the joyously jazzy fun of an Edward Irvin screen print gesturing in a corridor. The Jones was commissioned by the hospital even before it was opened; the vision of art's power to heal preceded the opening of the building itself.

Most surprising of all is the presence of a great old master painting of *The Resurrection of Christ* by Veronese (c. 1587) in the hospital's chapel on the first floor. It commands the high altar directly in front of you as you step into this relatively small space of retreat and contemplation. Christ, his wounded and recently crucified body elegantly lapped about by a gorgeous pink modesty robe, strides out to greet you. His left arm is raised; his right hand grips a banner topped by a crucifix. I ask the friendly chaplain for details of visiting hours. He says 24/7. After all, this is a hospital.

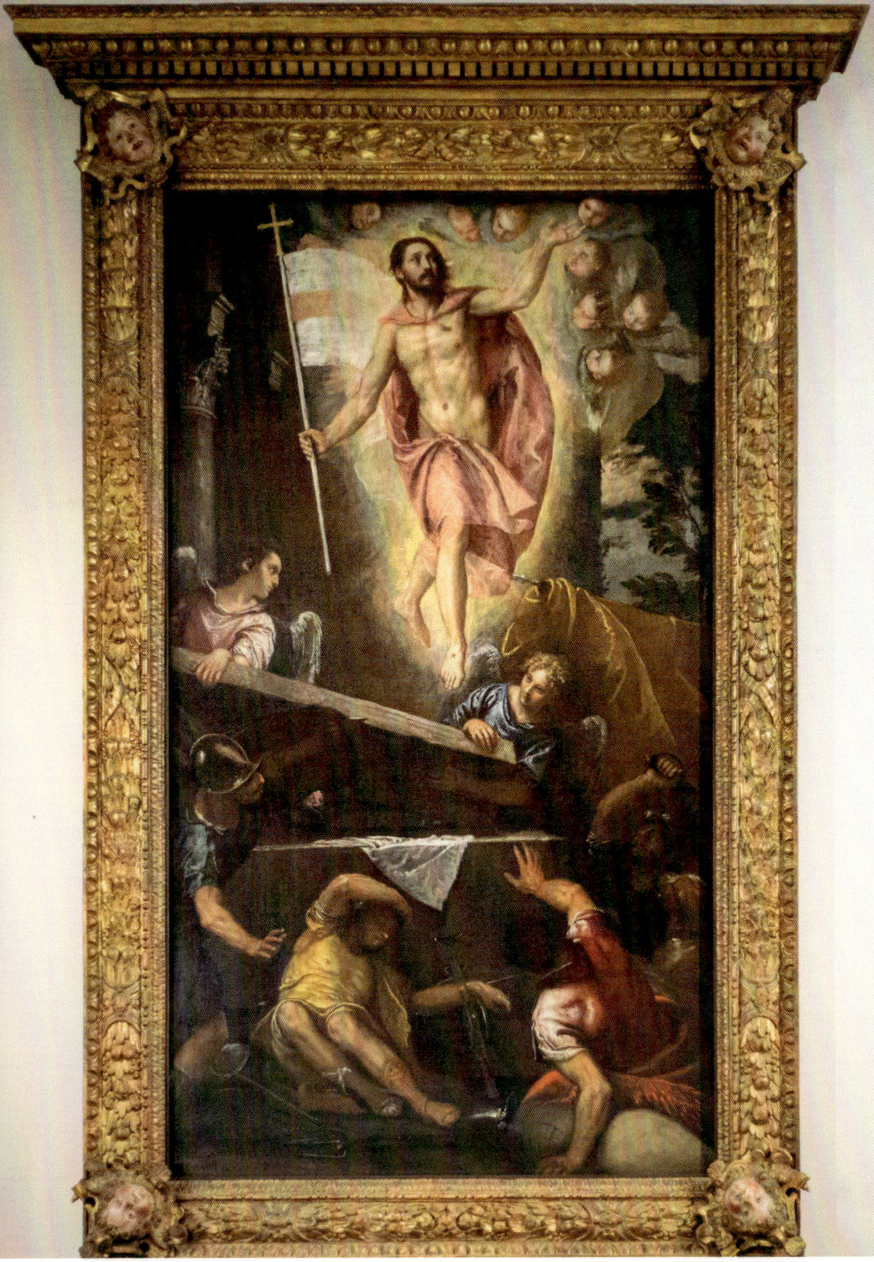

Address 369 Fulham Road, SW10 9NH, +44 (0)203 315 8000, www.chelwest.nhs.uk | Getting there Underground to Fulham Broadway (District Line), then a 10-minute walk | Hours Accessible 24 hours, but advisable to check before visiting | Tip Five minutes away is Brompton Cemetery, one of London's most famous Victorian cemeteries. It's full of spectacular monuments, but is also a beautiful and tranquil place teeming with wildlife and wild flowers.

107 Warm Shores

In praise of the Windrush Generation

Monuments paid for by governments, local or national, are often characterised by a degree of self-serving pomposity. They are elevated by fine plinths, which sets them high above us in order to enable us to pay homage. Horses and fine clothing are often a part of the rather awe-inspiring mix. Quite otherwise is Thomas J. Price's tribute to the Windrush Generation in Hackney, one of London's poorest northern boroughs. These were all citizens of the British Empire who came to Britain from the Caribbean diaspora in the aftermath of World War II to work in essential services, and they were often treated like non-citizens. It is as if they barely existed at all as significant human presences.

The bronze sculptures – they are two figures, slightly larger than life, set at a slight angle to each other – are sited on a stretch of pavement in front of Hackney Town Hall, facing a public information board that invites us to look out for Ghost, a small local lost dog, or to report domestic abuse, or to enjoy getting a little slimmer this month, amongst friends. The figures are looking in the direction of the famous Hackney Empire, where Mother Goose is about to begin her Christmas run.

There is something utterly ordinary and casual about these two human presences, both black, the shorter a little older than her companion. The younger's hair is fashionably styled, in neat cornrows. Otherwise, he is dressed much like the rest of us – his top hangs fairly loose. The older seems a little more fashionably dressed – look at the shapeliness of the jacket, and the casual knotting of that scarf at the neck.

The fact that they seem arrested here in their motion, on this stretch of pavement, at the same level as the rest of us, makes us feel that they are a part of everything that goes on around here, and that they deserve our respect. They are a part of our space.

Address Hackney Town Hall, Mare Street, London E8 1EA | Getting there Train to Hackney Central, then a 10-minute walk | Hours Accessible 24 hours | Tip Book tickets for a show at the famous Hackney Empire nearby.

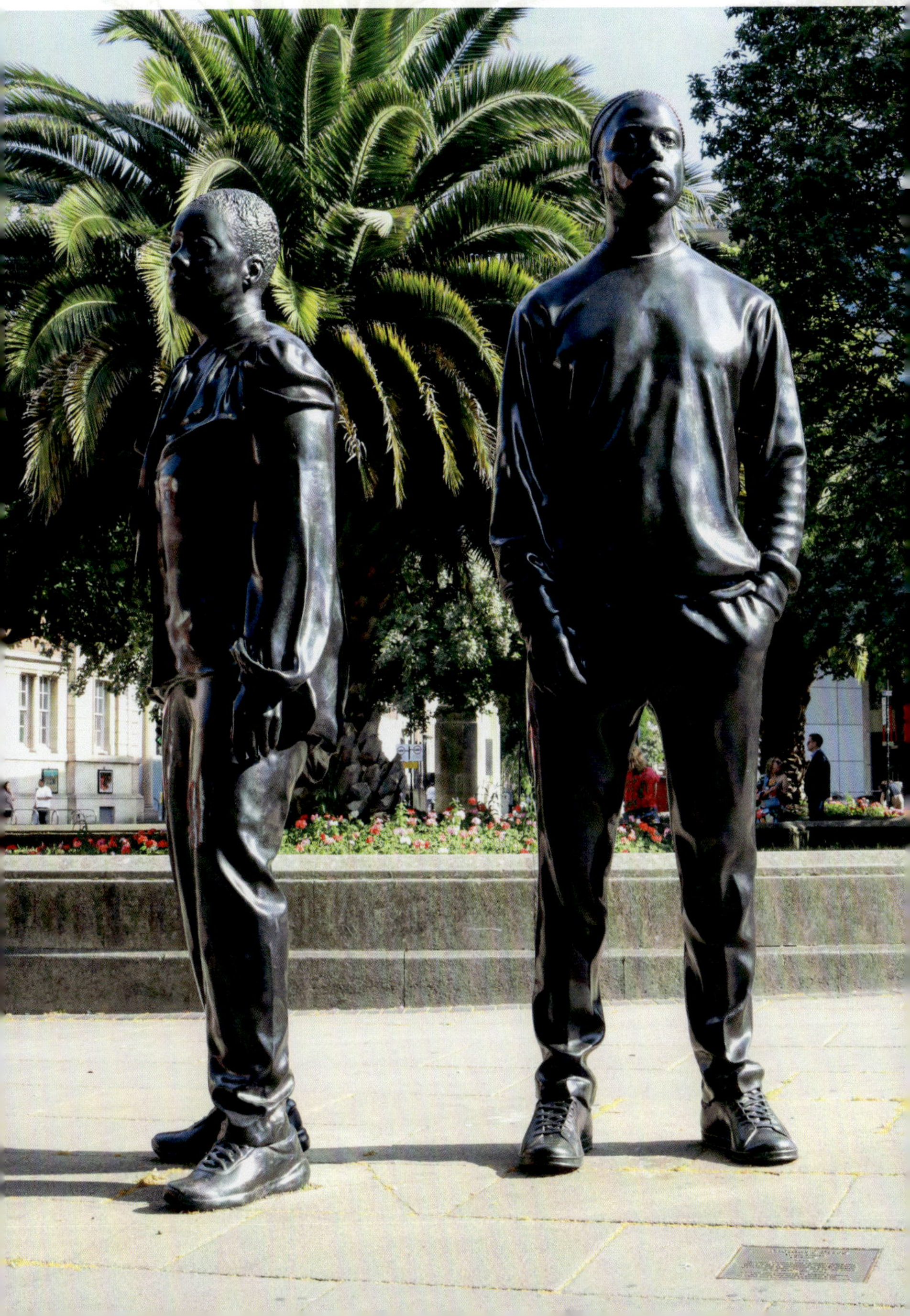

108_Watling Street

The 2,000-year story of a great London road

There is something unforgiving and unremitting about the passage of traffic along the Old Kent Road in the general direction of central London. This has been the case for at least two millennia, as has been recorded in a remarkable sequence of murals in ceramic created in 1965 by an artist called Adam Kossowski. The story, told in a series of low-relief panels, wraps itself around the first-floor frontage of an unoccupied and sadly neglected building still called the Peckham Civic Centre. Only these tiles gleam as brightly as ever, as if to say to us: history must not die!

The story begins at the intersection with Peckham Park Road, when this road had its Roman name: Watling Street. On this corner the Romans have already established their presence here: a legionary holds a Roman standard as if in proof of the success of the invasion. Shifting around the corner to the scenes that now face directly onto the Old Kent Road, we enter the era of Chaucer – there is a quotation from the *Canterbury Tales*, written in the 15th century. Those pilgrims, with their horses drinking from a stream, would have taken the road out to Kent in this general direction. Banners unfurl and dogs frisk. Lords and ladies disport themselves.

Then other great historical markers appear, one by one: the Jack Cade Rebellion, the triumphs of Henry V over France, the Restoration of the monarchy marked by the return from exile of the dissolute Charles II.

The story draws ever closer to our own day: the Industrial Revolution is marked by smoke pothering out of a chimney stack. And then we move into the near present of the artist himself: here is a family of traditional Eastenders tricked out as Pearly King, Queen and Child. A helicopter circles overhead, with an aircraft nearby; residential tower blocks are sprouting up. A London copper keeps a wary eye out for a spot of bother.

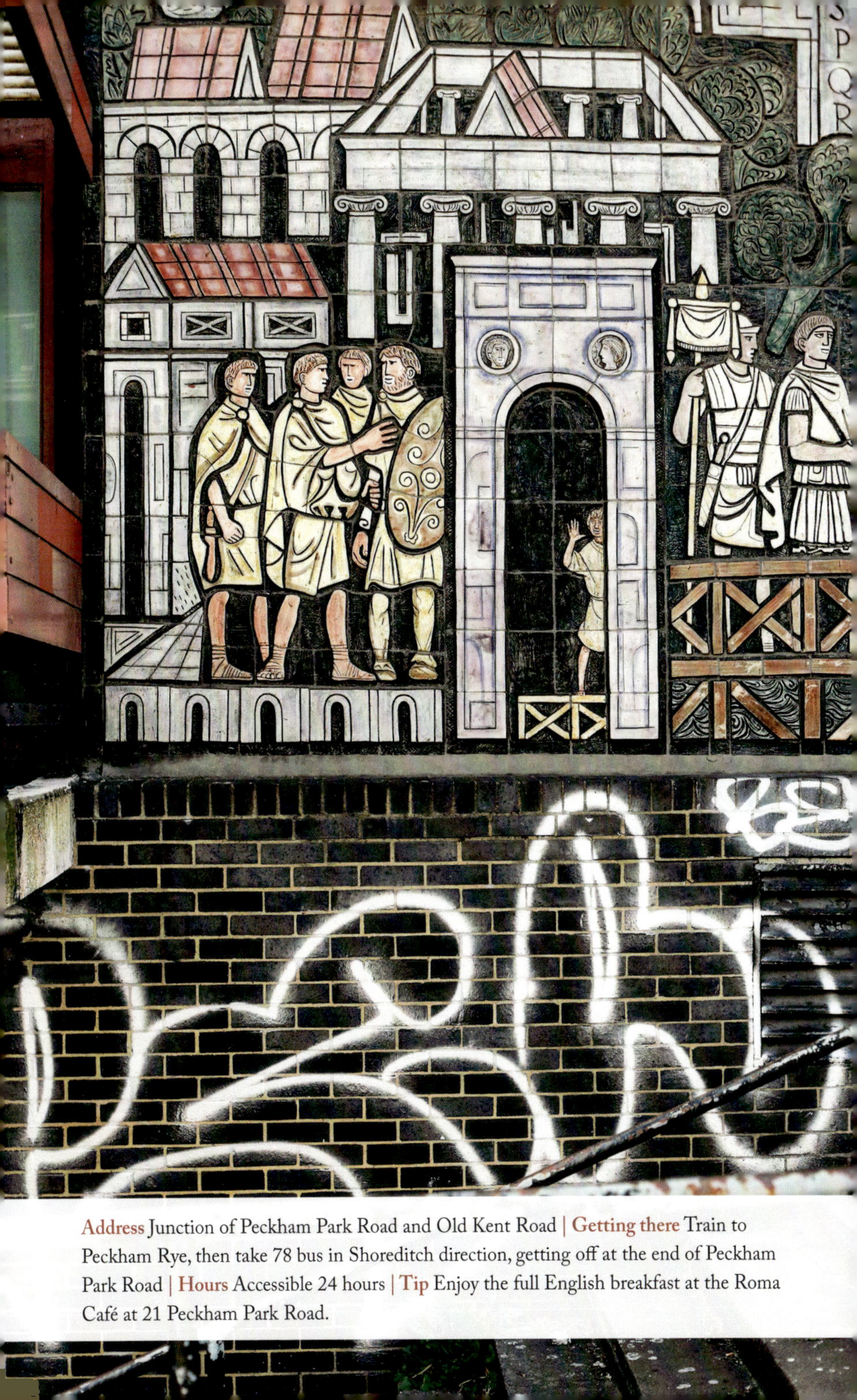

Address Junction of Peckham Park Road and Old Kent Road | Getting there Train to Peckham Rye, then take 78 bus in Shoreditch direction, getting off at the end of Peckham Park Road | Hours Accessible 24 hours | Tip Enjoy the full English breakfast at the Roma Café at 21 Peckham Park Road.

109 Westminster Cathedral

Showing off the saints and martyrs

Like some basilica that might have been seen and admired by the senators of Ancient Rome, Westminster Cathedral, the mother church of Catholicism in London, situated in a piazza off London's Victoria Street, is a building still in the making and the growing – its unfinished state makes us think of Gaudí's great Sagrada Família in Barcelona. So too are its decorative schemes. Some of its finest sculptural works were made by the young Eric Gill, who created a sequence of 14 Stations of the Cross, low-relief panels, all pale beige in colour (with gilded halos), attached to the pillars flanking the nave.

The culminating point is the altarpiece in the Chapel of St George and the English Martyrs, flanked by columns with byzantine capitals, where a crowned Christ is shown on the cross as a triumphal presence, arms spread embracingly. To the left is Sir Thomas More, and to the right John Fisher, Bishop of Rochester, grasping a chalice in his right hand and a shepherd's crook in his left. Two angels hover in the air above the cross, their playfully pudgy arms and hands reaching down to take hold of its horizontal beams, as if to steady it and claim it as a symbol of victory. The head of Jesus is averted. The look is staunch, composed and authoritative, as if this trial is one that he will overcome.

The entire chapel, with its barrel-vaulted ceiling, is so eye-beguiling: look down, for example, into the magnificent glass coffin of St John Southworth, for example. His body is gorgeously apparelled in rich maroon vestments. His head rests on a plump cushion. His face is a golden mask. His eyes remain forever open. Or up at the ceiling mosaics by Tom Phillips, dabs of orange flame representing (and also naming) various English martyrs, flitting around against a blue ground – evidently a homage to Botticelli's saints in his version of Dante's *Paradiso*.

Address Victoria Street, SW1P 1LT, +44 (0)207 798 9055, www.westminstercathedral.org.uk | Getting there Underground to Victoria (Victoria, District and Circle Lines), then a five-minute walk | Hours Mass times run from 7.35am–5.30pm and visitors are welcome to enter at any time | Tip Walk to Westminster Cathedral Hall (entrance in Ambrosden Avenue), a fine Edwardian hall designed by the Cathedral's architect, John Bentley, and now a venue for a wide range of concerts, recitals, theatre and lectures.

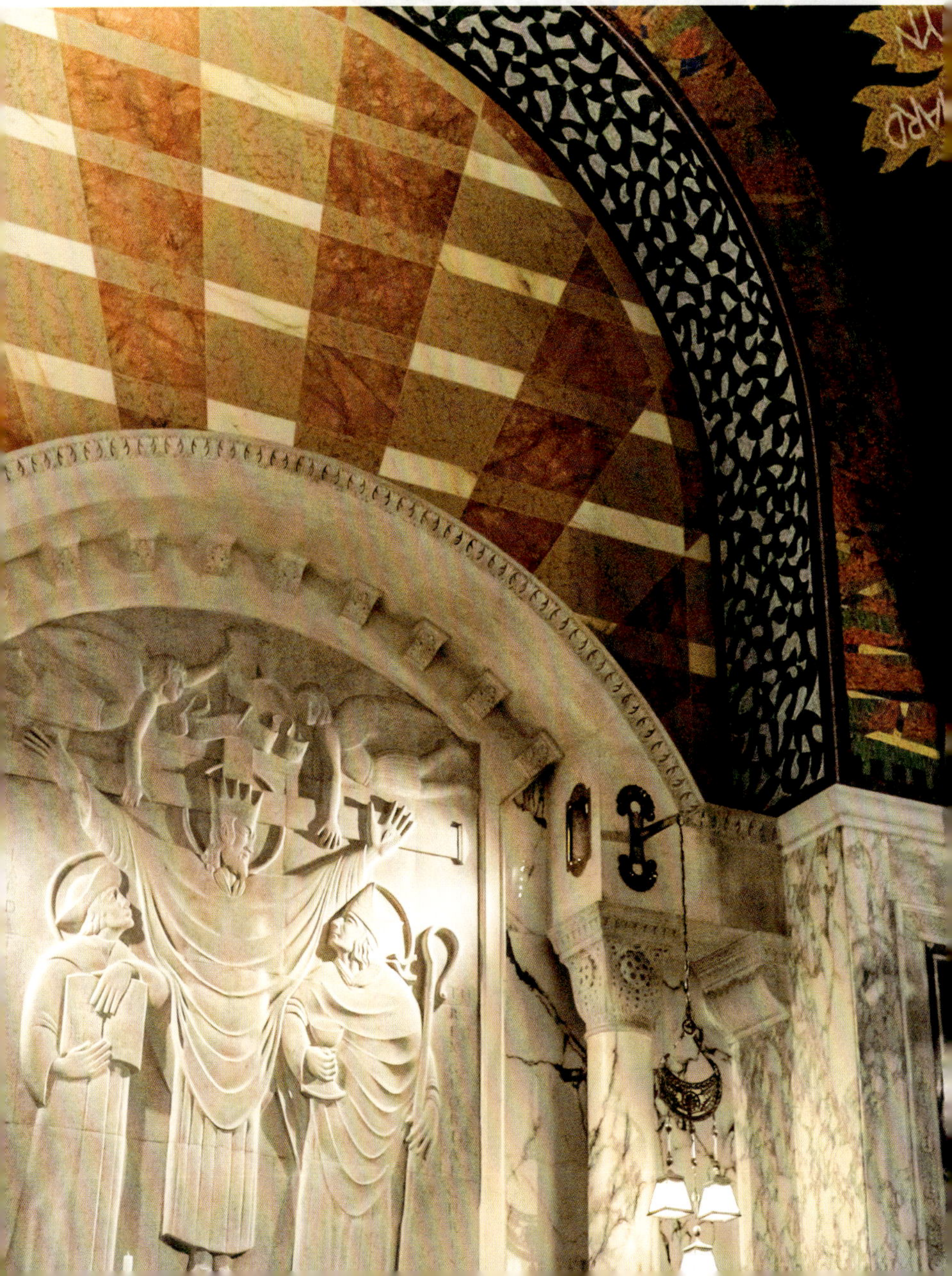

110 The Wigmore Hall

The healing spirit of music

Where do we go to find art that embodies the spirit of music and gaiety? Much of it is hidden away, seldom much noticed, and almost always unacknowledged, in the theatres and concert halls of London. The Wigmore Hall, for example, first opened its doors to the public with a gala performance in 1901. The only concert hall in London entirely devoted to presenting classical music on an intimate scale, it was built by the Bechstein company next door to its showroom, where the finest of grand pianos were on sale to those with the means.

Disaster struck in 1916. The Bechstein premises were sequestered by the government as the property of enemy aliens, and all the 157 grand pianos then in stock sold off to Debenhams. After the Great War ended, the hall re-opened as the Wigmore Hall – all reference to its former owners had been expunged.

The art embodying the spirit of music can be seen every time you turn up to enjoy a concert. Above the small stage where a grand piano usually sits, black shark's fin ever open at the ready, you will see a half-dome decorated in a style somewhere between German Expressionist and Art Nouveau. A naked figure yearns upwards. Its fingers are emitting golden rays. The rays represent music and her universal appeal as a healer and a peacemaker. A naked figure plays a wind instrument off to the side, as if in demonstration of the theme. Smoky arabesques resembling the spreading of thorns represent the forces against which music must contend in order to get its healing message through to its audiences. A man who bears an uncanny resemblance to the great Florentine poet Dante Alighieri, author of *The Divine Comedy*, kneels in front of a scroll in the foreground. He is busy writing some music. The scroll itself extends and extends outwards from the dome onto two flanking walls, which are also decorated.

Address 36 Wigmore Street, London W1U 2BP, +44 (0)207 935 2141, www.wigmorehall.co.uk | **Getting there** Underground to Oxford Circus (Bakerloo, Central and Victoria Lines) or Bond Street (Central and Elizabeth Lines) | **Hours** See website for concert times | **Tip** The Danish bakery Ole & Steen is just five minutes from here, serving excellent coffee and pastries.

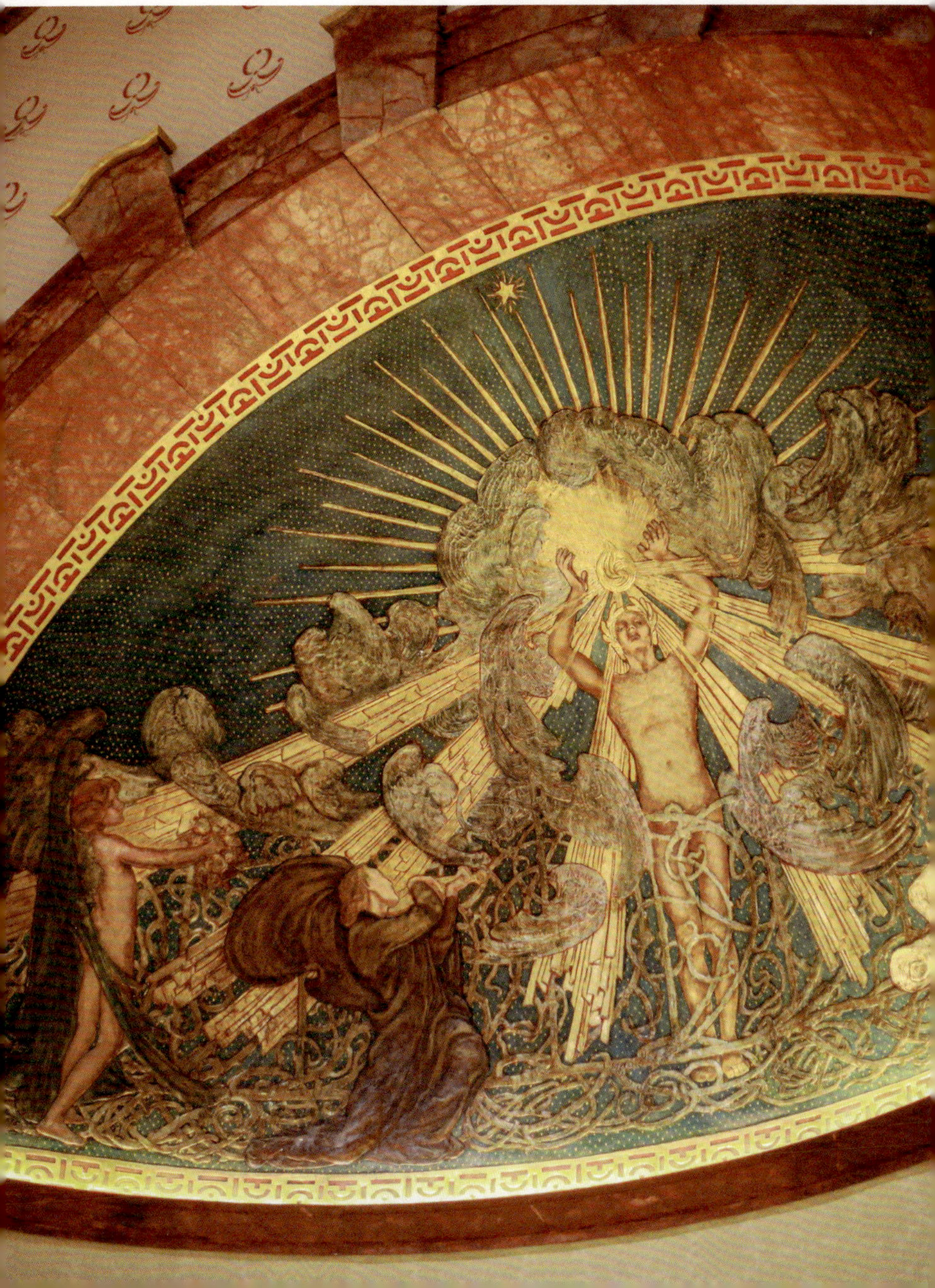

111 William

On the wilder side of life

Renzo Piano's Central Saint Giles, a mixed-use development of 2010 at the north-eastern edge of Covent Garden where High Holborn changes its name to St Giles High Street, is loud, colourful and shouty. Is it newly set down there as a challenge to any of the surrounding, more sober-suited, low-rise buildings of the 18th or the 19th century?

It seems that way. Each of its four blocks is faced with thousands of glazed tiles of strikingly different colours, ranging from lime green to yellow, from orange to red.

At street level, a piazza has been scooped out to accommodate contemporary art. The first example you see, a sculpture facing out to the street itself on a tall white plinth tucked in beside a bristle of bean-pole-slender metal columns that pretend to support the weight of the building that looms over it, has a name – *William* – which makes it sound familiar, if not accommodating and homely.

Its maker is Rebecca Warren, an artist shortlisted for the Turner Prize in 2006. In fact, Rebecca Warren is the least accommodating of makers when it comes to the representation of the human form. She works with clay, but in a way that's both freakish and gestural. Most of the sculptures of the human form you can see on public display in London are well mannered and recognisably human. They are often based on classical forms. Not so *William*. Warren is too wild for that sort of thing. She works with lumps of raw clay, and builds forms that are shaky and off-kilter, as if delving not so much into the polite faces we show off to the world, as exposing the raw and ill-mannered interiors of our lives. Is William boy or man? Perhaps one or the other. Perhaps neither, quite. He looks so rackety and lumpishly provisional. And what of that flourish of pink at his top? Is that a bow? What gender is William then? Trans? Hetero? Your throw of the dice.

Address Central St Giles, St Giles High Street, London WC2H 8AG | **Getting there** Underground to Tottenham Court Road (Central, Elizabeth and Northern Lines), then a five-minute walk | **Hours** Accessible 24 hours | **Tip** Try a cake and buy a book at the LRB bookshop in Bury Place, five minutes from here.

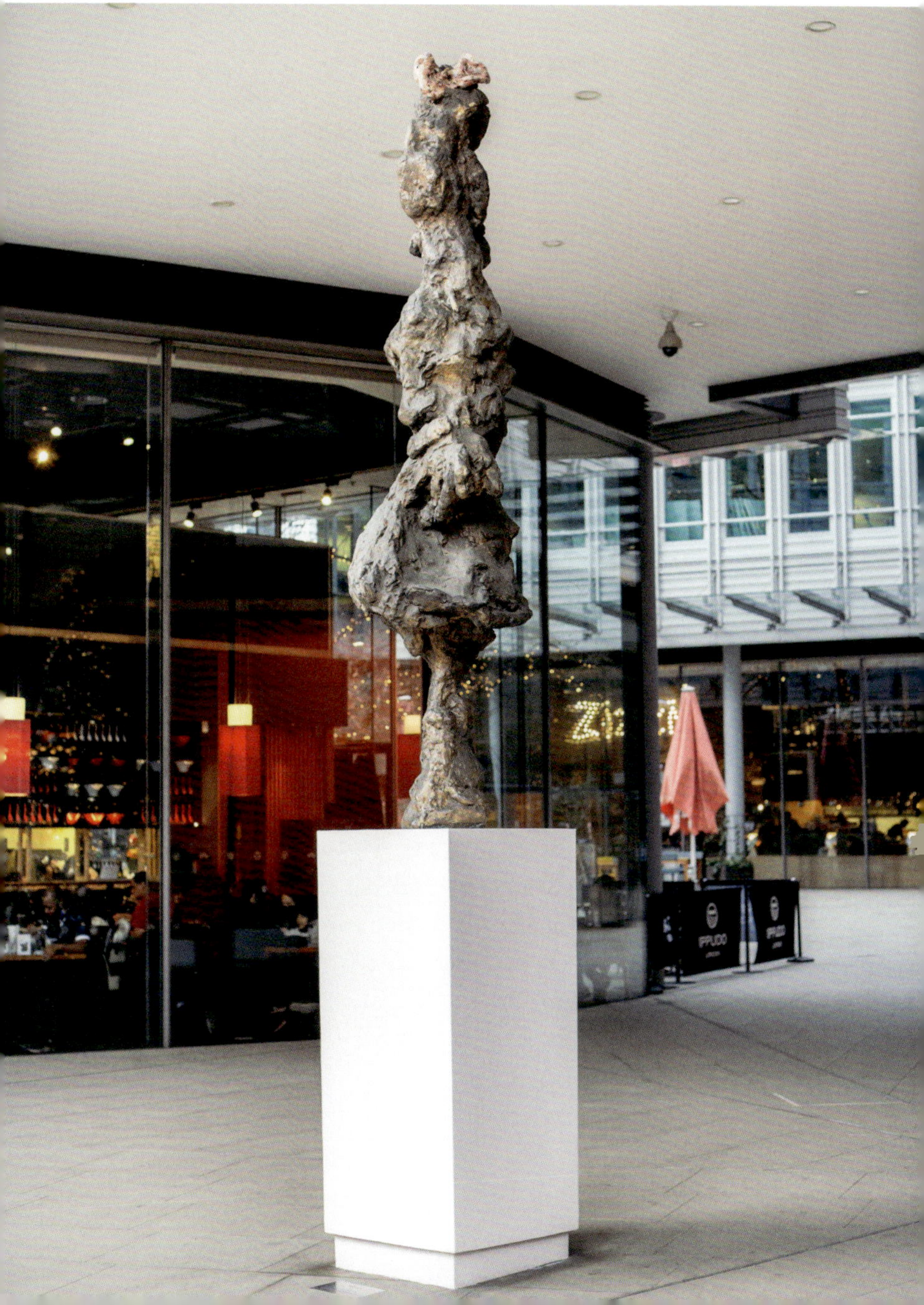

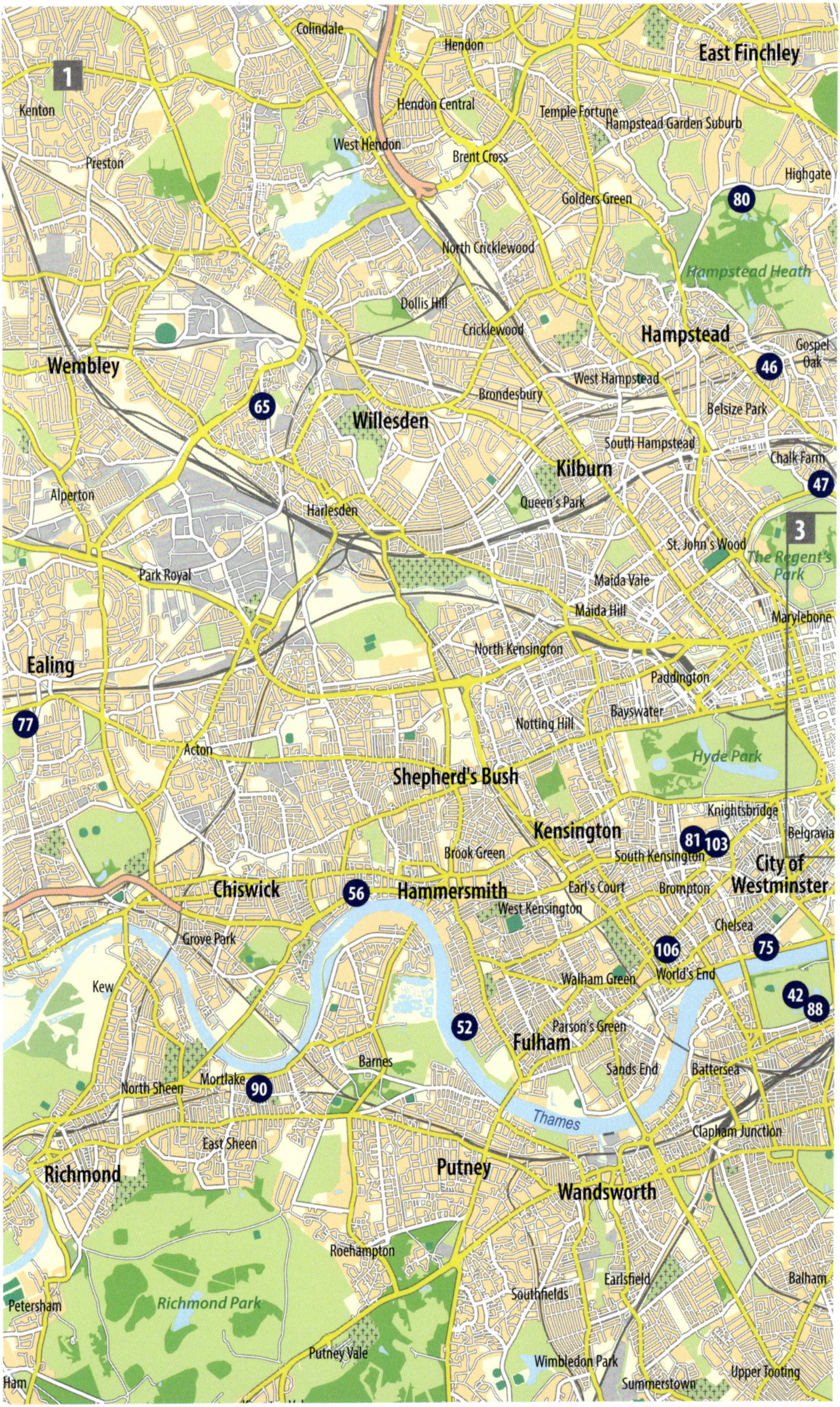
1
Colindale
Hendon
East Finchley
Kenton
Hendon Central
Temple Fortune
Hampstead Garden Suburb
West Hendon
Brent Cross
Highgate
Preston
Golders Green
80
North Cricklewood
Hampstead Heath
Dollis Hill
Cricklewood
Hampstead
Gospel Oak
Wembley
46
West Hampstead
Brondesbury
65
Willesden
Belsize Park
South Hampstead
Chalk Farm
Kilburn
47
Alperton
Queen's Park
Harlesden
3
St. John's Wood
The Regent's Park
Park Royal
Maida Vale
Maida Hill
Marylebone
North Kensington
Ealing
Paddington
Bayswater
Notting Hill
77
Acton
Hyde Park
Shepherd's Bush
Knightsbridge
Kensington
81
103
Belgravia
Brook Green
South Kensington
City of Westminster
Chiswick
56
Hammersmith
Earl's Court
Brompton
West Kensington
Chelsea
Grove Park
106
75
Kew
Walham Green
World's End
42
88
52
Parson's Green
Fulham
Barnes
Sands End
Battersea
Mortlake
90
North Sheen
Thames
Clapham Junction
East Sheen
Richmond
Putney
Wandsworth
Roehampton
Earlsfield
Balham
Southfields
Petersham
Richmond Park
Putney Vale
Wimbledon Park
Upper Tooting
Ham
Summerstown

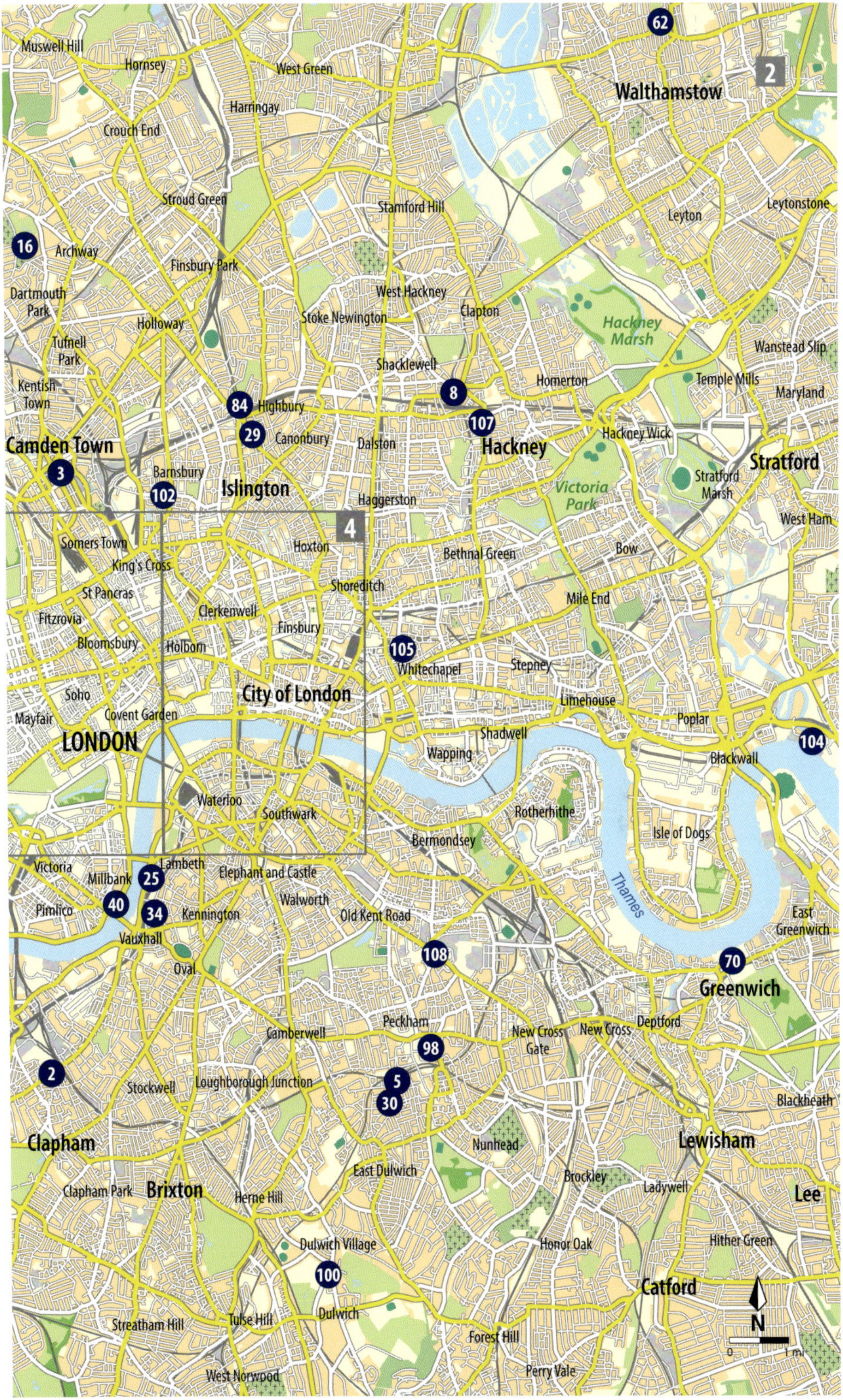

62
2
Muswell Hill
Hornsey
West Green
Walthamstow
Harringay
Crouch End
Stroud Green
Stamford Hill
Leyton
Leytonstone
16
Archway
Finsbury Park
Dartmouth Park
West Hackney
Clapton
Hackney Marsh
Holloway
Stoke Newington
Tufnell Park
Wanstead Slip
Kentish Town
Shacklewell
Homerton
Temple Mills
Maryland
8
84
Highbury
107
29
Canonbury
Dalston
Hackney
Hackney Wick
Camden Town
Stratford
3
Barnsbury
Stratford Marsh
102
Islington
Victoria Park
Haggerston
West Ham
4
Somers Town
Hoxton
King's Cross
Bethnal Green
Bow
St Pancras
Shoreditch
Mile End
Clerkenwell
Fitzrovia
Finsbury
Bloomsbury
Holborn
105
Whitechapel
Stepney
Soho
City of London
Limehouse
Mayfair
Covent Garden
Poplar
LONDON
Shadwell
104
Wapping
Blackwall
Waterloo
Southwark
Rotherhithe
Isle of Dogs
Bermondsey
Victoria
Lambeth
Millbank
25
Elephant and Castle
Walworth
40
Pimlico
34
Kennington
Old Kent Road
Thames
East Greenwich
Vauxhall
108
Oval
70
Greenwich
Peckham
Deptford
Camberwell
New Cross Gate
New Cross
98
2
Stockwell
Loughborough Junction
5
30
Blackheath
Clapham
Nunhead
Lewisham
East Dulwich
Brockley
Clapham Park
Brixton
Ladywell
Lee
Herne Hill
Dulwich Village
Honor Oak
Hither Green
100
Catford
Streatham Hill
Tulse Hill
Dulwich
N
Forest Hill
0
1 mi
Perry Vale
West Norwood

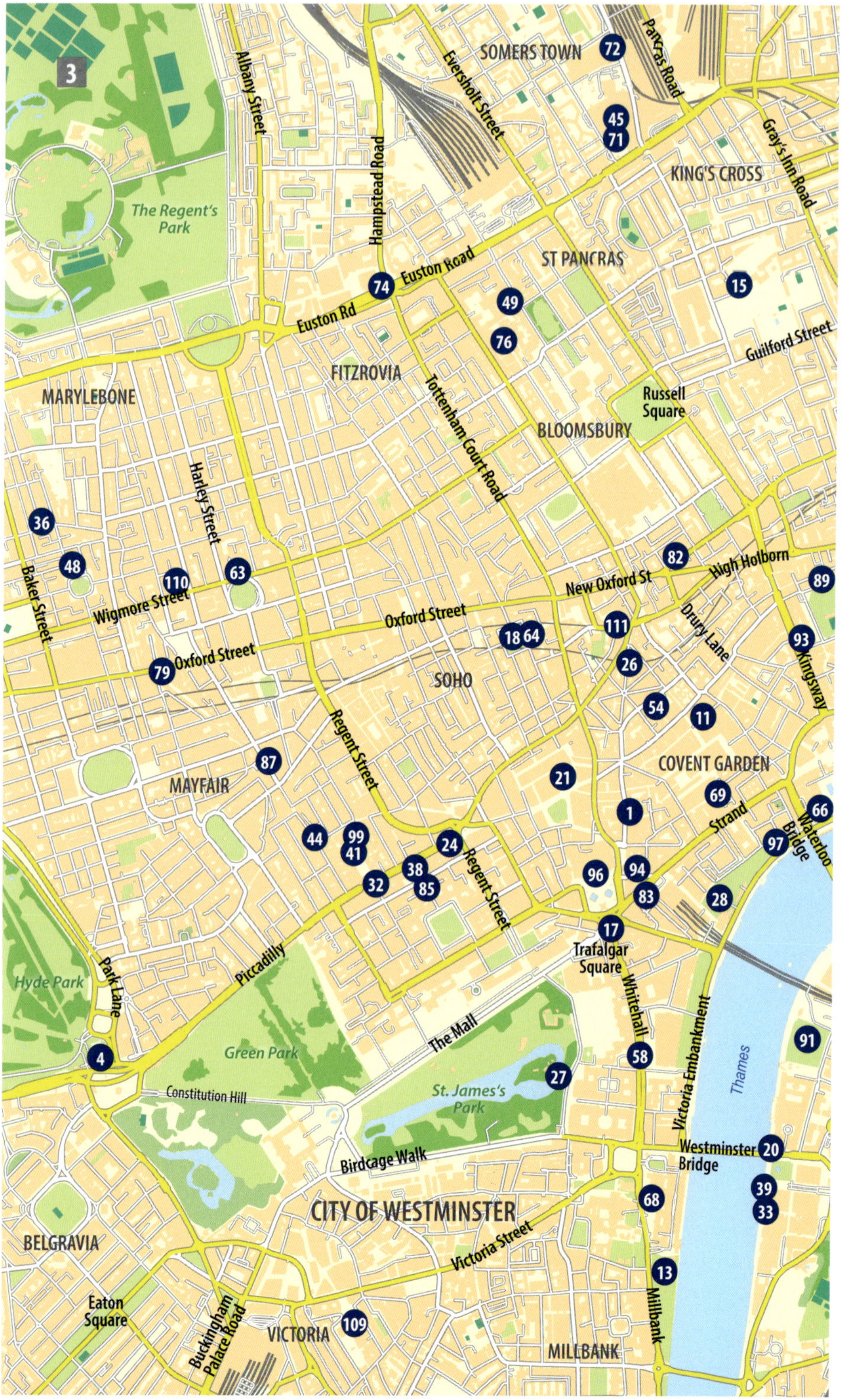
3
SOMERS TOWN
Pancras Road
Eversholt Street
Albany Street
Hampstead Road
KING'S CROSS
Gray's Inn Road
The Regent's Park
ST PANCRAS
Euston Road
Euston Rd
Guilford Street
FITZROVIA
Russell Square
MARYLEBONE
Tottenham Court Road
BLOOMSBURY
Harley Street
Baker Street
Wigmore Street
New Oxford St
High Holborn
Oxford Street
Drury Lane
Kingsway
SOHO
Regent Street
MAYFAIR
COVENT GARDEN
Strand
Waterloo Bridge
Trafalgar Square
Whitehall
Hyde Park
Park Lane
Piccadilly
The Mall
Green Park
Victoria Embankment
Thames
Constitution Hill
St. James's Park
Birdcage Walk
Westminster Bridge
CITY OF WESTMINSTER
BELGRAVIA
Victoria Street
Eaton Square
Buckingham Palace Road
VICTORIA
Millbank
MILLBANK
72
45
71
74
49
15
76
36
48
110
63
82
89
111
18
64
93
79
26
54
11
87
21
69
66
1
44
99
41
24
97
38
32
85
96
94
83
28
17
91
4
58
27
20
39
33
68
13
109

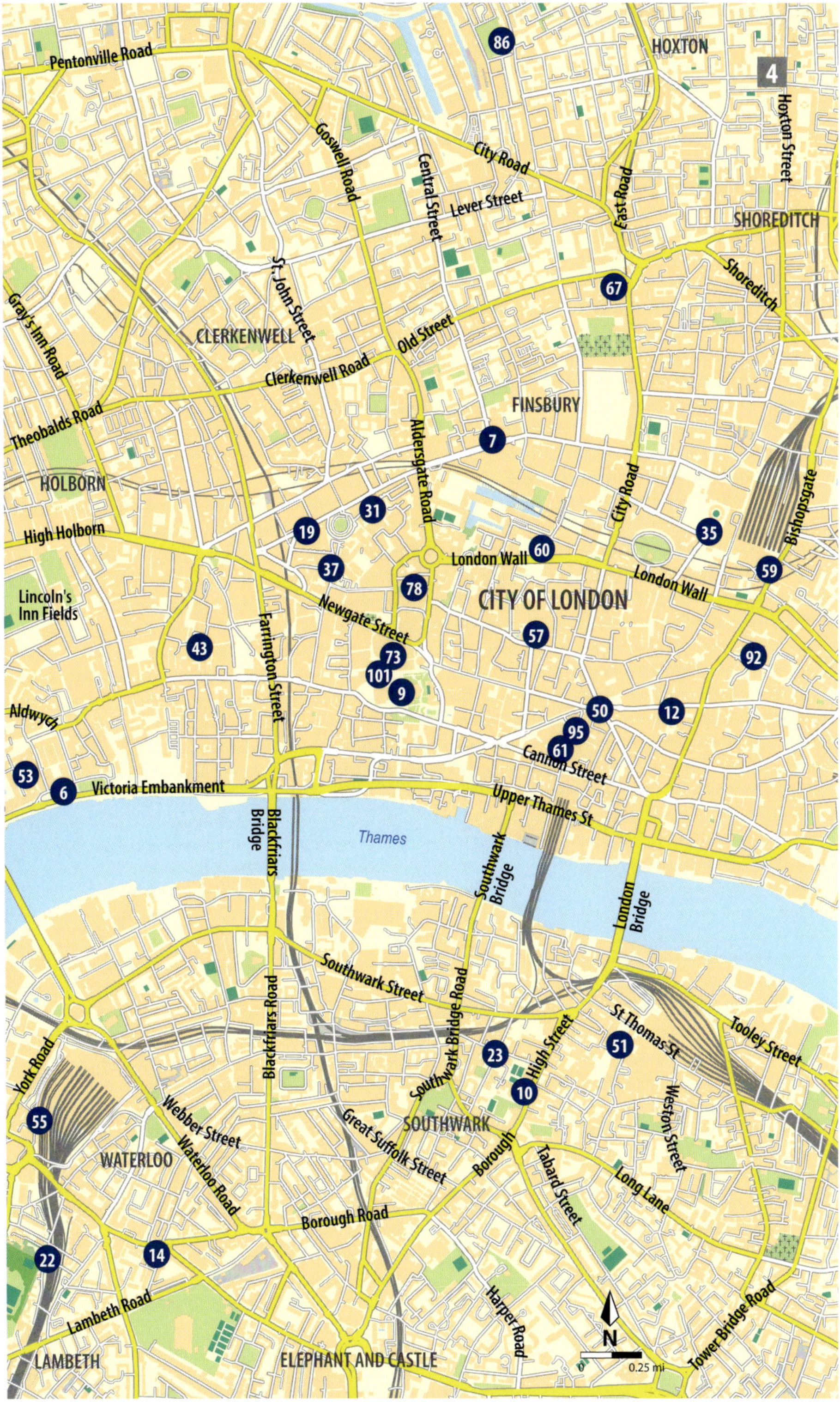
4
HOXTON
SHOREDITCH
CLERKENWELL
FINSBURY
HOLBORN
CITY OF LONDON
SOUTHWARK
WATERLOO
LAMBETH
ELEPHANT AND CASTLE
Pentonville Road
Goswell Road
City Road
Central Street
Lever Street
East Road
Hoxton Street
Shoreditch
St. John Street
Gray's Inn Road
Old Street
Clerkenwell Road
Theobalds Road
Aldersgate Road
City Road
Bishopsgate
High Holborn
London Wall
London Wall
Lincoln's Inn Fields
Newgate Street
Farringdon Street
Aldwych
Cannon Street
Victoria Embankment
Upper Thames St
Blackfriars Bridge
Thames
Southwark Bridge
London Bridge
Southwark Street
Southwark Bridge Road
St Thomas St
Tooley Street
York Road
High Street
Blackfriars Road
Webber Street
Waterloo Road
Great Suffolk Street
Borough
Weston Street
Tabard Street
Long Lane
Borough Road
Lambeth Road
Harper Road
Tower Bridge Road
N
0
0.25 mi
86
67
7
31
19
37
78
60
35
59
57
43
73
101
9
92
50
12
95
61
53
6
23
51
10
55
14
22

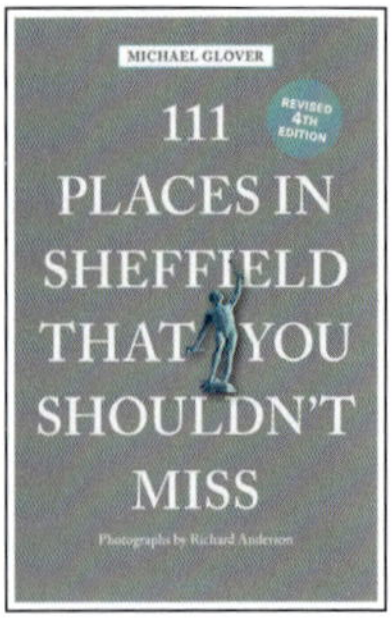

Michael Glover,
Richard Anderson
111 Places in Sheffield That You Shouldn't Miss
ISBN 978-3-7408-2348-1

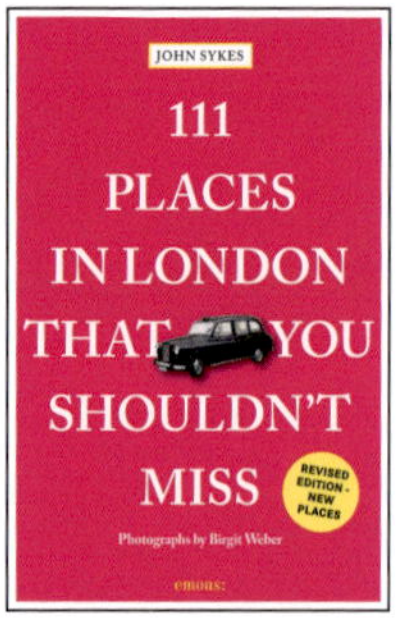

John Sykes, Birgit Weber
111 Places in London That You Shouldn't Miss
ISBN 978-3-7408-1644-5

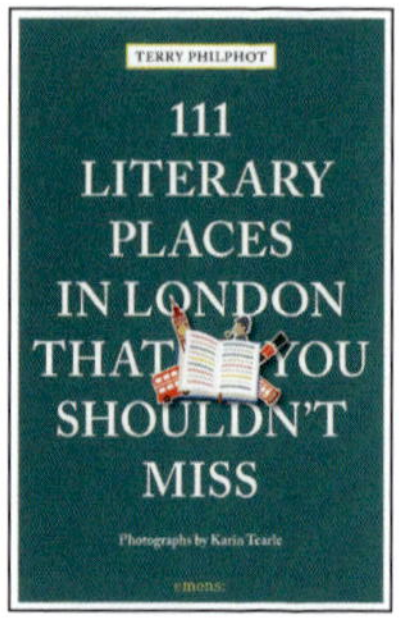

Terry Philpot, Karin Tearle
111 Literary Places in London That You Shouldn't Miss
ISBN 978-3-7408-1954-5

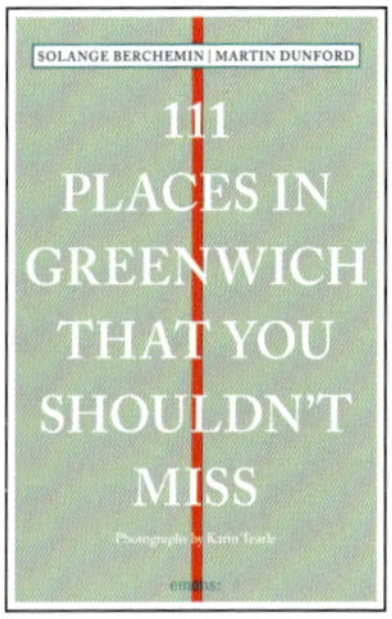

Solange Berchemin,
Martin Dunford, Karin Tearle
111 Places in Greenwich That You Shouldn't Miss
ISBN 978-3-7408-1107-5

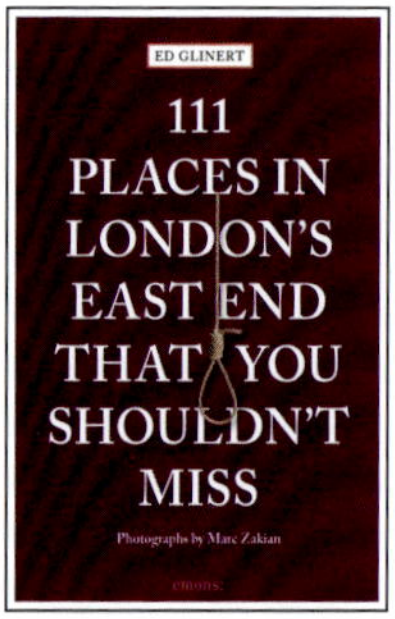

Ed Glinert, Marc Zakian
111 Places in London's East End That You Shouldn't Miss
ISBN 978-3-7408-0752-8

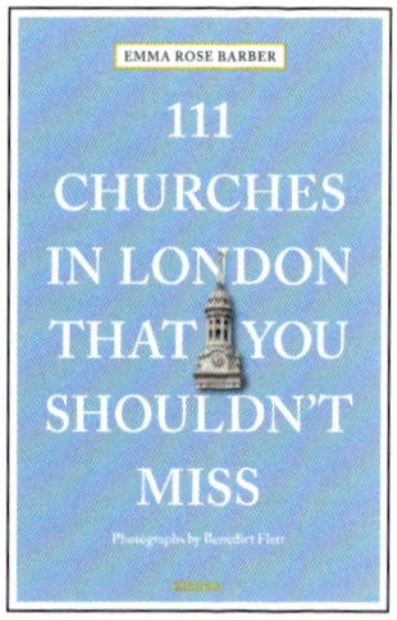

Emma Rose Barber,
Benedict Flett
111 Churches in London That You Shouldn't Miss
ISBN 978-3-7408-0901-0

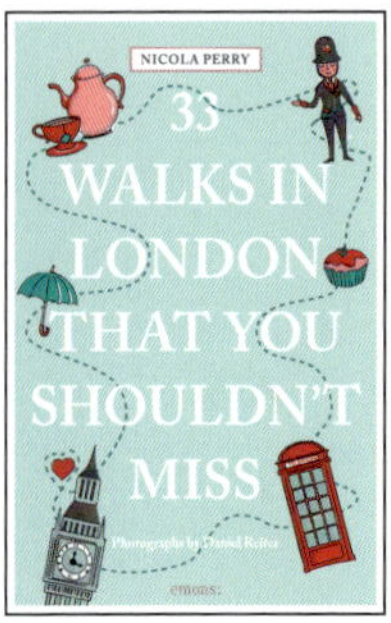

Nicola Perry, Daniel Reiter
33 Walks in London That You Shouldn't Miss
ISBN 978-3-7408-1955-2

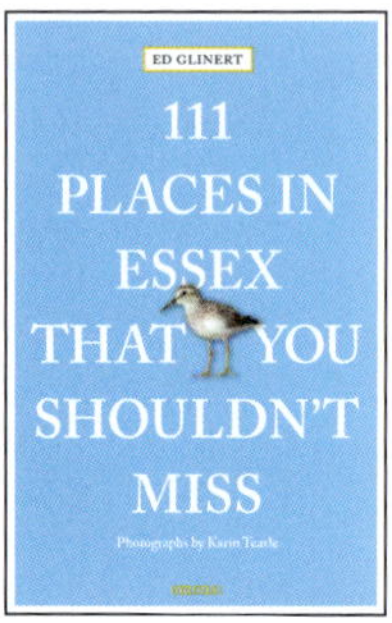

Ed Glinert, Karin Tearle
111 Places in Essex That You Shouldn't Miss
ISBN 978-3-7408-1593-6

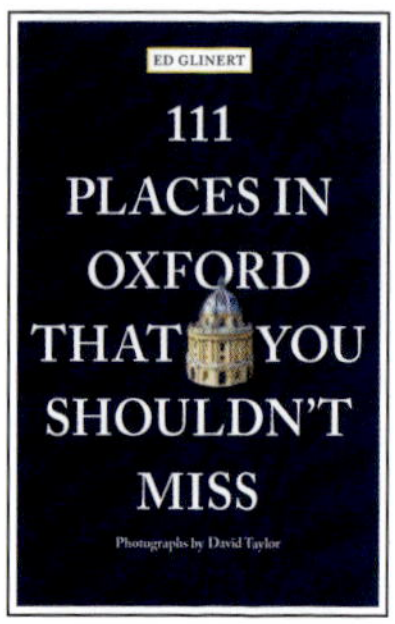

Ed Glinert, David Taylor
111 Places in Oxford That You Shouldn't Miss
ISBN 978-3-7408-1990-3

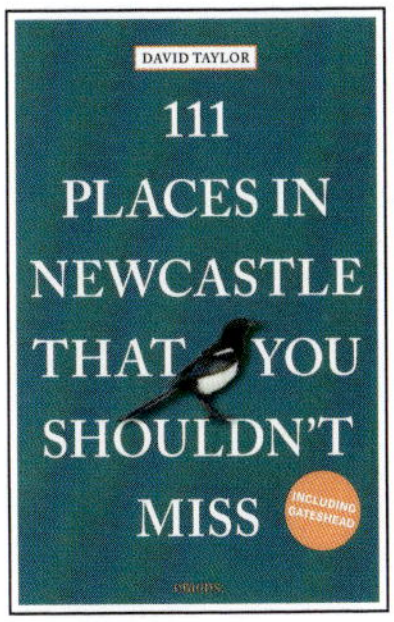

David Taylor
111 Places in Newcastle That You Shouldn't Miss
ISBN 978-3-7408-1043-6

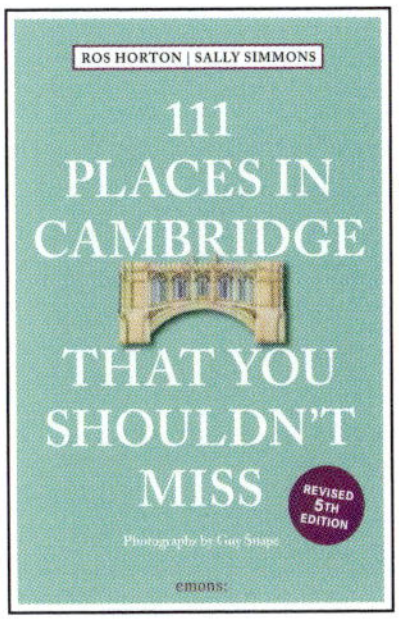

Rosalind Horton,
Sally Simmons, Guy Snape
111 Places in Cambridge That You Shouldn't Miss
ISBN 978-3-7408-1285-0

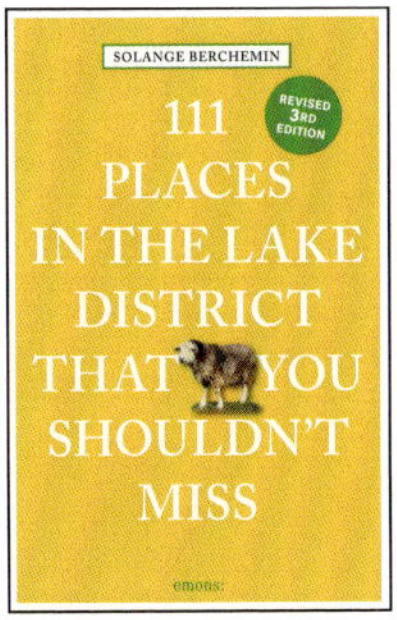

Solange Berchemin
111 Places in the Lake District That You Shouldn't Miss
ISBN 978-3-7408-1861-6

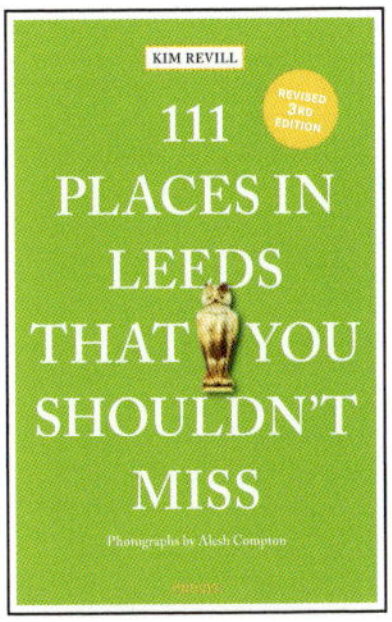

Kim Revill, Alesh Compton
111 Places in Leeds That You Shouldn't Miss
ISBN 978-3-7408-0754-2

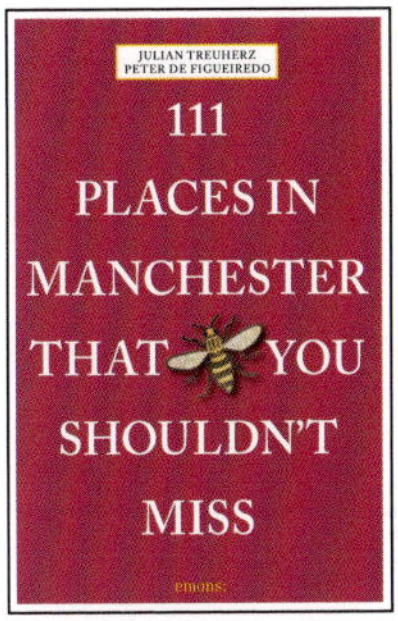

Julian Treuherz,
Peter de Figueiredo
111 Places in Manchester That You Shouldn't Miss
ISBN 978-3-7408-2246-0

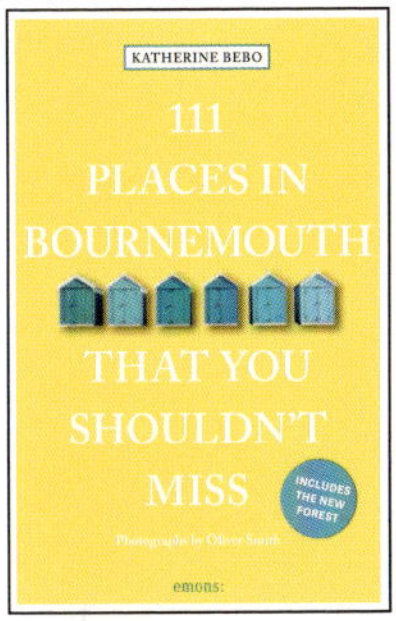

Katherine Bebo, Oliver Smith
111 Places in Bournemouth That You Shouldn't Miss
ISBN 978-3-7408-1166-2

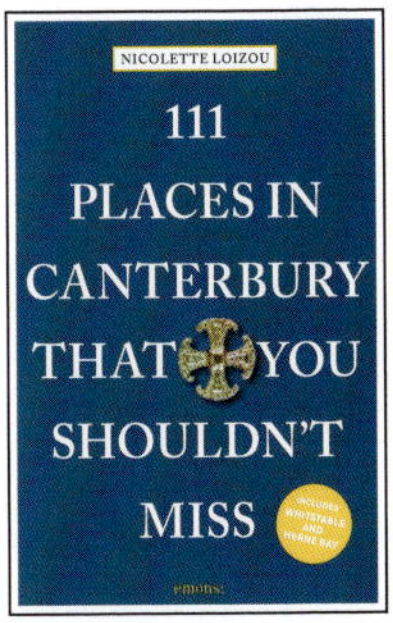

Nicolette Loizou
111 Places in Canterbury That You Shouldn't Miss
ISBN 978-3-7408-0899-0

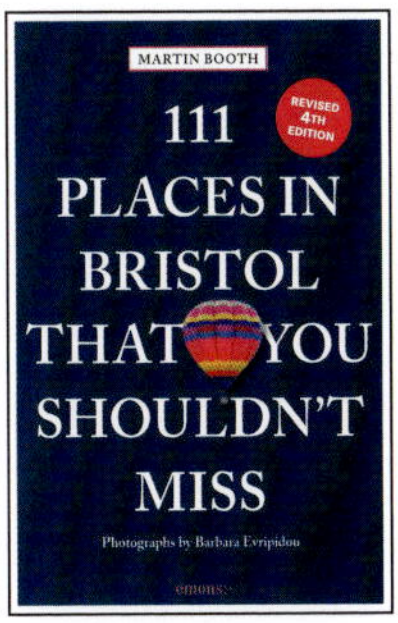

Martin Booth, Barbara Evripidou
111 Places in Bristol That You Shouldn't Miss
ISBN 978-3-7408-2001-5

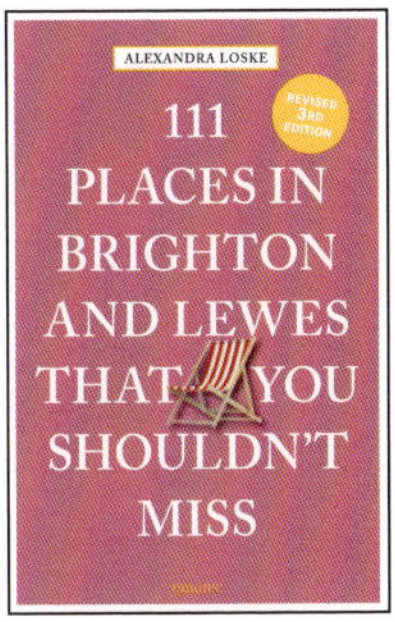

Alexandra Loske
111 Places in Brighton and Lewes That You Shouldn't Miss
ISBN 978-3-7408-1727-5

Photo Credits

The Crossbones Graveyard (ch. 23): Crossbones Graveyard & Garden of Remembrance is managed by Bankside Open Spaces Trust.
The Flayed Saint (ch. 31): WikimediaCommons/Davepastor
Ivon Hitchens' Mural (ch. 47): © Estate of Ivon Hitchens and Jonathan Clark Fine Art.
The Mithraeum (ch. 61): © MOLA
The Painted Ceiling (ch. 70): Jaime Ian Genovese, 2023
Paradigm (ch. 72): Marc Wilmot
Racing Against Time (ch. 79): GG Archard
Sullivan (Sans Gilbert) (ch. 97): Kaye Song

Art Credits

Anthony Caro Centre (ch. 3): © VG Bild-Kunst, Bonn 2024
The Cocteau Chapel (ch. 21): © Comité Cocteau, Paris / VG Bild-Kunst, Bonn 2024
The Flayed Saint (ch. 31): © Damien Hirst and Science Ltd. All rights reserved / VG Bild-Kunst, Bonn 2024
Ivon Hitchens' Mural (ch. 47): © VG Bild-Kunst, Bonn 2024
Paradigm (ch. 72): Conrad Shawcross, *Paradigm*, 2015. Commissioned by The Francis Crick Institute. © Conrad Shawcross. Courtesy the artist and Victoria Miro.
Racing Against Time (ch. 79): Darren Almond, 'Horizon Line', 2017. Bond Street station (Elizabeth line). Commissioned as part of The Crossrail Art Programme. Courtesy of the artist and White Cube.
St Martin-in-the-Fields (ch. 94): © VG Bild-Kunst, Bonn 2024

This book, which has been several years in the making, could not have been written without the contributions of others – multiple conversations, insights, suggestions, tips, and general encouragement. Here is a list, alphabetically organised, of the names of some of the people to whom I am so deeply beholden. The book would not have existed without their multiple acts of kindness. Forgive me if I have not acknowledged your help.

Mark Ashworth, Nicholas Bateman, Judith Bronkhurst, Martin Caiger-Smith, Hilary Davies, Richard Deacon, Jesse Dupré, Joseph Glover, Charlotte Grinling, Paul Hodgson, Marius Kociejowski, Maddy Nicklin, Celia Paul, Catherine Pepinster, Marietta Ryan, Imran Sabur, James Scott, Diana Wilkinson, Barnaby Wright, and last but never least, my wonderful wife Ruth Dupré, with whom I have discussed this project from end to end and back again.

Michael Glover

I would like to express my particular thanks to Callan Davies for the wonderful tour of the Palace of Westminster after photographing New Dawn, to Alex Farzad for lending me her camera after mine started playing up half-way through the project, and to Kaye Song for stepping in last-minute to shoot a missing place when I was not in London.

Benedict Flett

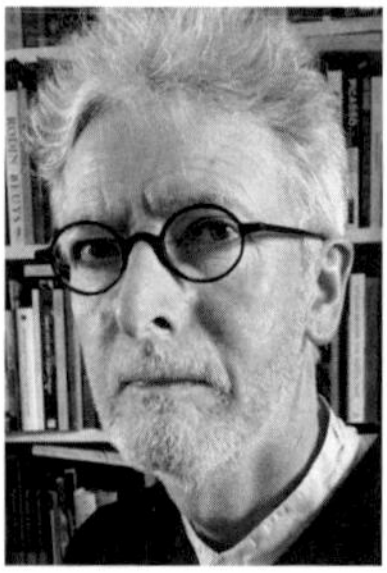

Michael Glover is a Sheffield-born, London-based poet, art critic, editor and publisher who has contributed regularly to *The Times*, the *Financial Times*, the *New Statesman* and *The Economist.* He was born in Fir Vale, Sheffield, was educated at Firth Park Grammar School, and read English at Queens' College, Cambridge. He has been a London correspondent for ArtNews, New York. His international poetry journal, *The Bow-Wow Shop* (www.bowwowshop.org.uk) first went online in 2009. His most recent books are: *Great Works: Encounters with Art* (Prestel), *Headlong into Pennilessness*, a memoir of growing up in Sheffield, and for Emons, *111 Places in Sheffield That You Shouldn't Miss.* Two collections of poetry are coming soon: *Hypothetical May Morning* and *The Book of Extremities.*

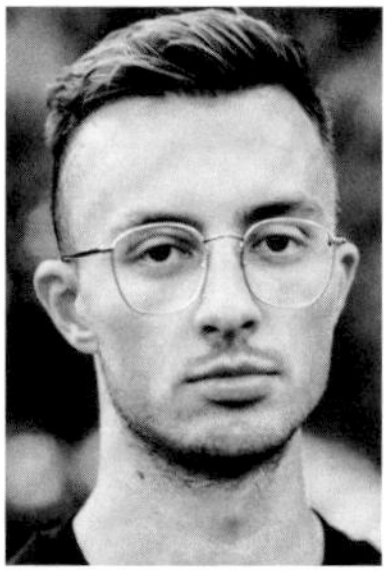

Benedict Flett was born in London, and has been using a camera of some sort since he was twelve. He studied Human, Social and Political Science at Queens' College, Cambridge, and Anthropology at the University of Leipzig. He previously worked on *111 Churches in London That You Shouldn't Miss*, in the same series, and published a book of photos made in Belarus with ZONE6 Press in 2021. He is passionate about exploring, documenting and writing about landscapes – mythic, wild and rationalised.